KILL
THEM ALL

KILL THEM ALL

Cathars and Carnage in the Albigensian Crusade

SEAN McGLYNN

For George & Margaret

First published 2015
This extended edition first published 2018

The History Press
The Mill, Brimscombe Port
Stroud, Gloucestershire, GL5 2QG
www.thehistorypress.co.uk

British Library Cataloguing in Publication Data.
A catalogue record for this book is available from the British Library.

ISBN 978 0 7509 8431 7

Typesetting and origination by The History Press
Printed and bound in Great Britain by TJ International Ltd

CONTENTS

ACKNOWLEDGEMENTS

Despite this book's frequently dark and disturbing content, with all too many parallels with conflicts in the world today, I have enjoyed writing it tremendously. Much of this was owed to getting back to the basics of immersing myself in the main contemporary evidence provided by the four main war reporters of the conflict: Peter of Vaux de Cernay, William of Tudela, the Anonymous and William of Puylaurens. In this regard, I would like express my gratitude and debt to Janet Shirley and Michael Sibly, who, between them (and with Michael's late father, William), have produced the essential English translations and editions of these writers. I have enjoyed and appreciated their support and correspondence while writing this book and I am grateful for their permission to use some plans of medieval towns that first appeared in their works. Some of the other maps are based on a selection from Michel Roquebert's five-volume history in French of the Albigensian Crusade.

There is no doubt that the influences of John Gillingham and John France are present in this book; both remain leading figures in the world of medieval warfare studies. I have enjoyed many discussions at conferences and talks with Paul Webster, Matt Bennett, Dan Power and others, as well as my regular contact with Simon Barton at the University of Exeter. The patience and encouragement of Shaun Barrington at The History Press has again made working with him a pleasure. Mention should also be made of Dirk van Gorp and his editorship of the excellent new magazine *Medieval Warfare*. Work continues to be stimulating at The Open University and at Plymouth University's Strode College, where special thanks go to my colleagues on the History, Heritage and Archaeology degree programme, Andy Pickering and Katherine Dray.

When I first drew up the proposal for this book some years ago, Laurence Marvin's excellent *The Occitan War: A Military and Political History of the Albigensian Crusade, 1209–1218* had yet to be published. Both being scholars of medieval warfare, it is inevitable that Prof Marvin and I focus on similar material much of the time and often reach the same conclusions. His book frequently clarified my understanding of some events or alerted me to an alternative reading of others in the chronicles. However, there is also plenty that is dissimilar as we very often present differing interpretations and analysis of aspects of the military episodes for the period 1209–18. The main difference is that Marvin finishes his account in 1218, while I continue to 1244 to cover all the warfare of the Albigensian Crusade, including the last military episode against the Cathar heretics at Montségur. I also add a broader introduction to encompass a discussion of heresy and emphasise throughout the wider European picture, especially the role of England; I also seek to explain the warfare of the crusade in light of military practice in medieval Europe. Thus the additional material that these 35–40,000 extra words explore makes *Kill Them All* a different book, the first to offer a military analysis of the whole Albigensian conflict.

On a personal level, I owe much to the ongoing support of friends: Stephen Rigby, Stephen Forrow, Glenn Renshaw, Anthony and Jackie Cross, Mary Beeken, Michael Owen, the Ottaways, Cath Hanley (herself a medieval scholar and also a historical fiction writer) and others. Very special mention goes to my great friend Robert Purves, who accompanied my son Sam and me to Languedoc and who, with Sam, took the majority of the photos in this book – bringing back warm memories of a tremendous trip that helped to make the writing of this book so enjoyable.

As always, my love goes to Sam, Maddy and Jenny, and to Marie, who is doing wonderful things and without whom so much would be impossible.

A Note on Names

Medieval names are notoriously flexible in the permutations of their forms. As a general, but far from inviolable, rule, I have anglicised the names of leading protagonists. I have kept the original names of some ecclesiastics such as the legate Arnald Almaric to emphasise their southern origins. Rather than employing the familiar academic use of names and titles in the style of, for example, Raymond Roger Trencavel, Viscount of Carcassonne, I have simplified it to Viscount Raymond Roger of Carcassonne. For the most part, I have retained *de* for French toponymns (e.g. Bouchard de Marly). Simon de Montfort is simply Montfort. I refer to him predominantly as viscount to emphasise his early territorial position in Languedoc. The French proclivity for hyphenation is not replicated here, hence Pierre des Vaux-de-Cernay becomes Peter of Vaux de Cernay. Castrum and castra are such recurrent terms and constant features of the landscape of the book that I have not italicised them.

THE ALBIGENSIAN CRUSADE: A BRUTAL WAR OF CONQUEST

Just over 800 years ago, the brutal Albigensian Crusade began as a war waged initially against the Cathar heretics in southern France. Much has been written about the Cathars, the progress of the crusade and the ultimate suppression of the heresy by the Inquisition – but the military history and warfare of the whole crusade has not hitherto received a book-length study.

The emphasis of this book is very much on the incredible drama of the battles and sieges of the crusade and the brutality with which the wars were fought. My intention has been to provide an exciting narrative of the military operations together with expert analysis of strategy and tactics, and an assessment of the leadership of the commanders – the famous Viscount Simon de Montfort and the arguably less familiar but equally important Louis the Lion and the Count Raymonds of Toulouse. Other books' narratives of the crusade understandably intersperse its progress with politics and religion, but for my purposes this would be detrimental to conveying the intensity and drama of the warfare itself. I deal briefly with religion in the first chapter; important developments in politics are covered as and when they influence the military arena and therefore are discussed in their military context rather than as detailed studies of their own. My focus throughout is on the war, how it was fought and what it tells us about the nature of warfare in the High Middle Ages, making this book the first dedicated military history of the entire Albigensian conflict.

I intend to show that military operations took precedence over all else; religion and politics, vital as they were, depended on the outcome of the battlefield. Ultimately, this was a war not fought simply for religion (as is commonly supposed, even by many academics) but for territorial conquest. Thus, in 1213, at the pivotal battle of Muret, the crusaders under Simon de Montfort took on the forces of King Peter II of Aragon, acknowledged as a champion of the Catholic cause by the papacy. National identity was far more important than religion: in the south, Catholics and Cathars alike united to resist the French, whom they considered to be barbaric northerners. The south fought to preserve its customs, laws and language against the northern invaders and the military occupation of its cities.

The book is structured around chapters which relate pivotal and dramatic military events as well as the overall course of the fighting. The chapter titles are quotes from contemporary sources that reflect phases of the conflict for the period under discussion. These are related and analysed in considerable depth to reveal the tactics and strategy of crusading warfare. The book starts by looking at the origins of the crusade and its logistical preparations before covering its launch and horrific start with the massacre of Béziers and the fall of Carcassonne. The brutal progress of the early years of the war is then charted, marked by many massacres, climaxing with the remarkable battle of Muret in 1213, which saw the death of a king. We then continue with Simon de Montfort's ruthless, relentless leadership during a period when the southerners co-ordinated a successful counter-attack, culminating in 1217–18 with the second (and most significant) siege of Toulouse, a huge military operation that resulted in grievous losses for the northerners. In the period that follows, Louis the Lion, heir to the throne and then King of France, takes up the crusaders' cross with a major siege of Avignon, after which the scorched-earth operations of the French saw the land itself and the people who lived off it as the primary target in a period of anarchy. The final chapters examine the last phase of the war – no less bloody or less marred by massacre – and include important, extremely rare accounts of the siege of Carcassonne in 1240 and the battle of Saintes and Taillebourg in 1242; the latter, though fought outside Languedoc, were decisive in sealing the fate of the Cathars.

The title of the book derives from the infamous reported remarks of the papal legate heading the crusade in 1209. The immediate result was the dreadful massacre at Béziers. Historians have generally doubted that the legate actually gave the command, 'Kill them all! God will know his own.'

Further to my detailed study in *By Sword and Fire: Cruelty and Atrocity in Medieval Warfare* of what we would today consider war crimes, I argue here that the order was indeed given and I explain why. The command set the tone for one of the bloodiest and most savage conflicts of the entire Middle Ages, during which commanders frequently ordered a policy of no quarter. The military thinking behind this and the implications of this strategy are explored.

It has recently been argued that the Albigensian Crusade was not as bloody as it has traditionally been depicted. The case has been made by a leading historian of the Cathars, but one who specialises in religious matters rather than military ones. This historian also doubts the extent of Catharism, which may well therefore inform his position of mitigation; however, as I argue here, the war was not primarily a confessional one but instead one about the land and its people. Other estimates reassert the terrible toll of the conflict. Harvard Professor Steven Pinker, in his recent bestseller *The Better Angels of Our Nature: A History of Violence and Humanity* (2011), states his belief that the crusade claimed some 200,000 victims (some put the figure as high as an implausible 1 million). He writes that 'The reason you have never met a Cathar is that the Albigensian Crusade exterminated them.' He goes on to say, 'Historians classify this episode as a clear instance of genocide.' Statistics are notoriously slippery creatures at the best of times; those relating to the medieval period are even more elusive. But as readers will discover, the vicious nature of the war and its numerous massacres kept the victim count consistently high.

As mentioned above, military concerns overrode all others and the crusade can only be fully understood if one comprehends the nature of medieval warfare. The Albigensian Crusade really was one of the most brutal conflicts in Western Europe in the entire Middle Ages, and perhaps the most brutal of all.

The massacres of the crusade are generally regarded as being religiously motivated, and are seen in terms of heretics killed in sieges and, more especially, burnt at the stake following the capture of a Cathar stronghold. Here I stress that most massacres were, in fact, motivated primarily by military considerations and were frequently indiscriminate as to the victims' religious beliefs. This important aspect is reflected in the book's title. Religious fanaticism certainly did add to the bloodiness of the war, but its shocking scale and extent were motivated more by pursuit of the military imperative to win at whatever cost and by the fact that this was a war of conquest and regional survival. It was the struggle for the control of land that made the conflict so bitter.

The war is made especially vivid by a number of factors. Some chronicles devote great attention to the conflict, recording the acts of war and brutality that marked the crusade. They also record the remarkable heroism of those involved on both sides: Simon de Montfort, who led his troops from the front, winning unexpected victories and rescuing his men from deadly situations; and southern Catholics who refused to hand over Cathars to be burnt by the crusaders, and fought bravely to defend their way of life.

The protagonists are imposing characters. Among these are the brave and ruthless Simon de Montfort, an experienced and highly capable general of great ambition, ready to risk his life in combat to inspire his men; the equally ambitious and even revolutionary Pope Innocent III, determined to support the spiritual presence of the Church with muscular and practical force; the neglected but colourful figure of Louis the Lion, King of France for only three years, who died while completing the main conquest of the south; and the resourceful counts of Toulouse, defending their territory from the northern invasion.

The crusade is replete with dramatic and detailed accounts of sieges and battles, many of which have received relatively little military analysis: Termes, Muret, Minerve, Toulouse, Beaucaire, Castelnaudary, Avignon; massacres from the war's beginning to its end, from Béziers to Montségur; and, in the war's final phases, the much-overlooked siege of Carcassonne (1240) and battle of Saintes (1242). This provides a rarely taken opportunity to analyse the warfare of the crusade in terms of battles, sieges and campaigns, and interesting features of these (such as the military innovation of the new, precision trebuchet, a siege machine with a reputation for demolishing the walls of cities and castles).

The war also marks the first use in medieval history of a crusade against a Christian enemy – for the Cathars were not the military enemy, this status falling to the Catholic counts of Toulouse and Trencavel. Thus the savagery for which the crusade is famous should not be seen in purely religious terms, as ultimately this was a war between the north and south, the former looking for territorial gains (underlined by grants of enemy lands to the crusaders, fuelling their self-interest), the latter defending their different laws, customs, language and independence. It is considered, probably correctly, that the southern lands needed to be transferred to rulers who were unreservedly orthodox in their Catholic beliefs so that the Cathar heresy could finally be extirpated by firm leadership and by the Inquisition; that said, the transfer of land was to be implemented by military means – and that, in simple terms, meant conquest. In fact, as noted above, some recent scholarship has raised the question of whether Catharism was much of a phenomenon at all, and suggested that its threat was manufactured and massively inflated so as to provoke a military response. After the war council of Lavaur in 1213, the crusade made little pretence of using heresy as a *casus belli*, and focused on all-out conquest of the south.

Identity is more important than religion in explaining the crusade's ferocity. When tied to land, group identities – whether tribal, regional or national – invoke fiercely strong feelings of 'us' and 'them', the other threatening one's very way of life and existence. Cathar communities were dispersed among Catholic ones in the south of France; what brought many of them together was a united opposition to the invasion of foreigners from across Europe, but mainly from northern France. For this reason, and to emphasise the primacy of territory, I have largely avoided referring to the enemies of the crusaders collectively as Cathars, using this term to denote religious persons rather than combatants. Instead, for those resisting the crusaders I generally use the cultural and broad regional identifications of Occitanians (some prefer the term Occitans) and, most frequently, southerners. This war spilled across the contested lands of Languedoc (*langue d'oc*), denoting the southerners' different linguistic heritage from the rest of France. For their enemies, which encompassed troops from Europe seeking either redemption or booty (and usually both), I have used the terms northerners and French (for they led and dominated the invading forces) and, of course, crusaders. For this was, despite many cynical motivations, a fully fledged crusade.

Travelling across the region researching this book, I was struck by how the beautiful landscape of Languedoc clarified my understanding of the war, not least the question of how such astonishing, formidable and vertiginous castles of southern resistance could fall to the crusaders by siege. I hope that this book explains to the reader the warfare and campaigning of the crusade. It is written for those interested in medieval history – especially its darker side – and medieval wars specifically. It is also designed to accompany interested visitors as they tour the region, especially the famous Cathar castles, so that they may have a full understanding of the remarkable and bloody events that surround these magnificent historical sites.

CATHARS, CATHOLICS AND CRUSADERS: 'THE GENERATION OF VIPERS'

The Cathar Heresy

Just before dawn on 14 January 1208, Peter of Castelnau was on the banks of the Rhône north of Arles, making ready to cross the river. Peter was the papal legate, sent to Languedoc by Pope Innocent III to root out the evil scourge of Catharism, a heresy that had taken hold in the region and which threatened the supremacy of the Catholic Church. As Peter prepared himself, 'an evil-hearted squire' galloped up to the legate and 'drove his sharp sword into his spine and killed him'.[1] Another account claims that the murderer ran the legate through with his lance. As the unknown assailant made his escape to kinsmen in Beaucaire, a stronghold of heresy, the mortally wounded Peter raised his hands, asked God to forgive his attacker and, as dawn broke, died a martyr to his faith. His death sparked the launch of the Albigensian Crusade and three and a half decades of vicious warfare in southern France.

Just as the assassination of Archduke Franz Ferdinand in Sarajevo in August 1914 was the trigger that unleashed the First World War, so Peter's murder is the moment at which words were replaced with weapons. In both cases, the precipitating murder was so momentous because it brought to a head, in one defining act, the long build-up of frustration, dispute and tension that was to erupt into open war. The combustible ingredients that sparked such an explosive outburst of prolonged violence had been stirred into the melting pot of Languedoc for some time.

That a crusade should be fought over religion is seemingly self-evident. The target of the crusaders was the heretical Catharism of southern France. The origins of the heresy appear to lie in the dualism of the Bogomils, who stemmed from tenth-century Bulgaria; French writers therefore sometimes called them *bougres*, a deliberate insult and accusation of sodomy. Less clear is when Catharism originally spread into Languedoc. It may first have appeared there in the form of Manicheanism (itself based on dualism) just after the millennium, a time of febrile religious activity, new thinking and the increased recording of heretical developments. Thus, at the end of 1000, we can read of the case of Leutard, a peasant from Châlons in France, who for some scholars displays Bogomil tendencies. The monk Ralph the Bald tells how Leutard, 'an emissary from Satan', fell asleep after exhausting himself with hard labour, and how he claimed that 'a great swarm of bees entered his body through his privates'. They passed though him, tormenting him with stings, before exiting through his mouth. They then started speaking to him, revealing to him a new spiritual life. He entered his local church and, in an iconoclastic rage, broke the crucifix and image of Christ. He then started preaching anti-clerical sentiments and the rejection of some aspects of the Bible. It is interesting to note that 'in a short time, his fame, as if it were that of a sane and religious person, drew to him no small part of the common people'. Although his career as a visionary was short-lived – before long he 'threw himself to death in a well' – it demonstrates that new religious ideas, however oddly inspired, could spread quickly and find a receptive audience.[2]

That Catharism had established itself in Languedoc by the mid-twelfth century is evident from the works of the great reformist preacher Bernard of Clairvaux during his anti-heresy mission to Toulouse; evidence of Cathar beliefs from the same time is also to be found in the Rhineland. Two decades later, it was concentrating the minds of church leaders. In 1163, Pope Alexander III condemned the heresy emanating from Toulouse but which had by now spread to northern France, Germany and Italy; heretics with Cathar beliefs were burned in Cologne in 1163 and Vézelay in 1167. The German episode prompted the monk Eckbert of Schönau to write his *Sermon against the Cathars*; he seems to suggest that heretics of similar beliefs had been burned in the city some twenty years earlier. However, a small group of Cathars known as *Publicani* failed to gain a footing in England in the 1160s: they converted only one Catholic and their group was broken up. A church council at Oxford condemned them and King Henry II, enforcing the secular arm of the law, had the heretics whipped, branded and cast naked into the winter, decreeing that no one should help them or associate with them in any way.

The situation proved very different in Languedoc, where tolerance rather than suppression was more widely the response; indeed, across the region Cathars were living openly among the orthodox believers without any hindrance and very little, if any, censure. By the early 1170s, the Cathars had established their first diocese at Albi, hence the name Albigensians given to them. And by the end of that decade, Count Raymond V of Toulouse sent letters of supplication to the Church calling for assistance:

> The disease of heresy has grown so strong in my lands that almost all those who follow it believe they are serving God … The priesthood is corrupted with heresy; ancient churches, once held in reverence, are no longer used for divine worship but have fallen into ruins; baptism is denied; the Mass is hated; confession is derided … Worst of all, the doctrine of two principles is taught.[3]

Raymond's letter captures how pervasive Catharism and some of its tenets, including dualism ('the two principles'), had become. Christian theology – which at this time meant Catholic theology as Catholicism was the monolithic religion – teaches that God is the 'Maker of all things visible and invisible'. Cathars rejected this doctrine and instead proposed a dualist one. For them, the real, tangible world was the creation of an Evil God of darkness, the demiurge, while the spiritual world was the work of the competing Good God of light. The demiurge kept the divine souls of humans imprisoned in their physical bodies (or other warm-blooded animals), condemning them to perpetual reincarnation. This cycle could only be broken by adherence to Cathar beliefs.

There are similarities and differences between Catholic Christianity and Catharism. Moderate dualists can be considered Christian heretics in that they believed Christ and Satan were the sons of one God and that Christ was sent to this world to free it from Satan's clutches and release men's souls to heaven. Absolute dualists offered a new religion (but still with very strong Christian influences) as they held the belief that the Evil God and the Good God were independent, of equal power and co-eternal. By the end of the twelfth century, following a successful preaching mission in the early 1170s by Bishop Nicetas of the Bogomil Church of Constantinople, the absolutist version had gained dominance in Languedoc. But we should allow for variances: different Cathars held their beliefs to varying extents, just as today many Catholics, for example, do not follow every single teaching of the Church in Rome. As the unorthodox new faith grew and developed, so it was received in different forms in different places by different people.

Nonetheless, there were some accepted basic tenets adhered to by the majority of the Cathars, many of which share a Christian heritage. Although Cathars obviously did not celebrate the Eucharist (as they would not rejoice in the body and blood), at breakfast and at dinner they did break bread and share it with the words: 'May the grace of our Lord Jesus Christ be with us always.' A more explicit sharing was the acceptance that the Bible was divinely ordained, but with some exceptions (much as the unfortunate Leutard had claimed). Cathars anticipated the Protestant reformers of the fifteenth and sixteenth centuries in reading the Bible in the vernacular and in rejecting most of the sacraments of the Catholic Church; for the Cathars, as with the Protestants, the sacramental focus was on baptism. In keeping with their rejection of the physical world, Christ became man to spread his message but his body did not rise again as his spirit returned to heaven, while his mother Mary was an angel. (These elements were present in the Docetic sect of the early Church.)

Central to their belief was the sacrament of *consolamentum*, their baptismal rite that also echoed Catholicism's sacraments of confirmation and, when applied to believers on their deathbed (as was common), extreme unction. 'Consolation' by the laying-on of hands was reserved only for those who had full knowledge and understanding of the faith, and for the dying. This ritual reconnected the recipient's soul with his spirit at death, breaking the cycle of reincarnation. Only those who had been consoled were actual members of the Cathar church; the other believers were followers guided by the clergy. The clergy were known as the 'perfects' and, crucially, these included women equally (hence *perfecti* for men, *perfectae* for women). They also went by the name the Good Men and the Good Women. The name Cathar itself comes from the Greek *katharos* ('pure'). Catholic antagonists played on these terms and used them sarcastically to mock what they tried to project as a holier-than-thou attitude. Becoming a *perfectus* or *perfecta* entailed enormous personal sacrifice. Once consoled, the perfect had to reject the world and live a life of extreme asceticism. On the less onerous side, the perfect could not swear oaths, lie or take the life of a warm-blooded animal even to save their own life (as human spirits inhabited the bodies of animals). More onerous on a day-to-day basis were prayers at set hours fifteen times through the day and night; a prohibition against consuming anything from a warm-blooded animal, be it meat, milk, cheese, fat or eggs (only fish was permitted in an otherwise high-carb diet); a requirement to undergo strenuous fasting; a total renunciation of all property (except for a habit and a Bible) and of family and social ties; and a lifetime of complete abstinence from sex (as procreation perpetuated the evil world). Given these severe stipulations, it is remarkable that Catharism had any followers at all. But the consoled were a small group of elite clergy and those facing imminent death; followers were free to pursue their own lives fully with none of the curtailments of the perfect, knowing that hedonistic indulgences counted for little when a deathbed *consolamentum* would spring them into heaven. Perhaps the most overindulgent good-timers would prefer to be reincarnated anyway.

The Cathars were virulently antagonistic towards the Catholic Church, but their own church emulated it in some ways. The relationship between the perfect and followers was not so different from that between more austere monasticism and the laity: most perfects seem to have lived in same-sex communes, some offering charity and others being more eremitically inclined, mirroring Christianity's holy hermits. Catharism had its bishops and dioceses divided into deaconries (though no church buildings: meetings took place in private houses); funding came from the bishops, donations and alms, and from the labour of the perfect, many of whom were weavers. Much of this reflected the structure of the Catholic Church, though of course on a much less grander scale. Despite the Cathars' anti-clericalism, which reflected some attitudes of the time, extreme deference to their version of the clergy was expected of believers: when meeting a perfect, the follower was to kneel down to him three times while saying 'Bless us, have mercy on us'. Other than that, believers (*credentes*) had little to do in the form of rituals that was absolutely necessary; many would still attend Catholic masses (whether for social or protective reasons) and fulfil Holy Day obligations that remained far more exacting than anything they had to perform for formal Catharism. However, devout believers would try to follow the challenging example of the perfects; more challenging again was that the authorities persecuted Cathars, so the heretical faith could demand the ultimate sacrifice.

Recently, an influential school of thought has challenged much of this picture, claiming that Catharism as a threat was little more than a fiction manufactured by a paranoid Church and avaricious princes, and that the heresy was not a counter-church but merely a localised, largely individual unorthodox expression of belief. Even one of the most important scholars of heresy has questioned his earlier work on the Cathars, which has been instrumental in shaping our views on the heresy, suggesting that the early heretics were discontents from monastic orders, especially the Premonstratensians, and otherwise orthodox reformers such as the Patarenes. It has also been argued that the dualism of the Albigensians was a useful excuse to vindicate the sacking of Constantinople by crusaders in 1204, as dualist beliefs were strong in the East, and thus as justification to move into Languedoc. While there is something to be said for medieval powers having overstated the extent of Catharism – it is a constant in warfare to inflate the danger of an enemy one intends to attack – this revisionist approach, which offers some extremely valuable insights, perhaps goes a little too far, and has already been challenged, with the reality lying somewhere in-between.

The extent of an established Cathar church and structure can be overemphasised as the revisionists claim; this structure may have represented an ideal rather than the reality, but may also have reflected the experience of disaffected monks in its ranks who were used to such structure and a chain of command. There was a formal organisation and hierarchy, however loose, as the Cathars imitated existing religious models after their own fashion. But Catharism's international connections should not be played down too much, either. It is the nature of new religious movements to proselytise, spreading their message far and wide. Missionaries from Eastern Europe, Catalonia and Italy ensured Languedoc had contacts with the wider movement of Catharism. Exaggeration of the heresy by Inquisitors eager to justify their livelihood was indeed common (in the same way that Matthew Hopkins, the notorious Witchfinder General, promoted his career in mid-seventeenth-century England), but they had plenty to work on. Evidence for the Cathar heresy is clear from before Church theologians began denouncing it; furthermore, clear distinctions were made between various forms of heresy, especially those of

Cathars and the poverty-inspired Waldensians, with Catholic churchmen holding documented debates with these two groups in the same meeting. While the extent of the threat of Catharism to orthodoxy may have been magnified by the Church, it was a direct and growing challenge to it and a very real phenomenon that required a response. That response was at first spiritual, but then martial.

Something of a benign myth has been created around the Cathar faith, whose adherents are known to us as gentle, vegan pacifists who would not even allow animals to be harmed. Yet their ultimate goal – as extreme in its belief as its chances of success – was the elimination of the human race through the ending of procreation. As mentioned above, the perfects constituted a very small group; followers might try to imitate them, but as a whole they do not seem to be that different from their neighbours in displaying nastiness and discriminatory behaviour; indeed, the slightly cultish feel of Catharism led to some unsympathetic treatment of those less fervent or inferior in their devotions. It is important that this less favourable picture is depicted, as it helps us to understand why the Albigensian Crusade was not a one-sided act of extreme violence with atrocities meted out just by those wearing the cross.

Ermessinde Viguier was a Cathar wife who lived in the village of Cambiac on the eastern side of Toulouse. In 1222 she was present at a Cathar meeting where other women mocked and belittled her for being pregnant. Having been told she was carrying a demon and bringing forth wickedness into the world, she understandably left the church, even though her Cathar husband beat her with a rod to force her stay. Some Cathar women were coerced into abortions. This attempt to counter maternal instincts ensured that male followers outnumbered female ones.

The famous Cathar village of Montaillou near Ax les Thermes offers more extreme examples. Sybille Pierre's daughter of under twelve months, Jacotte, was seriously ill. A perfect, Prades Tavernier, consoled the infant (the *consolamentum* was not usually administered to dying children) and told Sybille not to give her any milk; in effect, Jacotte was to undergo the *endura*, the final fast after a deathbed consolation that ensured release of the spirit. Sybille would not stand by and let her child die, so she strengthened Jacotte by 'putting her to the breast'. When her husband Raymond discovered this, 'he was very grieved, troubled and lamented'. Other villagers labelled Sybille a 'wicked mother' and a 'demon' for saving her baby daughter, and for a long while afterwards Sybille said that her husband 'insulted and threatened me ... and stopped loving the child'.[4] Insecurity heightened tensions in the village. Arnald Lizier was a Catholic and not trusted by the villagers; he was murdered and his corpse discarded at the castle gates. Mengarde Maury had denounced Pierre Clergue, the village's womanising priest, to the Inquisition; she had her tongue cut out. The gap between a religion's ideals and practices – common to all faiths – affected the Cathars as much as the Catholics. The Cathars were governed by human instincts and thoughts that they may have striven, but often failed, to overcome. Throughout history, beliefs – be they religious or political – have all too often been cited as the justification of an end, no matter how bloody or cruel, or how imperfectly adhered to by followers.

Nor was general morality very different between Cathars and Catholics, the records from Montaillou revealing rape of females and male youths at knifepoint. Pierre Clergue, the priest, encapsulates the crossover between the two religions: a Catholic by ordination but a Cathar by sympathy, he had over a dozen mistresses and took delight in deflowering virgins. 'One woman is just like another,' he said. 'The sin is the same, whether she is married or not. Which is as much as to say that there is no sin about it at all.'[5]

A great appeal of Catharism was the example set by the *perfecti* in their holy, simple and devout lives. But the perfects were often not perfect at all; being in the human form that they despised, they suffered as much as the next person from a willing spirit but weak flesh – and sometimes from a spirit that really wasn't very willing at all. We have little information on the perfects' private lives, but there are occasional glimpses to suggest that they were as prone to sin as their Catholic counterparts. Guillaume Bélibaste, considered the last perfect missionary in Languedoc, had a mistress called Raimonde. As a Good Man, his sole companion should have been male. Bélibaste passed her off as a servant (rather like many a Catholic priest at the time) and to those closer to him as his wife with whom he had no sexual relations, insisting that when they had to sleep in a bed (when travelling) they did so fully clothed so that no naked skin touched. This was all stretching it a bit thin, and the deception was revealed, along with much flesh, when Raimonde's sister walked into their room and caught them in the act.

The maxim that power corrupts and absolute power corrupts absolutely applies here. It was coined by Lord Acton in 1871: a Catholic historian, he applied it to Pope Leo IX's grab at papal infallibility when the Church lost its Papal States in the Italian Risorgimento; Leo hoped to replace the loss by accruing more spiritual powers. Whether communities were Cathar, Catholic or a mixture of both, spiritual leaders had both greater responsibilities to help their flock and greater opportunities to abuse it. (The paedophile scandal in the Catholic Church – and others – revealed at the start of this century is a stark demonstration of this truth.) It is therefore important to recognise that the Cathar–Catholic divide was not black and white, whether in terms of morality or compassion for those different in their beliefs. Being of one faith or the other did not somehow automatically strip a person of their human instincts for good, wrongdoing, self-promotion, defence – or their ability to commit horrible acts of violence on those perceived as a threat.

Southern France in the Early Thirteenth Century

Another 'pro-Cathar' exaggerated distortion exists in perceptions of the south being some kind of idyllic society that was trampled underfoot by the invading crusaders. It was not. Languedoc was a highly militarised society – just witness the proliferation of castles that still dominate the landscape – with its multifarious nobility waging constant war among itself and against others. Bands of mercenaries (*routiers*) terrorised the region as they made handsome profits from the business of war. Private armies consisted of these and retainers who were either paid cash or, in the more feudal sense, given land in return for military service. The lack of political unity among the southerners, a major cause of their military weakness, was exacerbated by the fact that much of the aristocracy's land was allodial, meaning that it was held in outright ownership (in contradistinction to feudalism) and so magnates often had less of a call on powerful overlords to help them or on a mutually reinforcing feudal structure locally. To add to their problems, the incessant warfare cost them economically, too, though the region remained prosperous as a whole.

Land holdings could be small, and even the main powers such as the counts of Toulouse had small parcels of land dotted around the south in a bewildering patchwork of possession. In 1207, Mirepoix, thanks mainly to the common practice of shared inheritance, was under the joint leadership of thirty-five heirs. Unsurprisingly, many knights sought to augment their income by diversification in trade and commerce, both of which abounded in the region (that the Cathars did not oppose usury may have added to their appeal among this class).

Political affiliation was fluid and confusing. Nominally, Philip II was king of all France; in practical terms, his direct authority was only just starting to expand beyond Paris and his influence in Occitania was extremely limited. In the south, the Aragonese crown owned some lands with vassals paying homage and ensuring its interest in the region. Areas of Provence owed allegiance to the Holy Roman Emperor while Aquitaine was ruled by the Angevin kings of England, following the marriage of Henry Plantagenet to Eleanor of Aquitaine after King Louis VII of France had divorced her; with the exception of Avignon in Provence, neither of these two territories suffered much in the way of prolonged encroachments from the crusade. The area of the Massif Central in the north of the region also escaped the ravages of war except for on its periphery, not least because here strong ecclesiastical lords dominated, ensuring that heresy was kept under control. The territories most affected by the northern invasion edged onto the Pyrénées. To the east, the nobility variously paid homage to their lords in Aquitaine, Toulouse and Aragon; here, the counts of Toulouse and of Foix play a major role in our story. To the west lay the crucible of war in the region, from Toulouse through Carcassonne to Béziers, and encompassing Montpellier, Narbonne and Nîmes. Here the Count of Toulouse held sway, although his lordship was far from all-pervasive as the great centres of Narbonne and Montpellier were beyond his grasp (the latter falling into the Aragonese orbit in 1204).

In this last area, where many of the crusade's worst excesses were to occur, lay the lands of the Trencavel family. The head of the family at the start of the crusade was the Viscount Raymond Roger of Béziers; he plays the leading southerner part in the bloodshed of 1209. Although only 150 of the 500 castles in their four counties of Béziers, Albi, Carcassonne and Razès owed them service, the Trencavels were effective at punching belligerently above their weight to cause trouble and gain influence. Like the Count of Foix, the Trencavels paid homage to the King of Aragon, but it did them little good. The Trencavel dynasty was the one to suffer most from the crusade, not helped by the enmity between its heads and the counts of Toulouse and by their overlord's reluctance to intervene on its behalf lest it upset Aragon's relations with the papacy. Not even Raymond Roger's subjects were altogether supportive: the inhabitants of Béziers had murdered Raymond Roger's father – a mark of how tumultuous the region was. Nowhere is the southerners' lack of unity and mutual support more exposed than with Raymond Roger; we have noted the region's fragmented nature which left individual lords vulnerable, especially if acting on their own against a massive force as presented by the crusade, and the Trencavels simply had too little support to resist the onslaught for any length of time.

Despite its political fragmentation, the south has been deemed a country by some historians. This is not meant in the sense of a state but in the sense of a *natio*: a defined area sharing common laws, culture, customs and, crucially, language. Modern historians and sociologists have been too ready to deny national groupings in the Middle Ages, but national identity according to the persuasive primordial school of thought was a very real feature of many societies; fighting for one's country, *pro patria*, is witnessed in numerous chronicles written during the time of crusade. Many of the place and street names the visitor encounters in this region testify to the strong linguistic links to the Catalan tongue; for southerners, the *langue d'oïl* of northern France was more of a foreign language. The peoples of the north and south of France also identified themselves in relation to each other, the southerner seeing the stereotypical northerner as crude, unrefined, brutish and bellicose, altogether lacking in manners and culture, while the equally stereotypical southerner was viewed from the north as sybaritic, indulgent, indolent and effete. Minor elements of veracity were blown up into caricatures, but war propaganda on both sides exacerbated these differences greatly so as to demonise the enemy. Once the enemy has been demonised, it is easier to kill him without troubling one's conscience.

It is also extremely important to recognise that the land being fought over was wealthy – hence the crusade attracting so many willing participants. It is no surprise that the war's main theatre of operations was in the prosperous regions of the Trencavel family. Recent scholarship suggests that initially the crusaders' aim was first and foremost the destruction of Raymond Roger, although for reasons other than the most obvious one of sharing out the spoils. Languedoc had large rural and urban populations. Its cities, many ancient in origin, were expanding rapidly, boosted by trade across the Mediterranean, including with Egypt and Syria; they exported wine, dyed woollens, olive oil and grain while importing spices, silks and luxury items. Travelling across the region today, especially between Béziers and Carcassonne, one is still struck by the expansive panorama of never-ending vineyards. The cities were also developing in a similar way to those of Italy, with independence and self-government growing in importance, and near autonomy being represented by magistrates, proconsuls and councils of oligarchs. The nobility collected dues from the urban centres, but had a decreasing say in their governance. Even villages attempted ambitious plans for semi-autonomy.

This independence asserted itself militarily, too. At the end of the twelfth century Toulouse, the largest of the region's cities, was spreading its influence in an attempt to secure castles that posed a threat to its commercial trading routes and outlying villages that supplied the city with food (an essential logistical consideration in times of siege). The city made wars, alliances and treaties to protect and expand its commercial activities and wealth; in this respect, it was similar to a great lord or prince. The urban centres could generally raise their own militias and they had the money to employ mercenaries. They were forces to be reckoned with.

Even before the crusaders came, the locals were squabbling over the region's bounty: the nobility, burghers and the Church could find themselves in a three-way contest for influence and control over the centres, as happened at Narbonne; in Montpellier the nobility was dominant; in Toulouse the burghers were the leading political force; in the towns of the Massif Central, the Church was very powerful. Such divisions enabled heretics – who could be influential townspeople – to play off different parties against each other, especially against the Church. The crusade added another unwelcome player jostling for position; this actually helped Catharism to grow in some areas, such as the Quercy, where the nobility allied with heretics in common cause against the northerners who were attempting to impose their more feudal rules and obligations on the independently minded south. Where the crusade did succeed in ostensibly preventing overt demonstrations of heresy, it was still left with the problem of political resistance, which, in turn, impeded the complete eradication of heterodoxy and thus encouraged its survival.

The Mediterranean influence on the region was also apparent in Languedoc's tolerance. The direct trade and contacts with a diversity of faiths – Jewish, Islamic, Greek Orthodox and others – created a more benign atmosphere of open-mindedness, not least because many locals depended on foreign trade for their livelihood. These contacts did exist further in the more rural north, but to a much lesser extent and were normally indirect through third parties. Catharism, stemming from Eastern Europe, was not such a seismic shock, as it was absorbed steadily into the mainstream of popular belief and could often co-exist with many elements of everyday Catholicism due to a relative lack of aggressive imposition or resistance. Most significantly of all, the majority of Cathar believers were notable for being completely normal in all things other than their religion; and as Catharism spread, that, too, became normal and accepted. Whether as neighbours, business associates or close relatives, most Cathars were integrated into the very fabric of society. When a bishop of Toulouse asked a Catholic knight from the south why he and others like him had not acted fiercely against the Cathars, the knight replied: 'We cannot; we were brought up with them, there are many of our relatives amongst them, and we can see that their way of life is a virtuous one.'[6]

The Church was on the frontline against heresy, but it could only prove effective when it worked in conjunction with the secular authorities. Elsewhere in Europe, especially the north, monarchs were often just as keen as the Church to suppress heresy: any unorthodoxy was perceived as a threat to the natural order and the great chain of being. Church and state had a symbiotic relationship, though it was often a disharmonious one. In southern France the close connection existed but was looser due to the fissiparous nature of society and the greater competition of polities. This competition weakened the Church, but while many abbots and bishops were fabulously wealthy, others were not: in 1200 the Bishop of Toulouse, a city of enormous wealth, relied on food handouts from the cathedral. The region's nobility reduced its economic competition and enriched itself by sequestrating tithes from the Church and seizing its lands. Nor was the nobility overly inclined to grant lands and rights to the Church as much as their counterparts did in the north. The rivalry had serious consequences. It has recently been suggested that Raymond Roger's poor relations with the powerful Cistercian order (to whom Count Raymond V of Toulouse made his appeal against heresy) were instrumental in his being targeted at the start of the crusade. A Church that was losing money and influence was less attractive for a career of the younger sons (and daughters) of the nobility and wealthy townspeople. For all the culture and learning that medieval Languedoc is famous for, the clergy there suffered from a relative lack of education, vibrant theological debate and reforming awareness, all of which were exacerbated by the distance from universities and centres of advanced study. The Church was therefore not as intellectually adept as it might have been in countering the teachings of the Cathars. The overall effect of these factors, combined with the lack of a unified ecclesiastical hierarchy, caused a relative weakening of the Church in southern France, rendering it poorly suited to countering the new heresy.

Competing economic and political powers, a weakened Church and the cosmopolitan air of tolerance all combined, therefore, to create an environment in which heresy could flourish. As different parts of local society vied to advance their own interests, heresy slipped in and flourished, so much so that in some communities Catharism utterly displaced Catholicism and became, in effect, the new orthodoxy. As Count Raymond lamented in his plea for help to the Cistercians, the problem was now too great to ignore. The authorities had to strike back.

The Outbreak of War

At first, the Church tried persuasion. It was responsible to God for the souls under its care, so reconversion took priority over simply killing heretics. A Cathar burnt at the stake was a sign of failure, even if it were hoped that at the same time the heat of the flames would drive others away from apostasy. When the crusaders came, they were not so concerned with theological matters; for them, eradicating heretics was the same as eradicating heresy. Niceties such as determining a suspect's unorthodoxy and offering them a chance to recant did not figure high on their list of priorities. It has been estimated that for the first five years of the crusade, between 1209 and 1214, the number of heretics who went to the stake without trial outnumbered all those executed by due legal process in the previous 200 years.

As Catharism progressed, it was clear that Languedoc was not dealing with the problem; all initiatives against the heresy came from outside. Count Raymond V of Toulouse saw an opportunity. Raymond was in a difficult position: Aragon had wrestled Provence from his grasp in 1176 and was now constantly threatening the western borders of his county of Toulouse; his ally Emperor Frederick Barbarossa was submitting to the pope; his capital city had been taken over by the burghers; and danger from Aquitaine hovered over him. Eager to get on the right side of the papacy (a temporal as well as spiritual power), he made his appeal to the Cistercians in 1178. Henry of Marcy, Abbot of Clairvaux, was one of many to express horror at Toulouse's open infestation by heresy, bewailing 'all the evil abominations which that noble city nourished in the bosom of its belief'. The city was now 'a place of abomination, of desolation … There the heretics ruled the people and reigned among the clergy … Heretics spoke out and all applauded'. As he walked through the streets, the Cathars 'railed at us, pointed their fingers at us, shouted at us that we were imposters, hypocrites and heretics'.[7] He also called upon King Henry II of England and King Louis VII of France for help. Here we see already the politicisation of the heresy issue and how regional power structures impacted upon anti-heresy policy.

Urged on by Raymond and Henry, Pope Alexander sent his legate in France, Peter of Pavia, to Toulouse as part of a joint papal and royal commission supported by kings Henry and Louis. That the heresy had spread to the city's elite is shown by the prosecution of Pierre Maurand, a prosperous merchant. His fate is instructive: having recanted his unorthodoxy, his penitential sentence was to spend three years in the Holy Land; when he returned, he was elected to high office as consul on the city's governing board. Two other heretics were also excommunicated at this time. Although missionary work was to continue as the primary response, Abbot Henry realised already that the problem was so entrenched it would take military force to expunge it: 'We know this triumph will not be denied to those who struggle for us, if they are willing to fight in the love of Christ.'[8] The Third Lateran Council, held in March 1179, took the message on board and, while acknowledging that the Church was not in the business of shedding blood, it called upon secular help to threaten physical violence. The heretical town of Lavaur felt the implications of this call in 1181 when Abbot Henry, by now papal legate, led Catholic nobles in a successful and relatively bloodless siege of the place. There was no concerted spiritual supervision afterwards so the action did not deracinate the heresy but merely displaced it; three decades later it was still staunchly Cathar, but its fate then was to be far, far worse.

Heresy continued to spread, helped by the distractions of those who might have quelled it. The papacy's focus was elsewhere. It had to contend with the fall of Jerusalem to Saladin in 1187 and the massive enterprise of the Third Crusade until 1192; the latter's failure meant that future plans for the Holy Land remained a priority, and the Fourth Crusade was launched in 1202. Closer to home, the papacy was preoccupied by the traditional German incursions into Italy, the Emperor Henry VI taking Sicily and leaving the Papal States feeling surrounded and vulnerable. There was also the matter of five papal elections between 1181 and 1198. One of the popes from this period, Lucius III, managed to address heresy in his decretal *Ab abolendam* ('On abolition') of 1184. This excommunicated Cathar, Waldensian and Humiliati heretics and, importantly, all those who offered them any form of support. It stipulated that bishops were to travel to places in their dioceses suspected of heresy and put on trial in their courts anyone denounced by reliable witnesses. Those who refused to recant were to be handed over to the secular authorities for unspecified punishment beyond removal of fiefs (which was temporary for those who reconverted). The measure of the decretal's lack of success may be gauged by Archbishop Berengar of Narbonne's failure to tour his diocese for ten years since taking up his office in 1191.

The last decade of the twelfth century saw the emergence of two figures who were absolutely central to the Albigensian Crusade: Count Raymond VI of Toulouse and Pope Innocent III. Both were 37 years of age when they came to power. Raymond inherited his title in 1194, by which time Catharism had become so ingrained that it was not so much an overriding problem for him as simply another facet of everyday life. To eradicate it would have taken ruthless single-mindedness, focused resolve and unrelenting energy. Raymond possessed none of these. He was more suited to a life of dilettantism than to political rule, especially in such a challenging environment. An admired patron of the arts and Languedoc's troubadour society, he indulged his love of luxury and sex with little restraint. He had at least five wives and any number of mistresses and, if we are to believe a hostile chronicler, so insatiable was his appetite even he committed incest with his sister. While confessing orthodox Catholicism to the end of his life, he was nevertheless completely at ease with heretics in his court and in his bed (his second wife, Beatrice of Béziers, was a prominent Cathar). His ultra-liberalism in confessional matters reflected, for his own lands, a sensible appreciation of reality. Others took a dim view of this misplaced tolerance. Peter of Vaux de Cernay deplored his inaction against the Cathars, the count even refusing to punish a heretic 'who emptied his bowels beside the altar in a church … and wiped himself clean with the altar cloth'. He denounced Raymond as 'a limb of the Devil, a son of perdition, an enemy of the cross, a persecutor of the Church, the defender of heretics, the oppressor of the Catholic faithful, the servant of treachery'.[9]

The Church's hostility towards the count owed much to its frequent run-ins with him. The Abbot of St Gilles protested when the count built the stone castle Mirapetra on his land without permission; the Abbot of Carpentras lost two castles to him; the Bishop of Agen was expelled from the city; the Abbot of Montauban and the Bishop of Vaison were imprisoned. Raymond's rough treatment of ecclesiastics was not unusual among the southern lords (Roger of Trencavel stood accused of incarcerating the Bishop of Albi in 1178) but when taken with his indulgent attitudes towards heresy and his power across the region, it marked him out as a major problem for the Church. In 1196 Raymond began his career as a serial excommunicate. But events such as those above and his appropriation of the fortified cathedral at Rodez reveal the primacy of his strategic and defensive concerns. This was the same for all the lords of Languedoc: religious matters, though they may have been important, always remained secondary to the concerns of local geopolitics.

In 1198, a 92-year-old pope, Celestine III, was replaced by a 37-year-old one: Innocent III. The youngest pontiff ever to be elected, Innocent remains one of the most formidable characters to sit on the throne of St Peter: brilliant, cynical, imposing, ruthless, skilful, authoritarian, obstinate and hugely ambitious, he resembled more a temporal prince than the spiritual leader of Christendom; he presented himself as the universal monarch and was the first pope to call himself the Vicar of Christ. He was the pope who called for the crusade against the Albigensians; in doing so, for all his outstanding ability, he probably worsened the situation. Catharism had directly challenged the supremacy of the Church and, as the latter saw it, was condemning increasing numbers to hell every year. For Innocent, the option of half-hearted countermeasures was no longer viable. The consequent crusade can be judged an overreaction that caused the situation to deteriorate in the short term due to the political reaction it provoked.

Innocent's attention to the dangers of the Cathar heresy may have been due to his experiences of Bulgaria and Bosnia, where Bogomilism had become a serious problem. Innocent had sent a legatine mission to the Balkans to help contain the spread of the dualist heresy and was directly involved in anxious correspondence with the region's leaders. The Fourth Crusade's taking of Constantinople in 1204 and Byzantine lands in Europe made him even more acutely aware of the internationalism of dualism.

For Innocent, this 'generation of vipers' (Matthew 12:34) in the heart of western Christendom was too great a danger to ignore.

Innocent began his fightback by sending legatine missions to Languedoc in 1198 and 1200–01. In 1199 his papal bull *Vergentis in senium* clarified the penalties against heretics: their lands would be expropriated by secular lords without regard to any Catholic heirs. There was no mention of the death penalty. The flaw in this approach was that it relied on these secular lords being orthodox in their beliefs in the first place, or at least nominally orthodox enough to comply with papal instructions. With Innocent's eventual preaching of the crusade, it is debated whether he wanted the southern lords coerced into stamping out heresy or their removal and replacement by men who were more willing to co-operate. In the first year of his papacy he had taken a radical step in launching a political crusade against Markward of Anweiler in Sicily; its success encouraged Innocent to employ fire and brimstone language alongside the missions in Languedoc: 'We concede the power to destroy, ruin and root out that which you know needs to be destroyed, ruined or rooted out'; to Count Raymond VI he wrote 'we will enjoin all the neighbouring princes to rise up against you as an enemy of Christ … Nor should the fury of the Lord be averted from you, but already his hand will be extended to strike you.'[10] To those who supported him in his work, he granted the same indulgences bestowed upon crusaders in the Holy Land.

This belligerent language was accompanied by a more reflective and persuasive approach through preaching and debate. In 1203 Peter of Castelnau and Master Ralph, Cistercian monks from Fontfroide, were assigned to head the legatine mission in Languedoc. They immediately asserted themselves, removing the Bishop of Béziers in 1203 for failing to co-operate fully with the anti-heresy drive. (In Carcassonne in 1207 the Catholic bishop was turned out by the city for being too co-operative.) In 1204 Carcassonne held a public debate with heretics; although it achieved little, it was notable for the presence of King Peter II of Aragon, anxious to pacify the disruptions among his feudal subjects. The presence of high-ranking preaching churchmen often had a deleterious, reactionary effect among locals who resented the elite, corporate face of the Church in an already anti-clerical environment that resented Church corruption and wealth; mocking, ridicule and contempt were common, as Abbot Henry of Clairvaux had discovered some years earlier in Toulouse.

A more concerted and successful preaching campaign took place amid a series of substantial public debates – some of these lasting from a week to over a fortnight – between 1206 and 1207 at Verfeil, Pamiers, Montréal, Servian, Béziers and Carcassonne. At Montréal, 'about 150 heretics were converted to the faith' reports William of Puylaurens.[11] Present at some of these debates were Arnald Amalric, the Abbot of Cîteaux, Bishop Diego of Osma and Dominic Guzman, who would found the Dominican order of friars ten years later. Dominic's simpler approach appealed to the apostolic leanings of Catharism and hence was more effective than earlier missions; he and his group preached 'not with an ostentatious escort of mounted men, but walking unshod on footways from place to place'.[12] Dominic set up base in Fanjeaux and established the nunnery at nearby Prouille, a positive alternative for Cathar women. But there were too few preachers and too many heretics spread out across the region's cities, towns and villages. Where they did make an impact, it was often fleeting as the converted slipped back into their old ways after the missionaries had moved on. By 1208 the missionary work had become ineffectual.

The political situation was even worse. In 1205 Raymond promised to make peace with the ecclesiastical powers in his region, restoring their powers (such as by knocking down the castle at Mirapetra), sending his mercenaries packing and persecuting heresy. But he did not. Peter of Castelnau, an intolerant, insensitive and intimidating man who incarcerated opponents at the drop of a hat, was active in Provence and stirring up animosity against Raymond so that the two regions were at war in 1207. Raymond needed his castles and mercenaries, and had little time and even less inclination for heretic hunting. Raymond was excommunicated once again and this time his lands were placed under interdict, which meant the withholding of church services and some of the sacraments (a move no doubt approved by the Cathars). In the summer Raymond found himself in a tight squeeze and once more made promises to accede to papal demands – and again he reneged on them. As one chronicler put it, the count 'had incurred the censure of the Church for the many grave outrages he had committed against her, and often – as might be expected of a person who was crafty and cunning, slippery and unreliable – had received absolution under the guise of feigned penitence'.[13]

Peter of Castelnau excommunicated him for a third time. Papal patience was wearing thin and tensions ratcheted up. The pope had for some time been aware that force might be the only answer. In 1205 he had written to King Philip II of France, asking him to lead a crusade against the heretics of the south. Philip declined. Innocent implored him again in November 1207; again Philip declined, still citing his war with England as his reason for doing so. This time Innocent had also contacted the great magnates of the north, men such as the counts of Nevers, Troyes, Vermandois, Blois and Dreux, offering them the lands of the conquered enemy and full crusading indulgences as granted to those fighting the Muslims in the Holy Land and Spain.

Raymond began to feel the pressure brought on by his procrastination. Either genuinely seeking a workable compromise or to buy more time, Count Raymond invited Peter to his court over Christmas 'and promised to give complete satisfaction on every heading under which he was accused'.[14] The resulting clash of interests and personalities only made matters worse, the meeting ending in acrimony; according to the author of the *Historia Albigensis*, the count made death threats against the legate. Peter left the court and on 14 January he and his entourage were encamped on the banks of the Rhône. By morning he was dead, run through by an unknown assailant. Fingers were pointed at Raymond; he was also accused of harbouring the killer. No evidence linking Raymond with the murder has ever come to light. It is most unlikely that the count had ordered the legate's death as this would have been political suicide; if the killer was somehow associated with the count, then the murderer may have had similar motivations to those who slew Thomas Becket. The assassination was the last straw for Innocent – an unforgivable insult and crime. Yet again Raymond, aware of the gravity of the situation, attempted to submit – probably genuinely for once – to the papacy. A measure of his concern was the poorly received embassy he sent to plead his innocence at Rome. But Innocent was not listening any more. The time for crusade had come.

Preparations for War

Pope Innocent was horrified and enraged when he heard the news of Peter's death in February. By 10 March he had already canonised this newest martyr to the faith. Without waiting for King Philip of France to take the lead (he had proven too reluctant in the past), Innocent took matters into his own hands. Arnald Amalric, the Abbot of Cîteaux, urged him to action: 'By Saint Martin, my lord, this talking is a waste of time! Have the indulgence proclaimed all over the world as far as Constantinople.'[15]

On the same day as the murdered legate's canonisation, the pope made his appeal to Christendom for an all-out crusade against the Cathars, concluding his long letter with a fiery call to arms:

> Forward, soldiers of Christ! Forward, brave recruits to the Christian army!
> Let the universal cry of grief of the Holy Church arouse you, let pious zeal
> inspire you to avenge this monstrous crime against your God!

The letter grants those who take up the cross a full plenary indulgence ('with our promise of remission of sins') and, in the very last sentence, the territory of the dispossessed by 'expelling him [Raymond] and his supporters from the towns of the Lord and seizing their lands, where Catholic inhabitants will take over from the displaced heretics and will serve God in holiness and righteousness according to the tenets of the true faith which you follow'.[16]

The letter reveals the intended crusade's objectives and motivations for those taking part. The spiritual element was central to recruitment. Indulgences granted sinners remission of temporal punishments for sins in this world and in purgatory and could be earned for just forty days' service – a stipulated period that was a constant problem for the crusading leaders trying to maintain the strength of their army. Purgatory was a recent addition to Catholic belief: a punitive demi-hell that purged souls to purify them for heaven. The less time spent there the better. If a crusader died while actually on crusade he would, as a holy warrior of God, skip purgatory altogether and move straight into paradise. For many, the notion that they were doing God's work, serving Him in a divine cause, was enough.

Financial motivations are more disputed. The costs and dangers of going to war were very high and enough to put many off enlisting. During the First Crusade at the very end of the eleventh century the Count of Blois performed his service in the Holy Land and, having had quite enough of the arduous campaigning and ever-present perils, returned home to France; his wife was not pleased to see him and promptly sent him back – to his death. The roll call of the dead at the siege of Acre on the Third

Crusade was long and sobering. Nevertheless, for some the danger and excitement was part of the appeal, while the opportunity for land and booty was not only enticing but also central for recruitment; the potential for enriching oneself in war was considerable, as we shall see. War offered a high-risk, high-reward environment.

For the knightly classes, the prospect of land was, I would argue cynically, the chief lure. Previous appeals for the north to descend on the heretics had met with a muted response. This time, however, the pope was unambiguously launching a crusade rather than trying to stir one up through others. The Count of Toulouse was, as already noted, serially excommunicated and then reconciled with the Church; this made intervention for northerners less attractive as they might have financed themselves and made lengthy preparations only to turn up in the south and be told that everything was fine again and that their services would not be needed as Raymond was back in the arms of Mother Church. This time there were greater prospects for their investment. The murder of Peter of Castelnau was a crossing of the Rubicon; it was not something that could be rectified by a hastily convened meeting, an apology and a settlement. The promise of the count's rich lands was now considerably less speculative.

Declaring Raymond's lands dispossessed was one thing; taking them was another altogether. This, essentially, is why the Albigensian Crusade was fought. Innocent's letter makes clear that he wanted orthodox sons of the faith to take control of Cathar territory so that heresy could be deracinated once and for all. Count Raymond had fallen foul of the papacy because he had not taken any action, despite numerous promises. Thus, the military strategy was necessary to support the spiritual one. It should be made clear that the lands could not be owned outright by their conquerors but would be subject to feudal restrictions. This was designed to reassure and reaffirm the rights of the great overlords of the region, most notably the kings of France and Aragon and the Holy Roman Emperor; without their support – or at least their acquiescence – the crusade would have had next to no chance of success. Lands taken would therefore be held as fiefs with incumbent obligations to a suzerain. In the case of Toulouse this was Philip II. This was the land-holding norm of northern Europe. Its imposition on the south, with its more varied form of tenure and independent allodial holdings, created real friction and opposition to the north's occupancy in Languedoc. An additional incentive was that the lands and property of crusaders would come under papal protection during their lord's absence and their interest payments on loans were cancelled and the capital payments suspended for the duration of their crusading service.

For most individuals, it was probably the combination of these factors rather than any single one that encouraged them to enlist. The danger was mitigated by less time in purgatory or even a straight path to heaven; by the opportunity for adventure and enrichment in an age when life was precarious anyway and where many existed on a subsistence level; and by the fact that self-interest could be wrapped up in an act of religious altruism. Arguably, the last of these is the most important. The Albigensian Crusade was a land-grab for God that served man equally.

The word went out across Europe via preaching missions to recruit men for the crusading army. Innocent dispatched to France his notary, Master Milo, as the new legate. Once there he joined with Arnald Amalric and visited Philip Augustus at Villeneuve in May. The French king, as ever, remained unmoved by religious fervour and resolutely put his own political interests above spiritual ones. This was the man who, although joint leader of the Third Crusade with Richard the Lionheart, left the Holy Land early to capitalise on his enemy Richard I's absence (Richard habitually got the better of him in their Anglo-French conflicts) to make territorial gains back on his home turf. There was nothing of the chivalrous knight in Philip: he was a cynical, calculating Machiavellian given to intrigue, who treated war as a business venture. An unattractive character, he nevertheless deserves some guarded admiration for his single-minded mission to extend the authority of the crown across his country. There is some merit in calling him the founder of the French nation.

Philip's reception of the papal mission was measured and cool. No, he would not lead the crusade as he was too busy with his own troubles: the 'two great and dangerous lions' Otto IV and King John were threatening his kingdom and demanding his urgent attention. In fact, Philip was once again taking advantage of his enemies' misfortunes, not least John's: England was about to fall under an interdict and the English king himself would be excommunicated; Philip's power, and that of France, was on the rise and the Capetian had no intention of stalling his momentum. However, he did make a concession to the legates. With him at court were the powerful barons the Duke of Burgundy and the counts of Nevers and

St Pol; these he permitted to take up the cross – but only after he had won the current round of the war with England.

Already this amounted to a significant core. Duke Odo of Burgundy was lord of one of the most prosperous territories in France; his contingent of troops was second in size only to the king's in any crusading army. Hervé de Donzy, the Count of Nevers, was a bellicose opportunist with an unenviable reputation for thuggish behaviour; he was to become a notorious figure in England. Between them, they could muster a maximum of 500 knights; although their entire contingents would not travel with them to Languedoc, as a significant number would have to remain at home to guard interests there (Nevers brought only eleven knights with him – a quarter of the total possible), they represented a considerable reservoir of manpower. The knights were well equipped and armed, and rode mailed horses. Medieval troop numbers are notoriously hard to ascertain and forever changing. Nor, of course, was the knightly contingent the sum total, as mercenary troops came and went according to needs. An army of 3–4,000 was considerable for this time; the numbers at the start of the crusade were to exceed this by some margin.

The pressure continued to pile on Raymond. Milo summoned him to Valence and the count came running. According to William of Tudela, he had tried to persuade his long-time enemy Roger Raymond, the Viscount of Béziers and Raymond's nephew, to 'stand together in defence and avert their own and their country's destruction. But instead of Yes the viscount answered No.'[17] The viscount may have miscalculated that his lord, King Peter II of Aragon, would protect him; this was not an unreasonable assumption, but it turned out to be the wrong one. Raymond had no choice but to submit. As security for his word, he handed over, as was demanded of him, seven strong castra (fortified settlements) in Provence: Oppède, Beaumes de Venise, Mornas, Montferrand, Roquemare and Largentière. He was still expected to bear the costs of their upkeep and garrisoning. Milo then compelled the proconsuls of Avignon, Montpellier, Nîmes, Valence, St Gilles and other places to swear an oath proclaiming that if Raymond went back on his word, all these towns and cities would instantly renounce their homage to him in a papally sanctioned act of diffidatio.

There then followed the humiliating ritual of penitence, important for both sides for its political symbolism. On 18 June, at his birthplace of St Gilles, Raymond stripped to his undergarments and was led to the doors of the church. There, in front of the legate, archbishops and over twenty bishops, he swore on holy relics to obey the Church henceforth. He acknowledged the charges laid against him, although by no means did he confess culpability to them all, but he did admit that his mercenaries had been employed to the harm of the Church, something it would have been foolish to deny and that would have undermined his credibility had he done so. The ritual was completed by the legate placing a robe on the count's shoulders and then scourging him to secure absolution. Mortifying as this was intended to be, the symbolism was more important; rather like Henry II of England's similar scourging for the death of Thomas Becket, one suspects that the strikes were administered with a light hand.

The submission might have seemed complete, but it was not. Raymond was still manoeuvring in what little room he had. His first aim was to protect his lands and in this he had succeeded. Six lords with local lands, including William of Raux, Prince of Orange, now had to swear oaths of their own that they would not attack Raymond's territories; they handed over castra as security for their word. Raymond's own predatory instincts were in play: he was hoping his conciliatory actions would allow him to gain a share of the spoils from the Viscount of Béziers's territories, as Raymond Roger was not fully co-operating with the Church. On 22 June, in a move of spectacular self-interest and hypocrisy even by the standards of the age, Count Raymond became a crusader. By so doing, he bought himself the immunity and privileges afforded crusaders for the preservation of their property. Raymond's taking up of the cross marked, or so it was hoped, the complete assimilation of the count into the ranks of orthodox suppressors of heresy and his full reconciliation with the pope. So why, then, did the crusade continue?

For a start, no one really trusted Raymond an inch. His reputation as a slippery, vacillating schemer was as widespread as it was deserved. Taking the cross convinced nobody. Peter of Vaux de Cernay protested: 'I declare the count a false and faithless crusader.'[18] This was not just the opinion of the southern orthodox but one that had spread to the north as well. Here William the Breton, chaplain to Raymond's overlord, King Philip, denounced the count after he had taken the cross as 'a wicked defender of enemies of the Catholic faith, war-maker of the heretics, unhesitatingly fearless in declaring himself against the faithful and the clergy'.[19] Furthermore, the problem of heresy remained in areas where proconsuls and local lords were apathetic or permissive towards it, or were themselves Cathars. Raymond had been both unwilling and unable to deal with the problem in his lands before; it required concerted, large-scale outside help if heresy were to be destroyed once and for all.

Just as importantly, there was the issue of the crusade as instrument of papal policy. Innocent had worked hard to initiate this crusade; to have called it off now would have been disastrous for his future uses of it, for who would heed him next time he called a crusade if this one were to be abandoned at the last minute? England was already under interdict and before too long the pope would be signing up Philip of France in a crusade against the English king. (Philip made his expensive military preparations and when John reconciled himself with the papacy in 1213 to prevent the planned invasion against him – he had learnt a thing or two from Raymond – the French king was furious and still intended to proceed with invasion before military action stopped him.) England witnessed another political crusade during its civil war of 1216–17, and the Fifth Crusade to the Middle East was already on Innocent's to-do list. The viability of crusading was at the forefront of the pope's mind.

Linked to this, and perhaps most important of all, was the fact that the crusade's momentum was such that any attempts to stop it now would have been impracticable. Too many important people had invested too much in it. The leaders of the crusade had financed their own involvement – a massive expense that had to cover wages, arms and armour, horses, baggage animals, fodder, food, etc. – and this meant borrowing money. Duke Odo of Burgundy, the richest lord to go on crusade, only found this money by redirecting his income in mortgages to monasteries. All had to reach deep into their pockets. The financing of armies – just like the gathering of them – was a hotchpotch affair of multifarious means, with the papacy, Church and princes pitching in with donations, taxes, loans and provision of materials and transport. King Philip arranged for his churchmen to mortgage their incomes over two years while the episcopate and nobility (especially if they stayed at home) were encouraged to make a contribution equivalent to 10 per cent of their revenues. Medieval wars were always beset with financial problems, but that rarely reduced the number of conflicts. One reason for this is the speculative optimism of those taking part; we shall see, in graphic detail, how the spoils of war were a great attraction to leader and humble footsoldier alike. By the summer of 1209, the crusaders had gathered and were looking for a return on their investment.

The crusading forces began to muster in Lyons in late June. Count Raymond had been painfully aware of this when he decided that now would be a good time to join the crusade. Numbers are hard to ascertain. The sources offer little guidance. William of Tudela claims the army contained 20,000 knights and 200,000 infantry and others, but admitted that it was so large 'no one could reckon the numbers'.[20] William the Breton proudly announces that Philip of France alone sent 15,000 men, which would have meant, totally implausibly, that the exceptionally cautious king was prepared to dispatch almost his entire army. Contemporaries had few ways of quantifying accurately, and such numbers simply mean that the army was very large indeed. A very loose guesstimate that most historians would be happy with is a figure of 20–30,000. This total would cover all those with the army, including those whose primary role was support. But all might be expected to pick up a weapon and stand with the professionals. As time went on, this number would fall dramatically, and Count Raymond's forces would greatly outnumber the northerners'; but for now it was a highly impressive army. The problem was that in the second half of 1210, forty days' service became the norm to fulfil the requirements of a crusading indulgence, meaning that the size of the crusading army could fluctuate wildly, thereby hindering its commanders' consistency in applying long-term strategy.

The army was dominated by Frenchmen, but was truly international in scope, with Lombardy and especially Germany well represented in its ranks. The sources are keen to highlight the illustrious names of the leading crusaders. In addition to Duke Odo of Burgundy, the most important lord of the crusade (and who was to rejoin it in 1213), and the Count of Nevers mentioned above, the army included the northerners Gaucher of Châtillon, Count of St Pol (who returned in 1215); Count Peter of Auxerre and his brother Robert of Courtenay (like Philip of France, cousins of Count Raymond); Count William of Genvois; Gaucher of Joigny, Lord of Châteaurenard; Count Milo of Bar sur Seine (who was a crusader again in 1215); Lord Guichard of Beaujeu; and William of Roches, Count of Anjou. Many of these men fill the pages of the chronicles across France for their deeds beyond their involvement in the crusade. Among them was Simon de Montfort, titular Count of Leicester, the future leader of the whole crusade, mentioned for the first time on the campaign in the selective roll call of Peter of Vaux de Cernay's *History of the Albigensians*. Among the crusaders from the south were Count Raymond of Toulouse; his reluctant vassal Adhémar of Poitiers, Count of Valentinois and Diois; and Peter Bermond, Lord of Sauve (an older brother-in-law to Raymond who had earlier rather unfilially asked the pope to grant him Raymond's county of Toulouse).

While the likes of the Duke of Burgundy and counts of Nevers and St Pol were the tactical leaders of the army in the field, overall command was given, as befitted a crusade, to Arnald Amalric, the Abbot of Cîteaux and hence the head of the important Cistercian order. Being Catalan, he had a good understanding of the enemy; not that this made him any more forbearing: he was a fanatical and unmoving opponent to anyone who opposed the crusade and who stood in the way of his pitiless ambition to take the position of Archbishop and Duke of Narbonne. It is to him that we ascribe the chilling order: 'Kill them all! God will know his own!' Accompanying him were his second, Master Milo and his assistant, Theodosius. Theodosius was promoted to legate on Milo's death at the year's end. Also joining the crusade was an impressive array of other ecclesiastics: archbishops Robert of Rouen and Peter of Sens; and bishops William of Nevers, Robert of Bayeux, Gautier of Autun, Robert of Clermont, Renaud of Chartres and Jordan of Lisieux. A smaller contingent from the Agenais also participated in the crusade, led by Count Guy of Clermont and the Auvergne, Viscount Raymond of Turenne, Bertrand the Lord of Cardaillac, Bertrand the Lord of Gourdon and Ratier the Lord of Castelnau, joined by Archbishop William of Bordeaux and the bishops of Limoges and Cahors.

The main force stretched out as far as the eye could see; if it were stationary it would have taken a whole day to walk its length. It comprised the various classes of society geared up for war. Noble lords and knights were arrayed in their armour, as were their warhorses when riding into combat; banners and flags fluttered around them and their retinues of squires and others in the entourage. Sergeants and men-at-arms were usually less well equipped, as befitted their lower social rank; for many their body protection was the *cuir bouilli*, a tough leather cuirass, often with felt-padded jerkin beneath (knights also wore felt-padding under their armour). Infantry soldiers, like the cavalry, could be either heavy or light, depending on their armour and weaponry. They contained a thoroughly professional element, well able to defeat cavalry (it is a myth that this first happened in the Hundred Years War), and were far from the disorganised rabble often depicted. The most professional footsoldiers were likely to have been among the mercenary bands, the larger of which represented mini-armies with mounted, foot and archery troops, while smaller groups might specialise in infantry, cavalry or crossbowmen (the latter especially useful for garrison duties). The non-professional contingent of the army was represented by the *ribaldi* or *ribauds*, the common folk joining the crusade as pilgrim warriors. Unruly and unpredictable, they were soon to show themselves capable of being devastatingly effective. The ecclesiastical retinues were similarly arranged, with knights from abbatial and episcopal lands accompanied by a range of other troops. The church's proscription of mercenaries was conveniently forgotten. And besides all these, other men drifted in and away along the journey. The biggest contingent was almost certainly the Duke of Burgundy's, as we have seen. Many lords might have brought just a few knights, a dozen or more plus some infantry. It was an *ad hoc* affair of myriad contributions that somehow solidified into a reasonably coherent whole. It is simply impossible to do anything but guess the total which, as we have seen, is put at between 20,000 and 30,000. It was a massive and hugely impressive force, the likes of which the south had not seen for centuries.

Such an army required impressive logistical support. Camp followers included priests, cooks, victualling masters, tradesmen supplying food and wine, blacksmiths, carpenters, wagoners and mule drivers, often under the instruction of quartermasters. Again, this number would fluctuate as the army progressed through villages and towns, where further food and supplies could be requisitioned. Of course, many were expected to turn their hand to a whole range of practical roles. In the most powerful contingents were specialist engineers to operate the siege machinery and direct miners to sap the walls of the enemy. These formed an essential branch of any campaigning army. Philip of France's success at war owed much to his skill in poliorcetics (siegecraft). He was known to take his engineers everywhere and they proved their worth time and again.

This mass of men and materiel required a huge transport operation. A substantial proportion of the equipment – armour, victuals, siege equipment – was loaded onto boats and barges and moved south on the Rhône and then along the region's river systems, including the River Orb for initial deployment at Béziers. But many of these had also to be transported by land; armour and food, for example, needed to be close by and so were carried in wagons. The demand for horses and pack animals was phenomenal. Knights required at least two mounts: a prohibitively expensive *destrier* warhorse for combat and the palfrey riding horse as transport. Others, including the ecclesiastics, who were lucky enough not to walk, had their own horses and mules. These animals needed their own supplies, which had also to be transported and augmented. Fodder was to the medieval army what oil is to a modern one. It has been calculated that a pack animal would consume the fodder it carried after ten days if other feed was not provided. Grazing was relied on to supplement the animals, but the problem of feeding both them and the soldiers could be equally acute in friendly or allied territory, where the crusaders might have to buy their supplies (if they had money) rather than plunder them, as when in enemy lands. The importance of horses in warfare is hard to overestimate – and not just for the medieval period: it is a remarkable fact that in the mechanised twentieth century Hitler used more horses in his invasion of Russia in 1941 than Napoleon did in 1812.

When one sees the magnificent castles of Languedoc perched impossibly on their rocky crags looking disdainfully down upon all below, it is easy to think that the crusade, for all its being a massive enterprise, faced an impossible task. But inaccessible as these castles were (and still are), the journey to them was not notably hard for the crusaders. The region's long, sweeping valleys and river systems made it relatively easy for the imposing crusading machine to arrive in might before the castles and fortified places. It was then that the hard work really began.

At the start of July the crusade juggernaut left Lyons and started out for Languedoc to wage war against the heretics. Thus began the conflict that 'led to so much sorrow, that left so many dead with their guts spilled out and so many great ladies and pretty girls naked and cold, stripped of gown and cloak'.[21] It is now time to show the truth of these words.

2

1209: 'KILL THEM ALL! GOD WILL KNOW HIS OWN!'

The War Begins

As the main crusading force marched over 200 miles from Lyons to Béziers, the smaller, independent army of the Agenais and Quercy opened hostilities. It was not an auspicious start and it set the tone for the bitter conflict that was now unleashed. The crusaders' confluent motives and conflicting interests are here already on display. The expedition's most likely promoter, Bishop Arnald of Agen, was an intractable opponent of heretics; that he was also one of the churchmen in conflict with Count Raymond over land rights in the Agenais offered the opportunity for some temporal as well as spiritual gains.

The very first objective was taken without any resistance: Puylaroque had been left undefended. Leaving fortified places open to the enemy was standard strategy in medieval warfare throughout Europe. If the opposing force was too large to resist effectively, the best option for defenders was often to withdraw to somewhere stronger, taking supplies and weaponry with them if possible, and hold that place instead, thereby saving men and supplies for a fight that had more strategic significance. While small fortified places were important locally for control and often because they were part of a larger overall defensive network, the loss of a few was not a major issue.

From here the crusaders moved to Gontaud north-west of Agen and then south-east to Tonneins. Both were sacked; the army was already resupplying itself. That no heretics were reported as having being in the towns was of no matter. The logic of war and the momentum of Mars's juggernaut had already manifested themselves. The next move was eastwards to Casseneuil, where they encountered their first setback. William of Tudela says that the place was defended by many archers and knights under the command of Seguin of Balenx, as well as by expert Gascon javelin men. The place itself was protected by rivers on three sides and a deep ditch. William says that the town would have fallen but for Count Guy of Auvergne, who did not want it taken and who argued about this with the archbishop. The count was concerned for the safety of his property there and did not wish to see it destroyed by military action or looted by the crusaders, the latter being something hard to deny the many men who had signed up on the promise of booty. One can deduce that the town was spared the rigours of a siege because an agreement was struck, for although the crusaders did not take it, the first killing of heretics took place here. Presumably they were handed over to ensure the safety of the town. The crusaders 'condemned many heretics to be burned and many fair women thrown into the flames, for they refused to recant however much they were begged to do so'.[22] It was the first of many *autos da fé* in a war where flames and smoke did not just signal the burning of crops and buildings, but also of people.

It was no longer simply a matter of the movement of armies; the war had become real. Word spread and people panicked. Some 60 miles to the east the Cathar town of Villemur heard from a young lad that the crusading army had finished at Casseneuil and was on the march again. Around 21–22 June, the inhabitants burned their own town and defences and fled to the hills and woods. Such a pre-emptive, self-inflicted strike would hopefully keep the soldiers away from their region as there would be nothing left worth taking or defending now any threat had already been removed. This is the last we hear of this branch of the crusade, the region staying quiet for the next three years. Perhaps the crusade dissipated because it was felt that its objectives had been met or crusaders' obligations fulfilled; it is highly possible that many made their way to the main force at Béziers, where the outcome was to be far more conclusive and far bloodier.

Peter of Vaux de Cernay seems to prepare his audience for the horrors that were about to unfold in Béziers and to justify them with his condemnation of its citizens 'entirely infected with the poison of heresy'. This was enough to condemn all within the town. 'They were robbers, lawbreakers, adulterers and thieves of the worst sort, brimful of every kind of sin.'[23] Peter illustrates his revulsion with an example of the kind of propaganda that war swiftly generates to demonstrate the inhuman nature of the enemy: a priest on his way to celebrate mass was set upon, beaten and robbed, and had his arm broken; as he lay on the ground, the assailants urinated on him. The tale sounds similar to that of the heretic the Count of Toulouse refused to punish for emptying his bowels on the altar. Such tales were designed to demonstrate the extent to which heretics were beyond saving.

War Reporting

Peter of Vaux de Cernay is one of our main sources for the Albigensian war. The crusade was a major event in an already crowded early thirteenth century, attracting the attention of writers across Europe. Historians are lucky to have four contemporary or near contemporary works by men closely involved in events that between them cover the conflict from start to finish. They are, in effect, our war reporters. How reliable are they? Does their bias hinder our understanding of how the war was fought? Do their accounts present a realistic depiction of medieval warfare at this time? As they are as much a part of our story as the warriors, they deserve some attention here.

Peter of Vaux de Cernay is the French author of the Latin *History of the Albigensian Crusade*. As he was a northern monk of the Cistercian order whose most important abbot, Arnald Amalric, was leading the crusade, and the nephew of another local Cistercian abbot and Bishop of Carcassonne, we cannot expect from the well-connected Peter much in the way of sympathy towards the Cathars; he makes no attempt to show any in what is a highly partisan account. His chronicle goes up to 1218 and is important because he was an eyewitness to many of the events he writes about; where he was not present, he had access to excellent first-hand knowledge. His age is uncertain, but he seems to have been a young man of about 20 when the crusade started. His family were close to the Montforts and he accompanied his uncle Abbot Guy on the crusade; Guy became Bishop of Carcassonne in 1212. His closeness to military activity is shown by how he narrowly escaped being hit by a crossbow bolt in 1212. It is thought that he was dead by the start of 1219. As he was at the siege of Toulouse in 1218, it is possible that he died as a result of being there, perhaps from disease or illness. His chronicle was widely disseminated and known by other writers of the time, such as Alberic de Trois Fontaines, William the Breton and the English monk Ralph of Coggeshall. Although highly prejudiced, as one would expect of a northern monk, Peter is nevertheless prepared to criticise the crusaders. His chronicle is biased but generally truthful, accurate and reliable.

William of Tudela is responsible for *The Song of the Albigensian Crusade* (also known as *The Song of the Cathar Wars*). Here we are in the troubadour tradition. William also became a cleric, who served with Count Raymond's stepbrother, Baldwin of Toulouse, a prominent ally of the crusaders. The work is therefore written in rhyming Provençal Old French (Occitan) rather than Latin; a language as colourful as it is variable. William was a man of the south, having come from Navarre and then Montauban. He claims that he began writing (or, if one prefers, composing) his work in May 1210. He says that he left the region when he foresaw the destruction to come, which he had divined in geomancy (telling the future from lines, shapes, dots on the earth or shapes formed after earth has been cast on the ground). Whether he believed this to be true, or whether it was foresight from a keen political antenna or just hindsight, his song is more grounded than his geomancy. It is another reliable source with relatively few inaccuracies (always to be expected in medieval chronicles, even as it is in newspapers today) as William was generally either an eyewitness to events or collected his information from first-hand testimony wherever possible, often quoting his sources. He is a supporter of the crusade against the heretics, but less zealously so than Peter. Interestingly, he baulks a little at the brutal excesses of the northerners. This may be because coming from the south he had considerable empathy with its people as distinct from its heretics. That his old home town of Montauban was the site of a particularly vicious crusading massacre means he is likely to have known some of the victims and this may have heightened his sensitivity to violent excess against southerners.

His *Song* covers the years 1209–13, but is carried on by an anonymous continuator until 1219. This continuator is widely regarded as one of the great writers of the thirteenth century, who combined an enviable ability with words with a very different viewpoint on the crusade. Despite its concern for entertainment value, this is also a largely reliable text, the troubadour's information often being verified by charter evidence, and many events are likely to have been witnessed by the author himself. The writer, who many believe was a knight from Toulouse or, as has recently been argued convincingly, from Foix, has stirred a debate among historians: to what extent was he an anti-crusader? As a southerner, he was bitterly against the northerners' invasion and its destructive impact on the people and traditions of Languedoc; and whereas Peter idolises Simon de Montfort, the anonymous continuator of William of Tudela despises him. He presents a genuine sense of the war as one fought between different peoples of different regions, and not just between faiths.

The last main source, in terms of chronological composition, is William of Puylaurens's Latin *Chronicle*. Again, he was extremely well placed to write on events as he was from Toulouse; it is thought that he was in the entourage of its Bishop Fulkes and also chaplain to its count, Raymond VII, from 1245. He wrote from personal memory and also utilised written documents, possibly including the *History* and the *Song*. His claims to have been an eyewitness to events have recently been challenged as he was writing long after the crusade, in 1275 when his chronicle ends, and possibly as late as 1276. This would make him a teenager or even a boy at the start of the crusade. However, other chroniclers such as Henry of Huntingdon and Jean de Joinville were writing about events from their early lifetime during their final years, so we should not feel the need to distrust William too much on this point. The more recent his chronicle entry, the more confidence we may have in it as a first-hand source, but his connections make his early work, especially on Toulouse's involvement, very valuable, too. He is indispensable after the *Song* finishes in 1219, until the end of the crusade. His coverage can be patchy and selective, but this is not surprising for a work that covers sixty-five years. Omissions may be due to poor memory, the deliberate disregarding of events as not essential or because he did not possess clear facts or evidence for them and so deliberately left them out. His position on the crusade is more interesting than Peter's in that it is more moderate. He approved the original aims of the crusade to crush heresy, but distances himself somewhat from it after 1215 for a while because he deems its aims to have been corrupted by that stage; Montfort comes in for notable criticism. With the arrival of King Louis VIII of France's crusade in 1226, William favours the French, but his position as a southerner also ensures that he does not lump together the southern lords, the Count of Toulouse and Catharism as a monolithic whole. His factual account is therefore not marred by any lack of balance and as a consequence his chronicle is full of insights and important information.

How conversant were our war reporters with the reality of conflict? Historians have generally dismissed monastic writers as being only of limited usefulness in trying to understand medieval warfare, much preferring vernacular sources such as the *Song* over Latin ones for getting us much closer to the truth. This is because these used the everyday language of the soldier and were written by men of the world who knew the ways of war better than secluded monks who had their own spiritual agenda and preoccupations. The latter have been considered to have little comprehension of military affairs and next to no interest in tactics and strategy. This is an area I have researched in depth for the thirteenth century and I disagree strongly with this argument: the preference for the vernacular is both overstated and misplaced. Many monastic chroniclers, including Peter and William here, were acute observers of war. Their factual and largely accurate retelling of military events is in itself of great importance, but their understanding went deeper than this.

The Church was more than a bystander or passive observer of war, and its involvement went far beyond praying for its side's victory, producing propaganda and supplying armies with money, troops, transport and supplies. Such clerical writers as Orderic Vitalis, Abbot Suger of St Denis, Henry of Huntingdon and Gilbert of Mons wrote on warfare with considerable insight in the twelfth century; at the time of the Albigensian Crusade, Roger of Wendover and William the Breton were doing the same but in even greater depth. While both Latin and vernacular sources were prone to exaggeration, the latter could be worse as they strove to shock and entertain their audiences. Vernacular writers might spend twice as long describing a battle as Latin ones, but the extra pages are often filled with florid elaborations, imaginary dialogue and impossibly stylised one-on-one duels. (Latin sources could be guilty of this, but to a far lesser extent.) Monastic and ecclesiastical writers were overwhelmingly from the same fighting class of warriors (*bellatores*) as their fathers, brothers, nephews, uncles, cousins and patrons, so it is only to be expected that they would be very familiar with the martial world, especially when they researched it and wrote about it in their chronicles. Nor should it be overlooked that many knights retired as monks or were promoted to high appointments in the Church such as that of bishop; these veterans were able to inform many monastic writers of the reality of war. In the late twelfth century, Bishop Hugh of Auxerre enjoyed gathering knights about him to discuss military lessons from Vegetius's book on the art of war, *On Military Matters* (also known by its Latin title, *De Re Militari*, and as *Epitome of Military Science*). The culture of chivalry did not stop at the church door.

The Church was not only very comfortable with military language and imagery, it thrived on it. It promoted its monastic ranks as the spiritual battalions of God in the fight against the forces of Satan – the Cathars providing an obvious example. The Latin word *turma* is used in chronicles to denote a body of troops, but it can also be employed to mean a group of monks. Abbot Marcwald of Fulda, famed for his extensive castle building programme, opined: 'Not that it is proper that monks should inhabit anything but monasteries or fight battles other than spiritual ones; but the evil in the world cannot be defeated except by resistance.'[24] The Church might condemn war and mercenaries at one moment, and then hire the mercenaries it had proscribed and start a war the next. Germany in the High Middle Ages saw almost uninterrupted local wars waged between princes and bishops. The Church even had its own armies, the *milites Christi* (soldiers of Christ) in the military orders of the Knights Templar and Hospitaller. These orders were well entrenched in Occitania yet seemed not to play a significant role in the crusade, possibly because they saw their remit as fighting Muslims in Spain and the Holy Land. It is likely that their local knowledge and expertise was offered – but not necessarily to the crusaders. Some Hospitallers actually fought on the southerners' side, emphasising once more the political, regional nature of the conflict taking precedence over purely religious issues. The Church, with the belligerent Innocent III at its head, had never been so militant.

But even Innocent's bellicosity and militancy was not as fervent as that of his legate in Languedoc, the overall commander of the crusade, Arnald Amalric, a Cistercian abbot. Such military positions for a churchman were not unusual: in 1214, Guérin, Bishop Elect of Senlis, was commander of the French rearguard at their great victory at Bouvines; Bishop Anthony Bek of Durham was a commander in the English army at Falkirk in 1298; Archbishop Thoresby of York helped to lead the English to victory against the Scots at Neville's Cross in 1346. When Thomas Hatfield was Bishop of Durham in the fourteenth century, he had a seal made depicting him not with mitre and crosier but on his warhorse as a knight.

Our chroniclers Peter and William had, as we have seen, intimate connections with the leadership of the crusade: Peter was a white monk, a Cistercian, whose uncle, as we have noted, became Bishop of Carcassonne;

William was a familiar of Bishop Fulkes of Toulouse. Both places were at the heart of the war. William of Tudela had Roger Bernard, son of the Count of Foix, as one of his patrons. As we read of the nature of the Albigensian war and its horrors, it is fascinating to hear the voices of those writing about it who lived through this remarkable historical episode. As with any sources, medieval or modern, there are of course flaws and problems here, but all three of our war reporters were genuinely concerned to offer a truthful account of the facts of the crusade and to leave their work behind as an honest legacy. The story they tell is a brutal one.

The Siege of Béziers

The crusading army approached Béziers via Montpellier to the east, which they reached about 20 July. Here Raymond Roger, Viscount of Béziers, went to meet its leaders. The 24-year-old viscount was panicking and regretting that he had not agreed to a defensive pact with his uncle, Count Raymond of Toulouse, who had sewn the cross of the crusader on his right shoulder and was now directing the holy juggernaut against his troublesome nephew. Castellans owing allegiance to Raymond Roger who were close to the crusading army's path had already opened their gates as allies and deserted him. Nor was any help in the offing from his suzerain, King Peter of Aragon; he was busy fighting his own crusade against the Muslims in Spain as part of the *Reconquista* and would not be free to become militarily involved until after the great victory of Las Navas de Tolosa in 1212. The sight of the immense army that spread out before the viscount's eyes when he reached Montpellier confirmed his worst fears and his plan of action. He would follow his uncle's lead and transform his position by complying with the crusade's demands. He submitted.

Or at least he tried to. He apologised for his anti-clerical policies and for not dealing with the heretics under his jurisdiction, attributing this failure to inability rather than permissiveness. He was prepared to offer all that his uncle had. But Arnald Amalric paid no heed to his penitential advances and dismissed him. The viscount rushed to Béziers to make his arrangements for the coming onslaught. The reasons for the legate's rejection were similar to those we have seen for why the crusade was not abandoned after the Count of Toulouse has so shrewdly capitulated, but even more so. Disbanding the army at this even later stage would have been more disastrous: there was a real danger that the forces would split up and run amok across the region in quest of booty and compensation for their investment of time and money. This risk was even greater for the mercenary bands. The expedition's leaders had no fondness for the Trencavels so all agreed that the viscount's lands were the ones best suited to pay the costs – literally – of the crusade.

But there were other reasons for pressing on, too. The intransigent antagonism of the Cistercian order towards the Trencavels has already been cited, although not proven, as a reason for targeting Béziers. Looking at the most obvious explanation, the city certainly harboured over 200 named heretics, and Raymond Roger had done nothing about them; but belief that intimates in his family and court were Cathars has not been substantiated. William of Tudela declares that the viscount was 'certainly Catholic'.[25]

When the viscount's conciliatory advances had been rejected, the Biterrois – the people of the region – went on the defensive, refusing to surrender the city or to hand over the heretics. This in some ways played into the crusaders' hands as now they felt fully justified in laying siege to the city and issuing it with an ultimatum. This was intended to force the citizens' collective hand to declare themselves either for the crusade (by yielding to a foreign force) or for heresy and, more importantly, continued political independence. It was the latter more than anything that the Biterrois were defending. The crusaders had sound, long-term strategic motives interwoven with their more cynical reasons for targeting the city. Béziers was the first main sentinel into Languedoc for the crusading army. It needed to be secured by the crusaders before they made their deeper incursions into the region. It was too powerful a base to be left in suspect hands behind the front line.

Even if the viscount's attempts at submission along the lines of Count Raymond's had not been rejected, there would have been potential problems. A change of position by Raymond Roger – and medieval barons shifted frequently as they saw fit – would be very dangerous for the crusaders, leaving them with uncommitted allies in the rear in a hostile region. This might have happened had King Peter of Aragon decided to make a move in support of his vassal (the king's sister Eleanor was married to the viscount). The Biterrois also had a reputation for rising up against their masters; they had killed their Trencavel lord in 1167. The city had to be in the safe hands of a trusted lord, loyal to the papacy and hostile to heresy, ruling over a subdued people.

Momentum, money and distrust all led the crusading army to Béziers – as did Count Raymond of Toulouse, riding ahead to point out suitable camp sites as he encouraged this massive force against his Trencavel enemy. The army left Montpellier on 20 July. Along the way the crusaders took some minor places, including Servian, a small fortified town less than 8 miles north-east of Béziers. It had been left deserted by its excommunicated lord, who later repented for having allowed Cathars and perfects into his castle.

Ahead of them, Raymond Roger was making his desperate preparations. William of Tudela feels sympathy for the young viscount and sings his praises: 'Day and night, he worked to defend his lands, for he was a man of great courage. Nowhere in the wide world is there a better knight or one more generous and open-handed, more courteous or better bred.'[26] His problems, William believed, stemmed from his youth and amiability, which resulted in his vassals lacking an appropriate fear of his authority and treating him as little more than a good-humoured companion with whom to share a joke.

Raymond Roger rode frantically into Béziers at daybreak on 21 July. The inhabitants flocked to hear what he had to say about their frightening prospects. He urged them to make ready while he made for his principal fortress of Carcassonne to organise its defence and a relief force. With him went the Jews of the city and others, no doubt many of them Cathars. The *History* accuses the viscount of abandoning the people of Béziers, but it was a sound strategic decision. The crusaders would have to encamp in the open before Béziers, leaving them vulnerable to attack from a relief force from Carcassonne. By itself, Carcassonne's garrison would have been vastly outnumbered by the crusading forces but it could harass them and pose real problems if it co-ordinated activities with Béziers; and if the latter held out long enough, Aragon might be drawn into the conflict, which of course is what the Biterrois hoped for. Furthermore, at Carcassonne, Roger Raymond sent out the call for his vassals and their forces to come to him there from the Minervois, the Montagne Noire, the Lauragais, from Corbières and from Razès. If they all heeded his call, he would be able to muster a considerable force. Béziers' stand was to provide him time for this.

While the two cities urgently required an interval to allow them to fortify themselves properly, it would be a mistake to think that they were starting from scratch. Political tensions had been heightening all year and the northern army moving southwards into Lyon would have focused minds sharply on defence. The number of men in a garrison reflected the political situation: in times of peace, garrisons were small, often skeleton, but sufficient for everyday purposes; but when war threatened, they would swell to ensure that the battlements could be adequately manned against assault. Although we do not have numbers, we can safely assume that the latter was the situation in eastern Occitania in July 1209.

Béziers itself was already in a reasonable state of readiness. For a start, it occupied a formidable, elevated position high above the River Orb and was encircled by impressive walls. Its ditches would have been cleared and deepened, with perhaps an extra last minute effort directed here after the viscount's flying visit. Gates would have been reinforced and the walls inspected. Even churches such as that of St Nazaire had been constructed for defensive purposes as much as for religious ones, with loopholes and machicolations for fending off attackers; such church-fortresses were a feature of the troubled Languedoc. Attacking the place meant crossing the bottleneck of the bridge and fighting one's way up a steep hill and then breaking through powerful walls defended by many people.

In the early fourteenth century, the population stood at nearly 15,000; at the beginning of the thirteenth century it had an estimated steady population of some 8–10,000 people, which could provide considerable practical support to assist the strong garrison. This number may easily have been doubled during the siege. Ironically, one reason for this was the highly orthodox celebration of a saint's feast day, St Mary Magdalene, on 22 July, a major event which drew the crowds in; the city had a large church named after the saint that, as misfortune would have it, played a central role in the tragedy which unfolded that very day. Less festively, refugees from the surrounding countryside would have flocked into the city for safety against the invading northerners; we have already seen how castra, towns and villages were being deserted by their inhabitants. Thus although Béziers' defenders may have been outnumbered by enemy combatants, the discrepancy was not great. The city's reputation for strength made it a natural place of refuge. The numbers would have meant a drain on the city's resources in a prolonged siege, but at the same time the festivities would have meant extra food was already available, and refugees would have brought in supplies and livestock to provide for themselves, sell and protect. Obviously there was great fear in the city, but also confidence in its ability to stand.

When the crusading army appeared on the plain below the city on the far bank of the Orb during the evening of 21 July, their spirits must have dropped at the sight of the imposing, fortified cathedral of St Nazaire dominating the acropolis high above them. Even today, without the medieval walls that once surrounded it, the visitor can look up from this position to Béziers and obtain a sense of the crusaders' task. The first move, as always in siege situations, was to negotiate an agreement for surrender; most sieges were resolved this way. The Bishop of Béziers, Raynaud de Montpeyroux, had gone to meet the crusaders earlier. He now returned to beseech his flock to surrender. The conditions were clear: the burghers were to hand over some 222 leading heretics named on a list (which has survived to the present day); if they did so, the city would be spared. Peter has the bishop tell them that if the Catholics could not do this, they should leave the city so as to avoid being slaughtered with the heretics. One presumes the bishop would have overseen any such departures to ensure that the remaining Cathars did not leave among them. William has the bishop warning the citizens that now was their only chance to choose between life and death. He also confusingly suggests that if they were to surrender the town, any possessions seized from them would be restored. By this he probably means only a portion of their goods, as the crusaders would want their share. Nonetheless, it was made obvious in the starkest of terms that resistance meant death by the sword.

But the city remained resolute, refusing to hand over anyone and displaying an impressive solidarity. Surrender would have meant the imposition of a foreign garrison, oppressive rule and a huge penalty in reparations to the crusaders. The Biterrois cherished their rights and liberties too much to permit such a loss of independence. Their response makes this clear: 'the majority of the townspeople said ... that the crusaders should not get so much as a pennyworth of their possessions from them or in any way change their rule over the town'.[27] They placed their confidence in their city's defences, which they believed could not be stormed even after a month's siege. But they did not believe they would have to wait that long: 'They were sure the host could not hold together, it would disintegrate in less than a fortnight.' This confidence was due to the size of the army: it was simply too large to be sustained. They expected, as was common in extended siege situations, that many of the crusaders would simply drift away, either to find easier pickings or to go back home. It is not absolutely clear that the forty-day service obligation was fully in force at this time, but if it were it would have added to the Biterrois' confidence. (William of Tudela says that the forty days' duty did indeed apply at Béziers.) Though not mentioned in the sources here, in their minds the defenders would also have been anticipating the return of their lord, Raymond Roger, with help.

A few townspeople left with the bishop, who then reported back to the legate on the city's defiance. On the morning of 22 July the crusaders began a formal investiture of the city and started to settle themselves in for a lengthy siege.

Within a few hours it was all over.

Even as Bishop Raynaud was informing the high command of the outcome of his meeting in the city, a group of soldiers from the garrison of Béziers sortied from the fortress to attack the crusaders, hoping to catch them unawares as they made camp and ate breakfast. It was one of the most disastrous tactical blunders in the annals of medieval warfare. All the city's great defensive advantages were nullified by this one insane act of stupidity.

The sortie was highly unlikely to have been a reconnaissance party as suggested by one French historian: the panoramic view from the heights of the city told them much more than an encounter at ground level with the periphery of the army. An intelligence-gathering mission would have been more apposite as the army approached, not after it had encircled the walls. Reconnaissance sorties of the former type were common. In May 1217 the Anglo-French defenders of Lincoln sent out troops to gauge the size of the royalist army coming to lift their siege of the castle. The English scouts came back and advised the leaders that the oncoming forces were not too large and so they should go to meet them in battle; but the French scouts reported back that the enemy was twice as strong as the English had thought, so the fateful decision was made to stay in the town and defend themselves there. In fact, the French had miscalculated by counting the banners of contingents twice over, thereby doubling the size of their estimate, not realising that the ones at the back of the enemy column simply designated the accompanying baggage train. The consequence of their poorly informed decision was a decisive rout.

The sortie at Béziers was most likely a morale-boosting raid, taking advantage of the army's disorder as it pitched camp and ate breakfast. The attempt to demoralise the enemy backfired spectacularly. The garrison troops poured down the hill and over the bridge, shouting at the tops of their voices and waving their banners to intimidate the enemy, hoping to put them to flight and, says Peter, 'began to assail our men with arrows'.[28] William of Tudela offers a detailed account of what then happened. The French ribalds looked up to see a knight on guard duty at the bridge being hacked to death and thrown in the river. *Ribaldi* is a loose term that encompasses the basic, lightest infantry, pilgrims and camp followers. The leader of this group (and it would have been just one section of the ribalds) shouted out 'Come on, let's attack!', while in the main French camp, the cry went up: 'To arms! To arms!' With just their clubs ('they had nothing else, I suppose') they counter-attacked with animated fury. They quickly turned the tables, using the confusion to their own advantage. In just their shirts and trousers, many without shoes, they attacked the walls, jumped into the moat with their picks, and began to batter and smash down the gates, climbing up ladders and sweeping the defenders off the ramparts. The defenders abandoned the walls and the ribalds poured into the city.

Did the *ribaldi* really win the day in this manner as William of Tudela suggests? The *History* and a letter from the legates to Pope Innocent confirm that it was the camp followers who took Béziers; William the Breton and Roger of Wendover also attest to their central role. Other strong and fortified towns have been taken by the lowest order of troops; they were, after all, the cannon fodder of the day and so were expected to make frontal assaults over the top of walls and battlements. It does seem that the cream of French chivalry were left gawping as the common folk won the first great prize of the crusade.

However, the rapidity of the assault and its success raises some questions. The legates told Innocent that the city was taken 'within two or three hours' while Peter claims 'astonishingly, they captured the city inside an hour'.[29] It would have taken picks and battering rams days or even weeks rather than hours to have made an impression on the walls and gates of the fortress. The only way to have breached the walls would have been escalade – storming over them by ladder. Of our three main reporters, only William of Puylaurens, the furthest away in time from the events, makes mention of this: 'the attackers scaled and occupied the walls'.[30] Interestingly, Roger of Wendover also says that the walls were scaled while William the Breton mentions breaking through the gates. Peter's estimation that the city was taken within sixty minutes may sound like one of his exaggerations, but it may be accurate if we consider another strong possibility for what happened.

The sortie party must have been of considerable size to have had any impact against the crusading camp. That this party was itself taken by surprise, by the ferocity and swiftness of the ribalds' response, is clear. The sortie's only recourse was to retreat. There is no mention of its soldiers being struck down. Thus they would have rushed back to the city and its perceived safety. I think the most likely scenario to explain the rapid fall of the city is one that sees the sortie party piling back through the city gates that had been opened for them to attack the camp. As the gates stayed opened to allow the sortie party to return, the press of cavalry and men desperate to get back in meant that the gates could not be closed, allowing the *ribaldi*, quite literally on their heels, to pour through as well. The *Song* tells of the gates opening and of 'the crush you would have seen there as these lads struggled to get into the town!' This is exactly what happened at the siege of Taillebourg in 1179. Richard I had deliberately placed his camp near the town walls to provoke a foray from its defenders; his men got into the town the same way the sortie had got out, pressing behind the sortie party trying to get back into the town through its opened gates. At Béziers, the defenders were forced off the battlements; it is easy to imagine that many were pulled off the ramparts by their commanders in an attempt to stem the critical irruption into the city through the gates. Thus the dramatic fall of the city can best be explained by a combination of forcing through the gates and escalade.

The siege was over. Now the massacre began.

The Massacre

The crusaders stormed into the city and sacked it utterly, unleashing one of the most pitiless and notorious massacres of the entire Middle Ages. According to one relatively obscure source, Caesarius of Heisterbach, it was at this juncture that the crusaders urgently asked the legate Arnald Amalric: 'What shall we do, lord? We cannot tell the good from the bad.' To which the abbot, fearful lest Cathars pretended to be Catholics to save themselves, gave his notorious response: 'Kill them all! God will know his own!'[31]

Peter claims that they 'killed almost all the inhabitants from the youngest to the oldest', adding approvingly: 'What a splendid example of divine Justice and Providence!'[32] Just as the worst casualties on a battlefield usually occur during a rout, so it was at Béziers. The defenders, be they the garrison or urban militia, appear to have simply folded. The storming of the city must indeed have been remarkably rapid as there was seemingly no attempt to organise further defences or to hold the line within the walls; the narrowness and steepness of the medieval streets and overhanging buildings that can still be seen today were perfect for blockading and raining down missiles on the intruders. Instead, all ran to the city's churches, especially St Mary Magdalen's, whose feast day they had been celebrating; here they hoped to find sanctuary. William of Tudela recounts the horror:

> The priests put on vestments for a mass of the dead and had the church bells rung as for a funeral. They [the ribalds] killed everyone who fled into the church; no cross or altar or crucifix could save them. And these raving, beggarly lads, they killed the clergy too, and the women and the children. I doubt if one person came out alive. So terrible a slaughter has not been known or consented to, I think, since the time of the Saracens.

The killing nearly done, the city was systematically looted. Tellingly, only the *Song* reports this. As the knights moved into the city they snatched much of the booty from the first wave of ribalds. Their bloodlust already bursting through their veins, the outraged looters now vented their anger on the city itself. 'Burn it, burn it!' went up the cry as they used 'huge flaming brands' to set the town ablaze 'from end to end'. At St Mary Magdalene's, any survivors were soon finished off when the flaming roof collapsed in on them: the *ribaldi* 'burned the town, burned the women and children, old men and young, and the clerks vested and singing mass there inside the church'.

How many died? It is impossible to know for certain as we do not even have definite figures for the city's population at this time. The *Song* does not give a number; William of Puylaurens simply and starkly says 'many thousands'; Peter of Vaux de Cernay claims '7,000' were killed in the church of St Mary Magdalene; in a letter to Rome the legates wrote that 'none was spared' and that 'almost 20,000' were put to the sword. William the Breton heard that 60,000 perished; others take it up to 100,000. William of Nangis, writing towards the end of the century, claims all were killed, but interestingly gives a total of 17,000, close to the legates' figure. Some historians are prepared to accept the legates' figure approaching 20,000 – in effect, the whole town. (William of Tudela estimated that only between fifty and 100 people escaped death.) This is very much on the highest side, but it is not a totally unfeasible figure given, as we have seen, how the town's population would have been swollen on 22 July. But a total massacre would have been very difficult to achieve in terms of time and labour, and, to put it coldly, it would have been impractical. The *History*'s figure of 7,000 deaths in St Mary Magdalene church can be discounted. I visited the church with a police officer experienced with crowd control and supervision; he estimates the absolute maximum capacity of the church to be about 2,500. If the building had been packed, it is possible many of the victims were cut down in the precincts around it. Perhaps Peter was confusing his figure of 7,000 with the total deaths in the city. Other churches were also full of townspeople who would have run to their nearest sanctuary; these, like St Nazaire, were also burned. Only a minority of the dead were heretics. Roger of Wendover rather optimistically reported that God's protection ensured that 'very few of the Catholics were slain'.[33] But William the Breton confirms that the killing was wholesale: the *ribaldi* 'struck out indiscriminately at the faithful and at those who no longer believed, and they did not stop to find out who was worthy of death and who was worthy of life'.[34] Killing some 2,000 people or more using just knives and swords would have been a long, hard process; I suspect most lives were claimed when the church was torched and the roof caved in on the people beneath it.

Churches were not the secure sanctuaries they were often thought to be and many a non-combatant died in them during medieval wars. In 1440 Sir John Talbot had over 300 men, women and children burned to death in the church at Lihons, where they had taken refuge; even the pious King Louis VII of France did the same at Vitry in 1143. Béziers was more systematic; here sanctuaries became execution chambers. In the mid-nineteenth century, a mass grave was uncovered beneath St Mary Magdalene; the victims having died on consecrated ground, their bodies could remain where they fell. Whatever the total number of deaths in the city, it is clear beyond doubt that the slaughter was extensive even by the standards of the time.

The name Béziers has gone down in history to represent fanatical religious intolerance and large-scale religious massacre. It has recently been argued that the impact of Béziers was so great – news of the massacre spread across Europe – because the unusual suddenness of the event heightened its horror. There may be something in this, but what really shocked people was its scale and where it took place: in a cultured Christian country in the kingdom of France at the height of the period of chivalry. The most famous massacre of this magnitude previously was the taking of Jerusalem in 1099 during the First Crusade. Here, when the crusaders broke into the city, 'there was such a massacre that our men were wading up to their ankles in enemy blood'; 'the surviving Saracens dragged the dead ones out in front of the gates and piled them up in mounds as big as houses'; 'about 10,000 were beheaded'; the crusaders 'rode in blood up to their knees and bridle reins'.[35] But here the accounts are considerably more hyperbolic than in 1209. The religious element was also stronger on the First Crusade. Jerusalem was the holiest of all cities and so the massacre there was regarded by many (though not all) as a form of divinely ordained purification that restored the city to its pristine dignity. The element of purification was present for some at Béziers, but surely severely mitigated by the great loss of Catholic lives in the carnage. And where Jerusalem was the most important pilgrimage destination for Christians, Béziers was just an ordinary city.

Unlike Béziers, Jerusalem can also be explained by pent-up bloodlust. The crusade in the Middle East had lasted three long years of incredible hardship, deprivation and danger in a completely alien land; disease and agonising thirst killed as many as combat, if not more; extreme hunger caused some to resort to cannibalism. The attrition rate has been calculated as being nearly 70 per cent. By the time the survivors reached Jerusalem, the ultimate goal of all Christians, they were ready to seek revenge in a climactic orgy of violence that had been waiting a long time to erupt. By contrast, the Albigensian crusaders experienced next to none of this: they had marched a relatively short distance, mostly through friendly territory whose culture they could recognise as close to their own. And the siege had barely lasted a day since pitching camp. There were other, more calculated, reasons for the brutality at Béziers.

'Kill them all! God will know his own!' is one of the most infamous phrases to have emerged from the Middle Ages. For most historians it is entirely apocryphal: just a colourful phrase invented for dramatic literary effect at a later date. However, there is more truth to it than fiction.

The phrase originates in the *Dialogue on Miracles* by Caesarius of Heisterbach, written by 1224, thus still during the Albigensian Crusade. According to his account, when, as the massacre began, the crusaders asked Arnald Amalric what they should do as they could not distinguish Cathar from Catholic, 'the abbot, as well as others, fearing that as they [the heretics] were in such great fear of death they would pretend to be Catholics, and after they had left again return to their perfidy, is said to have said: Kill them. For God knows who are his. Thus innumerable persons were killed in that city.'[36] Translations of Latin texts can – and do – vary widely, and there is no exception here. 'God will know his own' and 'God knows his own' are equally good renditions, the former conveying the fuller meaning that when any Catholics killed in the city appear before their Maker for judgement, God will know they are not guilty of heresy; thus heavenly paradise awaits them and not Hell, to which the Cathars are condemned. When deploying the phrase, historians tend to add 'all' and exclamation marks for emphasis. Again, this is reasonable: historians often add quotation marks that are, of course, not there in the original – they are not used at all in Latin. Caesarius is being quite honest and open: he is not reporting hearsay as fact but reports merely what the legate 'is said to have said'. Although Caesarius was not present on the crusade, he was a white monk, a member of the same Cistercian order as Abbot Arnald that was so heavily involved in the crusade. The monk's compatriot, Conrad of Urach, succeeded Arnald as Abbot of Cîteaux and head of the order in 1217; Conrad was also papal legate in Languedoc to counter Catharism there from 1220 to 1223. And as was mentioned in Chapter 1, Germans were heavily represented among the crusaders. Thus it is highly likely that Caesarius had access to some relevant information that has not surfaced elsewhere.

Some doubters point to the sheer impracticality of Arnald Amalric being asked what should be done with the Catholic faithful in the midst of a frenzied slaughter. But butchery on such a massive scale is actually a lengthy process; there would have been time to raise this question, whether or not the response was acted on. If the legate had made the order at this moment, it may simply have been an acceptance of the reality of the situation and reflect that he was trying to look for some spiritual consolation from the atrocity; however, this is less likely than a calculated command. Whether the notorious words were actually said or not said at Béziers, the reality is that they reflect the crusading policy of no quarter. The intention from the start for any who resisted really was to kill them all.

This is seriously overlooked when studying the massacre. The plan from the outset of the crusade was to annihilate without mercy all who resisted the crusaders. The reason was simple: to strike terror into the enemy and to frighten into submission any others contemplating resistance. This was standard practice in the wars of the Middle Ages, as I have shown in a previous book (*By Sword and Fire: Cruelty and Atrocity in Medieval Warfare*). William of Tudela actually discusses this strategy. Perhaps the draconian nature of his comments has persuaded some historians to dismiss what he says as an exaggerated statement made for effect and typical medieval hyperbole; it may also be because he makes the relevant remarks a few pages before the massacre at Béziers and so they may have been overlooked. But in the context of medieval warfare, no quarter is not just plausible, it is to be expected. The decision for no quarter was taken in Rome at the first council of war to launch the crusade over a year earlier. Present were Pope Innocent III, Abbot Arnald Amalric and Master Milo (legates on the crusade), twelve cardinals and numerous ambassadors. 'There it was they made the decision that led to so much sorrow … From beyond Montpellier as far as Bordeaux, any that rebelled were to be utterly destroyed.'[37] William says he heard this from the Navarrese ambassador Pons de Mela, who was there. Pons was representing King Sancho VIII of Navarre, who was William's overlord for Tudela. William was therefore in a good position to offer us this invaluable insight.

The injunction was not forgotten when the crusade started – unsurprisingly, as Arnald Amalric was at its head. In the middle of recounting the carnage at Béziers, William makes space to remind the audience why it was happening:

> The lords from France and Paris, laymen and clergy, princes and marquis, all agreed that at every castle the army approached, a garrison that refused to surrender should be slaughtered wholesale, once the castle had been taken by storm. They would then meet with no resistance anywhere, as men would be so terrified at what had already happened. That is how they took

Montréal and Fanjeaux and all that country – otherwise, I promise you, they could never have stormed them. That is why they massacred them at Béziers, killing them all.[38]

The success of breaking into Béziers took everyone by surprise; but the killing was not carried out merely on a sudden impulse. William the Breton, who appears uncomfortable with the bloodshed, is wrong to try and exonerate the crusade leaders and knights when he writes that the *ribaldi* killed all 'without the lords having given them their consent';[39] they were, in a well-known modern phrase used to excuse atrocity, simply following orders.

The order for no mercy was a strategic decision. William of Tudela recognises the wisdom of it: by setting an example at the start the crusaders hoped to cow otherwise impregnable fortresses, ones they could not hope to storm, into surrender. Béziers provided them with the opportunity to do this and they seized it. It worked. The road to Carcassonne was left open as garrisons deserted their posts for fear of suffering the same fate as the sacked city. Thus it is misleading to focus, as many historians do, on the extreme religious prejudice of Arnald Amalric as the main factor behind the slaughter. It has been pointed out by historians that the following year he was prepared to give a fair trial and the opportunity to recant to heretics who yielded to him, and that this casts doubt on the veracity of the order to 'Kill them all!' But this later tolerance can be judged on the one hand as either completely irrelevant to 1209 or, on the other, as actually reinforcing the veracity of the infamous command. This is so because Arnald was prepared to offer the chance of life to those who surrendered and had not resisted, in keeping with the crusaders' strategy from the start to kill all those who did not submit. It is vital, therefore, to separate the religious element from the martial one: if the papal legate did issue the command to 'Kill them all!', he did so not as an intolerant, fanatical leader of the church, but as the pragmatic, strategising leader of the army. The military imperative overrode everything.

The crusaders were following the established siege practice of using terror as a weapon. A few examples will place Béziers in context. William the Conqueror took a satellite fort of Alençon in 1049; he ordered the hands and feet of the garrison to be cut off. The town of Alençon quickly offered its surrender. In 1381 the Duke of Bourbon laid siege to Moléon; he offered them one chance to surrender or face hanging.

They surrendered. What made such threats effective was the belief of those receiving them that they would be carried out. In 1224 King Henry III of England gave the same warning to the garrison at Bedford Castle; they ignored the intimidation and, when stormed, at least two dozen defenders were first beaten and then hung.

The purpose of such merciless behaviour was to bring sieges to a speedy conclusion. The longer spent on a siege, the greater the problems: more expenditure; more lives lost; the greater the risk from starvation, disease and attack from a relief force. At Béziers, there was the fear of Raymond Roger returning with forces from Carcassonne and pinning the crusaders between them and the garrison. There was also the problem of limited service, with crusaders potentially drifting away once they had served their forty days or terms of service. The town's refusal to surrender was therefore at first a grave concern for the crusaders; a few hours later, it had become a bloody blessing.

There is a misconception among most medievalists that the laws of war relied closely on biblical justification for the total slaughter of men, women and children when a place was taken by storm. Deuteronomy is cited in support of this as verses ten to twenty of chapter two lay out the rules of siege warfare. Deuteronomy 20:16 does stipulate 'of the cities of these people which the Lord thy God doth give thee for an inheritance, thou shall save alive nothing that breatheth'. Biblical exegesis is, by definition, all interpretation; that the very next verse clearly specifies that this dire ordinance is aimed against the Hittites, the Canaanites and other Old Testament tribes is conveniently sidelined by medieval commanders and jurists. Verses thirteen to fourteen state: 'And when the Lord thy God hath delivered it [a city] into thine hands, thou shall smite every male thereof with the edge of a sword; but the women, and the little ones, and the cattle, and all that is in the city, even all the spoil thereof, shalt thou take unto thyself.' Verse fifteen makes clear that men and only men are to be killed in 'the cities that are very far off from thee'. Thus one can slay all one's own subjects but not those of another nation.

No laws are more made to be broken than those of warfare. Béziers was part of the Trencavel lands, and the King of Aragon claimed overall suzerainty; this should therefore have exempted the city from the slaughter it suffered, as the foreign invaders should only have killed men (the prerogative to kill men, women and children belonged to Viscount Raymond Roger and King Peter). Perhaps this is one reason why Peter of

Vaux de Cernay and William of Puylaurens make so much of the murder of Viscount Raymond Trencavel I by his citizens in 1167. William opines that 'It was widely held at the time that the Lord had wrought vengeance on them for their having treacherously murdered their lord Trencavel', before adding, almost as an afterthought, 'although they were also charged with unspeakable acts by way of heretical beliefs and blasphemies'.[40] That the 1209 killing ground was focused on St Mary Magdalene's church was not just divine, but also poetic, justice, for the viscount had been assassinated in this very church. The *History* deemed it highly appropriate that the city 'met its fate on the feast of the blessed Mary Magdalene, in whose church so enormous a crime had been committed, and so suffered a punishment worthy of its crime'.[41] The monastic chroniclers therefore emphasise political vengeance and spiritual retribution in explaining the massacre at Béziers. But William of Tudela gives the real reason: it was a strategic decision and a deliberate act of terror.

Béziers, then, shows how the military imperative took precedence in medieval warfare. If that meant thousands were to be massacred to discourage resistance in other strongholds, then so be it. But Béziers was not just a military massacre; it was also a comprehensive sack of a city. This, too, could serve a clear military purpose in medieval warfare that helps us to understand its nature more clearly.

That the sack of Béziers was comprehensive is made clear in a range of sources, but of our three war reporters only William of Tudela records it. The mass looting combines with the indiscriminate slaughter and flames to create a Breughel-like picture of Hell. The *ribaldi*, being first in the city, took the lead: 'They were in a frenzy, quite unafraid of death, killing everyone they could find and winning enormous wealth.' By the time the cavalry had made their way into the town, the killing and looting was in full flow. The knights were utterly horrified at what they found: the common folk were helping themselves to the best plunder. They were not prepared to stand by and see such a terrible injustice being perpetrated. They moved in. The *Song* says of the first looters, 'Rich for life they'll be, if they can keep it! But very soon they'll be forced to let it go, for the French knights are going to claim it even though it was the lads that won it.' When the knights saw that 'the servant lads had settled into the houses they had taken, all of them full of riches and treasure ... they went nearly mad with rage and drove the lads out with clubs, like dogs'. The *ribaldi* had 'expected to enjoy the wealth they had taken and be rich for evermore', not unreasonably seeing it as their just reward for taking the town. When 'the barons took it away from them', their anger and frustration was such they torched the town to the cry of 'Burn it, burn it!'

The sacking reinforces the 'Kill them all' strategy: when the knights appeared on the scene they stopped the looting, not the butchering. They were not worried about the latter, as it was policy; their first concern was to grab their share of booty and they were prepared to use violence against their own men to get it. All – from the highest lord to the lowest camp follower – were desperate to gain the spoils of war. On a basic level, it was their reward for signing up to the dangers of campaign, covering the costs of their involvement plus an extra bonus. As such, plunder was an essential element of warfare as it paid the troops and helped to keep the army together. There was the chance for real or greater wealth at the high end of the social scale, and, for the lower orders, unimaginable wealth. After all, for the victorious army it was legitimate stealing. When Southampton fell in 1216, 'such was the booty taken in that town that the poor folk who wished to take advantage and had their minds on profit were all made rich'.[42] We see an interesting case of prioritising on the First Crusade when, in 1097, Bohemond of Taranto puts courage into his impoverished and imperilled infantry with the prospect not of spiritual rewards but of financial ones: 'Stand fast together united in the faith of the Christ and the victory of the Holy Cross, because today, God willing, you will all be made rich.'[43]

Looting was not necessarily chaotic, but was sometimes carried out as a formal closing stage of the siege. When Philip took Luxembourg in 1463 he commanded that his army remain outside the town walls while he entered to give thanks in the main church; only when he had come out was the army given the all clear to loot the place. But discipline could easily break down. One example where it did, but in a clearly intended, organised fashion, was at Fronsac in 1451, during the closing stages of the Hundred Years War. The English surrendered the town under terms that guaranteed it protection from sacking. A large contingent of French besiegers was very disgruntled that they were to be denied their plunder and hatched a plan to rectify matters. That night, they created a situation which made it seem as if the English had gone back on the agreement and were making a sortie. Horses were stampeded and war cries went up. It worked. The French seized their weapons and, no doubt led by those behind the ruse, scaled the walls and looted the place. The officers could do little but play their part in the sack. The prospect of loot was therefore central to an army's motivation. In 1358 Charles the Dauphin needed more men to take Paris; recruitment shot up when he promised the spoils of the capital to those who would enlist with him. The *ribaldi* at Béziers would have kept some of their allotted share of the booty, it was just not as much as they had hoped for and not as much as the knights took. Medieval armies often had strict policies on the division of spoils and how much was apportioned to combatants according to their status. Out of the diabolical anarchy at Béziers, order was restored.

The frenzied sacking undoubtedly added to the numbers killed. A looter would not often risk being stabbed in the back by the inhabitants of the house or the owner of the goods he was ransacking. Nor would he necessarily be prepared to spare a family member, especially if male, of the wife, daughter, mother or sister he was raping for the same reason. Although there is no record of rape at Béziers, we can be sure it took place. It was one of the rewards of soldiering. It was also another weapon of terror, of warning and vengeance: if you do not submit or flee we will rape your wives and daughters. In recent times we have seen rape used in this way in former Yugoslavia, Haiti, Sudan, the Congo and Syria. Froissart, one of the most famous chroniclers of medieval Europe, tells of how those involved in the Jacquerie uprising in France 'violated and killed all the ladies and girls without mercy'. One family suffered a particularly horrific end: 'Having seized the knight and bound him securely to a post, several of them violated his wife and daughter before his eyes. Then they killed the wife, who was pregnant, and the daughter and all his other children and finally put the knight to death with great cruelty.'[44] The pathos of rape as part of a profitable sack is captured by Roger of Wendover when he recounts the pillage of Lincoln in 1217: 'Many of the women of the city were drowned in the river, for, to avoid shame, they took to small boats with their children, female servants and household possessions, and perished on their journey. But there were afterwards found in the river by the searchers goblets of silver and many other articles of great benefit to the finders.'[45]

The victory at Béziers was almost complete, marred only by the burning of the town. As well as the structural damage caused, much of the booty went up in smoke: 'many helmets and padded jerkins and jackets made in Chartres, in Blaye or Edessa and many fine things had to be abandoned'.[46] William of Tudela says all the crusaders would have been made rich for life but for the conflagration. There were to be many more such fires in Languedoc over the next few decades.

The Siege of Carcassonne

It had been an astonishingly successful start for the crusaders: the first mighty fortress they had encountered fell within hours. It had offered up valuable supplies and allowed an object lesson in terror to be taught. After three days camped outside the city – perhaps conditions were too grim to stay within the walls – they headed south-west, passing close by Narbonne. Viscount Aimery of Narbonne and Archbishop Berengar had been rather lukewarm in dealing with heresy there; not any more. After Béziers, they were all too eager to sign up to the crusaders' agenda, offering full military, financial and spiritual co-operation and support; Cathars who had fled there were handed over. This was just one of many effortless successes following the terrifying victory at Béziers. Along the route to Carcassonne, place after place either opened its gates to the northerners or its inhabitants took flight, providing a bounty of supplies and forts. Roger of Wendover reported that news of Béziers caused the fearful to scatter to mountain hideaways, leaving behind 'more than a hundred unmanned castles between Béziers and Carcassonne stocked with food and all kind of stores'.[47] The number may be an overestimation (though it is given in a letter by the legate), but one can gauge from it the force of the Béziers effect.

The advance of the French might have taken weeks if any resistance had been offered, but now they made a simple and straight procession to Carcassonne, arriving there by the end of the month. The city is hugely impressive today, and was only marginally less so in 1209. The skirting wall was constructed in the mid-thirteenth century; today the visitor can walk around the city in the *lices*, the space between the old and new walls. Built atop the steep incline of an escarpment above the River Aude, Carcassonne had twenty-six wall towers, plus fortified gates and the comital castle. Two suburbs – the *castellare* to the south-east and the *bourg* on the north side – were walled; a third, St Vincent, was less well protected, and lay more exposed between the city's wall and the river. These suburbs are no longer there, the inhabitants having moved either into the city or into the *bastide* St Louis new town across the Aude, when the extra ring of defences was built. Opinion differs over the relative strength of the place, but both William of Tudela and Roger of Wendover attest to its power. In 1355 Edward the Black Prince managed to destroy its suburbs but left the fortress itself alone, deeming it too difficult to take. Its long wall would have been a weakness if insufficiently manned, but with a population estimated at around 8,000, and with refugees having flocked in from Béziers and the surrounding countryside, and also with Viscount Raymond Roger having called his vassals in, there was no danger of this. Its western side, some 600yd from the river (a serious drawback), was more vulnerable, but the castle keep dominated here.

The usual preparations for a siege had been put in place as best as time had allowed. Wooden hoardings were constructed to overhang the walls, allowing the defenders to better protect the bases against the works of enemy picks. The garrison and inhabitants were allocated sectors to defend and made ready to douse fires. The fabric of non-essential buildings was cannibalised to further shore up the defences, the cathedral losing some stone and its wooden stalls (much to the horror of Peter of Vaux de Cernay). Food was brought in and anything left outside was destroyed to deny the enemy provisions. Even the flour mills were destroyed so that the besiegers would struggle to make bread. The burghers of Rye did this in 1217 to hamper the French invaders, who were left desperate for food as a consequence. The Trencavel lord therefore had reasonable cause to hope that the northerners could be resisted and that time would see the besieging army dwindle through departures, disease and lack of supplies.

Remarkably, if true, the viscount seemed prepared to risk the same tactic that had been the ruin of Béziers: a pre-emptive sortie. 'To horse, my lords!' he cried, as he made ready to lead 400 knights into the crusaders' camp.[48] The young viscount was persuaded against this course of action by the veteran lord Peter Roger of Cabaret (part of the stunning Lastours castle group), who advised him to preserve his forces for the morrow, when the French would attack their access to water. That night, guards rode around the city as both sides readied themselves for combat.

Hostilities began on the morning of 3 August with an attack, as the Lord of Cabaret had predicted, on the suburb St Vincent. The clergy called on divine help, chanting 'veni Sancti Spiritus' ('come, Holy Ghost'). The History says the suburb was overrun immediately as the defenders retreated. The Song claims, whether truthfully or so as to excite its audience is not clear, that the fighting was fierce and both sides suffered heavy casualties. Within two hours the suburb had been cleared. Peter draws attention to the first notable deed of his hero, Simon de Montfort, who 'courageously advanced into the ditch ahead of all the others – indeed he was the only knight to do so and thus played an outstanding part in capturing this suburb'.[49] Peter says that the ditches were filled in and the town razed. The first action makes obvious sense as it made the walls more accessible, but the reasoning for the latter is less clear: it cleared the way for the siege machinery to be brought up, but it also denied the northerners cover. It is likely that only some obstructions were removed for the artillery, which battered the walls incessantly when they had been constructed and drawn up.

William of Tudela makes the important observation that the city was now cut off from its main water supply; the southerners were left with just the deep-sunken wells within the walls. Meanwhile, he says that the northerners were sitting pretty as they had an abundance of supplies; these had been boosted by the abandoned places the crusaders had come across *en route*. Nonetheless, their expenses continued to mount. The *bourg* was their next target the following day. With its stronger defences, it proved much harder to take. The crusaders in the ditch were forced to pull back under the barrage of stones raining down on them. A knight was left behind with a broken leg until he was rescued by Simon de Montfort and a squire. Montfort was quickly building a reputation for bravery which, despite the sycophancy of the *History*, was justly earned. Under heavy bombardment, a 'cat' was sent against the wall: this was a four-wheeled wagon covered in oxhides under which engineers and soldiers could sap the base of the defences.

Fire, wood and stones thrown down destroyed the cover, but not before the sappers had carved out a hollow in the wall that afforded them the protection to continue their work. On the morning of 8 August this section of the wall collapsed and the crusaders stormed the breach; the southerners retreated. However, Peter relates that when many of the crusaders had withdrawn satisfied with their work, a sortie from the citadel 'chased off any of our men they found still in the suburb, slaughtered many who could not escape and set fire to the entire suburb'.

At this juncture, politics intervened in the form of King Peter II of Aragon, come to mediate between the northerners and his vassal Raymond Roger. He arrived at dinnertime with 100 knights. Civilities were

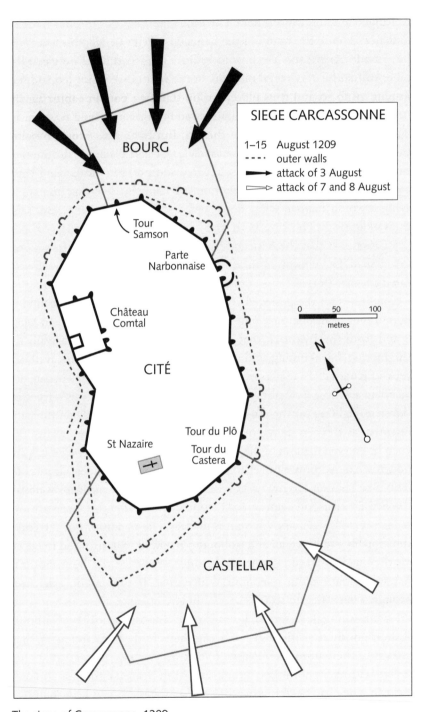

The siege of Carcassonne, 1209.

exchanged and discussions held. The king was there not to offer military assistance, despite the hopes of the besieged – Peter needed his forces for the crusade against the Muslims in Spain – but to arbitrate between the forces so that his territorial interests in the region were not jeopardised. He entered the city and told the viscount that little could be done against such numbers as the northerners possessed but that he would do what he could to secure decent terms for the city. But the legate Arnald Amalric was prepared only to allow Raymond Roger and eleven of his men to leave the city with what they could carry and nothing more. King Peter knew the viscount would not dishonour his name by deserting his people, saying it would 'happen when donkeys fly'. Raymond Roger rejected the terms indignantly. The king, both angry and saddened, returned to Aragon. Any false hopes that the besieged had entertained on Peter's arrival were now dashed. The tension in the city must have been unbearable as all now feared another Béziers.

Conditions for the besieged crammed into the citadel were dreadful in the summer heat. The *Song* tells of the stench from those who had fallen ill and from the livestock that had been brought within the walls for slaughtering and skinning, and of flies that tormented everyone. Within a week of King Peter's departure, another round of negotiations began; it is uncertain at whose instigation. William says that the viscount was warned by a kinsman fighting for the crusaders to surrender, or 'you will get the same treatment as Béziers'. Raymond Roger knew he had to seek terms. But when he entered the tent of the crusader Count of Nevers to begin talks he suddenly handed himself over to the custody of the crusaders, apparently of his own volition. 'To my mind he acted like a lunatic', exclaims William.

Whether terms had been agreed before or settled after this surprise move by the previously defiant viscount is unclear. The conditions of surrender were notably harsh: the inhabitants were permitted their lives and freedom, but they had to leave everything behind except for the light clothing they were wearing. On 15 August, William the Breton says they departed through a narrow gate so that they could be checked to ensure nothing was being smuggled out; they left 'to the disposition of the Catholics all their goods, their fields, their arms, their herds, their treasures, their vineyards, their homes'.[50] Peter of Vaux de Cernay mocked that they carried with them nothing but their sins. Most headed either for Toulouse or Spain. They had been impoverished in an instant. But at least their lives had been spared.

As was the city itself. The commanders did not want a repeat of Béziers; they were determined to keep the fortress intact as their headquarters. Roger of Wendover, confirming crusading sources, explains the northern barons' thinking at a council: 'if the city were completely destroyed, no nobleman of the army would be found to lead the government of that country.'[51] Without goods and infrastructure, the new lord would have no means of sustaining the garrison needed to guard it. If a stronghold was deemed necessary, as Carcassonne was, it would be re-strengthened after a successful siege and any damage inflicted repaired; if it was thought difficult or dangerous to hold, or that it did not serve a particular strategic purpose for the victor, it would usually be destroyed to deny its use to the enemy. With towns such as Carcassonne, as the barons pointed out, there was a need for a regional seat of governmental administration; for that to be effective, it had to be economically viable. Note William the Breton's list above of all that the citizens had to leave behind: it represents some of the basic forms of livelihood. A depopulated town, such as Béziers was to some extent, was one without markets and hence without economic benefits to its ruler. Furthermore, a scarcity of labour would, by the laws of supply and demand, place upwards pressure on wages, thereby increasing the costs of labour and decreasing competitiveness, as wage increases after the Black Death in the fourteenth century show. It could make sound military sense to kill a garrison and much of the male population as a warning to others and to keep survivors subjugated by fear, but to kill everyone made military sense only on relatively rare occasions. After all, vibrant towns and commerce were vital in creating the wealth that could be channelled into war.

At first sight, then, it would seem that the crusaders' policy for the defeated had been ill thought out. However, while our three war reporters make no mention of this, the well-informed William the Breton, much overlooked here as elsewhere, informs us of what happened after the city had been depopulated: 'the Catholic warriors filled the city with the faithful and worked to restore it'.[52] Who these faithful were and when they moved in is not specified. But just as field armies left garrisons behind to hold forts, as they did at Carcassonne, so it can be assumed that a large proportion of the camp followers settled into the city. To these might be added people from securely orthodox places in the Carcassès region and those from further afield who had heard of events and saw a new life for themselves in this part of Languedoc. War afforded such opportunities to settlers. When Philip II of France was invading Normandy in 1203–04, he spent six months besieging Château Gaillard. When his troops had taken the town of Les Andelys that lay beneath it, he filled it with settlers even before the castle had been taken. The crusaders' intentions at Carcassonne were therefore clear: this was a war of colonisation.

Having been spared the flames, Carcassonne offered up fantastic booty. This was piled up while the horses and mules were shared out. In the city, Arnald Amalric called the crusaders to him and, addressing them from a marble plinth, warned them to hand over all their plunder. If anyone so much as kept a piece of charcoal, they would be excommunicated. The wealth was to stay with the city so that it would remain strong enough to prevent the heretics from ever taking it again. All agreed to this, though no doubt reluctantly. The knights chosen to guard the hoard were not so keen: three months later, they were excommunicated for helping themselves to 5,000 livres of goodies from the pile.

The fall of Carcassonne leaves in its wake two mysteries: the submission of Raymond Roger and his ultimate fate. Did the young viscount hand himself over or was he grabbed by the crusaders during the negotiations? His open, heroic defiance less than a fortnight earlier had evaporated in the punishing summer heat. The failure of King Peter's mediation and his morale-destroying departure must have caused Raymond Roger to reconsider his bold stance. Conditions in the city were only worsening. A repeat of Béziers seemed ever more likely. William of Puylaurens suggests that Raymond Roger wanted peace talks as he was 'stricken with terror' and that he was taken hostage to ensure that the terms of the surrender were met.[53] The *History* claims that the viscount's imprisonment was part of these terms. Frustratingly, the *Song* appears to be on the verge of telling us what happened in the Count of Nevers's tent when … there is a gap in the single surviving manuscript. Just before this, as noted above, William of Tudela writes that the viscount had handed himself over completely voluntarily and judges that 'he acted like a lunatic, putting himself into custody'. At the time of writing, he knew the young man's fate. Perplexingly, William of Tudela also says that Raymond Roger only joined the crusaders in talks following the promise of his kinsman in the crusader army to 'take you there in safety and bring you back here to your own people'. Perhaps the viscount had planned to hand himself over but wanted to let his people think he had been taken by the enemy so as to avoid his reputation being besmirched. Perhaps he handed himself over on impulse after being warned of the dire consequences of further resistance.

We will never know what really happened in the tent that day. It seems likely that the viscount had thrown himself at the mercy either of his peers or of the Church. Whatever is the case, the might of the crusade had been directed against Raymond Roger and here was a golden opportunity to seize him, as some sources suggest, with no further expenses incurred. Yes, he was a fellow noble, but it would be easy for the barons and churchmen to convince themselves that in harbouring heretics he could be treated in an unconventional and unchivalrous manner.

The belief that he had been arrested dishonourably by his captors was heightened by the young viscount's fate: within three months he was dead. He died on 10 November, a prisoner in Carcassonne. Whether he died in a cell or confined in apartments (William of Tudela says he was 'lavishly supplied with everything he needed') is unclear.[54] Peter of Vaux de Cernay simply states that he suddenly fell ill and died; the *Song* says he was killed by dysentery ('I believe'). William of Puylaurens also says that dysentery claimed the viscount while he was still a 'hostage', but notes that 'news of his death produced widely current false rumours that he had in fact been murdered'. If merely rumours, they carried some weight: even Pope Innocent III wrote that the viscount had been 'wretchedly slain'. William of Tudela, sympathetic to Raymond Roger, vehemently denied the notion that 'he was killed at night by treason' and rejected the possibility of his captor, Simon de Montfort, ever allowing such a thing to happen: 'Not for anything in the world, by Jesus in heaven!'[55]

Raymond Roger might reasonably have calculated that he would not be treated too harshly in captivity; the Middle Ages are full of stories of noblemen and noblewomen being imprisoned in extremely comfortable conditions. Like his uncle Count Raymond of Toulouse, he was never indicted for heresy and his status would ensure his escape from public execution. The converse of this, however, is that any death would therefore need to be surreptitious. Nobility was no guarantee of safety. We are a century away from when English kings stared to be murdered in captivity (Edward II, Richard II, Henry VI, Edward V); the thirteenth century is seen, in contrast, to be generally a period of leniency to errant nobles.

But King John's recent activities might have shown the northern leadership how to deal with the viscount. In 1202 John captured his nephew Arthur of Brittany at the siege of Mirebeau. He was thrown into a dungeon in Rouen. Arthur, a contender for the English throne and an ally of Philip of France, was only 16; like Raymond Roger, he had plenty of years ahead during which time he could become the figurehead of resistance and trouble. After his incarceration, Arthur was never seen again. In a forerun of Richard III and the princes in the tower, John was suspected and accused of murdering Arthur. Stories abounded as to what had happened, two prominent ones being that John had killed Arthur in a drunken rage or had had him castrated, the shock of which killed him. Nothing was proven, but there can be little doubt a political murder had occurred. Six years later, he had the wife and son of William de Braose imprisoned in Corfe Castle. William, who had been one of John's closest familiars, had lost the king's favour. He had been with John at the time of Arthur's disappearance in Rouen and knew the duke's fate. When William fled from John the king targeted his wife, Matilda, and their child. He left them to starve to death in their cell. Stories went around afterwards telling how the bodies were found with Matilda slumped between her son's legs with her head lying on his chest, expiring that way after having gnawed at his cheeks for food. This death by neglect meant that John had not actually physically killed them, providing a rather empty case for non-culpability.

Such stories circulated rapidly throughout England and France, making news in nobles' courts. Many of the crusade leaders would have known about John's actions – the Angevins were important players in south-western France – and they may have decided to emulate his repulsive example in dealing with Raymond. It would have been a neat solution. Weighing up the possibilities, my inclination is to believe that Raymond Roger was not seized in the negotiation tent by the Count of Nevers, but agreed to become a hostage, something that was normal practice. I suspect that as plausible as dysentery may be, it is a little too convenient and that Viscount Raymond Roger Trencavel, the target of the first phase of the crusade, was either killed or left to starve to death as a political solution to a long-term problem.

In just three weeks of active military operations, the crusaders had crushed their Trencavel enemy and taken, with very little effort, the two most important hostile towns of south-eastern France. It was an astonishing achievement. For many, it was enough. Just as the first, independent crusade from Quercy and the Agenais had dissolved following its brief, initial success, so the great crusading host was now to shrink dramatically. And as

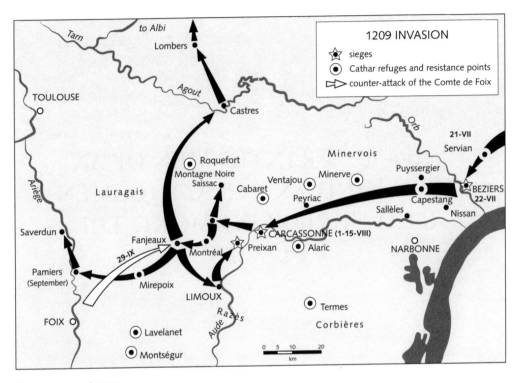

The invasion of 1209.

the remnants of the crusade prepared to extend its conquest of Languedoc, it also underwent a complete change of command. From this time onwards, the northerners had a ruthless and brilliant new leader, the most famous knight of the whole crusade: Simon de Montfort.

3

1209–10: 'Frantic Men of an Evil Kind and Crazy Women Who Shrieked Among the Flames'

Simon de Montfort Takes Command

A new phase of the war was about to begin: at first smaller in scale, more diverse and more intense, it would then escalate to an epic siege by the year's end. At a council held in Carcassonne at the end of August, the legate Arnald Amalric relinquished the military leadership of the crusade to Simon de Montfort. At first, the post was offered to the grandees of the crusade: the Duke of Burgundy and the counts of Nevers and St Pol. All refused. They had earned their indulgence and added renown to their family names by taking part. Their landholdings in the north were already plentiful and provided a secure power base for them. Any further involvement in the south would require considerable commitment and exposure to unnecessary danger; no doubt they had been rewarded by some spoils of war gained with remarkable ease and there was no need to put these at risk by staying longer. Nor did they want to be too far removed from the circles of political power around their king. It was also claimed that they felt it beneath them to take the inheritance of another man. The leadership needed to go to someone hungry for land, power and fame. That man was Simon de Montfort.

He was chosen by a council of two bishops, four knights and Arnald Amalric. They had a hard time persuading de Montfort to take the job – or at least he made it appear hard for them. His initial refusals were bargaining points to exact as strong a position as possible. This was not merely a cynical exercise but necessary if he were to have a chance of succeeding. He received an oath that all present would help him if he needed them and only then accepted (or was obliged to take) command of the army. The Count of Leicester and Lord of Montfort now added Viscount of Béziers, Carcassonne, Albi and Razès to his titles. That the Trencavel viscount was still alive and that the overlord, King Peter of Aragon, had not been consulted troubled neither the legate nor Montfort.

Montfort was in his mid to late forties when he took on his new role. His family lands were based in Montfort in northern France and extended to Evreux in Normandy. Through an inheritance to the earldom, he was known as titular Count of Leicester because, after Philip II's conquest of Normandy in 1204, Simon, as a vassal of the French king, was not permitted by King John to take up possession of his county in England (his son was able to do so in 1239). He married well, in all senses, to Alice of Montmorency, whose family were influential in the Île de France. Their marriage seems to have been a happy one, as well as advantageous to Simon. Alice is a truly redoubtable figure, Simon's truest ally throughout his decade of active crusading: undeterred by the rigours and dangers of war, she was to be found recruiting troops, organising defences and at the side of her husband at sieges. The business of crusading was very much a part of the family business with Simon's brother Guy and the viscount's sons Amaury and Simon accompanying him in the south at various times. He was a famously devout son of the Church, and a patron of the future St Dominic; but his orthodoxy did not extend to subservience as he repeatedly put his own political interests before the Church's spiritual ones.

His family had close ties with Peter of Vaux de Cernay's Cistercian abbey; Simon himself was old friends with the abbot, Peter's uncle Guy of Carcassonne. This ensured him a good press – indeed, a fawning one – at least from this quarter. Peter is keen (perhaps too gushingly keen?) to share what 'I know personally about the noble count of Montfort', a man of 'outstanding courage' who 'was tall, with a splendid head of hair and fine features, of handsome appearance, broad-shouldered with muscular arms, of excellent physique generally'. He then seems to recover himself to concentrate on 'his more important qualities' which cover all the characteristics that make the perfect Christian knight.[56] William of Tudela confirms his virtues, but in a more restrained fashion, observing importantly that Montfort was 'a tough fighting man'.[57] Many contemporaries held a similar view of this 'valiant knight', 'this illustrious count, with faithful heart and powerful arms'.[58] But, as we shall see, he was to incite hatred in others as he single-mindedly pursued his ambitions in Occitania.

Montfort was a true veteran. He had learnt his trade in the endless Anglo-French wars between Richard, John and Philip. He was already a crusader of some renown, having participated in the Fourth Crusade. To his credit, he had not continued to the siege and sack of Constantinople in 1204 as he would not sully his vows by fighting against the lands owned by the King of Hungary, a Christian monarch; instead, he went to fight Muslims in Syria. He was not so scrupulous in 1209; he may have felt that he had missed out on the wealth of the Byzantine capital and that this time he was going to get his share. As he proved in the ditches of Carcassonne, he was a soldier's soldier in every sense: a big, strong man and natural leader who inspired loyalty in his men through personal example and who was unrelenting in his prosecution of war. He was to demonstrate his consummate skills as a general time and again.

He would need these skills. At the moment of its greatest success, the crusade disintegrated, leaving just a tiny fragment under Montfort's command. Having fulfilled their crusading vows, most of the army left or soon drifted away. The *Song* says that most wished to go back north as 'the mountains are wild and the passes dangerous and none of them wanted to be killed in that country'.[59] Internal divisions did not help: the Count of Nevers, never on good terms with Duke Odo of Burgundy, departed with his contingent, unhappy with the duke's closeness to Simon. In vain, the count and the legate urged him to stay, as the enemy strongholds of Termes, Cabaret and Minerve needed to be taken next, along with the lesser castra of Ventajou and Alaric. The departure of such a leading figure served only to encourage (or discourage) the others and the crusading army melted away, great lords and lowly camp followers alike. As the crusade dragged on, some occasionally returned to the fight, but for now Montfort was commander of a small force rather than an army. He was left with the problem of how to garrison the more than 100 castra under his control and keep the country subdued. Great as the crusader gains had been, these would soon be challenged if the hostile lords and populace of the region perceived the occupying force to be weak and seriously overstretched. And it was not long before that challenge began.

The remnant of the crusading army was now a presence rather than an overwhelming power. The Duke of Burgundy would not be with Montfort beyond a fortnight. We know of twenty-three named knights who remained with Montfort out of a total of about thirty. These tended to be relatives, friends and younger sons looking for lands and wives (the two often went together) and generally not of high social standing. Some of the most important of Simon's entourage, and first in line for territorial fiefs, were Guy de Lévis, Bouchard de Marly, Peter des Voisins, Robert de Mauvoisin, William de Contres and Lambert de Thury. To these must be added the knights' own contingents (small as they may be), the sergeants and infantry, many of whom were to be found scattered around the region as garrisons and who would, where possible, form a field army. The army would recruit more men in the spring (William of Tudela says it was then 4,500 strong), but for now Montfort's force could be numbered in the hundreds, and probably no more than a thousand. This lack of manpower was an immediate problem for Montfort; he even felt compelled to spare one of his knights, Robert de Mauvoisin, to carry a letter to Rome explaining the seriousness of the situation in the hope of being sent more men and funds, the latter problem exacerbated by the fact that he had to pay the men who remained twice the usual rate. His small force was therefore immediately overstretched: it had an area of 10,000 square miles to cover. But it had some strengths: it was a highly disciplined, completely loyal, ambitious hardcore element led by one of the greatest generals of the Middle Ages.

Montfort had to move swiftly to make the most of the momentum the huge crusading army had generated; he needed to occupy all the towns and strongholds that had emptied in fear of the massive crusading force before the hostile lords of the south, under the loose overall command of the Count of Foix, organised a counter-thrust and re-occupied them. To this end Fanjeaux, Montréal and Limoux were garrisoned, the last of these being given to Lambert de Thury; meanwhile, Béziers and its environs were placed in the hands of William de Contres. Montfort took the strong castrum of Fanjeaux for his operational headquarters outside Carcassonne, as its central position placed it equidistant from there, Castelnaudary, Limoux and Mirepoix. Montfort then made a circuit of the south, west and north of his newly acquired territory at the end of August and into

September, doling out castra to his followers so that they might keep the population both subdued and economically productive. The bulk of the crusading army, still not fully depleted due to the continuing but short-lived presence of the Duke of Burgundy, was encamped at Alzonne just west of Carcassonne. Montfort was consolidating as much as he could at this time. It was a clear short-term objective. Strategically, long-term aims were not so easily achieved, especially with such a limited army. Eradicating heresy was a little nebulous; it meant taking and holding a whole region that was constantly on the point of uprising and then permanently dousing out the fires as they sprung up. The First Crusade was a much more taxing enterprise, but at least the objective was fixed and focused throughout on the taking of the all-important goal, Jerusalem.

The timings of these and the following episodes are hard to pin down, but historians can piece together a plausible chronology of events up until the end of the year. Amid the securing of the military aims, spiritual ones had also to be attended to. A delegation from the important town of Castres, halfway between Carcassonne and Albi, came to meet with Montfort and pay homage to him. There two male heretics, a perfect and a follower, were brought before the count. Montfort, unswervingly orthodox, ordered them to be burnt, even after the young heretic had broken down and recanted his heresy. He said that if the heretic was genuinely contrite, 'the fire would serve to expiate his sins'. The two Cathars 'were then tied with strong chains round their legs, middle and neck, and their hands were fastened behind them … A fire was lit round the stake, and burned vigorously.'[60] Peter of Vaux de Cernay then reports a miracle: the young man broke free, suffering only scorched fingertips.

Early September seems the most likely time for the crusaders' advance on Cabaret, the castle of Peter Roger, who had made his way there from Carcassonne. The Duke of Burgundy had advised Montfort to take the castle. As mentioned earlier, Cabaret was the chief fortress of the astonishing complex of three castles overlooking Lastours, only 9 miles north of Carcassonne but remote in the Black Mountains. The other castles there at this time are Quertinheux and Surdespine (the fourth that can be seen today is the Tour Régine, built in the mid-thirteenth century). Its master might have been a gnarly warlord, but his court at Cabaret was cultured and a home to Cathars, learning and troubadours. Not only that, it was sited in an area enriched by the mining of gold, silver, iron and copper. Like so many of the region's castles, these forts were truly inaccessible, high up on their jagged peaks. When the crusaders arrived they seemed to sense the impossibility of their task: they mounted a half-hearted assault and made a quick withdrawal the following day. It was at this point that Odo of Burgundy withdrew from the crusade with most of the army. It was the last major chance to obtain a sizeable victory.

With only around thirty knights (the *History* is quick to emphasise that he was now almost totally unsupported) and having made little of Cabaret, troubles were soon to mount for Montfort. But before they accrued, he made the most of the continuing momentum to gain further successes. With great energy he recommenced his whirlwind procession through his new lands. And beyond. He now moved south into the territory of the Count of Foix. Initially, Montfort was responding to a call from Abbot Vital of Mirepoix. This beautiful town was jointly owned by the abbey and the count (among other lesser figures); a vibrant Cathar centre, the abbot wanted Montfort here to restore orthodoxy and, of course, to displace the Count of Foix. Mirepoix, Pamiers and Saverdun all passed into Montfort's hands without a struggle, the last two seeking a more lenient lord than the harsh Count of Foix (except for the heretics, who fled further south and to the refuge of Montségur). A look at a map shows Montfort's strategic thinking: Mirepoix, enfeoffed to Guy de Lévis, secured the way to Carcassonne; Pamiers and Saverdun blocked the route of potential allies to Toulouse. It made sense, but it came at a huge cost: the Count of Foix, another Raymond Roger, was to become the crusaders' most implacable and savage enemy; and now his overlord, King Peter, was being provoked even further. Montfort then rode north again, accepting the allegiance of Lombres and Albi, at the northernmost point of his new territories; this was another possession of the Aragonese king. Peter of Vaux de Cernay claims that Lombres had over fifty knights who now offered their allegiance to Montfort; if so, this was a major boost to the viscount. Back south, he fortified Limoux, took a number of unspecified castra and, for good measure, hung some of the inhabitants on gibbets. Then, to further secure the perimeter around Carcassonne, he laid siege to the Count of Foix's castrum at Preixan. Here Foix came to meet with Montfort and seek terms: the swiftness and comprehensiveness of Simon's gains had kept the initiative away from the count, who now needed time to regroup. Raymond Roger submitted Preixan to Montfort, vowed to aid the Church, and offered his youngest son as hostage. Montfort was at the pinnacle of his success. But the landslide was about to begin.

The Fightback Begins

The spectacular falls of Béziers and Carcassonne had carried the crusaders on a wave to a position of seeming dominance. Time and again we will see how political and military momentum drove events. But now, for the crusaders, that momentum had petered out. Montfort wanted to consolidate his political position by paying homage for his lands to King Peter. The monarch met with Montfort at Narbonne and Montpellier, but talks in late November and early December lasting over a fortnight produced no agreement and Peter declined Montfort's allegiance. According to Peter of Vaux de Cernay, the king then sent secret messages to the lords of the region urging them to resist the northerners and promising them his help. The refusal of homage alone immediately weakened Montfort's position and encouraged many lords to break their recently proclaimed faith to him. Such breaking of allegiances might seem to go against views of feudalism and loyal service to masters, but, for all the gravity of allegiance, the service of a knight or a lord could be a fickle thing. Southern France was less feudal than northern Europe, but the latter saw just as much allegiance breaking as started to occur here. This is partly due to interpretations of legal ownership of land, and how this could easily be perceived in varying ways, but it is also because war could afford many new opportunities and be a great leveller. As Robert of Boves said to the Count of Flanders when breaking homage to him in 1185: 'Lord count, I was your man until now, but now by God's will I have been made your equal.'[61] The relationship between a lord and his vassal was a two-way contract, a deal that required constant supervision. Any number of things could, in the eyes of one or the other, render the contract null and void.

Montfort was reminded of this in the violent case of Gerald of Pépieux, a knight from the viscounty of Béziers. Gerald and his uncle were relatively rare examples of southerners fighting on the side of the crusaders. When the uncle was killed by a Frenchman, Montfort, extremely anxious to preserve the loyalty of such southerners and keen to demonstrate that he would show no favouritism, had the culprit executed by being 'thrown into a pit and buried alive', a method designed to shock.[62] This was not enough for Gerald, who broke faith with Montfort. It may have been the combination of his relative's death and King Peter's unaccommodating position that either pushed or encouraged Gerald into his new stance. Montfort had given Gerald control of Minerve and the area around it.

The *History* relates that Gerald gathered a force of other knights and infantry, and took the castrum of Puisserguier and imprisoned its garrison of two knights and fifty sergeants. The castrum may have been taken by surprise if Gerald had maintained a pretence of still being allied to the crusaders; William of Tudela says that he had not yet formally renounced his allegiance. Montfort rushed there with Count Aimeric of Narbonne and his men, the latter deciding belatedly that he wanted no part of the siege. His forces depleted, Montfort withdrew overnight to the nearby town of Capestang. Gerald, not knowing of Aimeric's departure and not relishing defending the less than formidable castrum, fled in the night with his two prisoner knights. Before he left, Peter says that he attempted to kill all the other prisoners by herding them into the ditch around the tower and bombarding them with stones and also with fire and straw as an incendiary material. Peter says these men were miraculously unharmed. There may been some element of truth to this story, but told as Peter tells it, it seems a remarkably inefficient way to kill prisoners. As Gerald made his way to the safety of Minerve, Montfort burned Puisserguier and ravaged Gerald's lands before returning to Carcassonne. The *Song* covers this event much more briefly and claims that Gerald burnt the castle. This is just as plausible and may be how he tried to kill his prisoners at the same time.

There followed an atrocity that was to further mark the bitter nature of the crusade. The two crusader knights in Gerald's possession were mutilated. He 'put out their eyes; more than that, he cut off their ears and noses and upper lips and sent them off naked' back to the viscount.[63] One stumbled into a dung pit where he died (he may have been seeking warmth) while the other made it back to Carcassonne with the help of a peasant. Montfort's reaction on meeting his barbarically disfigured knight is not recorded, but we can be sure it put even more steel into his heart. Later, he was to return the compliment to the enemy. Like Béziers and the attempt to massacre the garrison at Puisserguier, this atrocity was designed to shock and intimidate.

Such actions were not new in the wars of France and certainly were not new to Montfort. When Philip II of France massacred a large contingent of Richard the Lionheart's Welsh mercenaries, Richard hurled three of his French prisoners to their deaths from the rocky heights of Château Gaillard and blinded fifteen others, leaving one with one eye to lead them back to the French king. Not to be outdone, Philip responded in kind, 'so that no one', wrote William the Breton rather crassly, 'would believe him less than Richard in strength and courage'.[64] Philip's grandfather, King Louis the Fat, a larger-than-life character in all senses, was even more brutal in 1109, when he and his men defeated the castle of William of la Roche-Guyon:

> Attacking them with swords, they piously slaughtered the impious, mutilated the limbs of some, disembowelled others with great pleasure, and piled up even greater cruelty upon them, considering it still too kind. No one should doubt that the hand of God sped so swift a revenge when both the living and the dead were thrown through the windows. Bristling with countless arrows like hedgehogs, their bodies stopped short in the air, vibrating on the sharp points of lances as if the ground rejected them. When alive William lacked a brain, and now that he was dead he lacked a heart, for they ripped it from his entrails and impaled it upon a stake, swollen as it was with fraud and evil. They left it set up in a conspicuous place for many days to make public their revenge.[65]

Other corpses were tied to makeshift rafts and floated down the Seine to Rouen as further warning.

Gerald's actions in 1209 were part of the tit-for-tat atrocities that mounted up at regular intervals throughout the Albigensian Crusade. One leading historian of the crusade has suggested that the campaign was no more brutal than other contemporary conflicts in Europe. Given the examples cited above, it is understandable that such a view should be held. However, I would argue that the crusade was markedly cruel, even by the standards of the day, and especially for England and France. There are three main reasons for this. One is the scale and intensity of the war – a national war – within a relatively small geographical space, which increased the frequency of atrocity. The second is because the degree of familiarity between opposing knights was much less than was common in other theatres of war. In the rout following the battle of Lincoln in May 1217, there were only three notable deaths out of hundreds of knights; indeed, many of the victorious royalist forces were prepared to forgo lucrative ransoms and let their enemies escape, only pretending to pursue the fleeing enemy: 'had it not been for the effect of relationship and blood, not a single one of all of them would have escaped.'[66] The third reason has already been explored: this was a war of conquest and national survival of the southerners against the northerners. Religion adds to the bitterness of war, but wars over land and defending land from a foreign invader tend to be the fiercest of all. In this respect, the savagery of the crusade might be compared to the imperial invasions of Italy by the emperors Frederick I and Frederick II.

The mutilation of the knights was a cruel indication of the situation faced by Montfort, as the crusaders' position began to unravel amid a rising tide of open aggression. By the end of November, in addition to Gerald's breaking of homage, came news of more defections by knights across his viscounty. Two of his own knights, William and Amaury of Poissy, found themselves besieged in their castle near Carcassonne (believed to be Miramont). Montfort tried to relieve them but, says the *History*, heavy flooding of the Aude prevented him from getting there. The knights were taken. Worse was to happen at that painful thorn in the crusaders' side, Cabaret. The garrison at Saissac, a powerful castle and walled town north-west of Carcassonne, formed a body of fifty men to harass the territory around Cabaret. Saissac was under the command of Bouchard de Marly, a cousin of Montfort's wife Alice. As he approached Cabaret, Peter Roger and 'at least ninety' cavalry, infantry and fourteen archers ambushed and surrounded them. After a furious combat, the northerner Gaubert d'Essigny was killed and Bouchard was taken prisoner. He was to spend sixteen months chained to the wall with other prisoners in Cabaret's keep.

The clergy were targeted, too. The Cistercian Abbot Stephen of Eaunes and his party were attacked just a mile outside of the crusaders' capital at Carcassonne. Even though the abbot was on a mission for the Count of Foix, a southern lord called William of Roquefort, head of a Cathar castrum and family (his mother was a perfect), murdered the abbot and a lay brother in what seems to have been a frenzied assault: the abbot was killed by thirty-six wounds and the lay brother by twenty-four. Another monk was left half-dead having been hacked sixteen times. The fourth monk remained unscathed as, notably, the assailants knew him and were not hostile towards him. Roquefort's own connections reveal something of the personal situations some lords faced: some of his siblings were active Cathars and his brother-in-law was a Cathar bishop; yet William's brother Bernard Raymond was Catholic Bishop of Carcassonne until he resigned and was replaced by Guy of Vaux de Cernay (the chronicler Peter's uncle) in 1211.

And still the tide of reversals kept breaking at Montfort's feet. Castres reneged on its recent allegiance, capturing the knight in charge of the castrum, but not harming him as some of the town's people were being kept as hostages in Carcassonne. The counter-momentum, possibly pre-arranged, gathered strength. Within twenty-four hour of Castres, knights at Lombres took over the castrum and imprisoned Montfort's sergeants stationed here with the others in the tower of Castres; however, the prisoners, perhaps fearing a repeat of the episode at Puisserguier, fashioned a rope prepared from their clothes and made their escape through a window. The Count of Foix retook Preixan (and freed his son being held there), having submitted it to Montfort only a few days earlier. Aimeric of Montréal, a powerful local lord whose town was strongly heretical, also broke faith with Montfort. The viscount, short of manpower, had placed the town under the command of a local priest; but the priest now handed it back to Aimeric. It was to prove a costly mistake for the priest the following spring.

Any northerner victories at this point tended to be matters of survival rather than expansion. Foix led an assault on Montfort's field headquarters at Fanjeaux. His men managed to scale the walls and break into the castrum, but the garrison rallied in a successful counter-attack and expelled the enemy, killing several of them. But as William of Tudela writes of Montfort, 'all through the winter he lost ground'.[67] By the end of the year he had lost over forty strongholds, leaving in his possession Carcassonne, Béziers, Fanjeaux, Saissac, Pamiers and Saverdun in the south, and Albi and Ambialet in the north. The capture of knights, as well as others mutilated and sergeants killed, had also severely depleted his already straitened forces.

But Montfort was anything but a defeatist. The urban centres of his viscounty remained in his hands and hope was brought back from Rome in the form of Robert de Mauvoisin's return. It will be recalled that Montfort had sent him to the pope on his appointment as commander of the crusader army, so that Innocent could be fully informed of the precarious situation in Languedoc. The pope, at the centre of Europe's diplomacy, had all manner of pressing business to attend to, including the crusades in Spain and the Middle East; nonetheless, he promised his help and money, and wrote directly to Peter of Aragon, emperor Otto IV and Alfonso VIII of Aragon for support. The Albigensian Crusade was again preached in northern France, the Cistercians taking the lead, and by the spring of 1210 a steady, though not gushing, stream of new recruits moved into the south and revitalised Montfort's diminished forces.

The Siege of Minerve

The fighting eased off over the winter months but the politics continued. Southerner lords tried to lure Peter of Aragon into supporting them by promises of homage. In May he refused when Cabaret was not part of the deal and the lords would not agree to hand over their castles to him if

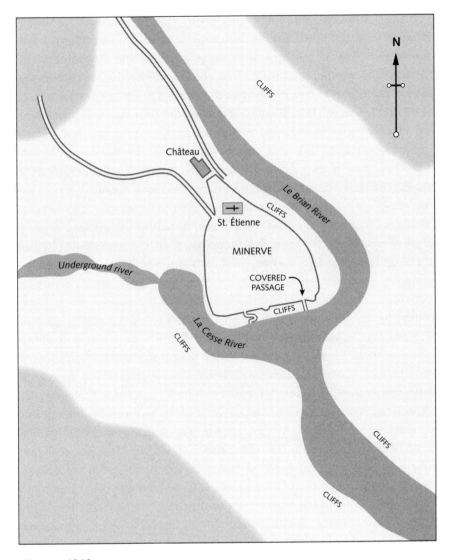

Minerve, 1210.

asked to, should the need arise; he was not yet ready to embroil himself in the war. Toulouse remained central to events, and while Montfort was waging war on all fronts, Arnald Amalric was doing his bit on the spiritual front, persuading the city to make a financial contribution to the crusade (not as much as he wanted, though) while lip service was paid to rooting out heresy in the city. Gang warfare broke out there. Bishop Fulkes, a former troubadour, organised faithful males into the White Confraternity, while the heretics responded with their own Black Confraternity; these two brotherhoods frequently engaged in violent clashes. The White Brotherhood became a militia; 500 were sent to support Montfort at the siege of Lavaur in the following year. While the city underwent interdiction and then had it lifted, its count was busy on the diplomatic circuit. Raymond visited Philip II in the north, Otto IV in northern Italy and Pope Innocent III in Rome, even while the count himself underwent yet another excommunication for still not having done enough to rid his city of heresy, only to have Innocent lift that, too. By the end of March 1210 he had been absolved of his earlier sins, only to be excommunicated again in late July, while the siege of Minerve was being executed. Raymond was attempting to keep his options open, even to the extent of a marriage arrangement between his son and one of Montfort's daughters, Amicia. Both were playing for time. Raymond knew that at some point before too long he would have to take on the crusaders if he were to regain his authority; Montfort, meanwhile, was waiting for reinforcements before he could act.

Just before they arrived, Servian returned to the crusaders' side in February 2010. Montfort restored its lord to his lands. It was a small but positive omen for the year to come for Montfort. At the beginning of March, Alice of Montmorency, the viscount's wife, returned to the region with new troops, including 'numerous knights', says Peter. However, the main reinforcements were not to arrive until the summer. Montfort went to meet her at Pézenas. As they returned to Carcassonne, intelligence reached him at Capendu that the inhabitants of Montlaur had defected and were besieging his garrison holed up in the keep. On Montfort's arrival on the scene, many of the townsfolk fled; others were caught and hung. William of Tudela warned at this time that the recalcitrance of the Cathars 'would lead to the death of many and the destruction of the land, laid waste and ravaged by foreigners, for the French of France and the men of Lombardy and the whole world hate them … and have gathered to attack them'.[68] This indeed pointed to what was to come. Campaigning now began in earnest.

Montfort headed to Alzonne, which he found deserted. From there he moved to the castrum of Bram, halfway between Carcassonne and Castelnaudary to its west. Here he put his new troops into action and introduced them to the savage nature of the war. The town, whose defensive circular street layout can still be seen today, was taken within three days by direct assault and without recourse to siege engines. Among the prisoners was the priest who had betrayed Montréal to Aimeric; he was taken to Carcassonne, dragged through the streets by a horse, and hung. Over 100 prisoners were mutilated: their eyes were put out and their noses cut off; one man was spared an eye to lead this pitiful group to strike fear into the hearts of the garrison at Cabaret. Montfort had his revenge for Gerald of Pépieux's atrocity in the autumn while economically combining it with a lesson in terror, like Béziers, that might prove militarily useful. He was also letting his own men know they would be avenged. The *History* is keen to point out that Montfort committed this act 'not because such mutilation gave him any pleasure but because his opponents had been first to indulge in such atrocities and, cruel executioners as they were, were given to butchering any of our men they might capture by dismembering them'. Montfort was, he hastens to add, 'the kindest of men'.[69]

The mutilation at Bram is one of the crusade's most notorious events. It marked the ratcheting up of the spiral of vicious reprisals that were to mark the conflict. While such acts show that any and all methods of terror were readily utilised as effective weapons to cow an opponent into resistance, there was an awareness among military commanders that they could be counterproductive. In 1347 Edward III had spent the best part of a year besieging Calais. When the city fell, he was not in a merciful mood, but he was talked out of severe punitive measures against its people by Sir Walter Mauny's pragmatic reasoning: 'My lord, you may well be mistaken, and you are setting a bad example for us. Suppose one day you sent us to defend one of your fortresses, we should go less cheerfully if you have these people put to death, for then they would do the same to us if they had a chance.'[70] Five years after Bram, Savary de Mauléon similarly advises the ever-vindictive King John not to hang the defeated garrison of Rochester:

My lord king, our war is not yet over, therefore you ought carefully to consider how the fortunes of war may turn; for if you now order us to hang these men, the barons, our enemies, will perhaps by a similar event take me or other nobles of your army and, following your example, hang us. Therefore, do not let this happen, for in such a case no one will fight in your cause.[71]

Though they would have understood this reasoning, the combatants of the Albigensian Crusade were not quite so ready to rationalise in this way, and once the atrocities started they were hard to stop.

Military activity was not restricted to one operation at a time, but co-ordinated to place pressure in different areas simultaneously. Much of this activity took the stock form of ravaging the enemy's lands. Ravaging was an essential part of medieval warfare and will be looked at in more detail later. It was not, as has sometimes been proposed, a pointless exercise in destruction carried out for want of being able to do anything else, but a tactic, often precisely employed, to destroy the economic base of the enemy and to undermine the authority of the territory's ruler, not least by generating in the affected people a sense that their rulers were incapable of protecting them. Thus in the spring we hear of the French uprooting the vineyards around Cabaret, a provocation that reduced Peter Roger's income. Peter of Vaux de Cernay relates here the miracle of a crusader shot in the chest by a crossbow bolt; even though he wore no armour, he was completely unhurt, the bolt not having even broken through his clothing. Mid-April time, Montfort was besieging Alaric between Carcassonne and Narbonne. His efforts were hampered by the snow and poor weather conditions, but after two weeks the garrison made a run for it at night; some made the escape but many more were killed. Count Raymond had recently handed over Narbonne, which was to become important in supplying troops for the crusading army.

Montfort was meeting with considerable success in isolating Minerve, the Cathar stronghold of the Minervois, with the intention of taking it later, but he also maintained the initiative by taking the war to the east, beyond his viscounty, and to the Count of Foix. Montfort's force went through Pamiers and, in a surprise thrust, found themselves on the verge of charging through the castle's open gates, which were then shut urgently in their faces. One thinks of the possibilities of Taillebourg and Béziers here. The *History* predictably shows Montfort in a heroic light, about to burst into the castle with just one fellow knight (the latter struck down by the bombardment of stones from the battlements). There was no intention to besiege Foix – Montfort's small force was not designed for that – but it was a show of confidence and intent, and demonstrated to its citizens that they were not beyond the reach of the crusaders. To emphasise that point, Montfort's force set about destroying the vines, trees and crops around the city before returning towards Carcassonne.

On his way he besieged the castle of Bellegarde, south-west of Montréal. No doubt he was concerned about King Peter of Aragon's recent arrival in the area for discussions with the counts of Foix and Toulouse and other lords, including Raymond of Termes, Peter Roger of Cabaret, and Aimeric of Montréal. The arrival of the king back on the scene encouraged the viscount to greater efforts: if any negotiated settlement were to emerge, he wanted to have as many bargaining chips as possible in his hands. He also wanted to show that he was not intimidated by the gathering; in this respect, Bellegarde may have been a diversionary tactic designed to break up the southerners' council. The castle soon fell and was enfeoffed to Guy de Lévis, who already held Mirepoix. The domino effect of Bellegarde's fall saw a raft of other castles in the area either abandoned or handed over to Montfort. While Montfort was at Bellegarde, King Peter had mediated a truce between him and Count Raymond Roger of Foix to last until the following Easter. (Though it stipulated nearly a year, the truce may in fact have lasted only a matter of days, according to some historians who place Montfort's *chevauchée* to Foix after the truce. The exact chronology of events is unclear and there is little to call between the difference – it is possible that the two events were almost simultaneous – but on balance I have gone with the attack on Foix being pre-truce as the truce itself would have eased the pressure for Montfort's planned campaigns in the Minervois and the east, where his strategy was geared to isolating Minerve. The reality is that the truce could have come either before or after the incursion to Foix.) Montfort returned to Carcassonne. Here, bolstered by the recent morale-boosting actions and, more crucially, the arrival of further reinforcements, he planned his campaigning for the next few months. They were to see the war intensify to a new level.

Minerve was the next objective. According to Peter of Vaux de Cernay, the Narbonnais requested Montfort's help in subjugating this centre of Cathar heresy, probably prompted by raiding parties emanating from there and disrupting trade. If true, this would have been a turnaround for

Narbonne's tardy support at the start of the crusade and Count Aimeric's non-committal support for the siege of Puisserguier. It has been suggested that Minerve was unimportant in military terms, but any successful, defiant display of political resistance served to further encourage military resistance: the two went hand in hand. And Minerve was a nuisance: it was a base for raids in the area and could threaten communications between Béziers and Carcassonne, especially if it co-ordinated its attacks with the mighty Cathar castles south of the Aude, such as at Termes.

Montfort gathered his forces and siege equipment for a major campaign. Innocent had been true to his word in organising help and preaching the crusade indulgence and by June significant (though undetermined) numbers had made their way south to gain their indulgence. They came from Maine, Île de France, Brittany, Frisia, Lorraine, Gascony, Champagne, Anjou, England and Germany (the Empire) to join the existing crusading army and the contingent from Narbonne under Count Aimeric. Montfort arrived at Minerve towards the end of June and began the siege. It was a major operation, of the type that the southerners were not yet in a position to mount. They might harass castra and look opportunistically to take one, but so far this had been done only by surprise and treachery. They were not yet centralised and organised enough to put together a large field army to match the crusaders on full campaign or to set up a full-scale siege action. While such disunity limited their ability to strike back at the northerners with a major blow, it also meant that the crusaders had, for the time being, no overarching primary objective; hence sieges such as at Minerve to subjugate piecemeal an enemy spread over Languedoc.

Minerve is one of the most striking sights in the region. Set on a rocky plateau spur high above the confluence of two rivers that have carved its protective cliffs nearly 100m high, the only approach to the fortified village is the narrow, sloping isthmus on the northern side that was protected by a strong castle. The sources attest to the strength of the place: it was 'incredibly strong', there being 'no stronger fortress this side of the Spanish passes, except Cabaret and Termes'.[72] That might once have been the case, but not now the crusaders were here. The gorges are deep, but quite narrow; while at one time this might have afforded the village protection from artillery bombardment, the recent introduction of the counterweight trebuchet into siege warfare negated the distance. The trebuchet, the heavy artillery of the day, was able to hurl large stones further than ever before with destructive accuracy. And the crusaders had one. Some historians believe the French used it for the first time at Minerve. The fact that the village's walls were actually lower than the besieger's positions across the gorges only served to increase the machine's effectiveness. Its crew were specialists, costing twenty-one livres a day to employ. William of Tudela called it 'the queen and lady of all Montfort's siege engines'; troops called it, with soldierly humour, 'Bad Neighbour' (this was the most common nickname for a trebuchet, but 'Wolf' and other intimidating sobriquets were also popular). It seems that such a weapon joined with at least one mangonel (a large catapult stone thrower), operated by the Gascons, and two other machines to bombard Minerve. A further weakness, always crucial as Carcassonne proved, was access to water. A well, situated at the foot of the cliff and protected by a three-sided tower, was as much a target for the siege machines as the village walls. As with previous sieges, the population was swelled, to bursting point this time, with refugees, especially Cathars from around the district and from Béziers nearly a year earlier. There were water cisterns in the village, but these would be quickly exhausted in the summer, especially in a protracted siege. And the crusaders had settled in for the long haul.

Montfort positioned himself across the River Brian to the village's north-east with the trebuchet; the Narbonnais under Count Aimeric and the Gascons under Guy de Lucy blocked the isthmus to the north-west and west respectively; while a fourth force camped across the Cesse to the south-east. William de Minerve conducted the village's defence from the castle. Bad Neighbour went to work, soon finding its range as 'he smashed openings in the high walls and in the stone-built hall, mortared with sand and lime'.[73] The bombardment was intense. The longer the siege went on, the worse the damage and the greater the depletion of the water and food stores. William decided to take action. He ordered the trebuchet to be destroyed.

Under the cover of darkness one Sunday night, some of the garrison crossed the gorge and climbed silently up the cliff face to where the trebuchet was positioned. They had with them baskets of dry wood, rubbish, oakum and fat. No guard saw them as they made their way to the great siege machine and attached their baskets to it with hooks. They then set them alight. The flames quickly sucked in the warm, dry night air. At the very moment they were igniting their incendiaries, one of the trebuchet crew, answering a call from nature, caught sight of them. He raised the alarm and was seriously wounded by a spear hurled at him. The camp responded quickly and put out the fire, and the trebuchet suffered only minimal, inconsequential damage. Whether the commando party made it back to Minerve or was captured (and, if so, almost certainly killed), we do not know.

The failure of the attack left William suing for peace terms towards the end of July. At this juncture, Arnald Amalric and Master Theodosius arrived on the scene. The abbot wished to demonstrate leniency, offering pardon – and life – to all those who recanted their heresy and returned to Mother Church – even the perfects. This shows Arnald in a very different light from Béziers (where, it should be noted, he had been present from the onset) and can be taken as evidence that the Béziers massacre was militarily and not religiously motivated. Robert de Mauvoisin protested against such leniency. He may have been voicing a military concern – perhaps he felt another sharp example was needed – or perhaps Innocent III's virulent hatred of heretics had rubbed off on him after their meeting in Rome. The legate reassured him that few would take up his offer. He was right.

After the crusaders had entered the village singing the *Te Deum*, the heretics refused to listen to Arnald's offer of life. The Cathar women were especially deaf to his entreaties. A pyre was built. Some heretics were hurled onto the fire; others rushed forward to throw themselves on. At least 140 died this way, 'frantic men of an evil kind and crazy women who shrieked among the flames'. The bodies were buried in shallow graves 'so that no stench from these foul things should annoy our foreign forces'.[74] Robert of Auxerre, a contemporary French chronicler, claimed the conflagration was necessary to strike terror into the Cathars and to curb their temerity. But this was not of itself a war crime. This was a spiritual punishment, an *auto-da-fé* before the Inquisition. It was not a military massacre like Béziers, but a religious one: those who died had the opportunity to save themselves; the other inhabitants were not harmed and their lord, William, was granted land elsewhere in the region.

There were immediate knock-on effects from Minerve. Peter Roger, the Lord of Ventajou submitted his castrum to Montfort, who destroyed its tower to render the place indefensible, lest Peter Roger reverted to his old ways. As one of the *faidits*, a southern lord deemed an outlaw by the French and who had lost his land as a consequence, Peter Roger had helped Aimeric regain Montréal some months back. Aimeric himself reconciled with the crusaders a second time on positive terms: he was granted comparable lands elsewhere, which had to be flat and unfortified so as to discourage further trouble making. Aimeric was neither so easily discouraged nor beholden to his word.

The Siege of Termes

Montfort paused to take stock with another council of war, this time at Pennautier, where his wife Alice joined him for a few days. William of Tudela says that the northerners' army was very large. Many crusaders who had served out their indulgence at Minerve would have returned home, but fresh reinforcements arrived from France and Brittany. Thus bolstered, the crusaders felt strong enough to take on the powerful fortress of Termes, in the south-eastern area of Termenès between Carcassonne and Perpignan. This was a major undertaking that would require a lengthy absence from Montfort's power bases, and the council gave much thought to who should protect Carcassonne while Montfort was campaigning. Seated on a silk carpet, the war council of the viscount, William de Contres, Robert de Mauvoisin and Guy de Lévis, the marshal of the host, chose Lambert de Crécy and Rainier de Chauderon for the task. Both declined, believing the task was beyond them in such a hostile area: Peter Roger of Cabaret threatened from the north, and Count Raymond Roger of Foix from the south, now that Preixan was back in his hands. In the end, Montfort appointed William de Contres to take charge of the city, but he did so only reluctantly as he had wanted Contres to accompany him on campaign. Supporting Contres in his new role as Carcassonne's governor were Crespi de Rochefort, Simon the Saxon and his brother Guy, and a substantial number of other nobles and forces from France, Normandy and Burgundy. Montfort dispatched Contres to the city to urgently prepare a siege train for the advance on Termes. Contres arrived there at the end of July and quickly set about carrying out his orders.

The engines and other siege equipment were hauled out of the city onto the meadow in readiness for departure; they had to be arranged for transportation and for ready assembly when they arrived at Termes. Their bulk would have meant delays in getting them to the viscount if they had remained within the confines of the city walls. While they were being loaded onto horse-drawn carts, a southerner spy made the short ride to Cabaret, less than 10 miles away, and informed Peter Roger of the crusaders' activity in the city and the plan for the siege train to be escorted to Termes by no more than 100 men. The Lord of Cabaret reacted immediately. With the Occitanian knights William Cat from Montréal and Raymond Mir from Fanjeaux, he swiftly gathered a substantial force, says William of Tudela, of over 300 men and rode under moonlight to the city. Peter of Vaux de Cernay says that there were two attacks, one at night and the other at dawn. However, the *Song* records just the one assault. When they did strike, they did so hard and decisively.

When the guards saw the enemy riding down on them, the call of 'To arms! To arms!' went up. The southerners charged into the camp and dismounted to attack the machines. These they hacked with axes and set alight with the help of straw. Fortunately for the crusaders there was insufficient wind for the flames to catch too quickly. It is clear, however, that some damage had been done by the time the city's gates opened to allow at least eighty sergeants and some knights from the garrison to rush out and engage with the enemy. The combat was fierce. The southerners seemed to have organised a defensive wall of men to allow the others to continue with their attempted destruction of the machines. Contres, one of William of Tudela's heroes, rode his Hungarian warhorse into the thick of the *mêlée*, at one point riding into the shallows of the River Aude, where he knocked one of Mir's men into the water with a blow on the shield; his heavy hauberk dragged him under the surface. Contres cut down two other fleeing soldiers with his sword. Crespi de Rochefort and Simon the Saxon are also picked out by the *Song* for their prowess. The southerners would have been aware that more men from the garrison would soon join in the fray against them, and so they withdrew to safety, having been unsuccessful in their daring mission.

This encounter rings true. Works like the *Song* and *chansons de gestes*, and often chronicles, too, frequently tend to pit one great lord against another in action, personifying whole bodies of troops in a one-on-one combat between leading characters. But here William has Contres fighting against unknown troops, and not against his main protagonist, the Lord of Cabaret. The *History* claims that Peter Roger was captured two or three times, only to give the crusader war cry of 'Montfort! Montfort!' to ensure his safety and hence escape. While this is clearly meant to defame him as being someone who did not adhere to the rules of chivalry – when taken, a knight yielded to his enemy and was expected to accept his captor's protection and give his word not to escape – such acts were common. William des Barres, arguably France's most chivalrous knight at this time, is known to have been claimed as a prisoner at least twice, only to have used the confusion of battle to make a successful break for freedom. This was a major issue at the battle of Agincourt in 1415. Here many French knights surrendered to the English to avoid the slaughter on the battlefield. Some, however, surrendered a number of times, extricating themselves while their captor continued fighting, and yielding again later when facing peril once more.

William of Tudela claims that Carcassonne's garrison was overjoyed at saving the machines and rejoiced in their victory. If so, this would have been the immediate effect of post-combat euphoria. In reality, the attack was an unsettling psychological blow, for the enemy had ridden up to the very gates of the capital of the Carcassès and announced a newfound boldness and confidence; in so doing, they had underlined the fragility of the French occupation of the south.

The large contingent of reinforcements from Brittany arrived at Castelnaudary at the end of the month. The town, which belonged to the Count of Toulouse, refused the troops entrance. Peter of Vaux de Cernay uses this as evidence of Raymond's surreptitious undermining of the crusade. However, the burghers of the town were no doubt worried about the potential impact of a substantial force of foreign soldiers billeted amongst them. The preservation of their goods and of their women's honour would not have been far from their minds; and there were Cathars among the townspeople. The Bretons did not stay long, but accompanied the siege train to Termes.

Termes was under siege by the first week of August. Like Minerve, its importance as a focus of resistance outweighed its strategic value, though the latter should not be underestimated, for the same reasons as Minerve. Indeed, the lords of Termes had close matrimonial ties to those of Minerve. It was the one major castrum in the area that had not succumbed to the crusaders. Set in the mountainous Corbières, it was a truly formidable fortress, imposing in its sheer mass. Set on top of a rocky hill (some refer to it as a mountain) looking down on the river valley of Sou and the stream of Caulière, its only approach is a slender strip of land, narrowing towards the top. While the village of Termes nestled unprotected at the foot of the hill, the approach was defended by two walled suburbs with the castle and wall of the bailey at its top. Around it are vertiginous cliffs with some spectacular drops. On a tall crag just outside the northern side of the castle, protecting its access to the river below, was a small tower known as the Termenet. Many such castra were deemed unconquerable, but Termes appeared to deserve its reputation for being 'marvellously, unbelievably strong ... quite impregnable'; 'no one ever saw a stronger castle than this'.[75] Termes was one of the 'five sons of Carcassonne' (the others being Puilaurens, Quéribus, Aguilar and Peyrepertuse), a fortress system to guard the southern border of Languedoc. But for now the threat came from the north.

Montfort set up his camp in the village; events would reveal that it was a little too close for comfort. With him was his international army, a multinational force now further complemented by the arrival of the Bretons, Italians from the north and south of their country, Gascons, Provençals and more Germans, this time from Bavaria and Saxony. Spiritual representation came in the form of the Archbishop of Bordeaux and the bishops of Chartres and Beauvais. Philip, the Bishop of Beauvais, was accompanied by his brother Count Robert of Dreux; these powerful men, cousins of the King of France, were very experienced in the ways of war. The number vacillated as men came and went to serve out their forty days, but it grew from a modest size at the outset to be an impressive force. It had to be to have any hope of taking the castrum.

They faced a very large garrison, strengthened in preparation for the siege, comprising veterans and mercenaries from Aragon, Roussillon and Catalonia. Their commander was the elderly but still robust Raymond of Termes. Long used to asserting his independence from the counts of Toulouse and the Trencavels, he had no intention of now prostrating himself before the upstart Montfort. A man with close Cathar connections in his family (it was said that the sacraments had not been celebrated in Termes's church for over thirty years), he was the most important figure of the Corbières, his lordship extending to about sixty castles, villages and hamlets. From these, he called his vassals to Termes to fight against the crusaders; among the lords with him was William de Roquefort, the man responsible for the murder of the Abbot of Eaunes. Raymond supplied his castrum with plentiful stores of fresh and salted meat, bread, water and wine. He was ready for Montfort.

The siege of Termes was one of the great setpieces of the whole crusade. It captured the imagination of writers for generations to come, and is featured in at least ten chronicles. At first Montfort had insufficient men to fully invest the fortress: the garrison and inhabitants could collect fresh water at will and hurl down abuse from the battlements at the crusaders. But when the reinforcements arrived, both these activities stopped. These reinforcements did not always reach Termes unscathed. Peter Roger of Cabaret was harassing them on their way there, either killing them or mutilating them by putting out their eyes, and cutting off their noses and other body parts. The southerners' knowledge of their region was a clear advantage in laying ambushes and withdrawing into the safety of the mountains. With his full force assembled there, however, Montfort could complete his investiture of Termes. It has been estimated that at least 1,500 men would have been needed for this task and it is reasonable to assume that Montfort had at least this many troops under his command. He drew up his petraries, his stone throwers, to the southern outer wall of the suburb and began his bombardment.

It was not just the knights and lords who won glory at Termes. The case of Archdeacon William of Paris reveals the role of less prominent military men. That said, it is possible that William was an ex-soldier for he showed great knowledge of siege warfare during the crusade. In his spiritual role, he exhorted the besiegers to offer up funds to contribute to the upkeep of the siege machines: crews had to be paid, engines repaired and built, and missiles had to be supplied from stone that was hard enough not to break up on impact with walls. He conducted work parties to the nearby woods to cut massive amounts of timber for the machines and their platforms. At Termes, ravines hindered the erection of a machine in front of the walls. William oversaw an operation to fill these ravines with earth, stones and timber that allowed the machine to draw up closer as intended. Filling in moats and ditches around fortresses was an essential part of siege attack, allowing battering rams, cats and belfry towers to reach the walls. At the siege of Acre on the Third Crusade Richard I paid soldiers a going rate for each stone they carried to fill the ditch, such was the danger. One female camp follower asked that, should she die, her corpse be used to contribute to the filling of the ditch.

The ensuing bombardment had the desired effect: it weakened the wall to the extent that the crusaders readied themselves to storm through an anticipated breach. The defenders saw the preparations and abandoned the outer burgh, torching it as they withdrew to the upper one. The crusaders moved in, only to be ejected by a sudden counter-attack from the garrison.

The southerners put up a stout defence; even Peter of Vaux de Cernay reluctantly admitted that they were 'courageous and astute'. Every time the crusaders weakened the wall sufficiently to force their way in, they were successfully obstructed by an emergency, makeshift barrier of timber and stone that had been hastily erected to reinforce the vulnerable and damaged section.

The crusaders' attentions now turned to the Termenet at the north-western end of the castrum, across from the main castle. Some of the fiercest action took place here. The Termenet afforded the garrison access to water and prevented a complete encirclement of the fortress. This tower was now subjected to a dedicated siege of its own. The crusaders formed a guarded barrier at the base to prevent direct communication between the tower and the castle and similarly to prevent the castle from reinforcing the tower. Under extreme conditions, the crusaders managed to erect a mangonel between the two after three days' strenuous effort. This is turn was targeted by a mangonel in the castle (larger castles had artillery of their own). Despite the bombardment from the southerners, the crusaders' machine survived behind a protective wooden wall on the castle's side. There was no more dangerous place at the siege. The crusaders were exposed to great danger from the castle, the northern side of which was a sheer cliff down to the ravine between it and the Termenet. When one first sees the Cathar castles imperiously looking down from atop their steep mounts, it is hard to envisage the practicality of siege machinery against them. But one way around this was the construction of wooden platforms on stilts that formed level platforms for stone-throwers to do their work. Such platforms were evident at Termes and throughout the crusade. Cut off from the castle and under constant, effective artillery barrage, the knights and soldiers in the Termenet abandoned their posts and slipped away. The crusader sergeants at the base moved in and placed their banner at the top of the tower.

Elsewhere, in another 'inaccessible place at the foot of a crag near the wall', a further mangonel was constructed and used to good effect. Montfort was anxious that it have sufficient protection: he appointed it a guard detail of no fewer than five knights and 300 sergeants. Its awkward position meant that in an emergency the main army would struggle to reach it and offer assistance. One day, eighty soldiers of the garrison sortied to rush at the mangonel, forcing their way to it behind their shields. They were protecting a large number of men following them carrying incendiary materials to burn the machine. The guard detail fled in panic, followed quickly by four of the knights. The *History* then tells a highly improbable story of how the one remaining knight, William d'Ecureuil, heroically fought off the overwhelming forces.

> This knight, seeing the enemy approaching, began with great difficulty to climb over the crag to meet them; they made a concerted rush against him, and he defended himself vigorously. They saw that they could not capture him, and instead thrust him with their spears onto the mangonel, and threw dry wood and fire after him. This courageous man at once rose up and dispersed the fire, so that the mangonel was unharmed.[76]

Peter claims that this happened four times. Ecureuil was saved by a feigned counter-attack from the crusaders that scared the sortie back into the castrum. It seems possible that a heroic defence of the mangonel did take place, but perhaps the knight was assisted by some lowly soldiers whom the chronicler did not feel merited a mention.

Fire was always the first weapon of choice when it came to destroying constructions built at the site of combat. Hence, where practicable, many engines, especially those that went right up to the walls, were protected by treated ox hides. On the Fifth Crusade in Egypt in early 1250, King Louis IX's army was attempting to build a causeway across the Nile. Louis had two towers built to protect the engineering work. These came under constant attack and bombardment from Greek fire. Guard duty for the towers terrified the crusading knights. Jean de Joinville was on such a detail one night when they came under fire. A fellow knight said: 'My friends, we're in the greatest peril we've ever been in, for if they set fire to our towers and we remain here we'll all be burnt alive. On the other hand, if we leave the posts we've been sent to guard we will be dishonoured.'[77] His rather desperate advice, taken by all, was to curl themselves up into balls and hope for the best. Another time, Joinville had to join a group that was putting out a tower that had gone up in flames; every single member of his group was hit by arrows. Engineering works were usually essential to an operation's success and hence required considerable security.

Sorties could serve as useful morale-boosting operations for soldiers and civilians kept hemmed in a tight place for a long period of time and always on the defensive. At the end of 1216, Prince Louis of France, who was to lead the crusade later, was besieging the castle of Berkhamsted with his baronial allies. The commander of the castle, a German officer called Waleran, sent out a sortie that caused havoc in the besiegers' camp. They seized the standard of William de Mandeville, one of Louis' leading captains, a major loss of face. Later, the garrison sallied out again into the enemy, carrying Mandeville's banner before them 'so as to put the barons into confusion'.[78] While the mangonel sortie failed, others seemed to have worked. We are told that many ensigns and banners were snatched off the crusaders and borne back into the castle.

Montfort himself had two lucky escapes during the siege. One day, he was talking with a knight by a 'cat'. In a scene that captures something of Montfort's leadership style, the viscount 'as a gesture of familiarity placed his arm on the knight's shoulder'. At that very moment, a stone hurtled down at great velocity from one of the castle's mangonels crashed onto the knight's head and killed him. Even in his camp Montfort was not safe. One Sunday, he was attending mass when another of the castle's siege machines, a ballista (in effect, an enormous long-range crossbow) let loose a bolt the size of a small spear that reached the area where mass was being celebrated. The viscount was unharmed only because a sergeant standing directly behind him shielded him by being himself hit and killed. Peter of Vaux de Cernay, relieved that his hero survived, put both episodes down to divine intervention; rather unsympathetically, he is happy that God had obligingly arranged for the sergeant 'to take the force of the missile'.[79]

As the siege wore on, so provisions were depleted; even Montfort himself often went without bread. Archdeacon William lent a hand here, collecting money to help with supplies. The besieged were suffering, too; their worst problem was the lack of water, all the more pressing since crusader reinforcements and the fall of the Termenet had cut off their access to fresh supplies. As the *History* rightly notes, 'Lack of water produced lack of courage and of the will to resist.'[80] By the end of October both sides were ready to talk. Raymond offered to hand over Termes for a few months – until April the following year – if he were allowed to keep his other lands. This was a very poor deal for Montfort, but his hand was greatly weakened by the announcement that the counts of Dreux and Ponthieu, as well as the bishops of Beauvais and Chartres (it was the latter's men who first entered the Termenet), were leaving the following day with their contingents. No entreaties could persuade them to stay. Peter criticises them for not fulfilling their forty days' service. He suggests that without them Montfort's force would be a sorry shell and that this prospect forced him to agree to Raymond's terms, a poor return for the epic siege. Montfort tried to insist that he hand over the castle immediately, but Raymond refused, promising that he would do so first thing next morning.

The delaying tactic was seemingly an inspired move. That night a torrential downpour occurred, replenishing the defenders' water cisterns and reviving their will to resist. The next morning, Raymond went back on his word while his people taunted the crusaders by saying this divine intervention had proved them right. Their confidence soared all the more when they saw whole divisions of the crusading army departing, leaving an unthreatening core behind. However, two of Raymond's knights, their consciences pricked, did surrender themselves to Guy de Lévis. The code of chivalry was a flexible thing. While it was habitually exploited and ignored, for some it was a binding ethic. On the eve of the battle of Agincourt in 1415, Henry V released his French prisoners on the promise that, should the French lose the battle, they would return to him as his captives and be taken back to England for ransom; remarkably, after the French defeat, they did not melt away but kept their word and came back to the English king.

The departure of most of the crusading force towards the end of October emboldened the southerners. They made yet another sortie against a mangonel, which they were in the middle of destroying when Montfort rushed against them and put them to flight. The *History* reveals Montfort's indecision at this stage. Winter was now approaching, which, in the mountains, would make siege operations all but impossible. He did not wish to abandon the siege but there were no longer enough men to make a success of it. At that lowest moment, Montfort's luck changed. A large force of infantry from Lorraine appeared at Termes to reinforce the crusaders. The besiegers' morale lifted; re-energised, they renewed their operations with vigour. They managed to get their siege machines closer to the walls, where they started to have a greater impact. Over the next month the keep was weakened by an accurate barrage, while a covered trench reached the walls of the castle and threatened to mine underneath it and bring it down.

By 22 November, after nearly four months, the impregnable Termes was about to be vanquished. Its people were exhausted and sick. The rainwater that had been seen by them as a divine gift had led to the spread of illness in the woefully unhygienic conditions of the siege. William of Tudela believes that without this Heaven-sent outbreak of 'violent dysentery, they would never have been defeated'.[81] Peter attributes the end of the siege to Montfort's unflagging tenacity, determination and leadership. Both he and William of Tudela tell of a mass attempt that night 'to escape being killed'. Leaving the women behind in the castle keep, the men left the fortress in the dead of night and attempted to slip away in the darkness. They left everything behind but some weapons and money. Such an exodus could not go unnoticed, and the crusaders rushed to capture the enemy. The plan was designed to allow as many of the garrison as possible to escape in the confusion. Many did, but the majority were either taken prisoner or killed. According to Peter, Raymond of Termes was found hiding outside the castle by a commoner and taken to Montfort. The viscount incarcerated him in a dungeon of Carcassonne, where he died three years later. His sons continued the southern fight for years to come. There is no report of any atrocity at Termes. According to William of Tudela, Montfort 'behaved very well and took nothing from the ladies'.[82]

The taking of Termes led to a windfall of strongholds for Montfort, all of which came to him without any further need for sieges. Termes initiated a new crusading momentum as Montfort headed westwards, having secured the east of the region. 'All the strongest castles were abandoned' after the fall of the mighty Termes, says William. Le Bézu and Coustaussa were found deserted and Puivert negotiated its surrender after just three days of encirclement. The garrisons 'never supposed that the crusaders would get that far'.[83] The southerners did not even have winter on their side to stall Montfort's progress, as the weather was unusually mild until the end of the year. Montfort then headed north towards Albi, where the recalcitrant castra of Castres and Lombres offered no resistance: the former opened its gates while the latter, fearful of Montfort's revenge for breaking faith with him, was left deserted and bulging with supplies for the crusaders. In this way Montfort regained nearly all the castra in the Albigeois south of the River Tarn by the year's end.

This was the importance of Termes. As indicated above, its inherent strategic value did not match its symbolic value; but when this symbol of resistance was crushed, there then followed an abundance of strategic gains. The effort Montfort had expended on Termes had therefore paid off due to the all-important military momentum that followed in the immediate aftermath; this materialised in solid achievements regaining lost territory. The crusading army was nothing like the overwhelming force it had been at the start of the crusade, but Termes ensured that it was regarded as a serious and effective force under an unrelenting and brilliant leader. It had been a hard year. But 1211 was to prove even more intense.

4

1211: 'THERE WAS SO GREAT A SLAUGHTER IT WILL BE TALKED OF UNTIL THE END OF THE WORLD'

The Failure of Diplomacy

With military operations curtailed by the winter and all protagonists taking stock after the massive crusading victory at Termes, energies directed towards the war were now spent not on the battlefield but in chilly castle halls and ecclesiastical palaces. The spiritual focus at this moment was shifting back to its origins: Toulouse. Count Raymond had lost his authority in eastern Languedoc following Montfort's strenuous and successful efforts there. With the count weakened, more pressure could be applied to his principal city, which, up to now, had dismissively fobbed off the legates' entreaties to do something about heresy. The omens had not been good over Christmas, when Montfort met Count Raymond near Albi; the former took exception to some of the men in the count's party, men Montfort thought had betrayed him. They had a traditional Christmas argument and separated wholly devoid of any festive spirit.

On 22 January important talks were held at Narbonne. All the main lay and ecclesiastical players were there: for the Crusaders, Montfort, Arnald Amalric, Bishop Raymond of Uzès, Master Theodosius; for the southerners, Count Raymond of Toulouse and Count Raymond Roger of Foix; and, for himself, uncomfortably perched on the fence, King Peter of Aragon. Positions needed to be hammered out and a satisfactory agreement settled on.

The Narbonne conference saw a success for Montfort when King Peter formally recognised him as his vassal for Carcassonne. This took some pleading from Arnald and Montfort, but in reality the king had little to gain by rejecting the homage: Termes had sealed the crusaders' success and Peter had to face up to the new political and military reality or find himself increasingly sidelined. The southern lords were not so easily won over. Raymond Roger of Foix rejected a deal that left him his land intact but which required him to leave the crusaders unmolested. As a guarantee of his good behaviour, King Peter would garrison his city and, should Foix renege, hand it over to Montfort. (Peter of Vaux de Cernay personally read the details of this proposal and reports them in depth.) This required a trust in his overlord that the cynical count did not possess; the monarch's somewhat equivocal positioning could not be relied upon. But such a move also represented a palpable loss of strength and an unacceptable emasculation of the count's power. In the end, a few token knights were sent to Foix as a political gesture to the crusading powers.

Count Raymond, on the other hand, was offered what seemed to be generous terms for making good his word and finally removing heretics from his domains: he would maintain all his possessions unhindered; he would also keep his rights to any of the castra identified as heretical within his lordship; and – the real sweetener – he would also be granted the rights of somewhere between a quarter and a third of the heretical castra that were not currently under his lordship. This last amounted to perhaps as many as 500 in total, a massive land gain as a reward for his less than ardent crusading duties. But Raymond refused the terms.

On the face of it, this seems an unusually obdurate stance. Raymond had seen first-hand the success of the northerners and the resolve of the tenacious Montfort, so why not share the fruits of victory? A positive perspective, not entirely without merit, would stress that Raymond was not prepared to attack his vassals when duty dictated that he protect them; circumstances had shown that it was often the case that persecution of heretics required warring against their lay defenders. He might then find himself not only in constant warfare against regional lords, particularly the Count of Foix, but also facing the prospect of open rebellion or civil war in Toulouse and elsewhere (the White and Black Brotherhoods did not bode well in this direction).

He had also recognised that the extent of heresy in his land was so pervasive he could do little about it without the help of the northerners. And this was perhaps the real rub: the level of outside interference would be intolerable. Not only would his territory remain destabilised by this foreign presence, not helped by all the financial obligations this would also entail; but the demands of the legates might become ever more unreasonable and impracticable, and hence impossible to meet, paving the way for the crusading army on his doorstep to be 'forced' to take action against the count and impose a new regime that would carry out religious policy.

The count's fear – expectation, even – of the escalation of unrealistic demands was borne out at another meeting at the end of the month in Montpellier. Again, the victorious Montfort was successful in making political capital. In a diplomatic coup, on 27 January he negotiated a marriage arrangement between his 4-year-old daughter, Amicia, and King Peter's 3-year-old son, James. At what must have been some personal cost, but one common to the age, the young boy was sent to Montfort's court for custody; our war correspondent William of Puylaurens, who now starts to file more regular reports, is right to call James a hostage. Montfort had established himself as a political, and not just military, power in Languedoc. Nonetheless, Peter was still not budging from his fence: less than two months later he had married his sister Sancha off to Count Raymond's son.

Meanwhile, Arnald Amalric tightened the screws on his antagonist, Count Raymond of Toulouse, seemingly intent on alienating and humiliating him to the point of either complete submission or to use the count's understandable rejection of terms as a sign of his perverse and unremitting intransigence. According to William of Tudela, the new, tougher demands were handed to the count as he waited 'for them outside in the wind and bitter cold' with the King of Aragon. Raymond called the king over to listen to the 'strange orders the legates say I must obey'. There certainly were some unusual requirements among the more standard ones, if we can fully trust William here (his list is detailed). Many old demands appeared again: the count should keep the peace, restore the rights of the clergy, expel Jews and, within a year, hand over all heretics to the abbot and his party identified by them, to be dealt with as they saw fit without any interference. The demand to dismiss the count's mercenaries was also included, but this time to be carried out within an impossible twenty-four hours. The unusual conditions are the ones that could possibly be considered suspect: the count and his men were allowed to consume meat only twice a week, were not permitted to wear rich fabrics, only coarse ones, and were to go the Holy Land for an unspecified time where the count was to join either the Knights Templar or Knights Hospitaller. Only if he fulfilled all these would Raymond receive back the castles he lost in the conflict. These demands appear a little extravagant, but make sense if seen as a penitence imposed on the count by the Cistercian abbot, who had clearly lost all patience with this harbourer of heretics. Another term mentioned by the *Song* was that the count's castles should be dismantled. This was a condition more usually dictated to a defeated enemy. Agreement meant acceptance of culpability and humiliating submission. When King Peter saw the list, he exclaimed: 'Almighty God in Heaven, this must be changed!'[84]

Raymond knew this meant that war was all but inevitable. He did not dignify the demands with an answer but instead immediately left Montpellier, anxious to prepare for what was to come. He raced back to Toulouse and thence to Agen, Montauban and Moissac. Here and elsewhere he had the legates' demands read aloud to gathered crowds. His intention was to shock his people at the arrogance of the intruders' demands and to provoke an outrage that would be channelled into resistance. It worked. They responded that 'they would all rather be dead or imprisoned than endure those conditions or do what was required' as it would place them under the yoke of serfdom to the north.[85] Religion is not mentioned; this was about independence. Raymond then wrote to all his vassals and allies for help as far as the Albigeois, the Toulousain side of the River Béarn and past the Carcassès. He also called for armed assistance from his cousin Count Bernard of Comminges, the Count of Foix and Savary de Mauléon, King John's seneschal for Poitou and an opportunistic warrior. For the first time, a concerted resistance was being organised. Meanwhile, the legates excommunicated Count Raymond yet again and once more placed Toulouse under interdict. The war was finally coming to Toulouse.

The Spring Offensive, 1211: The Massacres of Lavaur and Montgey

The crusade had continued to be preached and the recruitment drive brought a large number of new pilgrims and leading figures to the south in mid-March. Northern France was again well represented by forces under Bishop Peter of Paris; others who made the journey to Carcassonne, the great marshalling point of the crusade, included Count Raymond's cousins Count Peter of Auxerre (who had crusaded there in 1209) and his brother Robert de Courtenay, Juhel de Mayenne from western Normandy and Enguerrand de Coucy, great nephew of Philip Augustus. Thus reinforced, Montfort set about tidying up some unfinished business from 1210. He set out for Cabaret.

All the above reinforcements would not linger long beyond their forty days, so Montfort wanted to put them to work quickly. Cabaret was the last major centre of resistance in Montfort's newly enfeoffed lands that had once belonged to the Trencavels. Within its dungeon Montfort's close ally Bouchard de Marly was chained to the wall. But its lord, Peter Roger, was experienced enough to feel which way the wind was blowing. Following the fall of Termes, invincible castles were a perception rather than a reality. The victories at the end of 1210 were now being underlined by new reinforcements from the north. And now even his own men could see this and were defecting; most notable among the defectors were Peter Mir and Peter of St Michel, both of whom had been involved in the capture of Bouchard de Marly. Their mother, a perfect, would not have been proud of them.

Peter Roger sought terms. His captive and his castle ensured these were favourable: in exchange for his two greatest assets, he was to maintain his freedom and receive land in compensation elsewhere. William of Tudela relates how Peter Roger had a blacksmith release Bouchard from his chains, then set him free (one can make the assumption that this was a goodwill gesture for the coming talks). The Lord of Cabaret sent Bouchard to the count after the prisoner had been bathed, barbered, attired in fine clothes and given a bay palfrey to ride. Best of all for Bouchard was that he became Cabaret's new castellan. All the more surprising, for the ferocity and brutality with which Peter Roger had waged war, is that it was an amicable change over. That was not to be the case for Lavaur.

Lavaur lies to the north-west of the area between Toulouse and Albi, near the border between the lands of the Trencavels and the Count of Toulouse. A Cathar stronghold (for some, it was the epicentre of dualism), it had experienced military action back in 1181 to rid it of heretics. Then, the outcome had been anti-climactic and mild, with the recanting of just two heretics; it was not to be the case this time.

Lavaur is positioned on an escarpment above the River Agout with hills to its east beyond the river, a wide and deep gorge to the south, and plains to its west, the latter affording the crusaders their only practical approach. To its strong defences were added a garrison of eighty knights plus other soldiers, and between 300 and 400 Cathars and sympathisers (the higher number is the one usually accepted). The terrain made it relatively easy to bring crusading forces here, but the town itself was strongly fortified and unlikely to yield. There were two main reasons why a lengthy siege was expected. There was a predominance of Cathars among the defenders, including perfects, a presence swelled by an influx of refugees. Their resistance was stiffened further by its commanding officer, Aimery de Montréal; unhappy about his agreement with Montfort, he had rebelled and joined his widowed Cathar sister, Giralda, who was the Lady of Lavaur. For Montfort, it was a toxic combination of bad religion and bad blood.

On his arrival here at the start of April, Montfort was immediately beset with logistical problems. The first was temporary: with about 500 men, he did not have enough troops to fully encircle the town. He lost a knight when a sortie grabbed one, took him back into the town and killed him. The crusaders based themselves on the town's eastern side, in two camps across the river, from where they loosed their siege engines and controlled the river and the town's port. When reinforcements shortly arrived from France with Bishop Jourdain of Lisieux, Bishop Robert of Bayeux and Count Peter of Courtenay, the town could be completely invested. As always in sieges of this scale, major engineering works began; before long, a wooden bridge was built across the river, allowing the crusaders to extend their line of communications and attack. 'The besieged', says William of Puylaurens, 'had no respite, by day or night, as they were continually beset by petraries, large rocks and other forms of attack.'[86]

The second logistical problem was of a longer duration: the Count of Toulouse hindered the supply of food and weapons to the crusaders from his county. The French were drawing closer to his city – Lavaur is about 22 miles to its north-east – and any damage and delay Lavaur could inflict on the northerners was welcomed by him. Raymond had not yet resorted to open warfare; he even visited the crusaders' camp. Here he was harangued by his cousins the Count of Auxerre and Robert de Courtenay. Raymond left Lavaur with a display of anger and indignation, reiterating his orders not to supply the crusaders with provisions or siege engines.

The political divisions within Toulouse that so worried the count manifested themselves at Lavaur. Toulouse's bishop, Fulkes, had arranged for a large force from the White Brotherhood to help the crusaders at Lavaur. The *History* says the force from Toulouse was 5,000 strong, probably too high a number as this would have left the city vulnerable to a Black Brotherhood backlash. A letter from the consuls of the city to Peter of Aragon in July confirms that they helped Montfort with provisions and armed support, against Raymond's orders. Their arrival greatly demoralised the defenders at Lavaur, who at first thought that the Toulousains had come to their aid; they were soon disabused of this notion when the force camped among the crusaders. In vain the count had attempted to physically block the departure of this battalion from his city. Fulkes rubbed salt into Raymond's wounds when, according to the proscriptions of the excommunication, he refused to celebrate mass for him. Thus provoked, Raymond ordered the bishop to leave his principality on pain of death. Peter of Vaux de Cernay portrays the bishop in heroic mode, defying the count and daring him to do his worst: 'Let him come if he dares. I am ready to embrace the sword … Let the tyrant come surrounded by knights and armed; he will find me alone and unarmed.'[87] The legend of Thomas Becket was an inspiration to bishop and writer alike. After a fortnight of waiting for martyrdom – or perhaps after organising his affairs and packing his bags – the would-be Becket exiled himself from the city and headed for the siege of Lavaur at the start of April. The *History* reports that the count also helped the besieged by sending 'several' knights there. Later records suggest that only two knights were sent, probably either as observers for Raymond or as advisors in a token gesture.

The siege is reported in detail by Peter of Vaux de Cernay. He says that the besieged 'defended themselves vigorously' and even rode their armoured horses along the walls 'to show their contempt for our side and demonstrate that the walls were substantial and well fortified'.[88] The main thrust of the assault was on the town's southern side; other attacks would have been made around the defences to keep the southerners stretched and guessing as to their enemy's intentions. A siege tower was brought up close to the walls. On its top there was a cross, which lost one of its arms to defenders' missiles, 'whereupon the shameless dogs started howling and cheering'. Defenders used hooks on ropes to try and snatch up anyone working at the base of their walls. A cat machine was built and dragged to the town's ditch. As at Termes, 'a great effort' was made to fill the ditch with bundles of wood to allow the cat to reach the walls. This elicited a major response from the besieged. They dug a tunnel through which they went at night to remove the wood and carry it back in the town. One night they used the passage to attack the cat machine with incendiary material in an attempt to burn it. Two German knights and their men were on guard detail for the machine that night. They sent up the alarm and attacked the raiders in the ditch, repelling them and causing a number of fatalities.

The tunnel continued to pose a major threat to the crusaders. They filled it up during the day; the defenders excavated it at night. The crusaders began to despair of ever taking the castle when a simple plan was devised to neutralise the threat: the tunnel was filled permanently with smoke. The southerners could not now enter the passage without asphyxiation. The moat was then filled with material that could not be removed and the siege engine was dragged up to the wall. The sappers went to work under the cover of the cat, which was the target of a constant barrage of 'fire, wood, tow, stones and heavy sharpened stakes', but the machine could not be destroyed. As the crusaders began to make some real progress, a few miles away they were struck by disaster.

The chronicle of William of Puylaurens passes over this episode briefly: 'Whilst the siege was still going on the Count of Foix attacked some newly arrived crusaders as they were on their way to join the army. He caught them unawares in wooded territory and slaughtered a great many of them.'[89] The ambush seemingly took place at the end of April, just north of the small hilltop castle of Montgey. From here, one can see for many miles across the undulating landscape. The area is one of gentle hills and sweeping plains, easy country for troops to pass through physically. Lying south-east of Lavaur, it was on the crusaders' route from Carcassonne, just over 20 miles away.

The force from Carcassonne comprised some 1,500 troops, according to Alberic de Trois Fontaines. William of Tudela gives an unrealistic figure of 5,000 – too many to be absorbed by the siege. They were mainly Germans and Frisians, led by the Frenchman Nicholas de Bazoches. The southerners were under the command of the Count of Foix, joined by his son, Roger Bernard, and Gerald de Pépieux, who had famously and brutally broken faith with Montfort. With them were, notably, some men from the Count of Toulouse, and a large mercenary force; they bolstered their numbers further by the inclusion of squires and youths.

The *History* and the *Song* offer two different versions of what happened. William of Tudela relates the combat in a more heroic fashion, depicting events as a battle, rather than an ambush, in which the crusaders donned their armour and advanced in tight ranks. However, William does confirm that the action took place by a wood and that the southerners 'attacked from every side'. Peter of Vaux de Cernay is in agreement with William of Puylaurens in saying that the crusaders suffered a surprise attack, and thus 'they were not wearing their armour and were unaware that they had been betrayed'.[90] Ambush seems the more likely option, as the southerners had yet to engage openly with crusader field forces in a major engagement, though his may have been the first time they did so arrayed for battle. The fact that the crusaders were unarmed suggests, on the one hand, that they were unready for battle; on the other, defeats in medieval warfare are often explained away by embarrassed chroniclers as being the result of the enemy's sneaky, underhand and dishonourable tactics. Perhaps, as the *Song* indicates, some of the crusaders, possibly in the vanguard, had time to prepare themselves for combat, but the column had too little opportunity to organise itself into an effective defence.

Armies in hostile territory usually advanced in a coherent line of march with a vanguard and rearguard. Often these guards had groups of crossbowmen in front and behind them to hold off any cavalry attacks. On an extended line, the sides would be most exposed. This seems a strong possibility for the southerner's focus of attack at Montgey. Richard the Lionheart famously had his men organised in a highly disciplined order of march as they made their way to Jaffa in August 1192: the army marched with protection from ranks of crossbowmen and spearmen, and did not break ranks until the end of the day despite the constant provocations of the enemy. However, they were in full armour, their mail and shields absorbing the arrows of the Muslims. It would have been strange if the crusaders had not been wearing their armour deep in what was Cathar country. Perhaps, as newcomers from far afield, they did not have good intelligence (although this is unlikely as they had been in Carcassonne); perhaps they were indeed betrayed as Peter says, having been lulled into a false sense of security.

One thing is clear from the sources: the crusaders were utterly annihilated. There is no mention of any prisoners, only of killing. One French source does not mention any combat at all but instead says that the crusaders 'were taken by the enemy who butchered them'.[91] The local inhabitants came out to lend a hand in the massacre: 'the villeins and filthy wretches of that district went and clubbed them to death with sticks and stones.'[92] The southerners – soldiers and villagers alike – pocketed a small fortune from the dead northerners. The line between combatant and non-combatant was blurred by episodes such as this. The villagers involved probably participated for a number of reasons, including revenge on a hated foreign invader and the desire to plunder them, the latter often simply to recoup some of their own losses in a time of war. When the French were defeated at the battle of Lincoln in May 1217, their retreat to their stronghold of London was a bloody one, not unlike what passed at Montgey: 'Many of them, especially nearly all the infantry, were slain before they got there; for the inhabitants of the towns through which they passed in their flight went out to ambush them with swords and clubs and killed numerous of them.'[93] At the end of May, Montfort exacted his revenge on the people of Montgey by destroying their village.

One survivor made it to Lavaur. Typically, Montfort responded instantly, but the Count of Foix, a master of hit-and-run tactics, had made for the safety of Montgiscard, 20 miles to the west. By the time the viscount arrived at Montgey (having garrisoned the deserted castrum of Puylaurens on the way and given the place to Guy de Lucy) the enemy had gone, leaving behind a plain strewn with the bodies of nearly 1,500 crusaders. It was a massive psychological blow to the crusaders: 'When the French heard of it, they almost went out of their minds.'[94] All recognised that this was a very significant event. In their first open encounter with the enemy in the field the crusaders had been wiped out. In terms of scale, it was the worst massacre of the war, comparable with Béziers. It established the Count of Foix as the leading general on the southerners' side. The southerners had now organised themselves into an effective field force. Count Raymond was no longer attempting equivocation: he had sent men to join the Count of Foix in a military action against the crusaders. He was as exasperated with the legates as they were with him. His personal intervention to prevent the White Brotherhood from assisting the besiegers at Lavaur had failed; he was now evening the score a little. But the greatest persuasion for him was that the southerners were finally coming together in ambitious joint action against the invaders; now greater unity meant some capacity to match the enemy in size and defeat them.

The first consequence of the Montgey ambush was felt at Lavaur. Here, the siege had finally been approaching its final stages. Had the crusaders reached the siege unscathed, things may have gone easier for the defenders, but their presence would not have affected the outcome of the siege. The constant battering of the walls and the sapping carried out under the protection of the cat had taken their toll on the town's wall. On 3 May it was breached. William of Puylaurens says that the town surrendered unconditionally; Peter of Vaux de Cernay seems to suggest that the breach was stormed; William of Tudela opts for a combination of the two (probably meaning that the storming led to surrender). After the hardships of the siege, but especially after the crushing humiliation and massacre of Montgey, the crusaders were not in a merciful mood. 'There was so great a slaughter', writes William of Tudela, 'I believe that it will be talked of until the end of the world'.[95]

All the sources attest to this latest massacre, just a few days after the first one at Montgey. Most shocking for the time was the hanging of a leading lord, Aimery de Montréal, and the killing of somewhere between seventy-four and eighty knights. Peter of Vaux de Cernay's report claims that Montfort ordered that the garrison be hung from fork-shaped gibbets. However, these were hastily erected and at least one began to fall down after the strain of bearing the weight of Aimery, who was a big man. Montfort could see the whole business taking up too much time, so instead told his men to put them to all to the sword. This was a small blessing for the victims, as hanging was considered the most shameful death for a knight, for it was the usual punishment meted out to criminals of the lower classes. Thus the *Song*, which believes all eighty met their end on the gallows, says 'four score they hanged there like thieves on a gibbet'.

Decapitation was the execution of choice for the higher orders. Hanging could be devised to be made even for more humiliating for them. In 1127 a rebellious knight named Berthold was strung up on the gallows but kept alive. A dog was suspended next to him. The dog was beaten so that it turned its fear and anger on Berthold next to him. The dog savaged Berthold, 'eating up his whole face', and 'befouled him with excrement'. [96] The *Chronicle* says sensibly that both sword and rope were used at Lavaur. In this it is in agreement with Robert of Auxerre, who wrote that there were 'about seventy-four knights' who 'all perished either by hanging or by the sword'. [97] The discrepancy between seventy-four and eighty knights may be due to the fact that some townspeople pretended to be knights in the vain hope that this would save them. There were some survivors from the garrison at Lavaur: the two knights that Count Raymond had sent were spared and thrown chained into prison.

Nor was there any mercy for the heretical townspeople: between 300 and 400 of them were taken to a meadow and thrown onto a huge pyre. It was the largest mass burning of the crusade. Historians have said that none was offered the chance to recant because our three main sources do not mention such an opportunity, as happened at Minerve. But Robert of Auxerre, a generally reliable source with good connections to the crusaders, states that 'all were given the choice to come to their senses from their error or to die in the fire'. [98] He goes on to say they obstinately refused and that with mutual exhortations they climbed into the flames as they preferred to be burnt rather than abandon their beliefs. The offer of recantation may well have been made as the Church felt it had an obligation to save souls. But one must consider the state of mind of Montfort and the crusaders. The joy of their hard-won victory had been denied them by the shock of the Montgey massacre on the eve of their success. The desire for revenge comes to the fore in such situations and Montfort would have found scant rational argument against killing his prisoners. He could avenge the crusaders and give yet another lesson in terror.

That this mindset dominated can be seen in the appalling treatment meted out to Giralda, the Lady of Lavaur. We have already encountered some of the most infamous episodes that the crusade produced, but Lavaur, Montfort not satisfied with the mass execution of its knights and the burning of its Cathars, was to add yet another beyond even these. Giralda, whom William of Tudela portrays as a generous and hospitable woman, was seized and as 'she shrieked and screamed and shouted they held her across a well and dropped her into it'. [99] The crusaders then heaped stones on her. She was broken from her fall and then battered and crushed to death by rocks.

There was no repeat of Béziers: 'The ordinary people were spared, on conditions.'[100] The town gave up a huge amount of booty: warhorses, high quality armour, linen and expensive clothing, plentiful provisions of wine and corn. The business of war was conducted when much of the plunder went to Raymond of Salvanhac, a merchant of great wealth from Cahors, who had funded the campaign.

The usual benefits accrued from the victory at Lavaur. When its outcome was assured, Roger de Comminges, the Viscount of Couserans, abandoned his uncle, the Count of Foix, and threw in his lot with the crusaders (for the time being, at least). Raymond of Toulouse left the defences of Castelnaudary, on the main route between Carcassonne and Toulouse, in flames, while the garrison at Les Cassès, 25 miles to the south-east of Toulouse, quickly realised that defence against the northerners, who were still strong even after the departure of the contingents that had joined them at the start of the siege of Lavaur, was not a realistic option: they surrendered and handed over up to sixty perfects; William of Tudela says there were at least ninety-four heretics all told. The perfects were consigned to the flames.

The next objective was Montferrand, 6 miles north-west of Castelnaudary. Here a garrison of fourteen knights and nobles, with a number of sergeants and mercenaries, were under the command of Baldwin, Count Raymond's brother. Baldwin was a successful warrior but a man shrouded in sadness. He had been born and raised in the north, never met his father and was for a while disowned by Raymond, who was loath to bestow lands and respect upon him. By now nearly 50, he was wondering if the northerners, with whom he was more familiar, might treat him with more esteem.

At first, the Montferrand garrison put up a vigorous defence. The defenders cleared the material being used to fill the fosse by burning it. The mercenary captain, Raymond de Périgord, would have been especially dedicated: while knights might be able to bargain for their lives with ransoms, captured mercenaries could expect immediate execution. The northerners knew Baldwin and understood that he was fighting for family. They persuaded him to end an unwinnable defence when they offered him favourable terms. As a sign of respect for a worthy opponent, Baldwin and his men were granted the right to leave the castle in honour, keeping their arms and armour on them. Only the castle's supplies were left behind. Baldwin had lost patience with Raymond and so pledged himself to the crusade. He was never to be reconciled with his older brother.

Such honourable surrenders were common in medieval warfare, especially when the victor acknowledged that the defeated enemy had put up an honourable fight. At Odiham in England in 1216, a small garrison of three knights and ten soldiers held out against a powerful French army for over a week; when the terms of surrender were agreed, the besiegers were amazed to see when the garrison emerged on their horses and in full armour that there were so few of them. Interestingly, William of Puylaurens notes that Baldwin surrendered at Montferrand only after 'the help which the count [Raymond] had promised did not arrive'.[101] This is very possible. Most medieval sieges ended in agreements whereby the defenders would open the gates to the enemy if they did not receive help from their lord; in this way, much bloodshed and expense was avoided.

Montfort moved into Castelnaudary, rebuilding its defences and leaving a garrison there before heading north. Baldwin negotiated control of Bruniquel while town after town fell to Montfort without opposition: Rabastens, Montégut, Gaillac, St Marcel, Laguépie, St Antonin, Lagarde Viaur, Puycelsi, Cahuzac. The *Song* says the reason is clear: 'fear'. Montfort was now master of the Albigeois, having successfully gained old Trencavel lands or areas disputed by Count Raymond. He had secured the east and now the north of his territories; now it was time to look west towards Toulouse.

Summer 1211: The First Siege of Toulouse

The Count of Toulouse, despite his military interventions, had not yet declared open war on the northerners. Even at this stage he was still trying to negotiate an agreement with them as he knew his city was next in line and that the summer would bring substantial reinforcements from the north. All his approaches were rebuffed. His first attempt after Lavaur saw him offer the concessions he had rejected before: his territories, except for Toulouse, were to be temporarily given over to the crusaders and complete compliance was promised in all matters of faith and eradicating heresy. The legates then summoned him to a meeting under the protection of a safe conduct; but Montfort, whose already strong animosity towards the count had been heightened after the Montgey massacre, ignored the clerics and attempted to ambush the count. (Was there collusion between the legates and Montfort on this, perhaps trying to trick Raymond into capture as

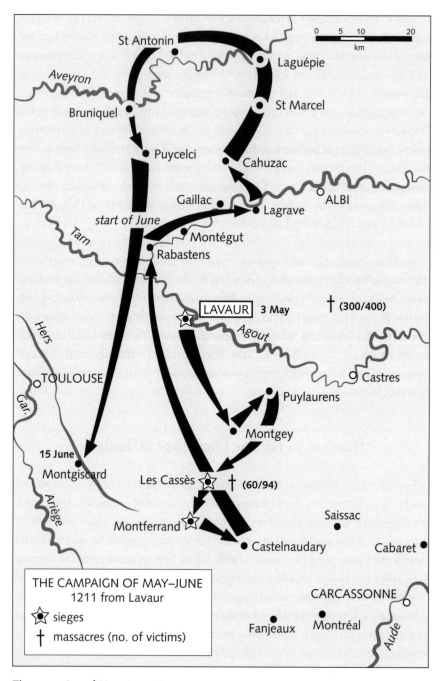

The campaign of May–June 1211.

many believed they had done with Viscount Raymond Roger Trencavel?) The attempt failed and next time it was the city's consuls rather than the count who entered talks with the northerners. The legates and crusaders now showed their hand: they wanted regime change. Any accommodation with the Toulousains depended on them rejecting their allegiance to Count Raymond and offering it to a new lord chosen by the crusaders. The consuls were not prepared to reduce themselves to such disloyalty or to accept foreign rule. They carefully laid out all these efforts and events in a long letter to King Peter of Aragon; they were anxious to gain his support by showing him how reasonable and flexible they had been in their search for peace, and conversely how unreasonable and untrustworthy the northerners were.

These attempts can be seen as either a genuine search for an agreement, or as cynical delaying tactics or, most likely, a combination of both. While negotiations were carrying on, both sides were preparing for war. For the count, talks were a fall back option should he be unable to unify his city or marshal sufficient strength through his allies. Neither was to prove a problem for him. The combined policies of the crusaders as to lordship and the Church as to religious practice helped to unite the divided city of Toulouse. After a last attempt to reach an accord, the legates, following the interdict placed on Toulouse earlier that year, ordered the withdrawal of all clergy from the city. This left the orthodox faction deprived of a key protector and feeling very vulnerable. It also made it even easier for the count to remove religion from the equation and to depict the northerners as foreigners intent on nothing but conquest and occupation. Even the White Brotherhood, back from Lavaur, was persuaded: 'the count devoted great effort and energy to winning them over to his side, and succeeded in persuading both sides to join together. United, they applied themselves to fortifying and defending the city against the invaders.'[102] Inflexible in their position, the crusaders had united the Toulousains against them. Religious and political policies weakened military potential because they strengthened and rallied the enemy in a common cause.

Large numbers of crusading reinforcements from France and Germany arrived in the first half of June under the leadership of the illustrious Count Theobald of Bar and Luxembourg. Montfort went to meet the new army at Montgiscard, 18 miles to the south-east of Toulouse and from there they made for Raymond's city in a show of strength. On the morning of 16 June they broke camp and were led by guides to cross the bridge on the River

Hers. As they did so, they were attacked by a large force of southerners (William of Tudela gives a figure as high as 500 knights and countless infantry). Word had reached Count Raymond of the northerners' advance and he quickly organised a body of troops to counter them. Among these were Count Raymond Roger of Foix, Count Bernard of Comminges and a force of Navarrese mercenaries. The southerners urgently set about the destruction of the bridge there, forcing the crusaders to look for a fording place. They came across another bridge, possibly at Montaudran, just 3 miles from Toulouse (where the *Song* places the action) which was also in the process of being destroyed. They crossed the river by swimming and by clambering over the damaged bridge, pursuing the retreating enemy to Toulouse. William of Tudela writes that a pitched battle had taken place for over 180 men lost their lives in the encounter. Bertrand, one of Count Raymond's sons, was taken prisoner; he was later ransomed for 1,000 livres. As the crusaders drew near to the city, they rode into a meadow where peasants were working. The northerners slew thirty-three of them.

Bridges, whether of long-standing strategic importance or made momentarily important by troop movements, are frequently the focus of military actions in history, and the Middle Ages are no exception. The Anglo-Scots battle of Buroughbridge of 1322 is one example. At Nantes exactly three years after the Hers episode, the Albigensian crusader Robert of Dreux came out of the city with soldiers and crossed its bridge, protected by a barbican, to block King John's forces. He taunted John, but his manoeuvre backfired: he and between fourteen and twenty other knights were, like Raymond's son, taken prisoner. At the battle of Bouvines three years later, the French army of Philip Augustus had just crossed the village's bridge, reinforced to take the strain of his large army and baggage train, when the enemy engaged with his rearguard and placed it in a precarious position. Philip recalled all his troops back over the bridge, then ordered it destroyed to reinforce the resolve of his men: there was to be no retreat.

The crusading army, estimated to be around 4,000 strong, arrived before the massive walls of Toulouse stretching out before them on 17 June. Theobald and Montfort did not have nearly enough men to invest the city completely; instead, they concentrated their attack on the eastern and southern sides. The Narbonne Gate on the city's south side was protected by the Château Narbonnais, making the siege all the more unlikely to succeed. But the crusaders needed access to the road to Carcassonne via Castelnaudary for supplies and reinforcements; their fear of another Montgey was to prove a very real one. This area outside of the city was also where the main orchards and gardens were, offering the northerners some food while denying it to the enemy. Without a full blockade, the townspeople would have made for this area and destroyed it. An attack from the northern side would have concentrated on the *bourg* and left the crusaders' line dangerously elongated from the main road; to the east the city was protected by the wide River Garonne.

The crusaders' intentions are not clear. This may have been exacerbated by a suspected split in the leadership now that the powerful Count of Bar was among the pilgrims. The northerners were woefully ill prepared for the task. Their numbers constituted a sizeable field army, but one utterly inadequate to the task of besieging a massive stronghold with at least 30,000 inhabitants, and probably many more than that if refugees from the countryside are taken into account. The large numbers would only prove a disadvantage if the city was sealed in and denied provisions, which was clearly not the case here. In fact, the Toulousains could pretty much sortie at will. The crusaders did not even have any siege machines for the task; this may have been due to lack of both money and materials, and also because the brevity of the siege (twelve days) did not allow enough time for machines to be brought up or constructed. Some sources indicate that the plan to go to Toulouse was a last-minute decision taken only in the aftermath of the victorious skirmish at the River Hers, when Count Theobald joined with Montfort. This would explain the lack of the necessary siege hardware and perhaps the importance of Theobald's influence. The Count of Bar was another forty-dayer and perhaps hoped for some quick, impressive victory to take back north with him; it is hard to envisage Montfort, with his military planning and understanding of the situation, wanting to embark on the biggest siege of the crusade without a capable force.

The siege offered nothing but hardship for the crusaders. In Toulouse with Count Raymond were the counts of Foix and Comminges, plus an army of their knights and infantry, the city's militia and the mass of townspeople. William of Tudela's 'fierce and wonderful' crusading army, 'a proud and terrible host', may have been outnumbered by an active defence of five-to-one or more, protected behind the city's thick, high walls.[103] Sorties were common. The counts of Bar and Chalon initiated the attacks. The first task was to fill the ditches so that the northerners could get across and presumably escalade the walls; all the wood and vines they could find were cut down for this purpose. They issued their men with large, boiled leather shields to protect them from the quarrels and arrows of the enemy as they made their way to the fosses and threw brushwood into them. The besieged sortied out to stop this work and a major skirmish occurred, resulting, says the *Song*, in over 100 dead and over 500 wounded (it is quite rare to be given figures for wounded as well as fatalities). One high-profile fatality was a cousin of Comminges called Raymond At of Castillon; another was William de Roquefort, brother to the Bishop of Carcassonne and the man behind the murder of the Abbot of Eaunes and two of his mission. The defenders seized three of the attacker's large mantlet shields.

Patrols were mounted day and knight to watch for sorties, which were causing the crusaders great concern. This was a job for the cavalry: when the enemy broke out from one of the city's eleven gates or various sally portals, the knights and mounted sergeants could respond swiftly and ride to meet the threat. The camp was on constant standby, with armour being worn all the time. Count Raymond, an indecisive and uninspiring commander, was reluctant to launch sorties, given the dangers these presented and the possibility of compromising the security of the city's gates. However, some of his officers wished to pursue a more aggressive form of defence. Two of these were Hugh of Alfaro, the Seneschal of Agenais, and his brother Peter Arcès. On a Wednesday afternoon they saw a supply convoy about to reach the northerners' camp and they launched a two-pronged attack, one force presumably to draw the soldiers away from the convoy while the other attacked it. 'What blows you [the reader] would have seen struck on both sides, what spears ringing on helmets, what shields shattering', writes William of Tudela in his dramatic but not unjustified fashion. The crusaders escorting the convoy were Eustace de Cayeux and Simon de Neauphle; they rode too far ahead of their group – perhaps drawn away by the decoy attack – and Eustace was killed as he tried to make his way back when a javelin pierced his side. He died before a priest could reach him to offer last rites. Simon just managed to fight his way back to safety.

The besiegers were by now suffering severe food shortages. A loaf of bread cost 24 deniers; at Carcassonne bread had been so plentiful that thirty loaves could be bought for just 1 denier. The army had stripped most of the fruit trees in the area and now all they had was what was left of these and some beans. William the Breton has written of strongholds under siege that 'hunger conquers all', but this applied equally to besiegers if they had exhausted the resources of the area and supplies were not reaching them. The weakness of the crusading force also meant that foraging parties were especially vulnerable to ambush in hostile territory from an enemy with far greater numbers. Dissension set in in the crusaders' camp. There was much moaning about the Count of Bar's limited contribution. William of Puylaurens does not mention supply problems but claims that the siege was raised when the bulk of the crusaders had completed their forty days' service. William of Vaux de Cernay writes that Montfort realised that the siege had achieved nothing and that it was preventing progress from being made elsewhere. He struck camp on the morning on 27 June. The crusaders left the area shrouded in smoke from the fires they had lit to destroy the vineyards and fields of crops.

The attack on Toulouse may be understood in one of two ways: as a probe forward rather like that Montfort carried out at the gates of Foix; or as a shaking of the tree to see what fruits might fall to the ground. The crusaders may well have been over-optimistic about the disunity within the city; as we have seen, Raymond had moved quickly and assiduously to repair the internal divisions. The crusaders would have hoped that their very presence might have been enough to show the Toulousains that the war had now come to them and that they should expel their count and open the gates. That would have been a sweet, easy and quick victory. A few weeks earlier that strategy would have had much to recommend it, but now the city was unified against the northern invaders and there was no hope that the beleaguered army outside its walls, far from home with an overstretched supply line, would change that. The mistake was compounded greatly by staying for nearly two weeks. All the crusaders had achieved was to prove to the townspeople the strength of their city and the weakness of the northerners. This was a significant, morale-boosting triumph for the southerners that served only to stiffen their resolve for years to come. It was the most serious blunder made by the crusade leadership.

Summer to Winter 1211: Counter-attack and the Battle of Castelnaudary

Montfort had lost face and the initiative. He now set about regaining both. With Raymond Roger of Foix in Toulouse, Montfort took the opportunity to raid south into his territory. First he took Auterive, a castrum of Count Raymond, and garrisoned it. Hardly had he left the place when a band of southern mercenaries retook it, the garrison surrendering on being granted their freedom. The fluid movement of warfare centred on strongholds is underlined by Montfort's return shortly afterwards to burn the place to the ground. Montfort rode on to the deserted and burnt castrum of Varilhes, which he refortified and garrisoned. Auterive and Varilhes lay exposed in enemy territory; it is hard to imagine many volunteers for garrisoning duties here. Montfort added insult to injury against Count Raymond Roger by the destruction of a number of other fortresses and by torching the suburb of Foix. For the next eight days the northerners rampaged throughout the countryside around the city, maximising the destruction of food stores, corn, crops, woods and vineyards.

Montfort then turned his men about and marched 150 miles to the northernmost part of the region. He made his way through Cahors and Calus (burning its suburbs) to Rocmadour, receiving homage from the barons of Quercy, who renounced their allegiance to the Count of Toulouse. Many of these men had participated in the brief Agenais–Quercy crusade of 1209. The success in the area was blighted by the sudden departure of the Count Theobald of Bar and his men, followed shortly by the Germans. This was a serious blow to Montfort as it seriously depleted his campaign army; he had begged him to stay. Peter of Vaux de Cernay does not underplay the invective and scorn poured onto the count for his withdrawal: 'he was the target of abuse to an extent that cannot easily be described; everyone in the army, from the lowest to the highest, pursued him with insults such as I would be ashamed to set down'; the count 'was universally derided, and despicable in everyone's eyes'.[104] This anger was due to a sense of desertion and of being left exposed to great danger; it was a betrayal of solidarity. Similar anger and disgust was directed against King Philip II when he abandoned the Third Crusade to head home; contemporaries wrote of 'contempt and hate' and 'immense opprobrium', 'how shameful and outrageous it was', and of 'frightened rabbits'; the blame for the ultimate failure of the crusade was then laid at Philip's rapidly retreating feet. The anger against the Count of Bar was merited. Montfort returned to Cahors with a small force while Count Raymond saw Theobald's departure from the theatre of combat as the ideal moment to launch his concerted counter-attack. The southerners were about to set out to reclaim western Languedoc.

While at Cahors more bad news reached Montfort: two of his leading knights had been captured by the Count of Foix. This episode is worthy of attention as it reveals something about the experiences of prisoners of war from first-hand testimony; as Peter of Vaux de Cernay writes: 'I can give a brief account of how they were captured, based on what they themselves told me.'[105] The knights in question were Lambert de Thury, who was very close to Montfort, and Walter Langton, and English knight who was brother to Simon, an ally of Prince Louis of France and also brother to Stephen, the Archbishop of Canterbury who caused King John such problems. They were riding with a large group of local men near the territory of the Count of Foix when the count heard of their movements. He set out with his men and caught up with them. Most of the knights' troops fled, pursued by the count, leaving just six to face the enemy. The crusaders' horses were killed, leaving the northerners surrounded and outnumbered. A respected southern baron, cousin to the count, called on them to surrender. Lambert, who knew this man, was aware that escape was impossible, and replied that they would hand over their swords only on five conditions: 'You will not kill us or cut off our limbs; you will keep us in honourable custody; you will not separate us; you will release us against a reasonable ransom; you will not place us under control of any other person.' If these conditions were not promised, they would go down fighting, taking as many of their opponents with them as possible, vowing to 'sell our lives dearly'.

The terms were agreed but not met, as the southern lord passed them on to his cousin, the Count of Foix. The count 'kept them heavily chained in a foul dungeon, so tiny that they could neither stand nor lie at full stretch. They had no light save only a candle – and that only when they were eating. There was only one tiny opening in that cell, through which food was passed to them.' They were not held for too long, soon being exchanged for three southerner prisoners plus a ransom. Their status as knights did not ensure them chivalrous and honourable treatment, as Bouchard de Marly had also found during his incarceration at Cabaret. Maltreatment even of knights was common in medieval warfare. During the Hundred Years War, Jean le Gastelier's job was to beat prisoners to extract from them the promise of the highest possible ransom. In the same conflict, François de la Paulu threw Henriet Gentian into a dungeon, which he shared with eighteen serpents and lizards. Henriet was connected to the Duke of Bourbon, so François sent letters to the latter and to his captive's family demanding prompt payment; any delay would be met by pulling out Henriet's teeth. He was as good as his word: when payment was not forthcoming, he grabbed a hammer and smashed out some teeth.

Montfort was soon on the move again. Accompanied some of the way by Arnald Amalric, he made his way back south to Pamiers via St Antonin, Lavaur, Gaillac and Carcassonne, inspecting his defences on the way. Near Pamiers, he took a southern-held castle (possibly Bonnac) by force, burning the gates and sapping the walls, and killing three of the six knights in the garrison. The three knights he took prisoner stood in peril of their death, but Montfort's officers advised him to exchange them for Lambert de Thury and Walter Langton. The exchange was arranged.

Meanwhile, Count Raymond had not been idle. By about early September he had amassed the largest Occitanian army of the war to date. He had summoned his host from Toulouse, Moissac, Agen, Castelsarrasin, Montauban and all his territories. With him were the counts of Foix and Comminges and Viscount Gascon de Béarn with their forces, Hugh d'Alfaro, the Seneschal of Penne, Savary de Mauléon and his cavalry from Bergerac, troops from Gascony and Puigcerda and just over 1,000 mounted mercenaries from the Apse Valley and Navarre. William of Tudela was impressed by this muster of southerners: 'Did anyone ever see an army so strong or so well equipped as that of Toulouse, or cavalry like theirs? … Not a man stayed behind.'[106] Beasts of burden carried bread, wine and other supplies; peasants drove oxen to haul the heavy siege machinery. This is the first time we hear of the Occitanians employing such equipment; it is a measure of the army's power and intent, for by now the southerners had formed themselves into a potent and coherent army of resistance of a size that dwarfed the remaining crusader forces. This great host headed east into Montfort's lands. This was a fully-fledged counter-invasion.

Just as Montfort had benefited from enemy desertions when he had the momentum, now he found himself on the receiving end. Guy de

Lucy's crusader garrison at Puylaurens handed the place back to Sicard de Puylaurens, who had owned it before the invasion. The knight Guy had left in command was accused of treason and of having been bribed by the enemy; when, a few days later, he refused to undergo trial by combat at Montfort's court, he was taken away and hanged. Montfort moved on to Carcassonne, on the way garrisoning Castelnaudary and Montferrand with knights and crossbowmen. The Montferrand garrison was the first in line to meet the oncoming onslaught; the troops did not relish this prospect so as soon as Montfort had disappeared over the horizon, they disappeared, too. The Castelnaudary garrison was ordered by Montfort to hold fast at all costs and await his help.

While southerners continued to flock to Count Raymond's banners at Avignonet and Montferrand, Simon de Montfort was holding a council of war in Carcassonne to decide how to meet this great crisis. The warden of Limoux had sent a young man reporting the enemy's great size and progress along the Toulouse–Carcassonne road to Montferrand, just a few short miles north-west of Castelnaudary. Montfort had called to his capital all those who could help him. Not all heeded the call: Count Aimeric of Narbonne deemed it safer and more politic to await the outcome of events from the safety of the Mediterranean coast. With Montfort were just over 300 men to face the combined mass of the Occitanians and the growing rebellion in southern Languedoc. To add to his problems, his family were dangerously exposed around the region: his wife could not be reached in Lavaur, his young daughter was in Montréal and his ailing son Aimery was laid up in Fanjeaux. Should any of these fall into southerner hands, the ransom demands would have involved crippling losses of territory. And only then if they were kept from harm.

At the council, Montfort, as a practical general, listened to his officers' ideas. Hugh de Lacy, an English crusader and veteran, counselled an aggressive policy that the best defence is attack. He said that holing himself up in a castle was the worst thing that Montfort could do. This would render the crusaders isolated and impotent; furthermore, the loss of momentum to the enemy would lead to an unending and ever-increasing stream of defections and the loss of most of his gains. Lacy therefore advised Montfort to bait the enemy into open battle by going to Castelnaudary. Here, he should wait until reinforcements came, and meet the southerners in the field. The crusaders voiced their approval in a unanimous shout.

This was a battle-seeking strategy, rare in the Middle Ages, when the norm was to avoid the risks of engagement in the open field. But for Montfort the risks of waiting behind the walls of Carcassonne were even higher for the success of his great enterprise. The following morning, a Tuesday in late September, the crusaders left a small garrison in Carcassonne and rode to Castelnaudary, eager to arrive there before the southerners had it surrounded.

Once there, he was joined by Guy de Lucy with fifty knights, bringing his total force of knights and sergeants to somewhere approaching 500. Guy's knights had been helping King Peter of Aragon against the Muslims in Spain but had been recalled by Montfort to meet this new crisis. Peter lost the battle of Salvatierra after this recall, and this is likely to have increased his already substantial antipathy towards Montfort. Peter of Vaux de Cernay claims that the king sent men to ambush Guy's contingent on their way back to Languedoc. The whole episode served to antagonise Peter and push him further away from the northern crusade. The Cathar-friendly town of Castelnaudary was of little help to the crusaders: it could offer only the most reluctant of conscripts and even fewer volunteers.

The Count of Toulouse arrived and set up camp, with tents everywhere, many crowned with a golden ball and a metal eagle. His men 'covered the whole ground like locusts'.[107] Seeing the approach of the huge army, many of the townspeople of the *bourg* jumped the walls and left the place to the enemy, who quickly took advantage to begin occupying it. The northerners were taken by surprise by the swiftness of events and were eating when this occurred. They responded quickly, driving the intruders out before themselves withdrawing. The besiegers' camp was pitched on a nearby hill to the north, Le Pech, and was strongly surrounded with ditches, fences and other barriers. This was a common precaution in long sieges, as it afforded protection against sorties and relieving armies. At the siege of Château Gaillard in 1203–04, the French camp suffered a surprise attack that left many camp followers dead. Philip II ordered that lines of ditches be excavated around both the castle and his men; these lines of circumvallation and contravallation were common features in major siege operations. The southerners re-entered the suburb but were driven out again the next day. They had anticipated such an event by cutting holes in the *bourg's* outside wall to facilitate a hasty escape.

For reasons unknown, the southerners did not invest the whole town, and this hampered their execution of the siege and has led to criticism of the Count Raymond's tactics. The crusaders were able to lead out their horses to water and harvest some of the fields outside the walls. This also made sorties easier and hence very frequent. During one engagement the crusaders unhorsed Roger Bernard, son of the Count of Foix. A siege engine set up on the road was embarrassingly ineffectual as the stone in the area was too soft and shattered on impact. This elicited much derision from the defenders. Three large stones were brought in from some distance away; one of these also shattered but the two others did damage to a tower and a hall. However, the threat that more stones of a higher quality would be brought in prompted a sortie led by Montfort to destroy it. The defenders' caution prevented the crusaders from reaching the machine as it, like the camp, was also heavily protected by ditches and fences.

But for all the lack of a complete blockade, the crusaders were soon running low on provisions. Montfort sent Guy de Lévis, the marshal of his army, to summon supplies and reinforcements urgently from Fanjeaux and Carcassonne. He returned empty handed: most of the area had decided that Count Raymond now offered them better prospects. Montfort sent him out again with Matthew de Marly, brother to Bouchard, who was now Lord of Cabaret since his release from its castle. They travelled all the way to the coast at Narbonne, where Count Aimeric again showed his disdain for the dangerous business of fighting. His disinclination to show any support revealed just how much the wind was blowing against the northerners; defections would continue apace until Montfort regained the initiative. More and more places were reverting back to southern lordship. Montfort had to force the issue. He ordered Bouchard de Marly to come to his assistance from Lavaur. Bouchard gathered 100 knights and was accompanied by Martin Algai, the veteran Spanish mercenary and King John's Seneschal of Gascony, with twenty of his own. Eventually the marshal collected 300 men from Narbonne and 500 from around Carcassonne, but many of these were to melt away on the march. The reinforcements mustered at Carcassonne and fitted out a supply train with baked bread, oats and other supplies for the beleaguered forces at Castelnaudary. The convoy of approximately 600–700 men set out westwards to the siege. They could not know that were about to be involved in the biggest field engagement of the war so far.

Southerner scouts reported back to the camp at Castelnaudary that a large convoy of reinforcements and supplies was on its way to the town; the southern knight William Cat, who had pledged allegiance to Montfort, also betrayed his new lord and passed on the news to the besiegers. As the town was not fully invested, these men and provisions would be able to reach the garrison unless action was taken to block them. The Count of Foix set out to do just this with his men and mercenaries, a force of 400 cavalry and 1,600 infantry. William of Tudela, ever keen to brighten his poem with detail, writes of their 'fast horses, hauberks or quilted jackets, strong shining helmets or good iron headpieces, sharp spears, strong ashen hafts and crushing maces'.[108] They blocked the crusader convoy between St Martin Lalande and Lasbordes, just over 3 miles east from Castelnaudary. When he saw large contingents of the southerners move away from the siege, Montfort sent forty knights under the command of Guy de Lucy, Simon the Castellan of Neauphle and Viscount Roard de Donges to the assistance of Bouchard de Marly and Guy de Lévis. His orders were clear and typical of Montfort's aggressive generalship: attack. The risk here for Montfort was that these men did little to redress the numerical imbalance, which stood at nearly three-to-one, and they left Castelnaudary with a reduced garrison of sixty knights and light cavalry plus infantry. The Count of Foix in turn sent back to the southerners' camp for reinforcements to maintain his numerical superiority against the relief convoy.

On the morning of the battle, the crusaders heard mass, made their confessions and took the Eucharist to prepare themselves for possible death that day. The southerners forged the traditional three divisions for battle into one solid line: at the centre was the heavy cavalry with armoured horses, with one flank comprising lighter cavalry and the other infantry with spears and, presumably, billhooks. They were exhorted not to rest until they had 'killed the foreigners' from France, Germany, Poitou, Anjou, Brittany and Provence. On the northerners' side, Bishop William of Cahors urged the troops to fight courageously in the knowledge that death would mean instant reward in heavenly paradise. The exact position of the battlefield has not been conclusively identified, but the area between St Martin and Lasbordes is not extensive; it is easy to stand there today on the road at the point marking entry into Lasbordes and envisage the open fields on a gentle incline being covered with 3,000 troops fighting across a broad front. The first on the scene would have been able to take up position on slightly higher ground, but the sources do not tell us who was where.

An opening barrage of crossbow fire initiated the engagement with such intensity that 'you would say the very sky was falling'. It would seem that both armies moved forward to meet, the crusaders with the intention, says Peter of Vaux de Cernay, of engaging first with the heavy cavalry. Though this risked the threat of encirclement from the wings, if the best troops were broken first then the likelihood was that resistance would quickly crumble; it therefore made sense for the crusaders to deploy their crack cavalry against the Count of Foix at the enemy's centre. As the lines broke on each other in a clash of armour and weapons, soldiers from both sides shouted out war cries for leaders and regions: 'Toulouse!', 'Foix!', 'Montfort!', 'Comminges!', 'Soissons!' Gerald of Pépieux, in the Count of Foix's contingent, charged into a Breton and ran him through with his lance; if William of Tudela is to be believed, the lance penetrated through shield and body deep into the rear saddlebow. Bouchard, with his silk pennon bearing Montfort's lion emblem, led his men into the fray. The mercenaries were targeted and in the combat here the son of the Castellan of Lavaur was struck on the nasal guard of his helmet by an arrow; the arrow glanced off and through the helmet's eyehole, killing the knight. The castellan was to lose another two sons in the bloody engagement. Riderless horses ran across the battlefield as the fighting intensified, shields and lances breaking and being discarded across the meadow.

Further down the line the mercenary crusader captain Martin Algai feared he was on the losing side of the encounter. According to the *History*, he ran off crying 'We are all dead!' before the reprimands of the Bishop of Cahors rallied him. (William of Tudela claims that the bishop accompanied Martin in his flight; after the battle, Martin claimed that he had been pursuing enemy mercenaries.) Some of the southerners punched through to the baggage train and began pillaging it. There, Master Nicholas, William of Tudela's close friend and one of his chief informants of the battle, had his mule and serving boy seized and carried off. William Cat felt confident at this stage to openly turn his back on Montfort and rejoin his Occitanian confederates. According to the *Chronicle*, the point had been reached in the battle when the outnumbered crusaders 'had almost succumbed'.[109]

Then, in the midst of the battle, Montfort dramatically appeared on the scene. With him were his sixty knights from the garrison. He had ridden out from Castelnaudary with nearly all his cavalry, having emotionally proclaimed: 'Heaven forbid that my knights should die gloriously in battle and that I should escape alive and in shame. I will either conquer with my friends or fall with them.' It was a desperate gamble but typical of Montfort's audacity; he had left only his infantry behind to guard the town to chance everything in battle. But it worked, as such bold, aggressive tactics often did. With cries of 'Holy Mary help us!' and 'Montfort!', his men launched themselves into the ranks of the enemy.

The southerners were dismayed to see Montfort's force approaching from behind their front line; they also knew that the presence of Montfort himself was a major advantage for the northerners. They now faced troops to their front and rear. The southerner mercenaries buckled, but the Count of Foix was not so easily overawed. He turned to meet the new onslaught, his shield splitting in the ensuing combat. Two knights broke through Montfort's line on the first assault: the count's son, Roger Bernard, and the *faidit* Porada, who was wielding a heavy mace. William of Tudela believed that if others had fought as hard, the southerners would not have lost. But lose they did. Montfort's intervention precipitated a rout as the southerners fled the field or died on it. As usual, the poor bloody infantry suffered the brunt of it, those on the flank being annihilated. The defeated troops called out 'Montfort! Montfort!' to save their lives and to make the crusaders believe that they were on their side. The crusaders then got these defectors to prove themselves by pointing to fleeing soldiers and ordering 'kill that fugitive'. Many thus killed their own comrades.

With the field of battle won, Montfort had to regroup his men urgently and lead many of them back to Castelnaudary, which now lay in imminent peril. Here Savary de Mauléon had led the besiegers to the gates to launch an assault on the greatly reduced garrison (Peter of Vaux de Cernay says this now consisted of just five knights and a few sergeants). Savary's men entered the *bourg* but were heroically held off by the defenders. When Savary heard of his army's defeat he immediately withdrew into the fortified camp. Montfort was advised that it was too heavily defended for his exhausted men to make continuous assaults on it; nor did anyone wish to put his great victory at risk. Besides, all were keener to return to the battlefield and the plunder to be found there. Late into the night under moonlight, they ransacked the battlefield: 'No one can describe the immense wealth they gained there; it will make them rich all their lives long.' After the crusaders later sang out their praises and thanks in a *Te Deum*, the remains of the southerner army quietly struck camp, loaded their tents and clothing into their carts, and retreated temporarily to safer territory. Behind them they left their trebuchet to stand as a symbol of their failure. The huge, concerted Occitanian counter-attack had been stemmed at Castelnaudary by a much smaller force, but one that was both more experienced and better led. Montfort's reputation for bravery and leadership was enhanced once again.

Montfort did not have the manpower necessary to pursue the southerners; instead, he rode to Narbonne to successfully recruit more men while the glow of triumph attracted them to his ranks. Here a small contingent of troops from the north under the command of the famous knight Alan de Roucy arrived to join in the crusade. But further west the fruits of victory were not all that they might have been. The Count of Foix and the Toulousains, anxious to prevent the expected flood of defections back to the northerners, spread the lie across the region that they had won the battle and even that Montfort had been killed. That the northerners were known to have moved eastwards to Narbonne was exploited and made to look like a crusading retreat. They backed up their words with force, their armies moving through the region while Montfort was absent. It was a highly effective ruse as many places defected back from Montfort: in the Albi he lost Rabastens, Montégut, Gaillac, Cahuzac, Laguépie, St Antnonin, Lagrave and St Marcel; in the dioceses of Toulouse he lost Puylaurens, St Félix, Montferrand, Avignon, St Michel, Cuq Toulza and Saverdun. Peter of Vaux de Cernay estimates that over fifty *castra* went over to the enemy. The southerners had seemed to gain more from defeat than the crusaders had from victory.

At Lagrave deception was employed. Montfort had left the knight Pons de Beaumont in charge here. One morning he was with the castrum's carpenter, checking repairs to a cask. The carpenter invited Pons to look inside the cask to inspect it; 'when the knight put his head inside the cask the carpenter raised his axe and cut it off'. This was the signal for the inhabitants to rise up against the garrison and kill them. Baldwin of Toulouse arrived the following day; seeing Baldwin's banner, which was similar to the Count of Toulouse's, the townspeople admitted his force within their walls. Baldwin, who was already angry at losing Salvagnac and the good wheat growing there, 'slew almost all of them from the youngest to the oldest'.[110] More places fell and the crusaders met with further reversals. Simon, Castellan of Neauphle, and his brother Geoffrey were ambushed by Roger Bernard, the Count of Foix's son, near Fanjeaux as they collected wheat for its garrison. Geoffrey and some others were surrounded and killed, another knight was captured and imprisoned, and Simon escaped. The victory at Castelnaudary therefore gave the crusade only a limited boost. Even major victories on the battlefield sometimes had little effect. Montfort and his small army of knights had much work to do if they were to gain anything from it at all.

5

1212–13: 'ALL WERE SEIZED WITHOUT MERCY AND PUT TO THE SWORD'

Winter 1211–12: The Long Haul Begins

As the year 1211 drew to a close, it was clearer than ever that there would be no quick resolution to the war by a knock-out victory and that it would drag on for some time. Wars were ever thus. For Montfort, conquest would be a matter of two giant steps forward and one giant step back, and often two or three; for the southerners, the sheer tenacity of Montfort's professional and dedicated force meant that at best the crusaders would remain for some time a huge thorn in their flesh, sometimes digging in painfully and moving dangerously close to vital organs and arteries, and always needing to be dislodged.

The first twenty-eight months saw some of the major encounters and episodes of the whole crusade, events that shaped the nature of the conflict for decades to come. We have seen how the war was being fought, especially its constant ebb and flow, the early experiences of the commanders and their troops, and the territory that saw most of the military activity.

143

The movement from castrum to castrum and from siege to siege; the importance of manpower and supplies; the need for active, intelligent, determined and brave leadership; the fickleness of southern lords' pledges of allegiance: the importance of all these have been established. After Castelnaudary, the frequency of major operations and campaigns on the scale we have witnessed decreased as the war settled in for the long haul with smaller-scale activity and searches for political solutions, punctuated by major campaigns and military operations. The aftermath of the battle of Castelnaudary in the autumn of 1211 demonstrated that now the southerners had shown themselves capable of full-scale mobilisation, that the rapid benefits the crusaders could previously expect in terms of all-important momentum were no longer guaranteed, and that what they held was as insecure as they had feared. They simply did not have the manpower to garrison the region's castra in strength with sufficient numbers of loyal troops to ensure that they could be confidently held. The year 1211 had seen the siege of Toulouse and the full-blown engagement at Castelnaudary; 1212 and much of 1213 were to see nothing on this scale, but instead a grinding away at the business of war.

Continuing military activity over the winter of 1211–12 indicates the start of this new, relentless war of attrition. This was due in no small measure to the mobilisation of the southern forces that year and the realisation that the war could no longer be either contained or curtailed. Medieval warfare is often seen as something of a seasonal sport, with the period from the onset of winter to Easter as a spell of respite, some hostilities even ending as early as harvest time. This is a myth. Warfare was far too important to be restricted in this way. Winter campaigns were common in Europe. Thus, at the end of November 1181 Count Philip of Flanders had invaded Picardy while his enemy King Philip of France was away campaigning in Champagne; after a Christmas truce, hostilities resumed in mid-January. Summer made army movements easier, but brought with it other serious problems, the chief of which was water for troops and animals, as seen at Termes. Dehydration was a major issue for men fighting in armour in the summer heat and there are accounts of men dying due to thirst and heat exhaustion. When Louis VI prepared his army for battle at Reims in August 1124, he formed his wagons into circles where men could retire temporarily from the combat for water and rest. Of course, local weather conditions were highly influential. In Languedoc, high altitudes and wind patterns could offer different conditions to the normal Mediterranean climate of the plains and valleys. In April one can clamber the heights of Montségur and place one's hands in the snow that lies around the castle, but come down sunburnt, or stand on the ramparts of Carcassonne and freeze in the biting Mistral wind.

The southerners still had their armies in the field in November. Montfort added further reinforcements to the Alan de Roucy and the Narbonnais contingents when the ever-trustworthy Robert Mauvoisin returned to Carcassonne from a recruiting drive in the north with over 100 knights. Another fillip was the arrival of Montfort's brother, Guy, also a veteran of the Fourth Crusade. The brothers were reunited at Castres over Christmas. Both sides could therefore remain active in the winter. But it is no surprise that Montfort tried to regain the initiative, moving back into the west to raid the Count of Foix's lands. He raised the siege of Quié and took La Pomarède; a number of castra such as Albedun returned to his allegiance. Campaigning continued in early January 1212, with the northerners attacking Touelles, a village belonging to the despised Gerald of Pépieux. Gerald's father was captured and exchanged for the crusader Dreux de Compans, who had been captured in the ambush at the end of 1211. The villagers were not so fortunate: Montfort 'killed every wretch he could find there'.[111] From there Cahuzac was taken, laden with supplies. The *History* relates how Montfort chased the counts of Toulouse, Foix and Comminges from Gaillac to Montégut and then to Rabestan, finally leaving them to retreat to Toulouse. Peter of Vaux de Cernay has Count Raymond taunting Montfort into battle, but then thinking better of it. Certainly, the southerners were very wary of full-scale engagements with the superior troops of the crusading army, but the reality was that Count Raymond was attempting, in vain, to draw all of Montfort's forces away from Cahuzac. As we shall see later in this chapter, this was a common diversionary tactic in medieval warfare.

A meeting at Albi in February with Arnald Amalric, now Archbishop of Narbonne, led to the siege of St Marcel, 12 miles north-west of the city and another possession of Gerald Pépieux. But the allied triumvirate of the counts of Toulouse, Comminges and Foix arrived with reinforcements. With too few men, too few supplies and too many enemies disrupting communication in the area, the northerners wasted a month there, their sole petrary attacked by a sortie led by the Count of Foix. The siege was abandoned on 24 March, an inexplicable repeat of the failure before Toulouse the previous year. Montfort attempted to save face by challenging the allies at Gaillac to open battle; sensibly they refused, no doubt as expected, and he was back in Albi at the start of April to come to terms with this latest setback.

1212: The Spring Offensive

But Montfort's fortunes changed that very week with a massive influx of crusaders from around Europe. Archdeacon William of Paris, one of the northerner heroes at Termes, and Master Jacques de Vitry had been on tour preaching the crusade. It was a great success, and this despite stiff competition from another crusade proclaimed in Castile in January at the behest of King Alfonso VIII. Luckily for Montfort, in 1212 much of Christendom had caught crusading fever; it was the year of the tragic and pathetic Children's Crusade, one of the most notorious triumphs of cynicism and exploitation over naive optimism and ideology in the Middle Ages, according to some historians. The warrior pilgrims in Languedoc arrived from northern France, the Auvergne, Germany, Lombardy; among them were some Slavs. The sources speak of 'incredible numbers' and an 'enormous' host. And more were to appear in the spring. Montfort quickly put them to good use.

On 8 April the crusading army stood looking up at the castrum of the well-named Hautpol, high above the town of Mazamet. The elevated crags and crevices rendered Hautpol one of the more inaccessible fortifications, as Peter of Vaux de Cernay, an eyewitness to events in 1212, affirms. The crusaders took three days to assemble their petrary, which was then put to constant use. But the bombardment of stones from the heights of the ramparts was much more intense and caused the besiegers great problems and a high number of casualties. However, unlike Toulouse and St Marcel, this siege was executed with conviction and the defenders knew it. When a mist descended on the night of 11/12 April, the defenders seized the opportunity to make a break for freedom, as the defenders at Termes had done. Some made it; others did not. The victory was mitigated by two episodes: the 100 knights who came with Robert Mauvoisin, having more than fulfilled their crusading pledged, returned home; and in Narbonne anti-Montfortian riots broke out with the viscount's 14-year-old son Amaury physically threatened and two of his men killed.

The departure of the knights was soon rectified by even more reinforcements, with contingents led by such powerful figures as Count William of Julich and Duke Leopold VI the Glorious of Austria. Burgundians, Frisians, Lorrainers, Normans and Bretons boosted the crusading host even further. So strong were Montfort's forces he could create two armies, placing one under the command of his brother, Guy. Over the next three weeks castrum after castrum bowed down to the inevitable faced with the might of this new crusading army, either being abandoned or offering only token resistance; these included Montmaur, Les Cassès, Montferrand, Avignonet and St Michel, the last of which was totally destroyed. Count Raymond of Toulouse was in Puylaurens with a large force of mercenaries, but on Montfort's approach he abandoned the place, which reverted back to the lordship of Guy de Lucy. Archbishop Robert of Rouen and the Bishop-elect of Laon then turned up with their forces; and especially welcome was the return of Archdeacon William of Paris. After this, Montfort continued his progress in the north of the region while his brother and Guy de Lévis moved southwards. Rabastens, Montégut and Gaillac all surrendered on the same day. As William of Tudela comments, 'never have I seen so many castles abandoned and captured with so little fighting'.[112]

It was a good time for Montfort, but revenge and bitterness remained to the fore. At St Marcel he had previously suffered the taunts and jeers of the townspeople while hearing mass on Good Friday; Montfort was a devout man and this demanded retribution. He rebutted the town's appeals to submit peacefully to him. The inhabitants fled. St Antonin refused the negotiated settlement offered by Bishop William of Albi; its lord, Adhémar Jordan, sneered: 'Let the Count of Montfort know that a crowd of stick-carriers will never take my castrum.'[113] (The southerners used 'stick-carriers' as a pejorative term to denote crusading pilgrims with their staves.) Montfort arrived there on 20 May; within a few hours the place was his. As at Béziers, the garrison had sortied out but were chased back by the lowly ribalds, who quickly took three of the town's gates under their own initiative. Peter of Vaux de Cernay called it 'a fight without swords', as these poor pilgrims used stones, clubs, knives and axes. The townspeople received some rough treatment: at least twenty-eight were killed, many while trying to flee across the river behind the castrum (ten did manage to escape); the men and women who sought sanctuary in the church were stripped of their clothes while the clergy were harshly abused by the peasant pilgrims.

Montfort was more lenient. The castellan and his knights surrendered and were imprisoned in Carcassonne while the inhabitants were spared punishment. Here a discussion took place reminiscent of the considerations in the summer of 1209 at Carcassonne. At dawn, Montfort 'ordered all the inhabitants to be brought out'. As they shivered with fear expecting to meet their end, Montfort consulted with his captains: 'if he ordered the defenders, who were mere untutored countrymen, to be killed, the castrum would be devoid of inhabitants and become desolate, so wiser counsels prevailed and he released them.'[114] Once again we see the cold, calculating logic behind life and death: here the military imperative was deemed best served by economic considerations. But only just. Had Montfort thought a harsh lesson took preference, the townspeople would have been slaughtered.

St Antonin and nearby castra were placed in the hands of Baldwin of Toulouse. Baldwin installed William of Tudela as canon there, where he spent the last year of his life writing *The Song of the Cathar Wars*. William had been with Baldwin all year and would have crossed paths with Peter of Vaux de Cernay accompanying his uncle on the crusade in 1212. The latter therefore offers even more detailed accounts for this year than usual.

Summer to Winter 1212: Conquest

With the Albi quelled, Montfort moved into the Agenais encountering little resistance: place after place was left deserted for the crusaders to destroy as part of their castle strategy, while the region's main city, Agen, opened its gates to him. He was expanding the breadth of his operations as he moved ever further north-west into unfamiliar territory owned by the Count of Toulouse, intent on applying greater pressure on Raymond and to demonstrate to the count that his sword arm extended even here. He was able to do so because the great influx of crusading numbers had allowed him, as we have seen, to create two powerful armies, the other one led by his brother Guy operating in strength in the south.

Montfort's progress stalled at the strong fortress of Penne d'Agenais on 3 June. The castle was, says the *History*, the most formidable in the Agenais, built on a huge rock and surrounded by powerful walls. In the

1190s it had been strengthened further by its previous owner, Richard the Lionheart. The place was commanded for the Count of Toulouse by Hugh d'Alfaro, the Navarrese mercenary, Seneschal of Agen and son-in-law to Raymond. With him were the mercenary captains Bausan, Bernard Bovon and Gerald de Montfabès. He had pulled in 400 mercenaries to garrison the castle in readiness for the crusaders' inevitable arrival. Alfaro stockpiled the place with provisions and weapons, including siege machines and plentiful supplies of wood and iron. He had two smithies, a furnace and a mill constructed. He evicted the townspeople and set the *bourg* ablaze; Alfaro had all the men he wanted to defend the place and he did not want his resources drained by a mass of useless mouths. His duty to defend the castle for his lord overrode his duty to protect the people under his care. He was ready.

The crusaders set up camp to the south-west and moved their mangonels and battering rams into the burnt-out *bourg*. The machines exchanged barrages with those within the fortress, whose thick walls easily withstood the crusaders' missiles, these only seeming to damage buildings within the castle's precincts. The defenders made many sorties, including a failed attempt on the northerners' petraries; the besiegers were constantly harassed. The crusading army was large but it suffered from a relatively low proportion of knights among its ranks, as its unarmed peasant soldiers were repeatedly driven away from the walls. Many crusaders started to melt away in the intense summer heat as their forty-day service expired. Montfort sent to his brother for help.

Guy had been attacking the lands of Raymond Roger of Foix along the edge of the Pyrénées. With him were the northern bishops mentioned earlier, Archdeacon William of Paris and the notoriously cruel and violent Berzy brothers. At the Cathar town of Lavelanet they massacred the inhabitants, which had the Béziers effect: resistance crumbled as they moved east towards Toulouse, 'since all the inhabitants of the area had been quite overcome by fear'.[115] Heeding his brother's call, Guy moved north, ravaging his way across the Count of Toulouse's lands. He left behind one knight killed in an ambush; after Guy's departure, southern mercenaries dug up the body, dragged it through the streets, tore it apart and left it to rot in the open.

Guy encamped on Penne's eastern side and erected a stone-thrower, bringing the total of siege engines deployed by the crusaders to about nine. But none was having much effect, so Montfort ordered the construction of a new, much bigger one under the supervision of that master of poliorcetics, Archdeacon William. As the siege moved into July, time was pressing as many contingents that had joined the crusade in May continued to return home. Some of those with Guy had only accompanied him to Penne because it was on their way back north. Duke Leopold the Glorious left to offer King Peter of Aragon his help against the Muslims in Spain. Only the Archbishop of Rouen's force committed themselves to staying until a fresh wave of crusaders reinforced Montfort. The archdeacon set his new machine to work and the wall it targeted began to weaken, much to the alarm of the defenders. Equally worrying for them was the depletion of their water supplies, which were drying up in the summer heat and leaving them dehydrated and ill. The women and servants who had remained in the castle were evicted in the hope of stretching what little supplies remained, but the crusaders forced them back in. With no sign of relief from the Count of Toulouse, and with the prospect of being put to the sword when the castle was stormed, Hugh d'Alfaro sought surrender terms. Montfort took counsel with his commanders and the surrender was accepted; they knew their forces would continue to disintegrate at a rapid rate and there remained important business to attend to elsewhere. The defenders were allowed to go free as Montfort took possession of the place and repaired its damage with mortar and lime. It was another significant victory for the crusaders.

Peter of Vaux de Cernay's unstinting admiration for Montfort's finer qualities is more uncritical than usual at Penne. When Alfaro pushed out the servants and women from the castle, Peter rightly says that 'he exposed them to the threat of death'. Montfort, however, 'refused to kill them but instead forced them to return. What noble and princely conduct!' This is a rather rose-tinted view: Montfort was rarely reluctant to kill the enemy non-combatants when it served his purpose; here, it served his purpose to drive them back into the castle. Montfort refused to let the poor wretches escape as he wanted them back with Alfaro, consuming his supplies and water. He knew full well what had happened at the siege of Château Gaillard near Paris nine years earlier. Then, Philip Augustus of France was besieging the castle held by Roger de Lacy for King John. Between 1,400 and 2,000 Norman peasants from around the area had flocked into the castle for safety. When an English relief operation failed to raise the siege, Lacy knew he would not have enough food for everyone in a lengthy encirclement (it was to last nearly six months), so in November he began expelling the useless mouths, the non-combatants, out of the castle. The French let the first pathetic band of around 500 of the weakest and the oldest through their siege lines. A few days later the scene was repeated. When Philip, away at another siege, heard of this he ordered any further refugees to be forced back into the castle, just as Montfort did. The difference at Château Gaillard was that when the third group of refugees were bundled out and then pushed back by arrows and spears, Lacy kept his gates closed to them. Neither besieger nor besieged relented and the non-combatants were left exposed to the cold and wet of winter on a barren rock for three months. There followed one of the most horrifying episodes in the pitiless annals of medieval warfare. The refugees resorted to cannibalism to survive. Those who made it to spring were saved only by Philip's return: not because the king had softened his stance, but because he wanted them out of the way of an assault and because he feared that disease might spread into his camp. The king's chaplain, William the Breton, similarly enamoured with his hero as Peter with Montfort, praises Philip to the skies for his act: the king was 'always kind' to those in need 'because he was born to have compassion towards the unfortunate and to spare them always'.[116] Compassion had nothing to do with Montfort's decision not to kill the non-combatants; he was using them as a weapon.

The campaign advanced even further from where the crusade had started three years earlier. Montfort had sent a force west under Robert Mauvoisin to successfully take Marmande, halfway between Agen and Bordeaux near the Atlantic coast, while he moved 17 miles northwards with reinforcements from Archbishop Alberic of Reims and others. At Biron he had a score to settle with Martin Algai, one of King John's favoured mercenaries. Algai had rather peremptorily taken to his heels at the battle of Castelnaudary; having soon afterwards changed sides, he now commanded the castle of Biron for the Count of Toulouse, from where he terrorised the surrounding area. The garrison knew it could not withstand a major siege and so struck a deal with Montfort: they could go free if they handed over their commander. This saved much time and trouble; it was a neat and convenient agreement for all except Algai. He was allowed to confess his sins before being dragged through the ranks of the crusading army and hung in a meadow.

Pushing his soldiers as they struggled through the fierce summer heat, Montfort arrived before Moissac on 14 August. His wife Alice had met him *en route* with some infantry reinforcements. The town of Moissac does not lie in an elevated position but on level ground. The problems for the crusaders were its strong walls, abundance of clear springs and the hardened mercenaries who garrisoned it. William of Tudela writes that the townspeople wanted to submit to the crusaders but the soldiers prevented them. Both sides exchanged artillery barrages with their machines and, as expected, one of the various sorties tried to destroy those on the crusaders' side. Montfort rallied his men to defend them; an enemy archer sighted him and let loose an arrow which struck the viscount in the foot. At one point his warhorse was killed under him and he was in danger of capture, but his men quickly saw his peril and rode to his rescue. Worse befell the nephew of the Archbishop of Reims: he was dragged back into the castrum, killed and dismembered, his body parts flung down on the crusaders from the ramparts. Any crusader caught or slain in combat was similarly hacked to pieces. There were other casualties in the combat. A young knight of Baldwin of Toulouse was struck by a crossbow quarrel that pierced his armour and 'drove through his guts as into a sack of straw'.[117]

It proved an especially difficult siege in its initial stages before crusader reinforcements started to appear. Even though the sorties became less frequent, the crusaders' working parties sent out to collect timber (for the northerner carpenters to shape into siege weapons) were still protected at all times by an armed escort; even the reinforcements had come under attack from Montauban and had to be rescued by Baldwin. Peter of Vaux de Cernay himself had a close call. While he was moving near the castrum to encourage the crusaders supplying the petraries with stones, a southern mercenary let fly 'an extremely sharp bolt from his crossbow at maximum power and tried to hit me; I was on a horse at the time – the bolt pierced my robe, missed my flesh by a finger's width or less, and fixed itself in my saddle'.[118] Arrows and crossbow bolts were the deadliest weapons of medieval warfare.

The intensity of the siege continued unabated into September. A siege cat was the focus of much of the fighting and the crusaders broke their way through wooden palisades positioned by the ditch and guarding the barbicans. But it was momentum that undid Moissac. As news came in of other towns in the region submitting to the crusaders, the defenders knew help would not be forthcoming and that they faced an imminent storm. The townspeople sought terms. Montfort agreed to spare them if they handed over the mercenaries and the Count of Toulouse's men. The citizens complied and paid a ransom in gold for their lives and freedom. The count's men were taken prisoner. The mercenaries were massacred, over 300 of them. The crusaders set about this task 'with great enthusiasm'. Much booty was gained at Moissac; the crusaders did not even have any qualms about helping themselves to the contents of the town's monastery.

Montfort continued to press ahead with his all-sweeping momentum into the autumn. He moved south-east, bypassing the isolated but troublesome town of Montauban under the command of Roger Bernard, the Count of Foix's son. Behind him he left William de Contres, Baldwin of Toulouse and Peter de Cissy in charge of Castelsarrasin, Montech and Verdun on the Garonne respectively to underpin his astonishing dominance of Count Raymond's lands. His next focus was on the south and the territory of the Count of Foix. The counts of Toulouse and Foix had been causing trouble from Saverdun, using it as a base for raids around Pamiers (both places were on the road north from Foix to Toulouse). Montfort and German crusading reinforcements from Carcassonne soon put the southerners to flight by advancing on the area. The counts retreated further north, closer to Toulouse, to Auterive; but the crusaders pursued them and they abandoned this castrum, too.

Montfort kept the relentless momentum going, now turning his attention to the lands of Count Bernard of Comminges. There was only token resistance, such as the burning of a bridge over the Garonne at Muret; the town, only 12 miles south of Toulouse, was seized. From here, at the behest of the local episcopacy, he progressed into Gascony and received the submission of the Count of Comminges's town of St Gaudens. This was followed by Samatan and L'Isle Jourdain. Montfort continued to mark his presence in the western counties of Bigorre, Armagnac and Astarac, and the viscounties of Lomagne, Béarn and Couserans – all new territories brought into the orbit of the Albigensian Crusade. Within a few days, most of the Count of Comminges's domains went over to Montfort. His next target was Roger de Comminges, the count's nephew, whose lands he now ravaged. From Muret and other places the crusaders were able to raid up to the gates of Toulouse itself. Toulouse was struggling under the weight of refugees, landless southern lords (the *faidits*), Cathars and mercenaries without towns to garrison. Monasteries and cloisters were turned into sheepfolds and stables.

Montfort ended the year with a general council held at Pamiers. Here, as conqueror of Languedoc, he oversaw the establishment of forty-six articles covering rights and rules for the governance of his new lands. These were drawn up by a commission of twelve men: four crusaders, four churchmen and four collaborating southerners (two knights and two burghers). The Statute of Pamiers was pronounced on 1 December. On religion, the church's extirpation of heresy would be supported by the secular army where necessary and, anticipating the religious laws of Elizabeth I's reign in Reformation England, but from the Catholic perspective, all, including lords and their wives, were compelled to attend mass and observe holy days on pain of a fine. The Church itself was to be restored all its rights and liberties. Economically and socially, the statute lowered taxes, abolished new toll gates, made justice freely available to all. The ways of the less feudally inclined south were recognised by an article that allowed serfs to be emancipated by moving into towns. Militarily, provisions were made for Montfort to call upon his vassals to perform service in the field. Among these was a clause that stipulated that the new French landholders had to provide French troops for the next twenty years. Montfort had learnt not to trust the southerners. Another clause gave Montfort the significant power to demand and receive any castrum at any time for any reason. Montfort and the northerners had laid down victors' rules.

The southerners' position now seemed hopeless; 1212 had been a year of unmitigated success for the northerners. Toulouse was surrounded and isolated by lands in the hands of Montfort's men, support only available from the count's men in the strong and still resisting town of Montauban a few miles north. Montfort had swept nearly all before him, the southerners unable to marshal an effective response. But the geographical extent of his power both belied his strength and undermined it. Winter saw the usual depletion of his forces; his garrisons would have to wait until spring to regain their strength. As it was, Foix remained unbowed and Montauban and Toulouse were stuffed full of troops who could – and needed to – sally forth on raids and test the overextended crusaders. The garrison at Montauban gave William de Contres all sorts of problems in the north-west. William of Tudela claims that they went on raids 1,000 strong; an exaggeration, no doubt, but it does denote a major force. They plundered the locality and stole sheep. Contres exhausted his men and horses tracking the enemy down, some of whom drowned crossing the River Tarn as he recovered much of their booty and freed their captives held for ransom. On another occasion, the Montauban garrison 'overran the whole Agenais. Their troops could hardly move for the weight of stolen goods.'[119] In yet another combat, Contres's horse was struck by five or six arrows and bolts, throwing its rider to the ground.

Even the heart of Montfort's territory was not safe. Roger Bernard, the Count of Foix's son, operated with mercenaries between Carcassonne and Narbonne, planning to ambush crusaders. This guerrilla warfare was typical of the southerners' tactics; while Montfort and the bulk of his forces were operating in the west, the Trencavel lands were not heavily garrisoned. Roger Bernard met one small group of new French crusaders on the road to Carcassonne. He approached them slowly so that they thought he and his men were crusaders, too. When they came close, the southerners pounced on the French and literally hacked most of them to pieces.

Others were taken off as prisoners to Foix where, says Peter of Vaux de Cernay, the southerners 'each day applied themselves diligently to thinking up new and original torments with which to afflict their prisoners'. He heard how the French were kept in chains and cut up from one of the knights incarcerated there, who witnessed and experienced the brutality. One punishment highlighted for its cruelty involved tying 'cords to their genitals and pull[ing] them violently'.[120] For many historians, such vivid descriptions of torture are examples of monastic hyperbole; however, such acts were common in medieval warfare and deserve to be treated with the utmost seriousness.

The overextension of Montfort's now greatly reduced force posed all sorts of military problems for the future, but the greatest weakness of all was political. Montfort's desire to maintain his momentum by obtaining sound military objectives in the west did more harm than good. More than once before he had shown himself willing to go beyond his crusading remit, but this time the vast extent of his operations caused a major political backlash. Montfort's incursions into the territory of Baldwin of Comminges had nothing to do with the deracination of heresy – unorthodoxy was not a problem in the count's lands – and everything to do with isolating Toulouse. But in so doing he greatly antagonised a powerful figure whom he needed to remain neutral: King Peter of Aragon. Peter had already shown his concern over events in Languedoc, where his vassals were being hammered by the northerners. He felt that he had to tolerate much of this as he was a loyal son of the Church and himself a leading crusader in Spain;

he had not, after all, gone to the aid of his vassal Viscount Raymond Roger of Béziers. But the move into Comminges's territory was blatantly about power projection. Montfort had moved into Bigorre, Couserans, Béarn and Comminges – all places, like Foix, where Peter was overlord.

Even Pope Innocent III, that implacable suppressor of heretics, appreciated that the crusade had now gone too far. In letters dated 17 and 18 January 1213, he wrote sternly to the leaders of the crusade. To Montfort he wrote 'you have induced to spill the blood of the just and injure the innocent, to occupy the territories of the king's vassals'. To Arnald Amalric, now Archbishop of Narbonne and so a major power in the region, he similarly aired King Peter's complaints to Rome:

> You, brother archbishop, and Simon de Montfort have led the crusaders into the territory of the Count of Toulouse and thus occupied places inhabited by heretics but have equally extended greedy hands into lands which had no ill reputation for heresy … It does not seem credible that there are heretics in those places. The king's messengers have added that you have usurped the possessions of others indiscriminately, unjustly and without proper care … Among these places are the territories of the Count of Foix, the Count of Comminges and Gaston de Béarn. He [Peter] has complained especially that although these three counts are still his own vassals you, brother archbishop, and Simon have sought to persuade the men of these territories they have lost to swear an oath of fealty.[121]

The pope ordered Montfort to restore the lands he had taken to King Peter's vassals. Montfort's political land grab was to be reversed.

Count Raymond, an ineffectual presence on the battlefield, had in the autumn left military matters in the more capable hands of the Count of Foix, while he used his time more productively: he slipped across the Pyrénées to press his case with the King of Aragon.

King Peter had stomached the upstart Montfort forcing himself onto the political scene in Languedoc but now he was going too far; the king was affronted. A continued lack of a robust response would undermine his authority as overlord. The year 1212 had been a good crusading year for him as well. In the summer he had co-led the Spanish and European crusaders in a crushing victory over the Almohad Muslims at the epic battle of Las Navas de Tolosa in southern Spain, the major turning point in the Christian *Reconquista* of Iberia. His reputation as a great crusading monarch was assured. The victory freed him to focus on his affairs north of the Pyrénées. The consequences were to be profound. The king began his journey to another major battle in 1213, this time in southern France; it was to be the biggest and most significant land engagement of the whole Albigensian Crusade.

Winter and Spring: The Diplomatic War

The first half of 1213 saw a respite in crusading, a war of words replacing the war of weapons. The diplomatic activity was intense as both sides pleaded their case with Rome. At the beginning of January, King Peter travelled with a large entourage to Toulouse, where he stayed for a month. In itself, this was a strong declaration of support for Count Raymond. At an ecclesiastical council at Lavaur on 16 January, the king put forward his case for Count Raymond, who was willing to make all amends with the Church, emphasising that the count's son was blameless and should inherit his father's lands, and that his vassals, the counts of Foix and Comminges and Viscount Gaston de Béarn, have their lands restored (as the pope was to insist in letters written in the following two days). The council of some twenty archbishops and bishops paid little heed to the monarch. They also refused his request for a truce until Easter, understandably fearing that this would result in the supply of crusade reinforcements drying up.

Peter's son, 6-year-old James, was still in Montfort's court as a privileged hostage, although that term was not employed. Nonetheless, the king felt not only compelled to act but strong enough to do so: insulted at Pamiers and rebuffed at Lavaur, he now openly sided with the southerners against his new, overmighty vassal in Languedoc. The attempts to disinherit Count Raymond's son upset many concerned about the precious rights of noble inheritance. King Philip of France was overlord of Toulouse; he was not prepared to let the crusaders dictate who should be the region's count, even though Montfort would pay homage to him for it. As the pope reminded the crusaders, the count was still not found guilty of heresy or of Peter of Castelnau's murder. Furthermore, the younger Raymond had powerful connections as nephew to King John of England and also King Peter's son-in-law.

Toulouse and Montauban offered homage to King Peter to come formally under his protection, thereby making all the chief southern lords his vassals. This encouraged other southern lords to follow. And, most of all, in mid-January, Pope Innocent suspended preaching of the crusade in southern France and instead redirected all new pilgrims to the new expedition planned for the Holy Land. The Albigensian Crusade was now officially on hold. It seemed that all Montfort now had available to him was his small permanent army of colonisation and what mercenaries and local troops his funds could buy. Leaving some troops behind in Toulouse, Peter returned to Aragon and prepared for war.

According to the end of William of Tudela's chronicle, King Peter 'said that he would bring at least a thousand knights, all paid by him and, if he could only find the crusaders, would face them in battle ... He summoned his men from his entire kingdom and gathered a great and noble company.' William wrote, 'And we, if we live long enough, shall see who wins and we will set down what we recall, we will continue to record the events we remember.'[122] Alas, William leaves us here. His poem ends a few lines later. Sadly, our colourful war correspondent did not live to see and record the outcome of the war. His great work was left for another to continue.

News of the crusade's suspension did not reach all quarters and some still planned to make their way south. One was the 25-year-old Prince Louis, heir to the throne of France. In February he took the cross and made his expeditionary preparations. It is thought that news may not have reached him of the pope's decision. This is possible but unlikely as Paris would have been one of the first to know. Like his father, Louis paid little attention to the papacy when it interfered with Capetian interests. The southerners' homage to King Peter was an insult and challenge to the French crown, the lawful overlord of Toulouse, and Philip saw the merit of combining crusading prestige in pursuance of restoring his rightful position in the south. The direct involvement of the French crown was potentially a move of enormous significance for the crusade. But Count Raymond's international alliances came to the rescue. Philip now had papal backing to invade England, a much greater prize. John had been excommunicated by Innocent and his kingdom placed under interdict for refusing to appoint the pope's choice of Stephen Langton as Archbishop of Canterbury. Just as Philip amassed his papally sanctioned invasion armada, John came to terms with Innocent. The pope called off the invasion, but Philip ignored him. A pre-emptive naval strike by the

English on the French fleet at Damme in May put paid to Philip's plans and left the French under pressure in the north. For the time being, Louis's crusade was cancelled.

Just as with military affairs, so the tides of diplomacy ebbed and flowed. The crusading authorities had not accepted the pope's judgement submissively and obediently. Montfort ignored the demands while the legates sent Theodosius to Rome to persuade Innocent of the justness of their cause. It worked. In spring the pope wrote angrily to King Peter, admonishing him for his distorted view of the situation in Languedoc and his less than full disclosure of the facts; he forbade him from interfering with the progress of the crusade in Languedoc. Now, somewhat contradictorily, he proclaimed that while he still wanted new crusaders to head east, he permitted southerners – and southerners only – the indulgence for combating heresy in Languedoc. Furthermore, in May he issued letters rescinding his instructions of January and raising the prospect of a new crusading indulgence for Occitania.

Letters from all sides crossed Europe in the pursuance of a resolution, in search of allies and to present justification of causes. All the while the southerners and the crusaders made ready for war; Count Raymond sent out word to towns to reject their allegiance to Montfort and retake control of their castra. In the spring, King Peter and Viscount Montfort renounced their feudal ties. When Lambert de Thury arrived at Peter's court with Montfort's letter of *diffidatio*, announcing his breaking of homage, the king had him thrown in a dungeon. Anger was now so high that some at court called for the killing of the messenger. Montfort rubbed salt in the wound at the end of June with the very public ceremony of the knighting of his son Amaury. This was a clear demonstration of dynastic intent and Montfort's statement that he and his heirs were a permanent political power in Languedoc.

Spring 1213: The Pujol Atrocity

Montfort had already sent a party north on a recruitment drive. In May, reinforcements had started to arrive in Carcassonne. The first tranche was headed by Bishop Manasses of Orléans and Bishop William of Auxerre; with them came a force of knights that included Evrard de Brienne and Peter de Savary. With these Montfort set out to wage war once again.

With too few men to invest Toulouse, he restricted himself to aggressive economic warfare in Count Raymond's lands, 'cutting down the fruit trees and laying waste the crops and vineyards' and seizing and destroying seventeen castles in the first week.[123] Meanwhile, Guy de Montfort besieged Puycelsi in the northern Albigeois. The castrum had twice before overthrown Montfortian rule. The counts of Toulouse, Comminges and Foix arrived with a relief army of mercenaries, hoping to raise the siege. Tellingly, they were accompanied by William Raymond of Montcade, a seneschal of King Peter. As usual, outside the walls the focus of combat was the siege engines; as at Termes in 1210, William d'Ecureuil once again found himself a solitary figure heroically and successfully defending the machines against an enemy sortie. Guy had to abandon the siege when his forty-dayers headed home. They were followed by the bishops of Orléans and Auxerre. Montfort took his newly knighted son into Gascony to bestow him with the lands he had recently won there. In his absence, and with the departure of the crusaders, the southerners became bolder in their military activity.

One of the seventeen castles taken in the spring by Montfort was Pujol, just 8 miles from Toulouse. Three veteran crusaders who had been in Languedoc since 1209 – Peter de Cissy, Simon the Saxon and Roger des Essarts – had requested its possession from Montfort, who granted it to them. Their purpose, says William of Puylaurens, 'was to threaten the Toulousains as they attempted to bring in the harvest'.[124]

It is at this juncture that the unknown continuator of William of Tudela takes up the *Song of the Cathar Wars*. We shall therefore henceforth call him Anonymous. It is strongly believed, for good reason, that he was a soldier and troubadour fighting for either the Count of Toulouse or the Count of Foix. It has been suggested that he was Guy de Cavaillon, a close friend of Raymond's son, the future Count Raymond VII. The Anonymous now brings a partisan viewpoint for the southerners' side, for he hated the French and the destruction they had wrought in his beloved Languedoc. Already at Pujol he is calling the northerners 'drunkards'.

Raymond, with his fellow counts in the triumvirate and a large force of Catalan mercenaries sent by King Peter, besieged Pujol in May. It was a large army that marked another major counter-attack. They surrounded the castrum and began the process of filling the fosse with branches and sheaves of corn, trying to keep the heads of the defenders down with a barrage of 'feathered quarrels' that flew into the teeth and jaws of the

French; the *Chronicle* says that Essart was killed by an arrow wound to the head. The sappers then struck at the base of the walls with massive picks, enduring 'blazing fire', 'a torrent of rocks' and boiling water poured down upon them. The siege engines pounded away and the castle, never very strong, succumbed. The Anonymous says that the southerners stormed the place. 'Every Frenchman there, rich and poor, they seized without mercy and put to the sword; a few they hanged.'[125] He claims that sixty knights, squires and sergeants died here. Peter of Vaux de Cernay believes that the French knights surrendered when they received a firm guarantee that their lives and limbs would be spared. It is also possible that they capitulated during the final attack, when the tower of Pujol was on the point of being taken. After the surrender, Simon the Saxon was killed by the infantry; Peter de Cissy and others were spared in the slaughter and dragged off to Toulouse. But here, 'a few days later they were slaughtered in their prison by a mob' and 'dragged out of the town like carrion' or 'dragged by horses about the city streets and then hanged from gibbets'.[126] The war was now all about land and not religion; this did nothing to diminish the bitterness with which it was fought – rather, it increased it.

The southerners returned to a rapturous reception in Toulouse: they had won their first siege of the crusade. Now news arrived that King Peter of Aragon was on his way with an enormous army. Many took up the offer to go over to him as an advanced force was sent ahead to Toulouse. Montfort recalled his forces from Gascony, where his son had just taken Roquefort and freed nearly sixty crusading prisoners being held there, so as to meet the threat from Spain. As Peter of Vaux de Cernay explains, 'the whole of the Albigensian area was now in a confused and unstable state'.[127]

The Battle of Muret, September 1213

The King of Aragon's army moved into Gascony and made for Toulouse. The city, already bursting at the seams, would not have been able to accommodate the Aragonese army within its walls; nor would it have been easy to provision it after all the crusaders' depredations in the area. Thus, as a practical measure, on 10 September Peter set up his siege camp at his first objective of Muret, about 12 miles south of the city. This was garrisoned by a northern force of thirty knights and some infantry – hopelessly

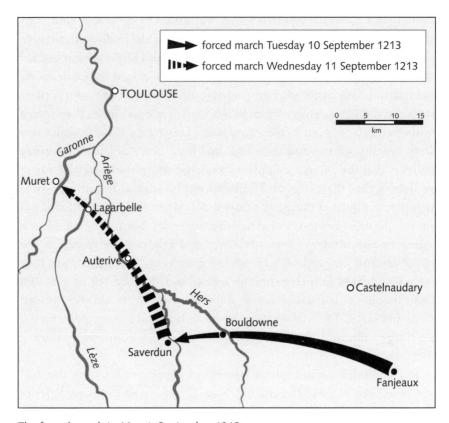

The forced march to Muret, September 1213.

inadequate to withstand a siege of any length against the formidable army of Catalan and Aragonese troops joined by those of the counts of Toulouse, Foix and Comminges, the largest army fielded by the southerners during the whole crusade. Before long Muret was being hammered by the siege machines of the Toulousain citizen militia and the southerners quickly made their way into the town, forcing the French back into the castle. When Peter heard that Montfort was approaching, he withdrew his forces from the town, not because he was afraid of the relief force, but because he wanted it trapped in Muret, too: 'Once he is inside there ... we'll surround and assault the town and take them all, every Frenchman and crusader.'[128] Peter was planning just what William of Tudela said he would do in one of the last comments in his work.

Montfort gathered his maximum strength as he headed from his headquarters at Fanjeaux to Saverdun. He sent his wife to Carcassonne to muster more men; there she persuaded Viscount Payen of Corbeil to delay his return north even though he had performed his forty days' service; he was unable to refuse a lady and so acquiesced to help Montfort. Montfort set out with seven bishops, three abbots and, more relevantly, an additional thirty knights who had just arrived from France. Among these was William des Barres, one of France's most illustrious chivalric figures and a veteran warrior of international renown. At Saverdun, Peter of Vaux de Cernay typically depicts Montfort as eager to enter Muret that very night, but

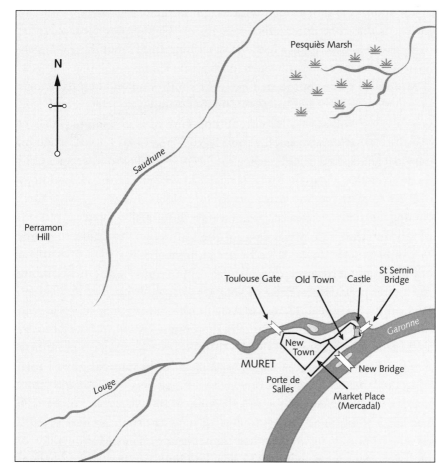

Muret at the time of the crusade.

his captains advised against this: their horses were exhausted and they would be in no fit position to fight their way in should they need to. He agreed. The next morning, 11 September, Montfort rode to the monastery at Boulbonne, where he made his confession, dictated a fresh will and heard mass. The bishops with him excommunicated the allied counts – but not Peter, as only the pope could excommunicate the kings of Aragon. He then set out to Muret and the greatest battle of the Albigensian Crusade.

The battle of Muret is one of the most important battles of the entire Middle Ages. At the time its impact was felt around Europe and accounts of it appeared in scores of chronicles. Even second- and third-hand accounts of it could be well informed as details were disseminated across the continent by the multitude of nationals who fought in the engagement. Naturally, each tells the story differently – remember Wellington's choreographic comparison of describing a battle to describing a ball – but there is largely broad agreement on what happened.

Montfort's force approached from the south-west and entered Muret unimpeded on the night of 11 September. Among the clergy with him were Bishop Fulkes of Toulouse, Bishop Guy of Carcassonne (Peter of Vaux de Cernay's uncle) and the papal legate, Theodosius. Montfort and his men had anticipated trouble – they had become used to southerner attacks on convoys as their main form of retaliation – but not the new strategy of Peter to draw them in. The Anonymous admits that among Montfort's contingent there 'were so many good men in so small a force'; as William of Puylaurens noted, it was easy for the southerners to count the force as it went into the town. What the exact number was is hard to ascertain beyond doubt. However, there is some approximate agreement among the figures provided by Peter of Vaux de Cernay, William of Puylaurens, William the Breton and James of Aragon (the son and heir of Peter, who offers numbers in his autobiography, the earliest known to be written by a Christian king). Peter talks of Montfort's force as being no more than 800 knights and mounted sergeants; William of Puylaurens gives a total of 1,000; James encompasses both with a range between 800 and 1,000 knights; while William, in the more reliable of his two works, records 260 knights, 500 mounted sergeants and, the only one to do so, 700 infantry composed of pilgrims rather than trained troops. Thus Montfort's force probably comprised about 800 heavy and light cavalry (and perhaps as many as 1,000) and some 700 relatively inexperienced infantry. Of the opposing Aragonese and Occitanian forces, the best-informed guesstimate puts these at some 1,600 to 2,000 cavalry (and perhaps as high as 4,000) and between 2,000 and 4,000 infantry militia. Thus, at worst, the crusaders were outnumbered by five-to-one; at best, by just over two-to-one. The highest ratio is unlikely, given that not all of Peter's forces were drawn up on the battlefield. Of course, Catholic commentators at the time portrayed the imbalance as approaching twenty-to-one, so as to exaggerate the extent of the challenge faced by the crusaders.

Montfort's position was not a comfortable one, hence his overtures to King Peter for talks of either a truce or a peace. This was in all likelihood a stalling tactic partly in the hope that he would receive further reinforcements (that night the Viscount of Corbeil arrived with thirty knights) and partly in the hope that dragging out negotiations would cause some of Peter's forces to drift away. Ultimately, as William of Puylaurens rightly noted, 'Count Simon thought it likely that if he gave Muret over to his adversaries the whole territory would rise against him and join the other side, which would create a dangerous situation.' He accurately captures Montfort's typical, belligerent attitude: 'he thought it better to risk all in a single day rather than strengthen the courage of his adversaries by ineffectual temporising.'[129] King Peter, confident in the might afforded by the largest anti-crusading army of the whole conflict, rejected all of Montfort's approaches out of hand.

The monarch appeared remarkably relaxed as the decisive battle loomed. Even his son reports him as having 'lain with a lady' just before going into combat.[130] Peter was an infamous womaniser, making it easy for the crusaders to make of him a propaganda target, depicting him as under the sway of women and even of fighting the war for a 'harlot'. Montfort's preparations were, of course, altogether more austere and pious, taking every opportunity to jump into a chapel rather than a bed, offering up his prayers to God. Peter, by contrast, when having finally made it to mass, is reported by his son to have been incapable of standing for the Gospel, so spent was he from his lusty exertions.

The sources provide us with a detailed account of the two opposing leaders on the morning of 12 September as they made ready for battle. The anonymous continuator of the *Song* tells of a grand council held in a meadow at which the king addressed the counts of Toulouse, Foix and Comminges (together, he omits to add, with all the Aragonese nobles who had accompanied him). Here the battle orations began. 'Be ready, each one of you,' he exhorted them, 'to lead your men and to give and take hard blows. If they had ten times the numbers, we should make them turn and run.' Count Raymond, unsurprisingly, cautiously advised a more defensive strategy: 'Let us plant barricades around the tents so that no cavalry can get through; then, if the French try to attack, we first use crossbows to wound them and as they swerve aside, we make our charge and rout them all.' He did not think any major engagement was necessary as the crusaders would eventually be starved out of Muret anyway. But one of Peter's leading commanders, Michael of Luesia, a hero of the great victory at Las Navas de Tolosa the year before, snorted contemptuously at this hesitant plan and talked of cowardice among the southerners. They would instead go immediately on the offensive. The cry of 'To arms!' went up and they began their approach to the town.

Meanwhile, Montfort had similarly taken counsel, as he always did, and he and his men heard mass and went to confession. Our three main war reporters do not record any rousing speeches by Montfort – the *History* has its hero simply say, 'Today I offer my soul and body to God' during one of his many visits to chapel[131] – but William the Breton offers a lengthy and almost certainly imagined oration by Simon, calling on the descendants of Charlemagne and Roland to vanquish the enemies of the true faith. His speech, focused very much on the honour and prowess of leading northern French noblemen, warned that defeat would mean certain death and that the enemy would 'disperse our bodies to be devoured by the beasts of the forests and by birds of prey'.[132]

Southerner cavalry and Toulousain infantry militia launched their first wave of attack against Muret, taking advantage of the fact that the main gates to the new town had been left open for an episcopal delegation of the bishops with Montfort to make a direct appeal to Peter. (While pursuing this one last diplomatic effort to avoid battle, they had put the services of their clerical entourages to more practical purposes, adding their energy to building up the town's defences.) The attack was repulsed after a combat in which 'both sides made blood spurt so freely that you would have seen the whole gate dyed scarlet', says the Anonymous.

It seems to have been at this point that Montfort finally decided on his plan of action. The *Song* has him claiming to have spent the entire previous night lying awake trying to decide what to do. His typically bold plan was to 'make straight for their tents, as if to offer battle'. If that failed, 'then there's nothing we can do but run all the way to Auvillar'. With that,

Montfort ordered his cavalry to saddle up. On raised ground, so that he was seen by his own men and the enemy, Montfort had his horse brought up and went to mount it. As he did so, the stirrup strap of his saddle broke and had to be repaired. This was followed by another bad omen on his second attempt: his charger suddenly raised its head and hit Montfort on his forehead, temporarily stunning him. The horses of the heavy cavalry wore armour and forms of protection, so the blow was quite heavy. This was actually the third ominous portent that had befallen Montfort immediately before the battle: earlier, while kneeling to pray in chapel, the leather binding of his leggings had snapped. The public embarrassment around the mounting of the horse must have unsettled his men as much as it delighted the predictably mocking southerners.

The Bishop of Toulouse then began to bless the crusader knights one by one. But Bishop Guy of Carcassonne, recognising the delay that this would cause, took the crucifix from his fellow bishop and blessed them *en masse*, promising Heaven to any who fell that day. While reviewing his troop, a knight advised Montfort to determine the size of the enemy forces before going out to meet them. This was standard practice, but Montfort dismissed the precaution. His mind was set on action and nothing should now delay the moment of truth. The Anonymous reports that Count Baldwin, the estranged brother of Count Raymond, urged the crusaders to 'be sure and hit hard. Better death with honour than a life of beggary'. On this, Montfort ordered his infantry to remain behind to defend Muret as he led his cavalry out of town and onto the field of battle.

It is likely that, as the *Song* says, the crusaders left Muret from the Salles Gate on the town's south-west side; this shielded their movements from the besieging Toulousain forces to the north. Here they formed up in the traditional three battalions – or 'battles' as they were known – for engagement. William des Barres, from a great chivalric family renowned throughout France, was given command of the cavalry in the front line, while Montfort headed the tactical reserve at the rear. The middle battle was commanded by Montfort's veteran captain, Bouchard de Marly. This was not timidity on Montfort's part – his personal courage had been proven beyond doubt on numerous occasions – but the usual positioning of the battlefield commander; from here, he could direct his troops, send out orders and launch his own battle into the fray where he thought it could best be used. Thus formed, William of Puylaurens says, they initially made a feint away from the enemy, to give the impression that they were retreating. William the Breton, however, says the crusaders 'headed straight for the enemy battalions like a lion'. Either way, they emerged from behind the wall, crossed the Louge, which feeds the Garonne, and advanced. Behind them they left the clergy praying for their victory; Peter of Vaux de Cernay says the latter created a deep roaring sound like a howling.

Facing them about a mile across the plain to the north-west of town were the ordered ranks of the enemy, similarly drawn up in three ranks. Count Raymond Roger of Foix led the first line of Catalans. Count Raymond of Toulouse was deemed too elderly to submit himself to the rigours of battle, so he withdrew towards the high ground of the encampment from where he could watch the battle. King Peter placed himself in the middle rank, a decision commented on by both contemporaries and historians. If the battalions were placed across the battlefield in line, even if staggered, rather than in column, this would make sense. However, the protection afforded to his flanks by the small River Saudrune on his right and by the Pesquiès Marsh to his left might also hinder his flight should this prove necessary. The river, little more than a stream, was not a major obstacle in itself, but in a rout the best crossing points could quickly become bottlenecks, and the banks would rapidly becoming slippery and boggy. At the battle of Towton in 1461, the retreating Lancastrians were slaughtered trying to cross a small beck close to the battlefield, their corpses forming a bridge of bodies. Furthermore, the western bank of the river soon rises up to an escarpment, which again would cause congestion in a retreat. The quick escape route from the battlefield was thus directly behind the centre. Peter's position was also strong in that it held the crest of a small rise, which gave him a good vantage point.

More notable is Peter of Vaux de Cernay's remark that the king disguised himself by wearing the armour of another knight. This was not common but not unheard of. On the one hand, a king's visual presence on the battlefield was important to his captains and troops, encouraging them to fight on; on the other, it did rather mark him out to the enemy. It was common practice to target an enemy king, as was to happen the following year at Bouvines. On that occasion, a squad of knights was formed with the sole intention of fighting their way through to either kill or capture King Philip of France. Although they did not break through, they formed a breach that allowed infantry to do so; catching his mail armour with a billhook, they pulled the king to the ground. He was saved only by the intervention of his bodyguard, who threw himself on top of Philip as a shield. The bodyguard died but bought enough time for Philip to be rescued. Capture would entail a massive ransom (as paid for King John II of France and Richard the Lionheart of England) as well as a complete transformation of the political scene. But disguise brought its own dangers.

Des Barres and Marly crossed the plain and plunged into the alliance ranks with their battalions, the one following the other into the fray, creating the waves of shock charges for which the Montfortian heavy cavalry was known. They both struck so deeply that they soon disappeared from Montfort's views as they penetrated the enemy divisions. William the Breton says that the Aragonese and southerners re-formed their ranks so as to encircle the northerners, while William of Puylaurens states that the impact of the crusader charge was so great that the southerners were given no chance to regroup in their rear line. The combat was ferocious. The bellicose Breton gleefully reports 'naked swords plunging into guts'. He is the only major source to speak of infantry; these would have been used by the southerners in ranks of spearmen to protect the knights. William describes how the knights attempted to knock the enemy cavalry to the ground so that the footsoldiers could despatch them, tearing out their entrails and cutting their throats. The horses were also targeted in an endeavour to bring down the riders, many mounts being killed or covered in wounds.

Montfort then made his move, ordering his battalion to advance to the right. To get to the enemy he had to cross some marshy land and a ditch; his way was eased by a pathway across these. He then unleashed his cavalry force into the left flank of the enemy as another full-scale *mêlée* ensued. The *History* gives a taste of the scrappy hand-to-hand fighting Montfort faced:

As the count was attacking them, they struck him from the right with such violent blows from their swords that his left stirrup broke. He tried to fix his left spur in the horse-blanket, but the spur itself broke and fell away. The count, who was a very strong knight, kept his seat and struck back against his foes vigorously. An enemy knight struck him violently on the head, but the count immediately hit him under the chin with his fist and forced him off his horse.

Back among the other divisions, the King of Aragon was in mortal danger. William and the Anonymous agree that the crusaders saw the king's standard and successfully fought their way towards it as the crescendo of battle filled the air. They set upon him; whether they recognised him or not is unclear. Peter tried frantically to identify himself with screams of 'I am the king!' but, relates the *Song*, 'no one heard him and he was struck so severely wounded that his blood spilled out on the ground and he fell his full length dead'. According to the less well-informed William the Breton, who at one stage fancifully imagines a personal one-on-one combat between Peter and Montfort, a squire named Peter, fighting on foot as his horse had been killed, approached the king and, ignoring his pleas for mercy, plunged his sword twice into his neck. Later in the century the honour of the kill would fall, according to Gérard d'Auvergne's chronicle, to Alain de Roucy.

The king struck down, together with Michael of Luesia and many other nobles, the Aragonese turned to retreat. Already, on their left wing, the Count of Foix was leading his troops in a headlong flight from the battlefield, pursued by Montfort. The viscount sensibly advanced relatively cautiously lest the enemy regroup and counter-attack: he did not want his men too dispersed to re-assume their battle formation. Des Barres and Marly's pursuit was more rapid, and southern casualties all the higher.

But the fighting was not yet over. Back at Muret, Toulousain forces were pressing to break into the town; if that were to be lost, the victory on the battlefield would have been a dramatic but hollow one. The besiegers were confident, not knowing at this stage the outcome of the battle. Bishop Fulkes of Toulouse tried to reason with his fellow citizens, sending out a priest to urge them to lay down their arms. Their response was to knock the messenger about with their spears. They soon rued their actions. They did not realise who had won the clash on the plain until the crusaders returned to Muret bearing the standards of the Aragonese and southern forces. The crusading army now turned its attention on them.

Montfort's cavalry, possibly assisted by the garrison infantry, chased down the Toulousains. The latter abandoned their fortified camp and rushed to their barges on the River Garonne. Those who could thus made their escape; but many did not. Most who failed to get away on a barge were either cut down or drowned in the river. After long years of dangerous campaigning and grievous losses, the crusaders were in no mood to show mercy. William the Breton says that they did not stop to loot the camp (that came later) or take prisoners; instead, they focused on 'reddening their swords with blows, taking the lives of the vanquished and shedding their blood'. The Anonymous reports that Sir Dalmals of Creixell, part of King Peter's intimate inner circle of advisors, jumped into the River Louge, shouting, 'God help us! Great injury has been done to us, for the good King of Aragon is dead and defeated and so are many other lords, all defeated and killed. No one has ever suffered such a loss!'

Chronicles misleadingly claim that some 15–17,000 southerners were killed – far more than the total of combatants on both sides. On crusader casualties, William of Puylaurens claims that not 'even one man on the Church side fell in battle'. Roger of Wendover repeats the evaluation given by the prelates present in a letter disseminated across Europe: 'a correct account of the number slain cannot be given by any means; but of the crusaders only one knight and a few sergeants fell.'[133] Guillaume de Nangis is more specific, reporting only eight fatalities on the French side. It was clearly a complete rout. With total victory assured, and their sword arms exhausted, the northerners took to gathering up prisoners and plunder, which Montfort shared out among his men. Many of the captured were ransomed; others were to die in prison. The *Chronicle* reports that 'it was pitiful to see and hear the laments of the people of Toulouse as they wept for their dead; indeed, there was hardly a single house that did not have someone dead to mourn, or a prisoner they believed to be dead'. News of the battle was to spread swiftly beyond Aragon and Languedoc throughout Europe, the Anonymous claiming that 'news of this disaster echoed round the world'. As the crusaders made their way to church to give thanks to God for their victory, the naked body of King Peter, stripped of armour and anything of either monetary or gruesome souvenir value, was retrieved by the Knights Hospitaller and prepared for burial.

Montfort's decisive action at Muret once again shows him as the embodiment of military command. His decision to engage the enemy at Muret has sometimes been considered unnecessarily perilous and risky, vindicated only by its improbable success. Significantly outnumbered, and, in the King of Aragon, facing his most experienced, powerful and successful opponent yet, the seemingly sensible option would have been to hold up behind the walls of Muret, the benefits of defence hopefully negating the enemy's numbers. Although the problems of provisions would weigh heavily on the crusaders – remember William of Breton's maxim 'famine conquers all' – the Aragonese and Toulousain forces would also have supply problems, especially with such a large army to feed. Disease would threaten those outside the walls as much as those inside them. The greatest clear advantage for Montfort was the potential for the southern alliance to fracture: the Occitanian counts had other affairs to attend to; the militia was away from its families and work; and Peter had a kingdom to run. The last factor was the most important: without the king, the southerners would have been extremely hesitant to face Montfort in open battle. The danger for them was that Peter would return home to attend to his concerns there (especially the *Reconquista*) as he had done before. It was his involvement in the great victory at Las Navas de Tolosa the previous year that freed him to make a full-scale intervention in Languedoc, but the full implications of this triumph were still unclear. The Almohad advance north had been decisively halted, but the temporary alliance of Navarre, Castile, Portugal and Aragon that had achieved the victory was a rare moment of temporary unity.

Without the benefit of hindsight, was Montfort's decision to force battle indeed a rash one? No. It made good sense on a number of levels. For a start, it was neither a hasty nor an idiosyncratic choice: the sources attest time and again to Montfort consulting with his commanders in a war council before taking any course of action and even altering his position because of their reasoning. The plan was a joint one, made by leading knights with impressive military experience. All were acutely aware of the gamble, but the consequences of a lengthy siege seemed to present the greater risk. Manpower was a perennial problem for Montfort; as forty-dayers completed their service and departed, he may have been in danger of becoming even more outnumbered. This problem was made all the more acute by Pope Innocent's focus on a new crusade to the Middle East, which would deplete the pool of potential recruits in Languedoc even further.

Two reasons dominated Montfort's thinking. The first was purely tactical. The northerners had a proven advantage on the battlefield, even when outnumbered: the shock charge of their heavy cavalry. This was a formidably effective tactic. The combined mass and momentum of experienced armoured knights and trained warhorses, packed tight in disciplined serried ranks and crashing into the enemy lines, constituted an overwhelming force, as the French had demonstrated at Castelnaudary.

We have seen how the charge of des Barres and Marly penetrated deep into the enemy ranks at Muret. This advantage of discipline and training was admitted by the future James I of Aragon (at this time a hostage under Montfort's roof and later an outstanding general), who explained his father's defeat at Muret thus: 'Those on the king's side knew neither how to place order in the lines nor how to move in formation, and each noble fought for himself, and broke with the rules of arms. And because of their disorder ... the battle had to be lost.'[134] Another factor was that Peter's army was not drawn up to its full extent: Count Nunó Sanchez and Viscount William de Montcada had not yet arrived at Muret and sent word to the king that he should wait for their arrival before engaging in battle (advice that was ignored). Perhaps Montfort's scouts and spies knew this, further persuading the crusaders to strike before their enemy's numbers increased even further.

The second reason was strategic and concerned the all-important phenomenon of momentum. Repeatedly Montfort had seen his great gains swept away, only to have to painfully win them back again. Delay at Muret would only weaken his precarious hold of Languedoc: it would reveal the weakness of his overall position as he had to concentrate his forces near Toulouse. Elsewhere throughout the south those hostile to French rule, encouraged by Montfort's enforced absence and by the powerful alliance now ranged against him, would, as they had so often done in the past, seize the opportunity to retake control of their castra. Like dominoes, when one fell the others would follow in swift succession. Montfort knew that behind him many who resented the northern invasion were waiting and willing to see him tied down and defeated at Muret. As noted above, William of Puylaurens put his finger on the danger when judging that events at Muret could result in the whole territory rising against Montfort and joining the other side. Delay risked losing all.

Peter's decision to join in battle mirrored Montfort's. He wanted to strike while he had the advantage of numbers and while he had such a large army mustered and ready for combat; he did not want to postpone the engagement lest his force dissipate during a siege. Besides, when the French attacked, the Aragonese and southern forces had little choice but to defend themselves; the only alternative was to scramble back into their encampment on the heights, which would have been a humiliating and unconscionable decision, and one that would have given a massive morale boost to the French. A Spanish historian has suggested that Peter ignored any counsel not to fight on the day because a victorious battle would bolster his reputation beyond dispute: having defeated the Muslims at Las Navas de Tolosa, he was already clearly a Catholic hero, and he wanted to capitalise further on this. Defeating Montfort at Muret would demonstrate to the papacy and all of Christendom that God was indubitably on his side against the French, just as He was against the Almohads. With such a divine seal of approval, Peter's ambitions for a Catalan–Occitanian empire could become a reality. For, again, we need to see the conflict itself in a territorial rather than a religious light. The stakes were huge: for Peter, it meant massively extending his influence and proto-imperial reach; for the crusaders, it meant the chance to consolidate their conquest of Languedoc.

Both sides were fully aware of the capricious fortune of battle. Count Raymond's defensive policy was not timid or cowardly as Michael of Luesia, now lying dead on the battlefield, had declared; rather, it was the standard strategy of battle avoidance to which commanders adhered as a general practice. Once contact had been made with the enemy ranks, little control was left to the commander. In the confusion of battle, trust had to be placed in the battalion commanders and their tactical units and lieutenants. Banners, heraldic devices and surcoats helped to identify individuals, but often little could be done to alter what was already in progress by those in the thick of the *mêlée*. Hence the need for tactical reserves, as Montfort showed at Muret, from where the commander could see the bigger picture of the engagement and deploy the reserve where it was most needed.

A commander might wish to avoid the danger of being killed or captured in battle – hence Peter's disguise. Harold Godwinson, Richard III and Peter of Aragon all met their end in combat, and many others, such as Henry V and Philip II of France, had close calls. Henry VI, Edward IV and King Stephen were just a few of the English monarchs captured on the battlefield; the French suffered this indignity, too, with Louis IX, John II and Francis I all seized in battle. In the latter stages of the Hundred Years War, French kings ordered their forces to avoid battlefield engagements with the English; the English, on the other hand, especially under Edward III, actively sought combat, as they were likely to be victorious. But for all their battlefield defeats, the French still won the war, as sieges and campaigns proved more decisive over the long run.

But avoidance was usually preferred because all could be lost on one throw of the dice: William of Poitiers claims that in 1066 Duke William of Normandy conquered England in a day because of Hastings; Richard III lost the crown at Bosworth in 1485; and the decimation of crusading manpower at the Horns of Hattin in 1187 decided the fate of the kingdom of Jerusalem. When a commander actively sought battle, he usually did so because the situation was such that it offered better prospects than avoidance, as proved to be the case at Castelnaudary and Muret. These were the exceptions in the Albigensian Crusade; like the vast majority of other medieval conflicts, the long grind of campaigns and sieges constituted the reality of combat more than the explosive drama of a brief battle.

Two major elements of battle are missing from the main accounts of Muret: footsoldiers and archers. We are familiar with the notion of effective infantry and archers from the great English victories of the Hundred Years War: Crécy, Poitiers, Agincourt. From this has arisen a myth of the late medieval military revolution: roughly stated, prior to this, cavalry dominated the battlefield, the other troops offering little more than ancillary support. Muret might seem to support this inaccurate view. But here Montfort not only needed his infantry to defend the town; he also needed to move quickly across the plain to fall on the enemy with as much surprise as possible. There would have been infantry pikemen in the southerner ranks, lined up as a barrier against charging cavalry. Such a disposition could be remarkably effective long before the Hundred Years War. At Gisors in 1188, English infantry beat off two French cavalry charges: the French 'launched into the press'; the infantry stood firm and 'did not evade this onslaught' as they 'received them with their pikes'.[135]

Archers and crossbowmen were also normally present. Field armies were commonly recruited from garrisons, as the Albigensian Crusade shows. The largest component of a garrison was its contingent of crossbowmen and archers, whose barrage of missiles was crucial to any defence. These men were then fed into a campaigning army. Arrows and crossbow bolts were the greatest cause of combat fatalities so their skilled operators were highly prized. Armies on the march would have their vanguards and rearguards protected by archers and crossbowmen to hold off enemy attacks on the column. A near contemporary illustration of the battle of Bouvines in 1214 actually depicts mounted crossbowmen in action. Archers can also be seen on the Bayeux Tapestry's portrayal of Hastings; here as elsewhere, archers were used to break up enemy formations and thin their ranks, especially against oncoming cavalry. At the encounter at Bourgtheroulde in 1124, forty mounted archers alighted from their horses and felled enemy knights with a barrage of arrows. Robert of Torigny reports that they directed their arrows against the knights' right side, as the left was protected by their large kite shields. The predisposition of contemporary writers to praise their lords and patrons often results in battles being represented as a series of individual duels between the great protagonists (hence William the Breton's poetic and imagined version of Montfort and Peter in face to face combat at Muret), but infantry and archers are nonetheless frequently mentioned as being participants. It is likely that the crusaders at Muret had to charge their way through enemy arrows and crossbow bolts, but the lack of heavy casualties suggests that any barrage would have been a light one. The speed of the cavalry charge (archers were ineffective once contact had been made), combined with the fact that many of the infantry soldiers and archers were besieging the town, may well have played to Montfort's advantage, and may even have reinforced his decision to launch the cavalry attack.

With King Peter of Aragon killed on the field of battle, Muret claimed the highest-ranking combat casualty of the entire Albigensian Crusade. The lauded hero of Las Navas de Tolosa and the southerners' greatest military asset had been dispatched in one telling blow. God had not favoured him again as he had hoped. Instead, once more, He blessed the pious, brutal Montfort and rewarded the Frenchman's audacity. The athlete of Christ had won one of the most impressive victories of the Middle Ages. But the war went on.

6

1214–17: 'We Shall Carry Death Across Your Land'

The Aftermath of Muret

Following the crusaders' stunning victory at Muret, the war resumed its normal pattern of post-defeat capitulations, with some previously defiant southern towns and castra such as Rabastens now being abandoned to the French. Despite some small-scale reinforcements from the north under Bishop Ralph of Arras, Montfort still had too few men to capitalise on his battlefield triumph for many of his troops had dispersed following Muret; they remained too thinly spread across his insecure lands of conquest. Pope Innocent's withholding of a crusading indulgence to those from outside the region severely restricted the potential for large groups of reinforcements for the time being.

Despite its significant losses in lives and prisoners at Muret, the city of Toulouse remained far too strong for Montfort to take, full as it still was of refugees and soldiers from across the county and beyond; he was not about to repeat the horrendous mistake of 1211 when a feeble, ill-thought-out attempt had been made on the city. Instead, the ecclesiastical negotiators were sent. Agreement was reached whereby the Toulousains, under advice from their count, swore their loyalty to Montfort. At first 200 hostages were demanded; then sixty. In a sign of how far Montfort still had to go to assert practical rather than verbal authority, none was ever handed over. Count Raymond himself made plans to plead his case in Rome again and spent time in England at the end of the year at the court of King John, his erstwhile brother-in-law, seeking his support and making plans. This was an intelligent move as John's recent rapprochement with Innocent III – which included the English monarch's mortifying submission of his kingdom as a fiefdom of Rome – had transformed him from papal pariah to papal pin-up boy. Raymond paid homage to John for Toulouse, for which he received 10,000 marks. The wily John was not seriously out of pocket, however: he simply penalised the Cistercians for their support of the crusaders, receiving 10,000 livres from them.

In October, Montfort made a raid into the Count of Foix's territory, menacing the town as he had done earlier in the crusade; this time he burnt some of the suburbs on top of widespread devastation in the region. Montfort must have taken pleasure in this, as Count Raymond Roger, who had escaped Muret with the Count of Toulouse and the other leading southerners, was a hardened and implacable foe of the crusader. As autumn progressed, Montfort led his force eastwards to Béziers to deter southern attacks on the supply route to Muret and the west. Moving north-east into the Rhône as far as Valence, this show of force subdued Pons de Montlaur and Adhémar de Poitiers. But there was some humiliation for Montfort: Narbonne and Montpellier refused him entry into their towns, compelling his men to sleep under the stars. Although towns frequently prohibited armies from entering for reasons of social order, this was still felt as a slight by the victor of Muret. By the time he reached Nîmes and was met with the same response, the exasperated Montfort began making threats; only then was he admitted. By November the Bishop of Arras had returned north with his men. Montfort stayed in the region until February, preoccupied with important dynastic matters: the marriage arrangement between his son Amaury and Béatrice, niece of the extremely powerful Duke of Burgundy, a match facilitated by Montfort's elevated status following Muret. The battle had not ended the war but had certainly gone a long way to consolidate his position. Now 50 years of age, his position in Languedoc strengthening by the day, Montfort must have felt some considerable satisfaction at the end of 1213.

Mercenaries, Messengers and Murder

Count Raymond's appeals to Rome had not gone unheeded. Innocent, looking eastwards for new crusades and suspicious of the motivations of

French crusaders and clerics in Languedoc, was not prepared to give free rein to Montfort. Arnald Almaric, Archbishop of Narbonne, was no longer to be the leading churchman of the crusade; in his stead Innocent sent Peter of Benevento, a cardinal and canon lawyer, as the chief papal legate. Crucially, Peter, the sixth legate appointed since the start of the crusade, was Italian; Innocent did not want him to become another apologist and supporter of Montfort like all the others. He arrived in the new year with specific, unequivocal instructions from his master which permitted little room for improvisation, restoring the legal position of all sides to the point immediately before the battle of Muret. Montfort's quest for the viscounty of Nîmes was put on hold pending an inquiry; Gaston de Béarn, a Gascon noble and vassal of Aragon, and counts Raymond Roger of Foix and Bernard of Comminges (both of whom had escaped at Muret) were to be reconciled with the Church, as were the citizens of Toulouse; Peter's son, James, was to be released to the new legate. In April the counts were to be joined by Raymond of Toulouse and representatives of his city in Narbonne to fully repair their breach with the Church, each offering a castle (the Château Narbonnais in Toulouse, Salies de Salat and Foix itself) as security. All rejected heresy and heretics in any form and promised not to employ mercenaries. The counts and their lands thus came under the protection of the papacy. All matters were to be conclusively resolved at the pope's planned great council in 1215. These instructions were communicated in the third week of January 1214; for many, they seemed to indicate that the war was effectively over: there were to be no more territorial conquests, only continued extirpation of heresy.

To read the Anonymous and William of Puylaurens, this might well have seemed to be the case for the time being: both move quickly on to 1215 and report no significant military activity until 1216. However, Peter of Vaux de Cernay's more detailed account records Aragonese activity and murder. In February, partly simply to harass the crusaders, but more to apply pressure for the release of their new king, James I, Aragonese mercenaries raided deep into Montfort's territory as far as Béziers 'and did whatever harm was in their power'.[136] Montfort had to counter this threat and enter Toulouse, where, in reprisal and attempting to reassert his authority, he demolished a number of castles. But the episode had shown how unstable the region was and illustrated the dangers of a border with a foe who remained active, for this was frontier territory. Such raids against the crusaders also encouraged local *faidits* and southerner lords to renounce their allegiance to Montfort. Probing attacks tested the resolve of the crusaders (hence the need for Montfort to respond forcefully) while trying to build an impetus of resistance. The added pressure of the raids, combined with Pope Innocent's instructions, led to the release of the 6-year-old king in April, James recalling that the pope 'Sent such forceful letters and such forceful envoys to count Simon that he had to agree to return us to our people. And so, the Franks took us as far as Narbonne, where a great part of the nobles and citizens of Catalonia came to receive us.'[137] The international aspect of the conflict at this time was also underlined by King John's arrival with an army at La Rochelle on the Atlantic coast of France in mid-February; he was eager to win back his lands from the French king, who, in turn, was keeping an eye on Montfort's expansionism in the south – territory for which he claimed ultimate overlordship. For the moment, Philip Augustus could do little to restrict John's support for Count Raymond – the maxim that 'my enemy's enemy is too strong' – but the time was soon to come when the French crown became militarily involved in Languedoc.

For the moment, Montfort was put on edge by John's forces heading southwards into the Agenais. The fear was that following Count Raymond's stay in England, the Angevin king was about to become actively involved in military support of Toulouse. Towns and castles that had sworn allegiance to Montfort now paid homage instead to King John. The political implications were serious, as Raymond in turn held his lands from John. It is also highly probable that John sent messengers and money to Montpellier and Narbonne to encourage resistance there. Montfort would soon have to campaign in the Agenais to counter the growing threat.

The bitter, personalised nature of the conflict was reflected by a violent episode in February. Baldwin of Toulouse, Count Raymond's estranged brother who had gone over to Montfort's side in 1211 and since served him loyally, was in western Quercy, part of the vast expanse of lands he had received from Montfort. On 17 February he was spending the night in his castle of Lolmie, some 5 miles south of his newly possessed town of Montcuq. With him amongst his men were William de Contres, who had defended the siege engines from attack in Carcassonne in 1210 and was a much-valued captain of Montfort's, and a northern sergeant named Simon. The garrison here, technically Baldwin's vassals, planned to betray him to the enemy. Bertrand de Montenard, Lolmie's castellan, surreptitiously locked Baldwin in his chamber as he slept. He sent word to the knights and mercenaries at the nearby southerner castle of Montenard, and also to Ratier of Castelnau, who had participated in the Quercy crusade of 1209 and sworn allegiance to Montfort in 1212, that they should come to Lolmie, where Baldwin would be handed over to them. They did not hesitate.

As this force made its way to Lolmie, Bertrand 'secretly summoned the townspeople and carefully ascertained from each of them how many of the count's entourage were quartered with them' in their houses. Ensuring he had twice as many as Baldwin's men, he positioned the southerners at the entrances, then lit torches and stormed the houses where Baldwin's men slept. Some of the French managed to escape in the confusion of the night; among these fortunate ones seems to have been William de Contres. Others were captured and some killed. One sought refuge in the church, where he received a promise of safety; he, too, was killed. Baldwin was seized 'asleep, unarmed and quite naked' and dragged off to Montcuq, where 'the townsfolk, thoroughly evil men, welcomed the mercenaries who were bringing their lord as a captive' according to Peter of Vaux de Cernay.[138]

Here a small French garrison guarded the keep of the castrum. The mercenaries demanded that Baldwin order them to surrender; instead, he defiantly 'forbade them to do so, even if they were to see him hanging from a gibbet'. He told them to resist until Montfort arrived with help. He was then locked up for the next two days without food and water; he was also denied spiritual sustenance as he was not permitted to take the Eucharist wafer. He was in a desperate situation but was perhaps sustained by the thought of his eventual ransoming. The mercenaries wanted one of their number imprisoned in the keep to be released, offering the garrison safety and freedom. The French soldiers grasped at this straw, knowing that Montfort was by now a long way off in Provence and lower Languedoc. They surrendered. They were all hung.

Baldwin was taken to Montauban and held in chains. Here, a few days later, he came face to face with his brother, Count Raymond of Toulouse, recently returned from England. With Raymond were the Count of Foix, his son Roger Bernard plus an Aragonese knight, Bernard de Portella. None was in the mood for mercy; as William of Puylaurens explains, Baldwin was 'condemned to death by hanging, to avenge the King of Aragon'.[139] Peter of Vaux de Cernay lamented: 'Who will ever be able to read or hear of what followed without tears?' Cold-heartedly refused confession according to Peter (but not William of Puylaurens), Baldwin was led out to a walnut tree where Raymond Roger, his son and Bernard put the noose around his neck and hung him. For the southerners it was an execution, and applauded as such by some, including the troubadour Peire Cardenal; for the crusaders and most others, it was murder. For all, it was another manifestation of terror as a weapon and a warning that rank did not guarantee the normal safeguards of chivalric security.

'The count damaged his reputation greatly by this fratricide,' wrote William of Puylaurens. 'He could have at least spared his brother death by hanging; there were other less ignominious means of executing him that he could have used, to avoid doing him this injury.'[140] Raymond had wished to remove his brother as a focus for a comital alternative in Toulouse more than he wished to preserve his name. But for the Count of Foix, his personal involvement in the actual stringing up of Baldwin cemented a notorious reputation without hope of rehabilitation. The *History* condemns the part played by Roger Raymond and his son, Bernard Roger, 'fully his father's equal in villainy' and inheritor of his father's dark traits.

Pro-crusading chronicles habitually condemned Count Raymond of Toulouse as the leader of the southerners, but the condemnation was not always universal or persistent. The one character they considered completely irredeemable and on whom unreserved opprobrium was always heaped was Count Raymond Roger of Foix. One can find features in this hardened warrior that one might respect, such as bravery and a bloody-minded tenacity, but he was a brutal, ruthless man, short on mercy and possibly long on sadistic cruelty. Peter of Vaux de Cernay's utter contempt for the Count of Toulouse cannot be matched by his horror of the godless Count of Foix, the 'monstrous persecutor' of the Church whose 'many exceedingly barbarous actions' rendered him God's 'most monstrous enemy', not least for his ransacking of monasteries and churches and his complete disdain for men of the cloth. In his dispute with the abbey of Pamiers, the count had the abbot and canons of the town locked up for three days without food and water or facilities for daily functions, before releasing them in only their undergarments with strict prohibitions against anyone helping them; elsewhere, besieged monks were forced to drink their own urine; and Peter repeatedly accuses him of acts of blasphemy, especially against the crucifix. The chronicler expends several pages denouncing the actions of the count against holy

Mother Church, rounding off with: 'This most cruel dog committed many other crimes ... His wickedness exceeded all bounds ... He excelled all others in cruelty ... The worst of all animals, a man no longer'.[141] The count was even more ferocious when it came to resisting the northern crusaders. He was always to the fore when it came to harsh treatment of enemy prisoners, as evidenced by his actions at the massacre of Montgey. He schooled his son in ruthlessness, Roger Bernard skewering a priest in the head with a lance when the latter had taken refuge in the church at Montgey to escape the slaughter of prisoners. No doubt Peter of Vaux de Cernay exaggerated some of the count's excesses, but Raymond Roger was a cold, pitiless warrior who struck justifiable fear into the crusading forces. His direct role in the hanging of Baldwin only served to justify his reputation as the *bête noire* of the French who threatened his brutal rule.

Meanwhile, Montfort once again found himself in mortal danger. The Narbonnais and their lord, Aimeric – always the last and most reluctant to offer any assistance to the crusaders – broke faith with the viscount and reinforced themselves with Aragonese and Catalan mercenaries in March, led by leading noblemen and ecclesiastics. These troops 'went to war against the French and the lands held by them'.[142] The mercenaries' aim, as mentioned above, was the release of their young king. Alberic of Trois Fontaines reports that at this point Montfort was reinforced by 200 crusaders (but, the crusade having been called off, these were in effect reinforcements), which allowed him to make his countermeasures against the incursions with large-scale raiding of Aimeric's territory. Outside the gates of Narbonne, he drew up his forces in three lines. His opponents, defending higher ground, repulsed his attack. Montfort's saddle was broken in the combat and he was unhorsed. As the enemy converged on him, his own tactical reserve broke through and drove them off, and the viscount was saved.

In April Montfort was back in the Agenais. King John had progressed as far as La Réole to receive homage for at least forty-three places before moving northwards once again, where his main interest lay. His recent itinerary was primarily concerned with securing his southern flank before his great campaign against Philip Augustus. But the transferral of allegiance to John and Raymond was a real concern. Thus Moissac, captured at some cost by the crusaders in 1212, went over to Raymond in late March, the northern garrison retreating to the castle. Raymond and a large force of mercenaries besieged them for three weeks, withdrawing when they learned of Montfort's approach. Montfort wished to mark his presence in the area and so marched far into the north-west to La Mas d'Agenais, a castrum some 30 miles west of Penne, which had been part of John's successful haul. Montfort was near here on 13 April and, perhaps rashly, attempted to take the place. First he had to contest a crossing of the Garonne against a superior flotilla sent from King John's town of La Réole; having achieved this, he arrived before La Mas. He besieged the castrum but, without any siege machinery and a long way from safe territory, he had to abandon the enterprise after only three days.

From here Montfort returned to Narbonne, where the legate Peter of Benevento had convened the major council discussed at the opening of this chapter. With James of Aragon returned home, the leading Occitanian counts and Toulouse reconciled with the Church from mid to late April. His work accomplished with astonishing success – five years of active and massively destructive campaigning had been brought to an end – the legate moved on to Aragon to help oversee the new king's succession there. Pope Innocent rejoiced that his will had been imposed and his great council of 1215 would finally settle the situation in Languedoc once and for all. But it was all just words. The papacy's crusade was over; Montfort's personal crusade was to continue. This pious, devout man simply chose to ignore God's representative on Earth. Within days he was leading the largest northern army since 1209 into action.

Montfort's War: Casseneuil and the West – Summer to Winter 1214

Montfort would keep up the pretence that he was waging war against heretics, but from May 1214 there was neither papal support nor, technically, any crusade at all. What was at stake now was not the protection of the Church from heresy, but the protection, consolidation and then expansion of Montfort's empire in the south of France. The invasion had, to all intent and purposes, long since ceased to be about religion, but now not even the veneer of that justification remained. There could no longer be any claim that the invasion and occupation was about anything other than naked ambition and land. The ferocity of the fighting did not abate in any way. And to add to the bitter mix, Montfort was out for revenge.

By the beginning of May, a massive army from the north had mustered at Montpellier – 100,000 cavalry and infantry claims Peter of Vaux de Cernay with typical hyperbole. No doubt he wished to inflate the figure as high as possible because he and his uncle Guy, Bishop of Carcassonne, had travelled north on what was palpably a hugely effective recruitment drive. Among others promoting the crusade was the famous preacher Jacques de Vitry and the veteran crusader Archdeacon William of Paris. Did these men knowingly preach a crusade even though Pope Innocent III had ended it? It is possible that Rome's instructions had not reached them, but highly unlikely as it was all too well known in Languedoc, so must have been communicated to the north, not least by the southerner counts. More telling is that Robert of Courçon, the papal legate in France, was just as involved in the crusade's preaching, and he would have been one of the first to know. At best, news reached them after the recruitment process had begun, and, seeing its early success, they simply chose to continue with it.

Montfort, then, had the largest crusading force at his disposal since 1209. (We shall continue to call them crusaders for the sake of continuity, though technically they were not pilgrims but reinforcements.) With this force were leading knights such as Viscount Geoffrey of Châteaudun. On 3 May Montfort went to meet them at Thibéry, 11 miles to the north of Béziers, where Bernard Aton granted the viscounties of Nîmes and Agde to him. Passing through Carcassonne, Montfort appointed his brother Guy and the Bishop of Carcassonne to lead most of this large force to the north-west of his territory (some would have been left behind to secure the recently troubled area), where he planned to take his revenge on Baldwin of Toulouse's killers. First in his sights was Ratier de Castelnau and his lands in Quercy; these were ravaged along with his home town. While Montfort himself stayed in the east for a few weeks to oversee the marriage of his son Amaury to Béatrice in Carcassonne on 4 June, the crusading army penetrated deep into Quercy; there was no resistance – most had fled this huge army – until they arrived at Morlhorn. This was taken within a day and destroyed. The northerners' policy was to demolish all the smaller forts and garrison the stronger ones; this helped to remove potential sites of resistance and any subsequent costly and time-consuming suppression, while securing for themselves places that could not be easily taken and from where the surrounding area could be controlled. At Morlhorn they found seven heretics of the Waldensian sect, rarely mentioned in the crusades. They 'confessed their unbelief freely and fully' to the legate Robert Courçon and so 'the crusaders seized them and burnt them with great rejoicing'.[143] The opportunity for the 'crusaders' to reaffirm their heresy-battling credentials with a large bonfire was too good a propaganda opportunity to miss.

Montfort caught up with this force by 12 June at Mondenard, the lord of which was his intransigent enemy, Bernard, the man who organised the capture of Baldwin of Toulouse. The place was destroyed, as were others that followed. Montfort's presence was needed as the crusading contingent that had arrived in May had served their forty days and most had now returned home. At Marmande, the deserted castle strategy of the southerners stopped. Here in the Agenais, at the westernmost point of Count Raymond's lands, Montfort came face to face with an English garrison under Geoffrey de Neville. The inhabitants of the castrum fled after a brief and very token resistance, while the English soldiers took to the keep before soon surrendering. While the castrum was pillaged, it was not destroyed and the English were allowed to leave unharmed. Montfort had marked his determination to see off all newcomers, but he did not wish to antagonise the unstable King John by any excessive actions and risk the monarch's great power being directed into Languedoc.

The main setpiece of the western campaign was the siege of Casseneuil from 28 June to 18 August. Lying about 15 miles north of Agen, it was an important satellite fort of the region's principal town. Such satellite forts needed to be taken under control not only to guard against their potential to become rallying points of resistance, but because they protected Agen itself. This lay downriver on the Garonne from Montauban and Toulouse, two powerful southern centres, and from there this central route followed through to Carcassonne, Béziers and the Mediterranean. Casseneuil itself lay at the confluence of the River Lot and two of its tributaries that provided a barrier on three sides; further considerable protection was afforded by a wide moat on its south-eastern land approach.

At the start of the whole crusade in 1209, the Agenais expedition had burnt the first heretics here. This time the violence was to be on an altogether larger scale. This was the third time the town had renounced the teachings of the Church, says Peter, even though its lord, Hugh de Revignan, was brother to the Bishop of Agen. As the last remaining major castrum of resistance in the area, it held a concentration of southerners,

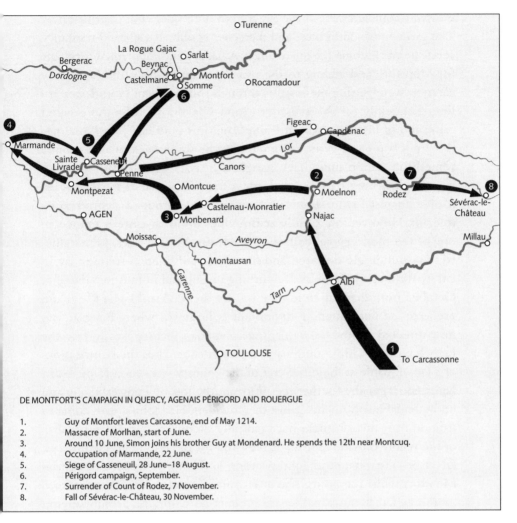

DE MONTFORT'S CAMPAIGN IN QUERCY, AGENAIS PÉRIGORD AND ROUERGUE

1. Guy of Montfort leaves Carcassone, end of May 1214.
2. Massacre of Morlhan, start of June.
3. Around 10 June, Simon joins his brother Guy at Mondenard. He spends the 12th near Montcuq.
4. Occupation of Marmande, 22 June.
5. Siege of Casseneuil, 28 June–18 August.
6. Périgord campaign, September.
7. Surrender of Count of Rodez, 7 November.
8. Fall of Sévérac-le-Château, 30 November.

Montfort's north-western campaign, 1214.

including some of those involved in the death of Baldwin of Toulouse. This added a personal element to the siege.

Montfort at first set his siege camp on the heights to the north-west of the town; he had insufficient men to invest the place completely. When reinforcements arrived, he moved to the plain to the town's south-east, leaving his son Amaury and Bishop Guy of Carcassonne (who was by now a papal legate) on the heights. They built siege artillery and began an incessant bombardment of the town from both sides with their petraries. The garrison of southerners and mercenaries offered a spirited resistance, at one point climbing the hill to attack Amaury's encampment. Worryingly for Montfort, and adding to the usual time pressures of besiegers, the garrison were getting messengers through to King John in mid-western France. Luckily for the crusaders, John was absorbed by the greatest campaign of his reign against Philip Augustus until late July. Nonetheless, John was close by in Périgueux by the third week of that month, something which must have weighed heavily on Montfort's mind. The English king had just suffered a major reversal at La Roche au Moine against Prince Louis of France, and was not of a mind to be tolerant. However, on 27 July at Bouvines in north-eastern France, in one of the most critical battles of the entire Middle Ages, John's allies were resoundingly defeated and his whole continental strategy lay in tatters. Although John delayed returning to England from Aquitaine until October, from that day in July he was on the road to Magna Carta and preoccupied with quelling discontent at home, to where his gaze was now directed. Conversely, this huge Capetian victory was to free the French crown to look southwards to Languedoc. Thus the ramifications of a far-off battle at the other end of the country were soon to be felt in Languedoc. For the southerners, it meant the loss of a powerful ally and his potential involvement against the crusaders. Had John's plans come to fruition in France, it might have radically altered the subsequent course of the whole crusade; instead, it removed for the crusaders a major risk factor of substantial hostile intervention in the north-western territories Montfort wished to pacify. The interconnection of events was reinforced by the fact that the papal legate Robert de Courçon, accompanying Montfort at this stage, had to leave the siege to arrange a six-year truce between John and Philip Augustus.

The crusaders continued to press the castrum, the artillery weakening several points in the wall. Montfort called his engineers to him to work out how to reach the town's walls. A pontoon bridge was devised (the defenders, as was usual in such cases, had destroyed the bridge before the enemy's arrival) and built on large casks. This major construction was drawn up the very wide moat (a width of some 80ft has been calculated) and lowered in. However, because the water level of the moat was considerably lower than its bank, the bridge's entry was too steep and it sank like a stone: 'So all our work on the bridge came to nothing in a single moment.'[144]

The engineers and carpenters then turned their efforts to the construction of a conventional bridge, completed a few days later. This was to be used in conjunction with some small boats built to transfer men across at the same time: a daunting prospect for the attackers, exposed to a slow crossing and highly vulnerable to being dragged beneath the surface by their armour. But the bombardment of enemy petraries and another miscalculation by the engineers – the bridge was too short to cross the span – meant that this attempt also failed.

The labour and resources put into these efforts to deal with water defences underlines the huge engineering efforts involved on such occasions. A decade earlier, at the siege of Château Gaillard on the Seine north of Paris, the river defences, which included a stockade, saw major engineering operations on both sides. Here, an English flotilla attacked the French pontoon bridge across the Seine; the bridge, constructed from flat-bottomed barges, was so substantial it had two towers erected on it for protection. Its defence was under the command of Simon de Montfort, which may have been what prompted the idea at Casseneuil. Under a deadly barrage of arrows, crossbow bolts, slingshots, timber, stones and boiling pitch and tar, the English reached the bridge and began hacking away at the cables and stakes that held the boats of the bridge together. They were only turned back when a huge oak beam smashed down on top of two of the attacking craft. The flotilla turned about and tried to make good their escape, pursued by French boats.

Disheartened but not deterred, Montfort convened a third council with his engineers. This time they came up with a new idea. They built a massive siege tower, a belfry, comprising six storeys. The first, most substantial level had a flat roof, on top of which five further levels were manned with crossbowmen behind defences. To protect it from fire, men were positioned with 'copious quantities of water in large bowls' while its front was covered with oxhides. With the crossbowmen laying down covering 'fire', the tower was brought up to the moat. In its first level men brought up wood and earth to fill the moat to create a causeway. The garrison could see that this posed a real danger that needed neutralising. 'One night, the enemy filled a small boat with dry wood, salted meat, fat and other inflammable material, hoping to propel it against our engine and set it alight,' reports Peter.[145] But the boat never reached its target, crusader sergeants succeeding in burning it as it approached.

The tower's defences prevented, absorbed and deflected the worst of the barrage the defenders directed against it. As the moat was successfully filled and the tower drew up closer to the wall, however, it became more vulnerable. On Sunday 17 August (as discussed before, it is a myth that Sundays and Holy Days were exempt from fighting) the tower was so close that the garrison on the battlement and the soldiers at the top of the tower were at times within reach of each other's lances. Fire was the great hazard for the crusaders, but for the moment the water held in the belfry dowsed any flames that caught. Montfort, fearing that at any moment a fire would destroy the siege machine, ordered an all-out assault. Armoured to the teeth, knights and infantry entered the tower. The lowest front defensive wall was knocked down and removed so that they could rush out from the tower, run across the constructed causeway and attack the enemy's defences on the opposite bank. Overnight they established a precarious defensive position between the walls and the moat – the crossbowmen in the tower charged with the task of clearing the battlements above them – from where they destroyed some of the wooden barbican outworks erected by the southerners. In the meantime, Montfort's carpenters were busily constructing siege ladders for an attempt at escalade. As the pressure mounted, the following day the garrison mercenaries launched what at first appeared to be another sortie, but which was in fact a fully fledged breakout. In the heat of the combat and the priority of taking the town, they successfully broke through and escaped what was now the inevitable outcome. That night the crusaders stormed the castrum, torching it and putting all to the sword.

Casseneuil took Montfort seven and a half weeks of concentrated and determined effort to win. The importance of the victory on the far western edge of his area of interest owed less to practical regional strategic concerns than to the message it sent out. But of course, both were connected. By showing he was prepared to go to literally any length to quell rebellion he was hoping to discourage any future uprisings against his rule; it was a naked statement of power and intent that reinforced his great military resolve and ability. At this stage, with King John's intentions as yet unclear to him and the monarch still lingering in Aquitaine, Montfort needed to show that he was prepared to fight for what he claimed was his, even this far west.

Casseneuil was the largest operation of Montfort's western campaign. But the expedition was not yet over and typically the chief crusader did not rest on the laurels of victory, but immediately moved on to his next objective, intending to make the most of the momentum of this significant victory and to utilise forty-dayer pilgrims in his army before they departed for home. He led them nearly 40 miles north-east – further north than he had ever ventured before – into the Périgord region and John's territories on the border of Aquitaine. News of the crusaders' victory had already reached here as the castrum of Domme was left deserted; Montfort had its stone walls undermined and brought to the ground, thereby denying it to any enemy invading from the north and thus rendering any plans for such impracticable. Three miles away lay the castrum of Montfort, also deserted despite its formidable defences, which took the crusaders some days to demolish. Simon de Montfort understood that the investment of time in sieges such as Casseneuil, if successful, reaped dividends in the form of other strongholds discouraged from offering any resistance.

The lord of this place was Bernard de Cazenac, a knight friendly to Cathars and hence a monster to Peter of Vaux de Cernay, who accuses him and his Jezebel wife of all manner of atrocities:

> They attacked crusaders, they persecuted widows and the poor. They cut off limbs of the innocent; in a single Benedictine monastery, at Sarlat, our men found 150 men and women whose hands or feet had been amputated, or who had their eyes torn out, or suffered other mutilations inflicted by this tyrant or his wife. She indeed, utterly without pity, had the nipples of women of the poorer sort torn out, or their thumbs cut off so that they would be useless for any labour.[146]

If the story is true in general outline, no doubt the number is exaggerated. But these were unlikely to have been victims of the war, which Montfort had only now brought to the region; the nature of these mutilations may suggest that many of these individuals had been punished for criminal activity and the monastery was a centre that cared for them. Peter's vitriol against any harbourers of Cathars is not reflected by the anonymous author of the *Song*, a partisan supporter of the southerners, who four years later deems Bernard 'a glory', a man of 'staunch courage … fair-minded … renowned for good sense and generosity'.[147] These writers' differing judgements were probably informed by Bernard's important role fighting against the crusaders in the years to come.

Having destroyed Bernard's castrum, Montfort continued his progress along the Dordogne. He garrisoned the deserted fortress of Castelnaud and at Beynac offered its lord, Gaillard, a choice: restore all he had seized from the churches or see his castrum knocked down. He was granted a truce for a few days to make his decision. Gaillard decided to keep the booty – or was unable to return it – and his fortifications were destroyed. By mid-September the northern Agenais had been pacified. Having created and secured his buffer zone, Montfort then ordered all the fortifications of the Agenais to be demolished, thereby creating a demilitarised region. Notable at this time are the political rewards that came with the success of the campaign. The *History* records that by the autumn in Figeac, Montfort was permitted 'to sit in judgement in the king's stead on lawsuits and prosecutions involving the local inhabitants, since the king had appointed him as his representative in the area for many purposes'.[148] As Figeac was part of Count Raymond's lordship, this in essence meant that King Philip of France, previously hesitant about fully endorsing Montfort, was now recognising the viscount's legitimacy in Toulouse. Other of Raymond's manors also accrued to Montfort while he was here. It is very likely that in the crisis over the summer, when he was faced with the two-front threat from John and his imperial allies, Philip had hoped to counter the English king's envoys to the southerners and to encourage, even perhaps partly fund, Simon's activities on John's southern borders, to hinder him from his plans against France. An understanding may very well have developed at this time between Montfort and Philip, and now the crusader's prize was to have his status recognised by the King of France.

By the end of the first week of November Montfort had moved 30 miles south-east back in the direction of Carcassonne, stopping at Rodez. Here, Count Henry tried to argue that he held his lands by the will of the King of England, but eventually he acquiesced to Montfort's lordship. Twenty-five miles to the east lay a mercenary stronghold at the castrum Sévérac-le-Château, the crusaders' next target. A surprise dawn raid by Guy de Montfort occupied the lower suburb and forced the garrison back into the castle, which lay further up a hill. Simon arrived and lodged in the town while a petrary was constructed to bombard the town. A duel then began with the castrum's own stone thrower. Attacked so suddenly, the garrison had no time to prepare for the approach of winter and were soon low on supplies. After a few days they sued for peace. As at Rodez, the

Béziers seen from the Pont Vieux over the River Orb. The cathedral of St Nazaire, scene of a massacre, dominates the summit. (Robert Purves)

View from Béziers showing St Nazaire cathedral and the strength of the fortified site even with the city walls long since gone. The crusaders camped in the plain below. (Sam McGlynn)

The early thirteenth-century municipal seal of Béziers reproduced on the wall of St Madeleine church. Note the armour and caparison. Viscount Trencavel was murdered here in 1167. (Robert Purves)

St Madeleine church, Béziers. The scene of the first and greatest massacre of the Albigensian Crusade in 1209, the result of crusading no-quarter policy and the alleged command 'Kill them all! God will know his own!' (Robert Purves)

The interior of St Madeleine church. Chronicles reported the massacre of up to 7,500 citizens of Béziers here, who had been seeking sanctuary. Its maximum capacity is estimated to be 2,000 people; many may have been slaughtered outside the church. (Sam McGlynn)

Carcassonne, showing the Château Comtal and the defensive works leading to the waters of the River Aude. The crusaders besieged and took Carcassonne in 1209, from which time it remained their headquarters for the whole Albigensian Crusade. It was frequently threatened by the southerners. (Sam McGlynn)

The north walls of the city of Carcassonne, showing the D-shaped towers of the current inner wall, which comprised the main wall at the time of the crusade. (Robert Purves)

Port d'Aude of Carcassonne at night. (Robert Purves)

Saissac. This strong castle and town was put under the command of Bouchard de Marly, a trusted captain of Montfort. At the end of 1209, Marly and his men were caught in a bloody ambush and he was taken prisoner. (Sam McGlynn)

Minerve. The town was taken by the crusaders in 1210 after a dramatic siege. The bridge across the gorge was built later. (Robert Purves)

Minerve from the south. The defences included covered passageways to a well and the River Cesse here, the latter of which dried up in the summer of the siege. A concentrated artillery bombardment took its toll on the town. The new trebuchet siege machine may have been deployed here. (Robert Purves)

Three castles of the spectacular Lastours system showing, from left to right, Cabaret, Tour Régine and Surdespine. (The second of these was built after the crusade to strengthen the suppression of any possible further southerner insurgency.) Peter Roger, Lord of Cabaret, was for a while a leader of the southerner resistance; he held Bouchard de Marly captive in his castle under harsh conditions for sixteen months. (Sam McGlynn)

The view of Lastours from Cabaret, showing, from foreground to background, Tour Régine, Surdespine and Quertinheux. (Robert Purves)

View through a north door of Termes to the gorge. The epic siege here in 1210 witnessed assaults, sorties, bombardments and heroic actions. Montfort was lucky to survive the siege. (Robert Purves)

Termes is built solidly on top of mountain rock. (Robert Purves)

The wall tower of Lavaur. In 1211 the crusaders stormed the city and a massacre ensued. Knights were hung or had their throats cut; heretics were burned; and, in one of the crusade's most notorious incidents, the Lady of Lavaur was thrown into a well and crushed with stones. (Sam McGlynn)

St Martin Lalande on the edge of Lasbordes, scene of Montfort's first major battle in 1211. He had deliberately provoked the southerners into an engagement, but the battle was a risky affair and a very close-run thing. (Sam McGlynn)

St Dominic's house in Fanjeaux. Dominic founded the Order of Preachers (the Dominicans) to counter the Cathar heresy in Languedoc by learning and example. Montfort used the small town as military base. (Robert Purves)

Couvent des Jacobins, Toulouse. Despite being the epicentre of political and religious resistance, Toulouse retained its orthodox elements, its bishop supporting the White Brotherhood against the Cathar Black Brotherhood. The city was subjected to a series of sieges. (Robert Purves)

St Cecilia cathedral, Albi, from the west. The cathedral, purportedly the largest brick building in the world, was built after the crusade, but still plainly constructed with serious defensive measures in mind. (Robert Purves)

The interior of St Cecilia cathedral, displaying its original, unrestored ceiling. Although the Cathars were first known as Albigenses and the city as the capital of their heresy, Albi itself was spared direct military conflict. (Robert Purves)

The interior of the cathedral of Saints Justus and Pastor of Narbonne. Although the city was not known as a centre of heresy, its support for the crusade was often lukewarm and spilled over into hostility at the political encroachment of the northerners. (Robert Purves)

The monastery of St Martin du Canigou in the Pyrénées. Even some monasteries supported the southerners in their struggle against the northern Albigensian Crusade, emphasising politics over religion. (Robert Purves)

The castle of Foix, attacked by the northerners but not taken by force. Its count, Roger Bernard, had an infamous reputation as a cruel and implacable enemy of the crusaders, and was responsible for atrocities. (Sam McGlynn)

Gateway into Labécède, whose garrison was slaughtered by the crusaders in 1227. (Sam McGlynn)

Padern. Despite its strength, it was a satellite fortification for even more formidable southerner castles. (Sam McGlynn)

Roquefixade, with the Pyrénées in the distance. A southerner stronghold, the fires of the Cathar burnings at Montségur (about 30km north-west) could be seen from here. (Robert Purves)

Roquefixade, perched on top of a precipitous cliff and built into the rock, as is common with castles in this region. (Sam McGlynn)

Montségur from the west, showing its formidable position. The Cathars thought it impregnable, hence its name, which means 'safe mountain'. (Sam McGlynn)

Montségur castle from the south-west. Here the Cathars made their last stand; over 200 of them were taken out from the castle and burned. (Sam McGlynn)

The castle ruins of Montaillou, still a Cathar village in the early fourteenth century. Inquisition records from here reveal tales of sexual licentiousness, a predatory heretic priest and murder. (Robert Purves)

The castle of Peyrepertuse, 'Pierced rock', a hugely powerful and typically inaccessible fortress, it was part of the Sons of Carcassonne, the network of immensely powerful castles designed to protect the frontier with Aragón. The other Sons are Aguila, Quéribus, Puilaurens and Termes. (Sam McGlynn)

The interior of Peyrepertuse castle. The castle was briefly besieged in 1240 before submitting to the French crown. (Sam McGlynn)

Quéribus, one of the Five Sons of Carcassonne. The last of the great Cathar strongholds, it submitted to French forces without a fight in 1255. (Sam McGlynn)

An army setting off from camp. This scene was repeated many times during the crusaders' sieges of southerner castles. (British Library)

Battle scenes and ambush of a supply train. The southerners relied heavily on guerrilla tactics and ambush, especially in the early stages of the conflict. (Pierpont Morgan Library)

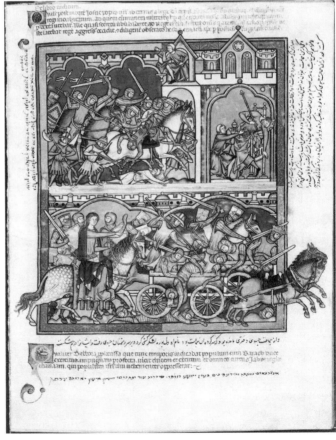

Above left: Sappers digging away at the foundations of a fortress as soldiers use their shields in an attempt to provide them protection. The crusade witnessed many huge engineering works at sieges. Early fourteenth century. (Christ Church, Oxford)

Above: The top panel shows a sortie against besiegers. This tactic was frequently used by defenders to harass besiegers, but at Béziers it backfired disastrously. (Pierpont Morgan Library)

Left: Disease taking its toll of crusaders at the siege of Avignon in 1226. Sickness also contributed to the fall of Termes in 1210. (Corpus Christi College, Cambridge)

Right: Escalade and storming of a fortress. Bombardment and starvation were less dramatic but more common ways of taking a stronghold. Early fourteenth century. (Christ Church, Oxford)

Below: Cavalry charging each other in a pitched battle. Montfort's crusaders were frequently outnumbered by southerner knights, but his cavalry was superior by dint of their experience and discipline. (Trinity College, Cambridge)

Bottom: Treatment of wounds. The contemporary source *The Song of the Cathar Wars* offers some precise details of the treatment of war wounds. (Trinity College, Cambridge)

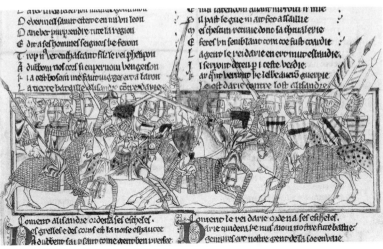

Cavalry duel. Note the horse armour (barding) on the right-hand mount. This was common by the end of the twelfth century among those knights who could afford it. (British Library)

The aftermath of battle and the spoils of war: stripping the dead for their valuable armour, a scene also to be found on the Bayeux Tapestry from two centuries earlier. (Pierpont Morgan Library)

lord of the place paid homage to the all-conquering crusader commander. Despite the fact that there was no papally sanctioned crusade, it had been an extremely successful year for Montfort's dominance of the south. His Christmas passed with considerable satisfaction.

1215: Interlude and Victory

While in 1215 the political turmoil in England was to erupt into open rebellion and the sealing of Magna Carta, matters were more settled in France. In the wake of his epoch-defining victory at Bouvines in July 1214, Philip Augustus was able to concentrate on local difficulties and stamp the authority and permanence of his Capetian regime in France. In Languedoc, severe tensions remained – how could it be otherwise when the northerners continued to occupy and dominate the region after their invasion and numerous campaigns? – but the scale, intensity and frequency of the fighting was reduced, for the moment, to small, relatively isolated incidents and individual acts of resistance. Pope Innocent was wholly preoccupied with establishing his earthly legacy with a major new crusade to the Middle East and a reform of the Church with the Fourth Lateran Council, two issues among others that absorbed his energies in 1215 as preparations were made for both.

The year in Languedoc was dominated by two great councils and one great military non-event. The legate Peter of Benevento returned from Aragon to chair an august council in the independent and, to Montfort's mind, hostile city of Montpellier in January, where five archbishops, twenty-eight bishops and a host of barons and nobles came together. Montfort wanted recognition from the Church for his conquests, but Peter understandably did not wish to go against the pope's instructions, not that his fellow clerics had any such qualms. Outnumbered, and with the powerful legate to France, Robert Courçon, appearing to run the council, it was agreed that Montfort should be bestowed with the glittering prize of the title of Custodian Count of Toulouse, temporarily, because Innocent, who had extended his protection to Toulouse, planned to settle the matter at the end of the year, and because Peter of Benevento had to send an archbishop to Rome to clear the decision with Innocent. The short-term settlement was recognition of the practical reality of Montfort's dominance on the ground. Count Raymond was at this time in voluntary exile, a move designed to keep the pope suspicious of Montfort since all the leading southerner counts had been reconciled with the Church the previous April; unsurprisingly, Raymond would press his case in Rome while Montfort held his county *in commendam*. Meanwhile, more and more of Raymond's lands continued to accrue to Montfort (for example, Beaucaire and Uzès) while Bishop Fulkes returned to Toulouse to occupy Raymond's residency in the Château Narbonnais (turfing out Raymond's son and heir in the process) and, in effect, to rule the city.

The military non-event — but a hugely significant political one — was the April arrival in Languedoc of Prince Louis, heir to the throne of France, at the head of a large army. This marks the beginning of the French crown's overt military involvement in the Albigensian conflict. It could do so now because the threat from England and the Holy Roman Empire had been neutralised (indeed, France was now planning to take the war into England). The move was partly an anti-heresy pilgrimage, but more a visible manifestation of the Capetian overlordship in the south. Events before and after the Montpellier conference showed little respectful cognisance of ultimate suzerainty in the region (where France, England and, in Provence, the Empire all had direct interests); now on its unceasing rise, the Capetian monarchy felt that the moment was right to make its presence felt in Languedoc.

According to the Anonymous, who omits from his song all the events from Muret to now, the 28-year-old Prince Louis was encouraged to come to Languedoc by Peter of Benevento (although it is more probable that the French legate Robert was behind this). Now, with the English and Imperial enemies vanquished, was the perfect time to fulfil his crusading vows from two years earlier — or it would have been, had there been a crusade. The army that accompanied Louis to Lyon that April on Easter Sunday was replete with the finest of French chivalry, most of whom had proved themselves previously in Languedoc and more recently at La Roche au Moine and Bouvines last summer: Bishop Philip of Beauvais, Count Gaucher of St Pol, Count Robert of Sées and Alençon, Matthew of Montmorency (Simon's brother-in-law), Count William of Ponthieu and Viscount Adam of Melun. Montfort went to meet them at Vienne, just south of Lyons, with great enthusiasm, says Peter of Vaux de Cernay (whose uncle was with Louis). Montfort was more likely to have been slightly apprehensive: on the one hand, he wanted to nurture strong relations with the French crown so that it would support his conquests as overlord; on the other, he may have preferred crusaders who would be under his direct control. While Louis was there, Montfort had to defer to him. Luckily for the count (as we can now call Montfort in Languedoc), Louis, an attractive character by the standards of the day, was 'a man of kindly and benevolent disposition', writes Peter (who is less favourably disposed to Louis's father) and for the moment made no attempt to be overly assertive.[149]

With the region pacified and awaiting the Lateran Council's decision at the end of the year, Louis was mainly interested in familiarising himself with the situation in the region – the counsel of the Albigensian veterans in his army was invaluable here – and to ensure that the rights of Capetian overlordship were protected in the transformed political environment. As he rode his Arabian horse from St Gilles to Narbonne via Montpellier and Béziers, his presence at the head of such an imposing force certainly cowed many southerners and bolstered Montfort's position: it also made the additional statement that, should future circumstances demand it, the might of France was ready and poised to intervene.

At Narbonne the archbishop tried to recruit Louis to his side in his dispute with Montfort. Narbonne had the previous year refused to support Montfort as he quelled the unrest in the east and the count now wanted the city's walls torn down. In a revealing new conflict of interest, we see how local power struggles could change the allegiance of even the most fervid crusader. For the Archbishop of Narbonne was Arnald Amalric, the leader of the first crusading army in 1209, and the man attributed the command 'Kill them all! God will know his own.' As a reward for his services he was appointed archbishop in March 1212. Arnald also claimed for himself the title of Duke of Narbonne. As the city was a fief of the counts of Toulouse, Montfort coveted this title for himself. The result was an ongoing and bitter dispute that was to see Arnald excommunicating Montfort – something that would have been utterly inconceivable a few years earlier – and the pope weighing in on Arnald's behalf, warning Montfort against sullying his reputation with the stain of ingratitude by acting against a man to whom he owed everything. Once again, the pious, devout son of the Church Montfort simply ignored the Holy Father in Rome. The walls came down in May.

As they did in Toulouse. As Louis and Montfort moved west through Carcassonne and Fanjeaux, the castle of Foix was handed over from legatine control (under which it had been held since Count Raymond

Roger's reconciliation with the Church in April 1214) to Montfort, who promptly garrisoned it with his men. Count Raymond Roger tried to meet with the legate and Montfort at Fanjeaux, but Montfort refused to see him. When Louis and Montfort entered Toulouse they stayed at the Château Narbonnais and ordered the city's walls to be destroyed. The Anonymous writes: 'all the towers, walls and battlements were to be razed right down to their foundations' – the enormity of this task might have averted the complete implementation of this command – and that it was decreed 'to have the ditches filled in so that no fighting man, however well armed, would be able to put up a defence'. William of Puylaurens later refers here only to 'towers of fortified houses', the 'earthen ramparts' and the removal of barrier 'chains at the crossroad', adding that the Narbonnais castle was then separated from the city by a wide fosse.[150] Peter of Vaux de Cernay's self-satisfied comment shows how well pleased he was by this: 'From this time forward the pride of the city of Toulouse was utterly humbled.'[151]

In June, Louis's forty days were up and he returned north. There was an isolated incident to be dealt with at Castelnaud in September – Bernard de Cazenac had retaken it, so Montfort took it back again, this time hanging the garrison – but otherwise all was quiet. So quiet, in fact, we hear no more of Montfort's activities until February the following year. That in itself demonstrates Montfort's masterful control of Languedoc in 1215.

The major event at the end of the year took place in Rome: the Fourth Lateran Council, a momentous General Council of the Church – the largest of the Middle Ages – which began in November. Count Raymond was there with his son and the Count of Foix to represent the southern lords; Guy de Montfort and Bishop Fulkes of Toulouse headed the crusaders' delegation. These pressed to have their cases heard by over 400 bishops and 800 abbots. The Albigensian Crusade was on the agenda but it was just one of many matters for debate. The partisan Anonymous devotes ten pages to the council, not entirely convincingly repeating the speeches verbatim, but revealing some genuine insights and information nonetheless. He uses the occasion to sing the praises of Raymond's 18-year-old son: 'never was a more charming child born of woman. He was alert, intelligent and well behaved.' The author paints an altogether different picture of the Count of Foix than does Peter of Vaux de Cernay: 'that valiant and delightful man ... had both sense and knowledge.'[152] The count opened for the southerners and a slanging match, albeit it an eloquent one as related by the Anonymous, began.

Both sides went into great supporting detail, knowing that the pope's decision would be of paramount importance. The southerners protested their orthodoxy (none had been convicted of heresy) and argued that the crusaders were just marauding bands of pillagers and land-grabbers. The bishops of the region naturally presented Montfort's case as a pious crusader; if he were not granted legitimate possession of his lands, these bishops could certainly expect to lose their seats in the south. Innocent's leadership had not offered a clear path after the start of the crusade and, for all the seeming decisiveness of his judgement at the council, his vacillations continued until he published his judgement on 14 December 1215. He awarded total victory to Montfort, succumbing to the pressure applied by the prelates and recognising Montfort's conquest as a *fait accompli*. The decision of the Fourth Lateran Council proclaimed that since Count Raymond had been found guilty of harbouring heretics and mercenaries and:

> his territory will never be able to be kept safe in the true faith under his rule (as has long been clear from sure indications), he is to be excluded forever from his rights of dominion, which he has exercised so badly. He is to stay in some suitable place outside his former territory … All the territory which the crusaders have won in their fight against the heretics, heretical believers and their supporters and receivers, together with Montauban and Toulouse (of all places the most corrupted by the stigma of heresy), is to be handed and granted to the Count of Montfort (a man of courage and a true Catholic who more than any other has laboured in this business).[153]

As the *Chronicle* succinctly summarises it: 'The decision reached was to dispossess the Count of Toulouse and award the territory to the Count of Montfort.'[154] Montfort had won – both militarily and politically.

It would be hard to gauge the devastating impact on the hapless Count Raymond: only five years earlier he had been one of the most influential nobles in France and one of its greatest landholders; now he was a landless exile condemned to survive on his wife's dowry and an annual pension of 400 marks. The only crumb of comfort was that his lands that had not been seized by Montfort would be kept safe for his son. The Count of Foix fared better: he was eventually to receive back his comital castle and Montfort was ordered not to wage war on either him or the Count of Comminges. The ruling on unconquered lands denied Montfort the marquisate of Provence, but otherwise Montfort had achieved all he had originally sought in recent years and far, far more than the days when he joined the crusade as a not particularly high-ranking noble. It was an astonishing achievement.

Now all that remained for him to do was to pay homage to the French king for these lands. Montfort duly rushed to Paris, where, according to Peter, Philip received him 'graciously and with honour' and invested him and his heirs with the duchy of Narbonne, Toulouse and all the territory he had won.[155] Philip, newly confident after his own dramatic victories and with grandiose family plans in preparation, was ready to accept Montfort's homage in recognition of the now settled situation.

And that might have been that, but for two dangerous loose ends. One was the remarks made by Innocent to Count Raymond, intended as conciliatory, but readily taken as encouragement to continue the struggle: 'If your claim is valid, God will help and support you.'[156] But far more pernicious and damaging was the fact that Pope Innocent reinstated the crusade with full crusading indulgences for pilgrims who went there from outside Languedoc. The crusade was back on. At first glance this seems a perplexing decision as not only was the crusading action effectively over at this time, but the pope's priority remained an expedition to the Middle East. A consideration of the decision must include recognition of the genuine desire to continue the deracination of heresy now that the region was under the control of a rigidly orthodox ruler. But another possibility, easy to believe in the world of political presentation and spin, is that the crusade was reinstated so as to justify the verdict of the council: in this way the northern land-grab was validated by the original intention to crush the generation of heretical vipers. It provided a veneer of retrospective justification. Whatever the reasons, it was, like his comments to Count Raymond, a remarkably inept move that encapsulates Innocent's equivocal reactions. It ensured that men from across Europe, hoping to achieve both spiritual and financial rewards, would still heed Montfort's call if he required assistance. This would serve only to rub salt in the southerners' raw, open wounds. The Albigensian Crusade was not over.

The South Strikes Back: The Siege of Beaucaire, 1216

Throughout the autumn and winter of 1215, Montfort had administered his lands like any other ruler; now, starting 1216 with Philip Augustus as his suzerain and the papacy having given its official blessing to his conquest, he basked in the glory of his achievement as he made a grand procession through France back to his officially recognised fiefdom in the south. Crowds turned out everywhere for him, some even hoping to earn part of his greatness by touching the hem of his cloak. The response to Count Raymond and his son on their return to the south, as the count made his deliberately procrastinated way to purported exile in Aragon, was also effusive but of greater significance. In February they were 'welcomed with joy and delight' at Marseille; at Avignon 'more than 300' men offered their homage to Count Raymond, greatly restoring his broken spirits and giving him hope. At Avignon, a leading noble by the name of Arnald Audegier expressed the deeply held feelings of the south: '1,000 knights, brave and experienced men, and 100,000 other valiant men have made oaths and pledged by sureties that from now on they will strive to recover all your losses … We shall carry death and slaughter across the fief until you have regained Toulouse and your rightful inheritance.'[157] It was a call to arms: the south was not prepared to accept the permanence of a French occupation sanctioned by Rome. Its men were readying for war and preparing to free themselves of the northern yoke.

This time the southerners rose up in the east. The towns of the Rhône Valley had enjoyed growing autonomy while Raymond and Montfort were preoccupied with their struggle, but Montfort's ascendancy and his consequent intrusion on their independence – unlike Raymond's light touch – was a great concern for them. The passage of crusading armies through their region further unsettled them for it was a constant and ominous reminder of Montfort's power and unrestrained ambitions. They were feeling vulnerable and nervous that the northerners had not yet finished their business in the south.

While the 60-year-old count made his way to Aragon to drum up support for a renewed campaign, the young Raymond, now 19, remained in Provence to gather forces mainly on the eastern side of the Rhône, especially from the Venaissan. He had more success than his father, who failed to deliver anything substantial on his part of the planned two-front attack from the south and the east, designed to stretch Montfort's thinly spread forces to breaking point. It was the most ambitious strategy yet devised by the southerners and had great potential. In the end, though, it was left to the son to lead the fight back with an attack from the east. The Anonymous constantly sings young Raymond's praises; it is highly likely that the author served in his entourage. The young count was to prove an altogether different character from his father, showing himself to be resolute and highly skilled in politics, leadership and warfare, and someone who learned from the experienced warriors around him. Almost perversely, he was also helped by Innocent's decision at the Fourth Lateran Council. This had simplified matters for the southerners: the clear judgement from Rome meant there was no point in attempting to work towards a political or diplomatic solution; with their hands now united by any such consideration, and with the south realising that words meant little, the matter had now to be resolved by war. This concentrated the minds and intentions of a large number of southerners, who now were more focused and united than ever on destroying their enemy. The Anonymous lists some of those behind the young Raymond: Avignon, Marseille, Tarascon, L'Isle sur la Sorgue (L'Isla), Pierrelatte, Guy de Cavaillon (a renowned troubadour and possibly Anonymous himself), Adhémar of Poitiers and his son William, William Artaut of Dia, Bernis de Mirel, Gerald Adhémar and his sons, Raymond of Montauban, Dragonet the Valiant, Aliazer d'Uzès, Ricaus de Caromb, and Pons de St Just. This constituted strong backing from a powerful combination of cities and nobles. Added to this was the latent support from resentful southerners under Montfortian rule across Languedoc. 'My lords,' Raymond told them, 'rich will be the rewards both God and I will give you.'[158] Montfort was about to face a determined foe.

The fight back began on the western side of the Rhône at the powerful town of Beaucaire. This meant crossing into French territory from imperial lands. Directly east of Nîmes and south of Avignon, the castle, Raymond's birthplace, looked down on the walled town to its south from a high rock; to its west lay the new suburb of La Condamine, while the approach from the north-west was protected by a tower outside its walls known as the Redoubt. The legal ownership of Beaucaire was a contested issue in 1216, but a later papal letter indicates that it was not part of Raymond's reduced inheritance that lay on the eastern side of the Rhône. Backed by his army, which included militia from Avignon, Marseille, Tarascon and Vallabrègues arriving in boats, Raymond entered the suburb and received the keys to the town from the council while his men took up their quarters. The castle, garrisoned by Montfortians, was his target. In early June he began his siege. It was an opportune moment to strike as Montfort was still in France and his brother Guy was in Toulouse. No doubt it was hoped that the castle would be taken quickly before either could muster a response. But the epic siege was to last until 24 August.

All the sources cover the combat that followed, but the Anonymous does so in remarkable detail and at considerable length, suggesting the possibility

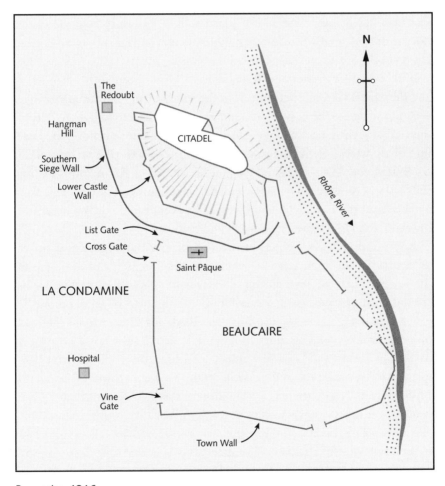

Beaucaire, 1216.

that he was present. It should be noted that much of this detail is absorbed by verbatim speech-making, which, though perhaps encapsulating some of the real sentiments expressed, is likely to contain a large element of artistic licence and literary flourish. William of Puylaurens takes no more than half a page to describe events, while Peter of Vaux de Cernay expends nearly four pages on it. Having reported in great detail on nearly a decade of the Albigensian conflict, Peter's account now loses its intensity in its final twenty pages, suggesting that he died before he had time to revise and augment events from this point onwards. (Unless otherwise stated, the quotes that follow on Beaucaire are from the *Song*.)

Montfort's men made the first move. As at Béziers and other sieges, the garrison attempted to take the initiative as the large southern force settled in. The seneschal and veteran crusader Lambert de Thury held the castle; one of the original Montfortians, he had experienced, as we have seen, harsh conditions while a prisoner of the Count of Foix.

With him were his nephew William de La Motte, Renier de Chauderon and Bernard Adalbert, a defector from the south; plenty of southerners had accommodated to the new regime and would be prepared to fight to defend their subsequent rewards. These sallied out of the castle and along the fosse into the town, bellowing the war cry 'Montfort! Montfort!' The Provençals responded with 'Toulouse!' and met the attack.[159] The Anonymous reports the plethora of weaponry involved: darts, lances, stones, bolts, arrows, axes, hatchets, spears, swords, clubs and staves. The French were driven back into the castle to man its towers, ramparts and brattices.

Raymond quickly tightened the investiture. Barricades and stakes were planted and men were positioned in the monastery of St Pâque in the town's north-western corner. The river, of central importance for its communications and travel, was secured with the help of Tarascon on the eastern bank. He made his first target the Redoubt. This guarded the road on which reinforcements and supplies might arrive, so it was a priority. A barrage of arrows and bolts was unleashed against the small garrison here in an action reminiscent of the assault on the Termenet tower of Termes in 1210. Here, however, there is no mention of the involvement of any siege machines at this stage (they were probably still being constructed on site). The northerners defended themselves vigorously in the exchange, hurling rocks down on the attackers. The gates were attacked and fires were lit. The danger from the fire and the choking smoke 'distressed the French so much that they were forced to come down'. Some of them sought safety higher up, but Peter de St Prais asked for terms and the first defence of the castle fell. The destructive power of fire at sieges could be matched by the deadly effects of smoke. At the siege of Château Gaillard in 1203–04, the fort on the Isle of Andely was set on fire and many of the garrison died from smoke inhalation as they sought refuge in the vaults.

There then followed a major engineering work of the kind prevalent in the sieges of the Albigensian Crusade and in so many sieges of the Middle Ages. Raymond Gaucelm of Tarascon and a leader of its militia suggested building a double siege wall and ditch between the Redoubt and the north-western corner of the town. From this the Provençals could shoot down on any sortie from the castle, and it would simultaneously protect the besiegers outside the town's walls from the expected relief force. It would be protected by short-range catapults, while longer-range ones could bombard the castle. A priest promised salvation to all who helped to construct the wall; little encouragement was needed as all knew that this construction would add to their earthly safety. The Anonymous delights in relating how all pulled together in this enterprise: 'No one hung back. They began building the wall, its platform and parapet … Knights and ladies carried the infill material, noble girls and youngsters the timber and dressed stone.' It was a total mobilisation of the town's people. A battering ram 'of enormous size' was also fashioned and placed under the command of Guy de Cavaillon, who directed it against the walls of the castle, which shook 'severely'.[160]

The garrison could not make any egress from the castle as the investiture on both the landward side and riverbanks was secure. While the garrison had to survive on what water reserves it had, the besiegers brought in plentiful provisions from the countryside: pigs, sheep, oxen, cows, hens, geese, capons, game birds, corn, flour and wine; such was the abundance 'the place looked like the promised land'. With the wall constructed and supplies gathered, they pressed the siege, hoping to take it before a relief force arrived. But if it did, they were prepared for it.

Montfort was still somewhere in France, basking in his homage to King Philip and the adulation of crowds, when he heard the news. The Lateran settlement had not lasted long. His brother and son, being at Toulouse, were closer and responded immediately. But they were still over 150 miles away. All rode hard to the siege. Accompanying Guy and Amaury de Montfort were the formidable veteran knights Hugh de Lacy and Alan de Roucy, as well as other experienced warriors such as Guy de Lévis and the notorious Foucaud de Berzy and their contingents. They were joined *en route* by Peter of Vaux de Cernay and his uncle, Bishop Guy. As Montfort urgently recruited soldiers with the promise of high wages, his brother's army travelled via Nîmes to Beaucaire. On their way they had received intelligence that the castle at Bellegarde had defected to the southerners; as it overlooked their road about 7 miles from Beaucaire they quickly seized it back and from then on used it as their siege headquarters – which, given its distance from Beaucaire, says something of the threat they faced from the southerners, who Peter says greatly outnumbered them (which was probably true when the townspeople of Beaucaire and Tarascon are included). They arrived at the siege on 5 June, just as Montfort's force arrived in Nîmes. Outside the walls of the town, Guy drew up his force into three battle lines and tried to call out the enemy; Raymond and his men were wisely having none of it. The only exception was a chance encounter between the French and Raymond Belarot and Aimon de Caromb, when lances were shattered. Instead, more men from Tarascon were ferried in across the river while horse and foot took up positions in gardens and other open spaces.

Exhausted from their rapid forced march, Guy and his men withdrew to Bellegarde, fearful that they were now on the front line with 'mortal enemies' at Montpellier, Marseille, Avignon and Beaucaire. At least in Bellegarde they had won a plentiful supply of food. Back in the town, the Anonymous paints a picture of high morale and an almost carnival atmosphere as all cheerfully busied themselves strengthening their defences further. Master craftsmen and engineers developed ramparts and galleries and constructed more barriers, palisades, breast-high parapets and siege engines such as mangonels and 'bitches' (a form of mangonel). Sentinels were posted everywhere, protected in 'double armour', while select boatmen guarded the river. And they made themselves stronger still as Raymond sent out the call to barons, vassals and mercenaries: 'Anyone who wants gold or silver or fast horses, let him come and earn them at the siege of Beaucaire.' Peter of Vaux de Cernay believed almost the whole of Provence rallied to the young Raymond.

The attacks on the castle continued, the defenders resisting strongly. They managed to destroy some of the siege engines by fire (Peter says 'all') and mitigated the blows of the enormous ram by countering its impact against the wall. Montfort arrived on 6 June amidst a blast of trumpets and joined his brother. He ordered the baggage train to be unloaded and a fortified camp behind stakes and barricades to be set up to the south-west of the suburbs in gardens and orchards (partly because there was nowhere else and also because he had taken a retreat route into consideration). Thus 'now the siege was complete, inside the place and out'. Montfort had to send armed escorts to protect supply trains from Nîmes and St Gilles, the only places he could secure them from.

At this time Prince Louis was campaigning in England, taking many of France's best knights with him, thereby severely denting the numbers available to Montfort in the south. Further problems arose from Montfort's lack of infantry, experienced or otherwise, so he was unable to haul siege machines into position, though his petrary was deployed effectively. Non-professional footsoldiers were often recruited from the locality, but here they had not been very forthcoming. A third of his knights had to be kept in a state of armed readiness at all times, day and night, to protect the siege engines and camp from sorties, which led to fatigue; but the southerners, confident in their strong position, did not feel the need to make any. Morale was further undermined by acts of atrocity. Peter of Vaux de Cernay lamented that anyone caught from the crusaders' side was slain pitifully, some by hanging, others by dismembering. Amputated feet were placed on mangonels and hurled into the crusader-held castle. Peter is quiet on any dishonourable acts the crusaders may have committed.

At a council of war, the Anonymous says that Alan de Roucy advised Montfort to negotiate with the honourable Raymond, but he rejected this, replying, 'battle is far better than disgrace'. Typically, Montfort instead led a bold frontal assault on the town as the only way of rescuing his men in the castle. The Anonymous relishes the fighting that ensued:

> Now came the clash of blades from Cologne and twice-tempered steel,
> of rounded maces and cold javelins, well-honed axes and shining shields,
> came flights of darts, arrows and polished quarrels, feathered shafts and
> brandishing spears, came brave knights, alert and active, sergeants, archers
> eagerly advancing, and the other companies, keen to strike hard. On all sides
> the rush and crash of men and weapons shook the field, the riverbank and
> the solid ground … What damaged hauberks you would have seen there,
> what good shields cracked and broken, what fists, legs and feet cut off, what
> spattered blood and skulls split apart!

For all the bombastic glorification of violence, it was indeed a brutal fight in which little quarter was given and there were no displays of chivalric behaviour. When Guy de Cavaillon struck down the crusader William de Berlit, he did not strike him down with a sword to grant him a death befitting of a knight, but instead had him hung 'from a flowering olive tree'. The attack was repulsed.

Reluctantly, Montfort settled in for the long haul. He called in carpenters and engineers to build a belfry and a cat of iron, timber and leather, which were manned around the clock. The catapult already constructed was in constant use, damaging the crenellations and seriously compromising the stonework around the gateway. Montfort badly needed reinforcements, all the more so as all the while southerner nobles, *faidits* and mercenaries continued to flock into Beaucaire to support Raymond's cause, many carried up the river from Marseille. Raymond's initiative in launching the offensive and his strategic timing had given him a telling head start. Montfort only made any progress through the operation of the catapult, but Raymond prepared for any breach by arranging a troop of knights whose only task was to defend the increasingly vulnerable gateway. 'If Count Simon dares attack the gate,' exhorted Ricaud de Caromb in response, 'let us scatter so much blood and brains around us, such lumps of sweaty flesh, that any survivors weep!'

Meanwhile, the southerners' assault on the castle had made some progress, damaging the keep and hoardings and breaking down beams and palisades with their petraries. But they were frequently countered by an inspired defence. The iron-tipped battering ram proved effective against the walls until the garrison lassoed it with a noose and 'held the ram's head'. One of the chief engineers then began a sapping operation, digging into the rock on which the castle was built to undermine the walls. They dug themselves far enough in to be protected by the overhang from missiles thrown down on them from the walls. But the garrison put an end to this with a response that is rarely seen in medieval sources: a rope was lowered in front of the sapped cavity on a chain to which was attached a concoction made up of sulphur and tow sewn up in a cloth bag that had been set alight; 'the flames and stench so stupefied [the miners] that not one of them could stay there'.

The garrison commander Lambert de Thury waved napkins and a bottle to Montfort, indicating that they were now without any sustenance whatsoever. William of Puylaurens says that they had even eaten their horses. This demonstrates the extreme precariousness of their situation. Trained war-horses were prohibitively expensive, and for a knight to resort to consuming them as food spoke volumes. Less than a year before in England, the Magna Carta rebels besieged in Rochester faced a similar dilemma: 'The provisions of the garrison failed them and so they had to eat their horses and even their costly chargers.'[161] Of the crusaders, William de la Motte is reported to have proposed cannibalism; this is possibly an embellishment by the Anonymous, but the eating of human flesh was not unheard of in medieval sieges in France and is widely and authoritatively reported in historical sieges through to the twentieth century.

Montfort had to act fast or face a rare failure. He was aware that his trapped men might surrender at any time unless he demonstrated that he could relieve them. He called out 'To arms!' and launched a charge up Hang Man's Hill to the north-west of the town. There the Provençals, having snatched up their swords, axes, maces and bows, went out to meet him in the open ground by the road. Foucaud de Berzy, Alan de Roucy, Guy de Lévis and Guy de Montfort led the charge, followed by Montfort himself, emulating the tactics of Muret. But the massed ranks of the southerners absorbed the shock of the charge and caused it to lose impetus. Gaucelin de Pertel, killed by Imbert de L'Aia, was one of many casualties in the combat. The Anonymous, like so many troubadours, relished the carnage: 'Slashed off and scattered you'd have seen legs, arms and feet, men's guts and lungs, jawbones and heads, scalps and spilled brain matter.' The attack was beaten off.

Immediately Montfort regrouped his men for another concentrated assault. His most experienced knights were sent out to scout and ascertain where their forces could best be concentrated. It was quickly decided to direct an assault on the Vine Gate at the south-western corner of the town. The crusaders' catapult broke through the gate and the wall protecting it, while the belfry tower and cat were manoeuvred into position. As the combat intensified even further, the people of the town rapidly effected repairs with lime and mortar and constructed barricades. Montfort's exhausted forces were driven off for a third time. Meanwhile, at the castle, the southerners applied a weasel to the walls; this was a smaller, wheeled version of the cat with a destructive pike. The garrison's engineer came up with yet another effective inflammatory counter-tactic: he accurately hurled a pot of burning pitch onto the contraption, engulfing it in flames.

Montfort held one of his regular war councils to try and find a way through the impasse. He could ill afford the steady attrition of losses and there was agitated debate on the problems of dwindling supplies and exhausted warhorses. The *Song* reports that Foucaud de Berzy put forward a new stratagem. The crusaders should remain inactive for a few days as though brow beaten before launching a diversionary assault on the Lists Gate at the north-west corner of the town, creating such a furore that 'the townsmen will all flock to it'. Then, at the height of the clash the cavalry would ride hard back down to the Vine Gate. Here, 100 of their best would be concealed behind the siege machine and beneath the cat. The two forces would then combine in a surprise attack on this damaged gate, in the hope that it had been left undefended to deal with the combat at the other end of the castrum. The report is a convincing one, but the timing is more suspect: at this critical stage a delay of a few days would have been sheer folly, unless the crusaders found it necessary to rest their mounts and to await the arrival of fresh supplies. (Another possibility is that the Anonymous has his chronology wrong and either this attack or the garrison's warning is out of sequence.) Montfort agreed to the plan and looked forward to hanging the traitors in the town from the palisade.

The plan altered as preparations were made. Now the crusaders would march first on the Cross Gate in the north-eastern wall rather than the Lists Gate; if this were seen to be too heavily defended, they would immediately double back to the weakened Vine Gate, where the other men concealed in the belfry and the hospital, a building outside the south-western perimeter, would rush out to join in the attack. At midday the attack began with great vigour and with the element of surprise, so much so that when the French swiftly broke through the palisades some of the southerners fled to the river and took to their boats. But the soldiers and townspeople of Beaucaire quickly rallied to the gate and held the crusaders back with the help of archers. The attackers now put the second part of their plan into operation and rode hard to the Vine Gate in the south-western wall. Here the crusaders in hiding burst forth and stormed over the barricades and trenches and were on the point of taking the defensive outworks. In the town, Ralph de Le Gua saw the danger and led a group of knights and townsmen to defend this sector, which was now under serious threat. Whether just from the battlements or combined with a sortie, these strove to drive the French away from the walls. The Anonymous gleefully depicts another gory and detailed combat, but also captures the messy, scrappy nature of fighting and the range of weaponry employed; in addition to the expected swords, maces, axes, crossbows and bows (what may be called professional arms), it is clear that anything that came to hand, including working implements, were also used to attack the enemy: stones and pebbles, scythe blades, knives, cudgels, sharpened stakes. The combat zone was made all the more perilous by the hot lime being thrown down onto the French in the dry moat. Such was the intensity of the defence that Montfort's men were beaten back. Both sides withdrew to attend to their wounded, doctors and, less reassuringly, farriers used 'water, tow and salt, ointments, plasters and linen bandages' plus egg whites for dressings, 'to treat the wounds and blows and deadly pain'.

The mood in Montfort's camp after this fourth failed attempt was naturally dejected. In seven years of active campaigning, Montfort and the crusaders had faced numerous tough military obstacles before, but none so obdurate as this. At another meeting in the wake of the latest setback, even Montfort showed signs of despondency, despairing that he could save his men. His brother Guy counselled abandoning the siege. A critical juncture was reached when a messenger from the besieged castle managed to get through to Montfort (he had either made a daring breakthrough of the southerners' lines or else Lambert had reached an agreement with the foe that he would urge his general to make terms). The messenger lamented that the garrison had been without water, wine and food for three weeks and were now at death's door. This was the turning point for Montfort: he could not rescue his men; nor could he let them starve to death after their heroic resistance in his name. The unthinkable happened. On 24 August Montfort conceded defeat.

Montfort dictated a private letter to Dragonet the Valiant in Beaucaire to settle terms. Peter of Vaux de Cernay attributes the defeat to the plight of the starving garrison and writes of an honourable settlement in which Lambert and his men were allowed to leave with their lives and armour intact. William of Puylaurens says only that their lives were spared, while the Anonymous convincingly reports that they had to forfeit their equipment and mounts (those that had not already been eaten).

The southerners had won a momentous victory over the French. For the first time they had triumphed at a major siege (Pujol should be considered a minor one); what is more, they had achieved this despite the presence of the mighty Montfort personally directing operations against them. They had been prepared, timed their uprising well and did not commit all their forces to open battle as the crusaders had hoped they would. Montfort's aura of invincibility had been shattered. The commander who had never led his men to a defeat had just done so. Peter of Vaux de Cernay accurately wrote that Montfort had feared that delay at the siege increased 'the ever-present danger that the city of Toulouse, and the territories he was holding, would desert him'.[162] But outright defeat was even more damaging. The news of Montfort's defeat and the south's victory resounded across the region. As William of Puylaurens records: 'As a consequence many who had concealed their opposition to him lifted up their horns and numerous strongholds and towns at once joined his enemies.'[163] The momentum was now with the south.

1217: The Rhône Campaign

Montfort now had to address the situation urgently or risk war on all fronts. Fearing the deadly combination of an uprising in Toulouse and an advance by Count Raymond at the head of an army from Aragon, Montfort rushed back to the city, covering over 150 miles in under four days to reach the nearby town of Montgiscard. Here he mustered men from the Carcassès, the Razès and the Toulousain. The situation had further changed with the death of Pope Innocent III in July; all were unsure as to how the new pope, the elderly Honorius III, an altogether less abrasive and less politically astute pontiff, would deal with Languedoc. What Montfort now needed was a reaffirmation of practical authority and the potent threat of a punitive response to all those considering defecting from him. For this he needed money to pay his troops, to recruit new ones and to buy loyalty; and Toulouse was to be his bank.

In a noxious combination of rage, vengeance and perhaps also panic, Montfort tried to fleece the city. In early September, he arrested a delegation of the city's elite that had come to meet him as he approached Toulouse in battle formation; Montfort was fully aware of the city's plans to rebel on Count Raymond's return. Ignoring the advice of Alan de Roucy and others to quell his anger, the count proceeded aggressively. An advanced party of soldiers entered the city, demanding and seizing payments and plunder to, they claimed, assuage Montfort's wrath. This provoked an instant response, with citizens and the militia taking up arms and erecting barricades. Fighting broke out all over the city. The northerners set various places on fire as a full-scale insurrection threatened. But Montfort withdrew his men into the Château Narbonnais overnight to let matters quieten down. The city's resistance did nothing but rub salt in his wounds: he threatened to execute his prisoners. Bishop Fulkes mediated between the two sides the next day. The violence was stemmed, but Montfort's direct rule only served to aggravate tensions even further.

Montfort, normally so effective under pressure, now began to lose his sense of proportion. His need for money drove him to find ways to justify it. In so doing, he stamped on the city's proud liberties and entrenched hostile positions even further. He took over 400 citizens hostage, who were carried off in chains, filling the Château Narbonnais; some nobles were expelled; weapons were seized; the city's remaining defences were torn down; and an indemnity of 30,000 marks was demanded, to be paid by November the following year. His men immediately set about harassing the inhabitants with threats and violence, coercing them to pay up in money or goods. Houses that had yet to pay were marked by a cross and many were demolished. As William of Puylaurens recognised with understatement, the Toulousains 'bore with difficulty the yoke which undermined the liberty to which they were accustomed'.[164] The Anonymous is less reserved: he reports the people wailing 'Oh God, what wicked rulers! Lord, you have delivered us into the hands of robbers! Give us back our own lords or give us death.'[165] This was not comital rule but a humiliating military occupation.

Resentment continued to fester in the city as Montfort spent Christmas there, soberly reflecting on the stark contrast to his celebratory one the year before. The military front remained quiet for the moment, but all knew this was the lull before the southern storm that had to break. Count Raymond was still building support in Aragon; Montfort had clumsily improved the count's position there by a brief incursion into an Aragonese fief in Gascony in the autumn. The Count of Foix also promised trouble. With a northern garrison still occupying his castle at Foix, he set about constructing a new one on a hill 3 miles to the town's south at Montgrenier. This was of immediate concern to Montfort as it presaged a potential focal point for southern resistance, and delay increased this risk. Ignoring the papal proscription of December 1215 and another from the new pope, who had ordered that Foix be restored to Raymond Roger, on

6 February 1217 Montfort besieged it. As discussed before, winter by no means precluded military campaigning. 'Despite the mud and the frost,' says Peter, Montfort 'strengthened the siege and launched a vigorous assault on the castle'.[166] The Count of Foix's son, Roger Bernard, commanded the castle and with him were powerful southern nobles such as Roger de Comminges, Peter Roger de Mirepoix and Baset of Montpezat, the last of whom died during the siege. The investiture was a tight one and the garrison, unable to bring in supplies or collect water, surrendered on honourable terms towards the end of March. Montfort garrisoned it and moved on to Carcassonne. Montfort hoped it was a positive sign of the year to come.

Other successes followed for him. In May, operations against mercenary-held castles near Termes in the Corbières gathered up a small bounty of places won by force or submission. The leaders of the southerners still not having made a major move, Montfort continued to consolidate his position in the summer as, for the first time since 1214, crusaders came from the north in force to undertake combat duties. Large numbers descended with Archbishop Girard of Bourges and Bishop Roger of Clermont. Although recruits came from across Europe throughout the crusade, France remained the chief reservoir of men. Between May 1216 and September 1217, Prince Louis had siphoned off the best of these as he fought in England to gain the throne there in the wake of the Magna Carta rebellion. This much-neglected invasion was an enormous affair, and came very close to being a second Norman conquest. Louis occupied over a third of England and ruled this massive area from London. The war there, fought in a very similar manner to that being waged in Languedoc (although with less barbarity), demanded considerable manpower; Louis, as heir to the Capetian throne and, during this period, *de facto* King Louis I of England, attracted the best knights and absorbed much of France's spare infantry and crossbowmen; the consequences were felt by Montfort at Beaucaire. Now, with Louis finally chased out of England and back in France, more reinforcements were being made available again.

With these Montfort returned to Provence in June with a determined mind and a hardened heart. Campaigning in the pro-Raymond region around Nîmes, Montfort took Posquières from its lord, Rostang, who had defected from him, and stormed the castrum of Bernis. Here he reverted to old form, hanging many of the inhabitants and killing some knights stationed there. The purpose was the same as ever: 'This inspired such terror in all rebels in the area that they became dumbfounded; they fled before the count and left empty all the castra in which they dwelt.'[167] The effect was dramatic: it greatly assisted Montfort in regaining most of the territory he had lost west of the Rhône in the uprising of the previous year. Marching 40 miles north along the Rhône, he took Dragonet's castle and the two men were reconciled. Beaucaire was now isolated but Montfort did not attempt a second bite at that sour cherry.

Montfort was bolstered in his task by the appearance of Pope Honorius's new legate, Cardinal Bertrand. The cardinal's disapproval of Cathar sympathisers was exacerbated by his arrival in the Rhône Valley, where the towns simply chose to ignore his proclaimed authority; indeed, such was the hostility that for much of the time he was holed up in Orange; at other times local archers took pot shots at him, wounding a member of his entourage. He excommunicated the towns and encouraged crusading military offensives in the region, prompting Montfort's crossing of the Rhône at Viviers, deterring an Avignon flotilla as he did so, and his march into new territory. All fled before him as he reached Montélimar, then moved nearly 20 miles north-east away from the river to besiege Adhémar of Poitiers's castle at Crest. They came to terms, Montfort offering his daughter Amicia in marriage to one of Adhémar's sons in exchange for loyalty and several castra.

This campaign deep into the east shows Montfort in confident mood once again, pacifying an area that had recently proven itself a centre of opposition to northern interference and also ensuring that the crusader route from Lyon was kept securely open. Despite the loss of the archbishop's and bishop's forty-dayers, Montfort now had the help of local episcopates and, significantly, of 100 knights sent south by King Philip of France (they were no longer needed by Louis in England) to serve for no less than six months – a massive boost to his operational ability and reach. Once again he was riding high. But the wheel of fortune refused to stop. As he reflected in Crest on the success of another impressive campaign in which most of his objectives had been met, in mid-September he heard the news that he had been dreading since his defeat at Beaucaire: Count Raymond had returned to Toulouse and the city had risen in his support.

7

1217–18: 'WHO COULD FAIL TO DISSOLVE IN TEARS?'

The Return of the Count

On 13 September 1217 Count Raymond returned from exile and entered his city of Toulouse. The scene was set for one of the epic military encounters of the Middle Ages: the siege of the city that was to last for nearly ten months and was made famous by its haul of victims. Raymond's son had delivered a bloody nose to Montfort in the east; now it was the elderly and previously ineffectual count's chance to make a decisive contribution to the southern resistance of the occupying northerners. He had made some headway in Aragon collecting forces, but nothing spectacular; however, the success of his son in the Rhône and the taking of Beaucaire had strengthened the will to resist amongst the southern nobility and the dispossessed and shown them what was possible. Roger de Comminges, the Viscount of Couserans and nephew to the counts of Foix and Comminges, joined with exiles from the city to rally support for Count Raymond, advising him that now was the opportune hour to return home and reclaim his title. With Montfort on the other side of the south in Provence, and the citizens of Toulouse seething with resentment at the northerners' draconian rule over their city and their ruthless occupation, Raymond seized the moment.

The Anonymous takes us through the events in rich and telling detail: the siege was close to his heart and strikes a central chord with his feelings about the French invaders and their brutish violation of his homeland. William of Puylaurens, ever succinct, covers the siege in a couple of pages, while Peter of Vaux de Cernay devotes the last ten pages of his work to events. The Anonymous, by contrast, goes into exhaustive detail over nearly sixty pages – one-third of his entire song – exceeding his coverage of Beaucaire by some distance, but again with much extended dialogue and speeches that, though not always necessarily accurate in the reported sense, do give voice to expressed sentiments and issues. (In what follows, any unattributed quotations come from the *Song*.)

The count approached Toulouse surreptitiously, successfully maintaining the element of surprise until the last possible moment. He did not have a large force with him, but that was not essential as his manpower was concentrated in the city and in the area around it. As he moved northwards he attempted a river crossing on the Garonne at La Salvetat, just under 30 miles south of his destination, but the way was temporarily blocked by a force led by Joris, a southern knight who had defected to the northerners. However, this was beaten off in a skirmish during which Roger Bernard of Foix distinguished himself. The southerners took this minor victory as a good omen. Count Raymond sent word ahead to his trusted men in the city to prepare for his arrival. The next morning, a fog descended, covering his troops as they approached the city from the east, away from the eyes of the northern garrison in the castle that guarded the west. He entered Toulouse as quietly as possible; ironically, the dismantling of the walls and defences made this much easier than it would otherwise have been. Once he was inside, the people flocked to cheer his return: 'they came to the count as to one risen from the dead'.[168] The scene was one of jubilation as all elements of the city, from the highest to the lowest, knelt before him and, whenever possible, kissed him. Their saviour had come to liberate them. However, as William of Puylaurens soberly notes, not everyone was pleased to see him: 'others judged the likely future turn of events by what had happened in the past' and 'were displeased'.[169] Their caution was justified; they anxiously withdrew to the castle (the Château Narbonnais) and to monasteries before the count coaxed them back out a few days later.

The jubilation of the majority of the citizens was matched by the panic of the French holed up in the castle. To add to the sense of urgency, among their number was Montfort's wife, Alice, and extended family. Some of the French garrison had tried to impede the count's progress, but they were quickly killed or pushed back by the vast numbers of a city in open revolt, moving against their oppressors with the rallying cry of 'Toulouse!'

as they picked up any weapons to hand, be it a club, pike or applewood cudgel. Those French who could made it back to the Narbonnais castle. Some knights emerged to face the mob, but none dared to venture into them. Inside the castle, confusion reigned as its inhabitants recoiled at the shock of this wholly unexpected episode. Gervase de Chamigny, Montfort's seneschal in Toulouse, caught sight of the banners of Bernard de Comminges and of Roger Bernard of Foix, behind which stood an army of dispossessed southerners; this immediately clarified the situation for them. 'Alas!' cried out Alice. 'And yesterday all was going so well for me!' A knight named Lucas urgently advised her to send to her husband for help and for him not to consider the cost of bringing a relief force, lest all should be lost. She instructed a messenger:

> Take bad news to the count: he has lost Toulouse, his sons and his wife. If he makes the slightest delay ... he'll find neither me nor any of his sons whole; if he loses Toulouse while he is over there trying to win Provence, it's a spider's web he's spinning, not worth a penny.

In a moment the only part of Toulouse that remained under Montfortian control was the Narbonnais castle. The citizens busied themselves immediately to cut off access between the fort and the rest of the city 'with pales and stakes, large wooden beams and ditches'.[170] Everywhere the citizens 'at once set about fortifying Toulouse by constructing barricades and ditches'; they were acutely aware of how their denuded defences left them cruelly exposed to the inevitable wrath of Montfort.[171] As towers, walls and fences were rapidly erected amidst a burst of intense and concentrated activity by the whole community, even the abbey of St Sernin and St Stephen's cathedral were incorporated into the new defensive network, their roofs and bell towers being heavily manned. Languedoc has an impressive tradition of fortified churches; those garrisoned in Toulouse had arrow loops and battlement walkways. Raymond also bolstered his position by the politically adroit move of reasserting the city's municipal government under a chief magistrate, thus ensuring the people that their interests were his. He had sensibly capitalised on the city's euphoric sense of regime change with a reversion to popular politics.

They had nine days before they were gripped in hand-to-hand fighting with the crusaders. The first northern force on the scene was led by

Guy de Montfort and arrived on 22 September. This was an especially anxious moment for him as his wife and some of his children were holed up in the castle. His troop included Simon de Montfort's second son, another Guy, and Alan de Roucy and Foucaud de Berzy with garrison troops from Carcassonne. Before the Montoulieu Gate at the city's south-eastern corner, where the rampart by the fosse had been destroyed, he gave his knights the order to dismount. Drawn up in squadrons and with swords drawn, 'they forced their way into the streets, smashing down and destroying all barricades'. They were met by soldiers, archers and the Toulousain militia, as well as by ordinary citizens, some of whom were flinging down missiles and debris from the rooftops. Roger Bernard of Foix rode swiftly up to join the fray with his company of men, dismounting and pushing the crusaders back, inflicting many casualties upon them. Guy's men jumped onto their horses and retreated, but quickly regrouped and rode into St James's gardens, outside the perimeter of the destroyed wall, before being repulsed a second time. Any French prisoners caught 'were dragged through the town and hanged'.

Meanwhile, Count Bernard de Comminges blocked Guy's baggage train from entering the castle. (It has been perceptively suggested that Guy might have been engaged in a diversionary attack so that supplies could reach the beleaguered French in the castle.) Guy's men now took up their positions in houses around the castle to deter a close siege of the place where his family was sheltering. As both sides drew breath for the next round of conflict, they sent out for reinforcements.

The southerners drew their men in first, mainly due to geographical proximity, but also because of the pool of willing manpower available to them. The Anonymous names numerous warriors such as Viscount Roger of Couserans and other knights and *faidits* who streamed into the city with their vassals. Alice de Montfort watched them enter the city in despair: 'I am afraid for myself and the children.' When word finally reached Montfort at the siege of Crest, he instructed the messenger to keep silent about the loss of Toulouse on pain of being 'burned, hanged or cut into pieces'; he did not wish for any difficulties to be raised during his current marriage negotiations regarding his daughter Amicia and Adhémar of Poitiers's son, William. Now more than ever he needed security in the east if he was to be able to deal with the crisis in the west. It seems that Montfort may have tried to buy time by declaring false information about the situation, pretending that all was well. But the news of such a momentous event could not be contained and those with Montfort feared that they would lose their lands.

Montfort knew well the danger of delay and so rode furiously night and day towards Toulouse. Messengers peeled off from the column to urgently seek reinforcements from all of Montfort's vassals on fear of forfeiting their lands and from the archbishops and the legate Bertrand. By the end of the first week of October he was at Baziège, 14 miles south-east of Toulouse. Montfort was met by his brother and some of his leading captains. The Anonymous relates how he berated them for failing to quell the uprising against civilians; increasingly, the writer depicts Montfort as irrational and making poor decisions, despite the advice of his right-hand men. The plight of the two Montfort brothers' wives threatened in the castle had unnerved the crusaders with an unwelcome added distraction.

Here, according to the Anonymous, a council decided on the Béziers option: a wholesale massacre was determined upon. As in 1209, the suggestion once again came from the papal legate, who insisted that all men and the counts of Toulouse, Comminges and Foix be hung. When Bishop Fulkes protested that those in his diocese who were in sight of an altar should be saved, Bertrand rejected his calls for sanctuary. The problem of Toulouse was to be dealt with once and for all.

The Siege of Toulouse Begins, Autumn 1217

The following day (8 October at the latest) the crusading army arrayed itself in squadrons before Toulouse, their imposing banners flying in the wind. This marked the beginning of the single longest military action of the entire Albigensian Crusade. The men of Toulouse came to face them on the levels and in the lists (the tourneying space between the town's former inner and outer walls; an excellent example of these can be seen in Carcassonne); behind them on the sentry walks and brattices were positioned archers and pikemen, the former with their ammunition ready in tubs full of quarrels and arrows. Montfort had not dallied to set up camp, but instead went straight into the fight. His front line advanced towards the enemy.

Leading the first assault were Guy and Amaury de Montfort with Sicard de Montaut and Foucaud de Berzy. They were met with an intense hail of 'slender steel-tipped shafts' in the arrow storm, but some were able to get to grips with their foes.[172] Their advance was halted by the recently excavated ditch, where a French knight by the name of Imbert de La Volp was struck down while retreating by Armand de Mondenard, who 'drove six inches of steel into his side'. A mangonel in the town was used as an anti-personnel weapon. The young Guy, Simon's son, was struck in the chest by a crossbow bolt said to have been shot by Count Bernard of Comminges (Guy's father-in-law!). Knights were well trained in such weapons, but in the confusion of battle the strike may just have easily come from an ordinary crossbowman. The unrelenting barrage of missiles eventually drove the crusaders back. Hugh de Lacy estimated that a third of the force had been lost in the frontal assault, which may have meant over 150 men either killed or wounded. The former were buried while the latter had their injuries attended to.

Having been 'vigorously driven back by the citizens',[173] Montfort took a pause to establish his camp by the castle and convene another war council within the tower. Foucaud de Berzy, ever ready with a military stratagem, devised a long-term plan so that they could 'destroy every man in there and kill them all'.[174] In sum, he planned for a siege town to be built – New Toulouse – to press the siege and where the crusaders, their supplies and reinforcements could be kept safe. From here they would mount daily raids to collect food from the region for their men or destroy it to deny it to the enemy. This was agreed upon. But for it to work the western approaches to the city from Gascony had also to be secure. Montfort divided his inadequate force into two: he crossed the Garonne to the suburb of St Cyprien, leaving his son Amaury and his brother Guy in command of the force at the castle. In this way he hoped to control the roads from Gascony into the city across the bridges as well as the river to the south.

New Toulouse was soon erected – a substantial construction of wood, 'barricades built all round it, with ramparts, levels and ditches, loops, gates, salients and chain-barriers'.[175] We have repeatedly seen at sieges that, when necessary, Montfort did not recoil at the prospect of a massive engineering project. This was standard procedure in lengthy investitures, especially those over the winter months, as at Prince Louis's siege of Dover in 1216–17. Here, 'to strike terror' into the besieged, Louis 'built shops and other buildings in front of the entrance to the castle, so that the place appeared to be like a market', and thus intimidated the garrison into surrender through fear of starvation as force had failed.[176] This was Foucaud's plan at Toulouse. Toulouse's great strength in numbers could be used against it if it could not be provisioned.

Montfort's main problem was, as so often the case, his lack of manpower. The enormous perimeter of the city meant that he could not invest it completely and so had to focus on just two areas – though even this proved to be too ambitious. The southerners' timing was well planned: they knew that beginning the uprising in the autumn would give Montfort trouble recruiting extra men from the north until the spring; meanwhile, they could be reinforced locally and have men active in the region. Thus Montfort's crossing of the Garonne into the suburb of St Cyprien was short lived as the occupation was too problematic to sustain.

The move was beset with difficulties from the start. The division of his army meant two smaller forces that were therefore more exposed to enemy strikes and more wary of taking the initiative. The Toulousains were ready for this manoeuvre and had strongly garrisoned the bridges' barbicans on the outer banks. The crusaders had to endure constant harrying from the archers and sergeants assigned to that sector, and morale slumped further when a French knight who ventured too close to the enemy was captured and hacked to pieces. The last straw seems to have been scouts' reports of the approach of the Count of Foix and the powerful Catalan noble Dalmas of Creixhell to reinforce the city. With his men in a state of great anxiety, and fearing being caught between this force and the Toulousains, Montfort ordered another assault on the city. But his men could not be persuaded to take this course of action. The Anonymous reports that his men managed to advise him against this rash move but the growing sense of unease may suggest an almost mutinous atmosphere in his camp. Either way, if true (and this seems likely) it was quite something that Montfort, that great leader of men, found himself in a position where his men were unwilling to follow. Montfort 'therefore re-crossed the river, thus to combine two weak forces into a stronger one'.[177]

Even this proved traumatic. As they retreated, they were closely harried by a sortie from the city. Montfort's men withdrew in close order, his best men forming the rearguard. When the French reached the boats, a panicked rush set in as they tried to board them, with the southerners' thrust pressing at the back causing those in front to be knocked down. The Anonymous reports that Montfort rode to the bank to calm his men and

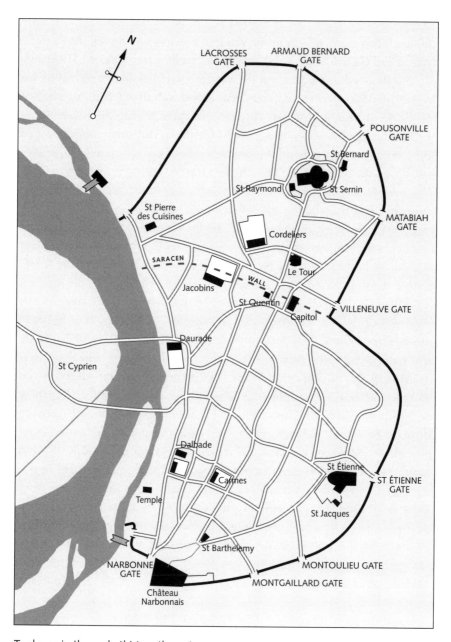

Toulouse in the early thirteenth century.

to restore order, but he went too fast and in his momentum inadvertently plunged into the river. (Peter of Vaux de Cernay says he fell into a deep part of the Garonne as he was trying to clamber into a boat.) His heavy armour dragged him under but he was grabbed by a soldier and saved; his horse, also heavily armoured, drowned. This was an ill omen, though before the battle of Muret, Montfort experienced three mishaps before winning the greatest battle of the Albigensian Crusade. But this culmination of the whole sorry episode on the western side of the river could only have dampened the spirits of the French even further.

Montfort had to rethink his tactics and accept the limitations imposed upon by him the sheer scale of the task before him and his lack of manpower. Once more he settled in for the long haul as he absorbed the bruising assaults of the southerners, their newly constructed petraries and mangonels bombarding the Narbonnais castle. Within its walls, the legate Bertrand often feared for his life, and with good reason: a fellow priest was killed by a shot from a trebuchet. Bertrand's part in the siege at this stage was to request a major preaching mission ordered by Rome, while throughout France, Flanders and Germany, Bishop Fulkes of Toulouse and Jacques de Vitry were to drum up reinforcements. The Countess de Montfort also departed from this dangerous situation, escorted by Foucaud de Berzy, to plead help from her powerful brother Matthew de Montmorency, the Constable of France. They also hoped to bring Prince Louis back down to the south, now that he had returned from his failed invasion of England. All travelled through the woods to avoid capture in hostile territory. But the city council was equally active in this area: on 1 November it had already sent out men to hire knights from as far as 80 miles away to come to the city's aid by Easter; these were to be protected by Arnold de Montégut on the way out and by Bernard de Cazenac on the way back. Vassals owing service would not be enough for this great setpiece; more mercenaries were needed. With both sides sending out for help, the great siege of Toulouse was about to escalate even further.

But first the winter had to be endured. The Toulousains continued to harness their vast resources of manpower in the construction of more defences and more siege machines that pummelled the Château Narbonnais. As seemingly desultory and ineffective fighting ploughed on into its fourth month, much of it concentrated around the site of the eastern Montoulieu Gate, around the end of the year Montfort wished to obtain hostages from the hostile town of Montauban nearby in an endeavour to secure its good conduct. He sent his Seneschal of Agenais, Philip de Landreville, and Bishop Arnold de Leocutre there with a small company of troops. In a plan reminiscent of the one that sealed Baldwin of Toulouse's fate, the townspeople sent messengers to Count Raymond to come there and seize these important figures and kill their men. Raymond dispatched a large force (perhaps not as large as the 500 Peter of Vaux de Cernay suggests) to carry out this scheme. At night, many of the 3,000 inhabitants of the town set to work as the crusading force slept: around their lodgings the streets were barricaded, guards were posted and firewood was piled up at the doors to burn them out if necessary. When the war cry of 'Toulouse! Toulouse!' was sent up, the crusaders, though 'heavy and dull with sleep', managed to respond quickly enough to put up a defence and forced their attackers to flee.[178] Their blood up, the French plundered the town and set fire to anything they could not carry away.

The winter also saw Montfort receive unwelcome news from Rome: at the end of 1217 Pope Honorius III finally restored the castle of Foix to Count Raymond Roger. This was to honour the agreement reached by Innocent III. The count returned to his city early the following year, but he left behind his son Roger Bernard with some of his men in Toulouse. Although the count was to take a well-earned sabbatical from fighting the French for the next year, Montfort could not have known this; this uncertainty and an apparent papal reward for a long-standing foe must have left him very uneasy. The Anonymous portrays an increasingly uncertain and pessimistic leader who can see no way to victory: 'My rage, bitterness and passion mount, and it is no wonder I cannot be cheerful when I see the hares turning on the hound!'[179]

In an attempt to break the winter deadlock, and perhaps also to improve the morale of the crusaders and their leader, a dawn assault was suggested by Guy de Lévis, Montfort's marshal. The idea was to catch the defenders unawares during the harsh chill of daybreak as they stayed warm in bed with their wives. But the crusaders' plan was quickly rumbled – the noise of their preparations alerted the inhabitants – and a defence was swiftly drawn up under Bernard de Comminges. The noise could not be helped as the attack was so large, led by the count himself. The size and weight of the attack meant that the French were able to break through the southerners' outer defences. But as with earlier assaults, this, too, was driven back after another bloody encounter and an equally determined defence.

Montfort could do little but fret about the situation and his money problems until reinforcements arrived in the spring. The Toulousains continued to bring in supplies and men and to strengthen both their city's defences and their lines against the Narbonnais castle. War weariness, casualties and expectations of the decisive battle to come saw fighting tail off. As the siege dragged on into its sixth month, all knew that the new season would unleash a new round of fighting on an even bigger and more intense scale than before. The clash was to be truly epic.

The Siege of Toulouse, Spring 1218

The southerners took the initiative in a pre-emptive strike in mid-April, just before Easter (15 April). They had learned at Beaucaire that their best defence in siege situations was to tough it out behind the relative safety of their walls and not seek a risky solution in battle. But by Easter 1218, they knew that northerners and crusaders from across Europe would once again flock to Montfort's banner and that the current regional advantage in numbers that the Occitanians enjoyed could soon be negated. They therefore decided on a massive sortie to attack the crusaders' camp. If it succeeded and the siege was lifted, new crusaders would be deterred from making the journey south.

It is not clear from the Anonymous and Peter of Vaux de Cernay whether the attack was launched on the siege camp of New Toulouse or on a tented site or, most likely, both. What is evident is the scale of the operation that was launched, with captains such as Hugh d'Alfaro (Count Raymond's son-in-law) and Hugh de la Mota leading the cavalry and infantry out of the city and straight into the crusaders' hastily drawn-up lines. The *Song* once again glories in the carnage: 'Sharp steel met flesh: noses, scalps and chins, arms, legs and feet, guts, livers and kidneys lay strewn on the ground in lumps and gobbets.' One of the first Frenchmen killed was Armand Chabreus, hacked 'into several pieces'.[180]

The danger of engaging with the elite crusaders in the field was brought home by Montfort's heavy cavalry charge, which burst from the gates of New Toulouse. The southerners turned tail and starting running back towards the city; but they were rallied by Hugh de la Mota with the loud exhortation (very frequently expressed in the pages of the *Song*) that it is

'Better to die well than live disgraced in prison!' Leading by example, he charged at a crusader and knocked him off his horse with his lance; 'reining back', he then drove his lance home into a man-at-arms. As maces and swords were wielded by the cavalry, another southerner, William Unaud, levelled his lance at an enemy knight with such force that the head of his lance snapped off and was left protruding from his opponent's body.

But the southerners had been learning from past mistakes. At this crucial juncture they launched a second wave of troops from the city. This tactical reserve poured from the trenches onto the plain outside the Montoulieu Gate and waded into the fight. The crusader Peter de Voisins was unhorsed in the ensuing *mêlée* and, according to Peter of Vaux de Cernay, surrounded. Montfort, seeing the danger his man was in, led a typically brave charge with just one other man into the fray to rescue Peter. 'Blows are rained on him from all sides,' says Peter.[181] He struck two men to the ground before his horse slipped and his saddlebow broke, hurtling him to the ground. But he was rapidly on his feet, fighting back at this moment of greatest peril, and managed to remount his horse.

Others were not so lucky. The crusader Sevin Gorloin was surrounded and cut to pieces; Bertrand de Pestillac ran an archer through with his lance. Among the other fatalities were the southerners Peter de Maurens and the Wolf of Foix, thought to be an illegitimate son of Count Raymond Roger. The southerner William Arnold was more fortunate: he was taken prisoner in the fighting, 'but cleverly he dropped down onto his knees and the Toulousains hid him'; abandoning his horse, he made it safely back to the city. The knight's *parole* – his word of honour – was not always the guarantee chivalry required it to be, especially when imprisonment and a crippling ransom were involved.

This second wave threw Montfort's men back. Although the sortie had been repulsed, the Anonymous portrays it as a morale booster for the Toulousains and another dispiriting moment for the crusading chief, whom he depicts as raging in its aftermath. Despite their losses, the southerners had taken the fight to the enemy and unsettled the French further, adding to the psychological strain of the besiegers and exposing their vulnerability to attack at any instant. However, the southerners' well-timed coup in retaking the city in the autumn had not paid off: the intelligent plan was devised so as to give them the numerical regional advantage over the crusaders during the winter. But during this time they had not managed to shrug off the ever-tenacious Montfort as they had hoped. Now, with spring arriving seven months into the siege, the French could finally expect large-scale reinforcements.

These reinforcements appeared in May, the result of a successful recruitment campaign initiated by the legate Bertrand and the preaching and beseeching of Bishop Fulkes, Countess Alice de Montfort and Jacques de Vitry: 'Their preaching mission resulted in a great many men taking up the cross.'[182] The countess and the bishop brought back with them an impressive army of men and leading nobles such as Amaury de Craon, Michael de Harnes and Walter Langton, brother to Stephen Langton, the Archbishop of Canterbury. Montfort's army thus augmented, he could now revisit his failed earlier plan to blockade Toulouse from the western side of the Garonne, which is where he wished the new crusaders to set up camp. In the meantime, he had assiduously prepared for their arrival with the construction of new siege engines: a cat, towers, catapults and mangonels. Montfort's general air of despondency dissipated now that he finally had a full force to implement his strategy. He went to meet the new army optimistic and resolute. 'Nothing', he is reported to have said, 'can hurt me now!'[183]

After a short delay while the new arrivals stayed in New Toulouse to rest after the rigours of the long journey, the crusaders then crossed the Garonne at Muret to make for the suburb of St Cyprien and position themselves there, laden with supplies. Scouts must have forewarned them of the large-scale excavations the citizens had carried out on the western side of the suburb since the last occupation, but the northerners still seemed to have been ill prepared for the system of defensive fosses that now lay before them. The Toulousains were well prepared this time, having anticipated such a manoeuvre. Throughout winter the citizens had busied themselves in preparation for the great showdown, all lending a hand in constructing walls, ramparts, crenellations and ditches. Count Raymond and the southerner leadership knew that a blockade from the west threatened the city with starvation, so St Cyprien and the western approaches were given vigilant attention.

The Toulousains also divided their forces to counter the two new fronts of the enemy. Count Bernard de Comminges and Dalmas of Creixhell kept sentinel for the south and south-eastern perimeter, while Roger Bernard of Foix led Roger de Montaut, Odo de Tarrida and the other militia, archers, knights and sergeants to occupy the bridges, banks, houses and gardens of St Cyprien on the far side of the river.

Michael de Harnes led the crusader charge into the town. Immediately they were confronted by the network of ditches. Peter complains that these served their purpose by preventing the crusaders from bringing their heavily armoured horses – their key weapon – to bear fully on the defenders. The French could not break the southerners' defences and so retreated, pursued hotly all the while. Montfort tried to rally his men to make a stand in the suburb, but Walter Langton and others persuaded him otherwise. They were forced to abandon St Cyprien and they withdrew half a league to pitch their camp at a safer distance. Peter of Vaux de Cernay, habitually ready with excuses for any setbacks suffered by his hero Montfort, actually makes no attempt to gloss over the episode: 'So despite the large size of our force we had to retire shamefacedly and pitch camp on the banks of the Garonne, some distance away from St Cyprien.'[184] The despair of the crusaders was matched by the demonstrative exultation of the defenders. Making the most of the victory, orders were given for a fresh bombardment of the Narbonnais castle. Somehow still holding out, it underwent a particularly punishing barrage that destroyed much of the fabric of the masonry.

But at that moment divine intervention came to the aid of the crusaders. The heavens unloaded a torrential downpour during a thunderous storm. At first this delighted the Toulousains as they hoped to see the level of the Garonne rise and flood the crusaders encamped on the embankment. In fact, after three continuous days and nights of heavy rain, it was their property and defences that became compromised by the storm damage, with bridges broken, equipment destroyed, ditches washed away and, particularly worryingly, flour mills impaired. With the new bridge now only partially intact and thus precarious to cross, the soldiers in its two barbican towers were left largely cut off on the far bank; any reinforcements could reach them in only small numbers at a time, perhaps too few to help in a crisis.

Montfort immediately capitalised on the moment, launching another move on St Cyprien, though his advances were hindered by the mud. This time he could enter with minimal resistance. He took up residence in the hospital built just a few years earlier, garrisoning it with mercenaries and crossbowmen, while his troops occupied the western bank of the Garonne that lay between the eastern side of the suburb and the city's perimeter. As a matter of urgency he fortified the area with ditches, barricades and walls with arrow loops while yet more siege machines were constructed and provisions brought in. As the Toulousains looked on with growing concern at the relentless Montfort making ever more preparations, Montfort himself simultaneously sent out urgent instructions for good boats to be brought in from the Agenais. He was planning an amphibious assault.

The defenders' first priority was now to provision the beleaguered garrisons in the towers. Carpenters and engineers were reluctant to risk themselves in making the necessary repairs. Inspiration came from an Aragonese knight called Peron Domingo: at immense personal danger to himself, he managed to clamber across on a rope with which he dragged over two boats full of supplies. A rope-bridge reinforced by timber was then thrown up to keep the link to the tower operational. The other tower remained out of reach from the city. But a long double rope was able to connect the two towers, with food and crossbow quarrels pulled across in reed baskets. With the southerners otherwise driven out of the suburb, the imperative was to get more men into the vulnerable far tower. Hugh de la Mota tried to get a boat full of his men across to them, but the strong current of the swollen river swept them downstream. However, a second boat manned with Toulousains did manage to succeed and reinforce the tower. Montfort, like a terrier with a rat in its teeth, continued to shake the exposed barbican. His engines launched a constant barrage of squared stones and rounded boulders onto it until 'the whole rampart was shattered and its mortar was knocked out'.[185] Their defences being pummelled into dust around their ears, the defenders withdrew back into the city, leaving Montfort master of St Cyprien at last. His banner was raised to flutter over the remains of the tower.

The fighting continued day and night with boatmen and archers taking the main roles in the exchanges while casualties mounted daily. Peter of Vaux de Cernay is keen to expose the bitter nature of the siege by recounting the atrocities suffered by prisoners. Of course, all the blame for these is laid at the door of the godless southerners, but the reality would have been that both sides were complicit in the brutality. Peter's descriptions of these barbarities may sound like hyperbole – and many historians would dismiss them as such – but, as I have shown elsewhere in my research and as I will discuss at the end of this chapter, such acts were disturbingly common in all spheres of medieval warfare (and, indeed, warfare in all ages). Peter's testimony needs to be taken seriously.

The least of the torments he describes involved humiliation. French prisoners were led bound through the streets of Toulouse with bags about their necks, into which citizens placed their money to show appreciation for their capture. What followed for many was the horrific part. Some had their eyes gouged out; others their tongues cut off. Some were dragged behind horses and then left to the dogs and crows; others were stoned to death. Some were burned; others hanged. Some had millstones tied around their necks and were thrown into the river; others were flung from the walls. To terrify and demoralise the northerners, some prisoners were hacked into bits and their body parts catapulted across to them, so that they fell on their heads in a gruesome shower. A Frenchman called Raymond Escrivain was buried alive up to his shoulders, his head then being used as target practice for stone-throwers and archers. He was eventually set on fire and fed to the dogs. The length of the siege, coupled with the length of the French invasion of the south, had served only to increase the savagery with which the war was fought.

Nemesis at Toulouse, Summer 1218

By the time June arrived, the siege still had nearly two months left to run. The crusaders remained unable to enforce a complete blockade, as was demonstrated by the ease with which Bernard de Cazenac entered the city with his force of Brabanter mercenaries (500, says the Anonymous), where he was met with much celebration. This rubbed salt in Montfort's wounds as he was experiencing difficulties in maintaining his own hired soldiers due to lack of pay. In other campaigns, smaller places would be taken and plundered, the booty therein going some way to satisfy the troops' demands. But at Toulouse, the lack of progress meant that pickings were rare indeed.

To deny the besieged the produce of nearby fields and vineyards after the growing months, on 2 June he led a ravaging party to destroy them in the Oratory Elm area north-east of the city. Roger Bernard of Foix in turn led out from the city a counter force to prevent this. In the intense skirmish that ensued, the Anonymous names nearly thirty knights on both sides individually. The combat quickly escalated. Some of the militia broke and ran back for the safety of the city, wading chin deep across the moat to do so. Some Bretons and Flemings carried torches and straw to the barricades, but were pushed back.

The following day, Pentecost (3 June), Montfort held another council, in which he expressed his growing concerns over money: his mercenaries were refusing to fight until they were paid. He planned to build a colossal siege engine, bigger than any before. The Anonymous calls this a cat, but the description suggests that it was a belfry tower designed to hold 150 archers and 400 knights. With it they would break into the city and kill all its fathers and sons. The crusaders received a great boost when Count Ralph of Soissons arrived with a strong force. Montfort, in his delight and relief, offered the count up to a quarter of the plunder of the city and all the finest warhorses; this was also an incentive for him to stay as long as possible. The Count of Soissons diplomatically advised Montfort to make the payment of the mercenaries his priority.

The arrival of this new force and, if known, the work on the new tower caused great anxiety amongst the Toulousains, who feared that the initiative was now firmly in Montfort's hands. However, their spirits were boosted by the arrival of count's son, the young Raymond. This was the cause of major celebrations across the city and some acts of bravado: men 'light on their feet' ran up to the crusaders' camp and shouted 'Death to the French, death to the pilgrims!'[186] In addition, reinforcements of sergeants and archers arrived on boats as the great conflict continued to suck in ever more fighting men.

This arrival underlined the need for Montfort to control the river. In an attempt to achieve this objective, he further intensified his fortification of St Cyprien, transforming his headquarters at the hospital into a castle surrounded by a deep fosse and squared stakes. He had to deprive the city of reinforcements and supplies if he were to make headway. His first objective was therefore to take the remaining barbican tower that defended the broken bridge on the eastern bank of the Garonne, beyond which stood the city perimeter. Once more the area became the scene of concentrated combat. The boats Montfort had ordered now arrived carrying some of his elite troops, with which he made a full-scale amphibious assault on the tower. This time it was taken. They broke the rope-bridge and placed Montfort's lion banner on the tower to display the victory.

This was an alarming development for the defenders as it severely tightened the squeeze on the city. They would not accept this defeat without a fight. They set up a mangonel, which bombarded the tower and drove out the crusaders, but only after they had torched it. It was another setback for Montfort, as the Anonymous makes clear that the river remained dominated by the southerners, who retained 'command of the waterways both up and down river and across it; they sought out and occupied all the landing places, bringing ashore foodstuffs and other supplies'.[187] Yet another tense moment in which the siege might have gone either way reverted back to a stalemate position.

This dominance of the river was reinforced when the Toulousains, renewed in their confidence, attempted to regain the initiative. A mercenary force of 163 Brabanters and Germans now made their own amphibious landing on the western bank and attacked St Cyprien. Armed with swords, clubs and their Turkish bows (shorter composite bows) they made the shore, where they were met by crusaders under the command of Peter de Voisins. On the riverbanks a desperate combat led to many drowning in the river, dragged down by their armour. Such was the fate of the Frenchman Rauli de Champagne. The outcome of the encounter is not clear, but it seems that the mercenaries were repelled. The relatively low numbers of attackers sent against the crusading force would seem to indicate that this was a probing attack designed to test the crusaders and also to demoralise and unsettle them by exposing their vulnerability.

Certainly, the strains in the crusader camp were becoming ever more evident. After the river assault, Montfort returned to the Château Narbonnais to confer with his commanders in a major council of war. Among those present were the Count of Soissons, Amaury de Craon, Hugh de Lacy, the legate Bertrand and Montfortian veterans Bouchard de Marly and Alain de Roucy. Count Ralph advised Montfort to come to terms with Raymond as he would remain Viscount of Béziers, Albi and Carcassonne. Amaury de Craon guardedly pointed out that the city was still receiving supplies and not suffering from any form of want and its morale was still high; all telling points that demonstrated the weakness of the crusaders' position after eight months of siege. The Anonymous has Montfort reminding them that he had conquered the Toulousain, Agenais, Quercy, Bigorre, Comminges and the Albigeois and that he would take this city, too. The legate Bertrand was in similarly uncompromising mood, apparently ordering Amaury to undertake a fast as penance for his defeatism.

Montfort's newfound positive outlook by now had the air of enforced optimism. He was repeatedly pinning all his hopes on one scheme after another. This time, the cat that he had constructed would win the day by 'spreading Greek fire throughout the town'. This cat seems to be a traditional cat to fill the ditches but with a belfry tower built on top, rather like the one deployed at Beaucaire. The morning after the council it was brought up to within striking distance of the wall near the Château Narbonnais. The problem with this was that it was also within striking distance of one of the city's trebuchets. This now redirected its projection to aim at Montfort's machine. Months of action pummelling the castle had sharpened the skills of the southern operators. A stone came sailing through the air and stuck the upper part of the tower, 'shattering all the hides and fastenings' designed to protect it. Montfort urgently ordered for it to be hauled back out of range lest more damage was incurred with its defences now weakened. It was moved a few paces back but struck again by another boulder that 'broke and cracked apart iron and steel, the nails and timbers, pitch and cladding'.[188] Many of those shifting the huge machine were killed; the rest ran for cover, despite Montfort's exasperated and ineffectual death threats if they failed to follow orders. The troubadour Raymond Escrivain captures the artillery duel in a song:

> When he saw her and recognised her, the Trebuchet said, 'Hard-bitten Cat, I will soon knock you down', and he hit her on the front of her helm with such a blow that she shook all over. 'You are foolish, Cat, for starting a fight with me, and I shall make you aware of that soon enough'. That made the Cat's hairs stand on end, for she is big, fat and bulky, and she said that she still had a strong skin, and that she would make it to the *lices*. She put her paws together and pounced ... This made the Trebuchet's hairs stand on end, for he is fierce and strong, cruel and true ... And he sent her a flying missile that not even three *ribaulds* could have picked up, and he shot it, hot, into her body ... And the Cat that felt the blow nearly died of grief, and cried out, 'Trebuchet, it was an unlucky day I saw you'.[189]

Meanwhile, Count Raymond held a council to discuss responses to the tower that Montfort had built. The Count of Comminges was unperturbed by it, saying that the crusaders' preoccupation with it kept them from destroying crops and vineyards. Bernard de Cazenac declared that the closer it drew up to the walls, the easier it would be to destroy. Estolt de

Linars was less sanguine, advising caution and the re-strengthening of the defences on the south-eastern perimeter. His plan, supported by Dalmas of Creixell, was put into action. Under constant harrying fire from the crusaders, the citizens undertook another great communal effort to protect the ditches and hence hinder the belfry's ability to reach the walls. The work was continued despite the cost in lives. All were unaware that the siege was soon to reach its shocking climax.

Montfort wanted to bring the belfry to bear before the new defences were completed. With his best-armoured knights now protected by latticed wicker shields, the repaired and reinforced belfry was drawn up closer to the city's wall. Many were still struck down by the barrage that met them as they moved forward; the tower itself was hit numerous times but its stronger protection prevented any major structural failure. Once again it withdrew to a safe distance, but this great tower was an ever-constant threat to the city, its presence warning of dire peril to come and all the time affecting morale in the city. Should the citizens lose the will to resist, there would be little Count Raymond and the other leaders could do. That the tower could be seen by the city's inhabitants might in itself be enough to make it effective without full deployment. The fear of a psychological collapse after more than eight months of unrelenting siege greatly troubled the southern command. Something had to be done.

On 24 June a knight by the name of Bernard advocated a sortie to destroy the siege engine. A plan was hatched and some of the southerners' best men assigned to the task. At dawn Arnold de Villemur checked over the men and their equipment as they made ready for the major attack, while the ramparts were lined with archers and crossbowmen with plenty of quarrels and arrows to provide covering 'fire'. On the left flank, Estolt de Linars had ladders ready for soldiers to clamber down the walls without opening gates or barricades. At the same time as the attack on the cat was launched, another group would charge the crusader camp; this was both a diversionary tactic and also a deployment of their greater manpower to keep the crusaders here from rushing to defend the siege engine. As Peter of Vaux de Cernay rightly noted, 'In this way they hoped that our men, unarmed and attacked on two fronts would be too disorganised to resist their foes and too weak to withstand a two-fold assault.'[190] Bernard de Cazenac exhorted the southerners to take their revenge: 'My lords, men of Toulouse, those enemies you see there have killed your sons and brothers and caused you great grief. If you can kill them, it will do you good.' The men went down the ladders crying out 'Kill them, kill them, it's the only way!'[191] As they shouted this, they could not have known that the moment of reckoning had arrived.

Montfort knew a sortie was likely; he was informed that the enemy was gathering behind the outer defences of the city between the castle and the Montoulieu Gate. He immediately donned his armour and, as was his pious habit before any major encounter, went to the chapel. He was still here when the fighting broke out, Bernard de Comminges having launched the southerners' attack in full force. Twice Montfort had to be urged to abandon his prayers and come to command the crusaders' defence. Only when he had completed his devotions did he finally stir into action. At last, says Peter of Vaux de Cernay, 'this most invincible of men hurried to the fight'.[192]

The attack on the crusaders' New Toulouse was co-ordinated with activity on the river to help protect the southerners from any threat from this direction and possibly to land troops as well to join in the assault. The crusaders are reported to have suffered a number of wounded and dead before Montfort's belated presence rallied his men to drive the Toulousains back to their trenches with a heavy cavalry charge that included the Berzy brothers, Foucaud and John. However, they could not press further as the barrage of crossbow bolts, arrows, slingshots and stones from the manned ramparts drove them back. The Toulousains themselves then rallied and turned to chase the French back. In this part of the combat Guy de Montfort was seriously wounded by an archer. When his horse was struck deep in the head by an arrow, it jolted sideways; a crossbowman targeting Guy seized his opportunity and let loose with a bolt that struck the crusader 'in the left side of the groin, leaving the steel deep in his flesh'. The Anonymous cannot resist making a joke in bad taste about enforced celibacy, reporting Guy as declaring to his brother: 'This wound will make me a Hospitaller!'[193]

Montfort and his men were still in the thick of the fighting, desperately guarding the belfry and other siege engines on which he had placed all his hopes. Here he and his knights sheltered as best they could behind large mantle shields against an intense salvo of arrows from archers and the stones from the enemy's trebuchets, mangonel and other stone-throwing machines. These were attempting to drive off Montfort's force so that their own troops could reach the machines and set about destroying them.

Peter of Vaux de Cernay states that Montfort himself was wounded five times by arrows, but the strength of his armour enabled him to continue the hazardous defence. One of the machines pounding his men was a mangonel dragged down from the St Sernin *bourg* in the north of the city and operated by women. Suddenly, a stone launched by it fell swiftly and heavily from the sky and struck Montfort's 'steel helmet, shattering his eyes, brains, back teeth, forehead and jaw'.[194] His head crushed in, he fell dying to the ground. He beat his breast twice and died.

Two French knights, Jocelyn and Aimery, galloped over to their lord and hurriedly covered his body with a blue cape. But many had already seen what had happened. Panic immediately set in. The count's body was carried out of the combat zone to Fulkes, bishop of the city Montfort had died trying to take. The churchman blessed his body. The shocking news spread rapidly, both sides hardly daring to believe what they heard: the crusaders were filled with despair; Toulouse erupted with joy and the sounds of celebration. Peter of Vaux de Cernay was distraught at the death of his hero. He likened the count's five wounds suffered before his death to Christ's at the time of his crucifixion. 'Who can fail to dissolve in tears?' he asks in anguish.[195]

The crusading army retreated in disarray. Those in St Cyprien returned to New Toulouse in such haste they abandoned many valuables in the camp: armour, money, pack animals, tents. They were pursued by the Toulousains and many were taken prisoner. The citizens poured out from the south-east of the city and set fire to Montfort's great siege tower, watching it burn with ecstatic relief. The crusaders holed themselves in the Château Narbonnais to absorb the monumental shock of their loss and to anxiously plan their next move.

At dawn the next day, Bertrand, the cardinal legate, oversaw the emergency council. He knew that Montfort's death must be quickly accepted if the crusaders were to move forward. The first order of business was to recognise the succession of Montfort's son Amaury as heir to his father's lands in the south. This ensured continuity of legitimate possession. This also made the young Amaury, possibly only 19 or 20 years of age, commander of the army. In some ways he was a figurehead, sorely needed to replace the irreplaceable. The wounded Guy de Montfort and the dead count's veteran captains were at hand to offer Amaury the benefit of their military and political advice. For four days the crusaders tried to come to terms with their loss. Then they acted.

On Sunday 1 June, amidst terrible storms, the crusaders finally emerged from their siege camp of New Toulouse and returned to the siege. The belief that they could still capture the place may have been encouraged by the deprivations the city was finally facing: William of Puylaurens reports that at the time of Montfort's death 'they had few remaining supplies and little hope of gathering their harvest that summer'.[196] Nonetheless, the plan was not to starve them out but to launch another assault. It is likely that the crusade leadership wished to offer a display of determination that would show the besieged that they still meant business and were not going anywhere, and thus deflate the confidence of the defenders. It was also a desperate undertaking intended to discourage the high desertion rate from the crusaders' camp in the wake of Montfort's death with the prospect of imminent plunder should the city fall.

The exact date of the attack in July is unknown, but it occurred before the third week of the month. It began with fire-carts filled with burning wood and other combustible material being propelled fast towards the Montoulieu Gate to burn down the wooden defences, helped by the dry, summer heat and a strong breeze. This caused instant panic in the city as the citizens rushed to the area with water to douse the fires and stones to deter the crusaders from drawing close enough to apply their incendiaries. The first wave withdrew to allow the second wave to move forward, making the most of the confusion caused by the flames; their intention was probably not to enter the city but to kill those fighting the fires so that the wooden defences continued to burn. With much of the Toulousain forces diverted to deal with the fires, the crusaders launched their third and final wave: the charge of their heavy cavalry. 'Thick on the ground lay feet, legs, arms, brain-matter and blood', the result of the fierce struggle that at times forced men to resort to wrestling with just hands and teeth.[197] The staunch defence broke up the ranks of the crusader divisions, forcing the northerners to withdraw. Across the battlefield the cries and moans of the wounded and dying echoed long after the battle was over, filling the night air.

The next few days were spent without any combat; the crusaders were too busy coming to a defining decision on what their next step should be. Guy de Montfort and Alan de Roucy both advised that the fruitless, costly siege be finally lifted. Amaury protested at this, fearful of how it would undermine his position in the south; but Roucy's point – that the logistical problems were now too severe to be overcome – carried the day. Peter of Vaux de Cernay emphasised the growing manpower shortages, too, as increasingly larger numbers of French returned home and desertion was rife in the wake of Montfort's death. The final decision was made by the legate Bertrand. The siege was over. On 25 July they departed, leaving their siege camp and the castle in flames. Even this last move was ineffective: the townspeople rushed out and extinguished the fires, profiting from the materials they had thereby saved and what the crusaders were forced to leave behind. After almost ten months, the longest military operation of the war was over. As they left, Bertrand is reported to have made a chilling promise: the crusaders would return: 'We shall destroy the town, and everyone in it shall be put to the sword. Sentence is given!'[198]

Aftermath

Count Montfort's body was carried to Carcassonne and buried according to French ritual in St Nazaire cathedral. In 1224 his body was exhumed and laid to rest in a priory church near Chevreuse. An unnamed tombstone discovered in 1845, thought by many to be that of Montfort, was placed on the cathedral wall in Carcassonne: it depicts an early thirteenth-century knight bearing Montfort's coat of arms. According to the Anonymous, his epitaph, now lost, declared that 'he is a saint and a martyr who shall breathe again and shall in wondrous joy inherit and flourish; he shall wear a crown and be seated in the kingdom'. With bitter sarcasm the Anonymous adds:

> And I have heard it said that this must be so – if by killing men and shedding blood, by damning souls and causing deaths, by trusting evil counsels, by setting fires, destroying men, dishonouring nobility, seizing lands and encouraging pride, by kindling evil and quenching good, by killing women and slaughtering children, a man in this world can win Jesus Christ, then certainly Count Simon wears a crown and shines in Heaven above.[199]

The news of Montfort's death shocked Christendom. Over the next century nearly seventy of 175 texts studied recount his end at Toulouse, nearly as many as those that recorded his victory at Muret. William de Nangis lamented the loss of 'a handsome man, firm in his faith and in combat, and worthy of eternal glory', while William the Breton exclaims

'O sorrow!' and says that Montfort 'received the crown of a martyr'. In England, Matthew Paris raises him to the pantheon of classical gods, likening him to Mars ('because he was warlike'), as well as Paris ('because he was handsome') and Cato ('because he was virtuous'). William of Puylaurens noted that:

> the man who inspired terror from the Mediterranean to the British sea fell by a blow from a single stone. I affirm that later I heard the Count of Toulouse (the last of his line) generously praise him – even though he was his enemy – for his fidelity, his foresight, his energy and all the qualities which befit a leader.[200]

This captures the qualities of Montfort the commander, but omits his complete ruthlessness and his unrestrained ambition.

The crusaders failed at Toulouse for a number of reasons. It was not through want of good tactics: they had launched a series of well-planned attacks that were all sound on vellum, especially the last one in July. But victory was always going to be difficult because of the sheer scale of the task. Toulouse was the major city of the region for a reason: it was an economic powerhouse whose sheer size alone in ground covered and population meant that Montfort simply did not have the manpower to successfully blockade it or even take command of the river. Despite its makeshift and hastily erected defences, it remained a huge and formidable stronghold. Supplies and men continued to make their way into the city and so its weight of numbers could not be used against it to starve it out. That the uprising had shrewdly taken place in autumn also meant Montfort had had to wait for spring before any sizeable reinforcements could arrive. Delay was a victory of resistance for the besieged, and a mark of failure for the crusaders tied down, not least because across the south Montfort was now losing the allegiance of southerners who felt confident enough to defy him. Although we do not hear of it in the sources, some of his men had to be garrisoned and active elsewhere to keep a lid on any trouble threatening to boil over thanks to the opportunities the great siege of Toulouse offered.

Montfort reluctantly had to settle in for the long run, but he still attempted frequent storms, knowing that this offered a greater chance of success than an impartial blockade. If his superior fighting men could break into the city itself, the chaos and fear created would have been to his advantage and may have secured success for him. The defiance of the Toulousains and their admirable communal spirit, so often remarked upon and praised by the Anonymous, was hugely important in keeping the French out. A steady supply of provisions kept the citizens loyal to their leadership and free from the hardships that might otherwise have led them to seek terms with the enemy. A crucial factor was therefore their psychological outlook, bolstered all the more by the fact that the invincible Montfort had ground to a halt at Beaucaire. He no longer had unstoppable momentum. The people of Toulouse exploited this to the fullest extent.

A notable feature of the siege was the brutality meted out to prisoners. This brutality has often been dismissed by historians as the hyperbole of hysterical monks and the near excess of troubadours sensationalising their stories. The accounts of siege atrocities here can be trusted; they fit into an all too familiar pattern. In some conflicts, relative restraint was observed, especially among the knightly classes; in others, such as German invasions of Italy and the Spanish *Reconquista*, atrocities were more common as reprisals and revenge escalated. This was the case in the Albigensian Crusade. At Toulouse, nearly a decade of northern occupation and southern resistance – all fought for control of the land – now focused on a claustrophobic ten-month siege where savage frustrations were bound to be vented.

Not that these atrocities were merely irrational or angry outbursts; as discussed previously, terror was a weapon frequently and successfully deployed in the crusade from its very start. Medieval commanders – like those before and even today – knew the worth of terror tactics. In 1049 at a fort near Alençon, Duke William of Normandy had the hands and feet of a defeated garrison amputated to cow the town into submission; it worked. The display of body parts and their use as missiles was a common psychological ploy. On the First Crusade, the Christian army stuck the heads of Muslim prisoners on poles in view of the besieged Muslims in Nicaea and Antioch; crusader heads were impaled on stakes at Tiberias on the Third Crusade. James I of Aragon, the son and heir of King Peter killed at Muret and the young hostage of Montfort, catapulted prisoners' heads over walls and at Lisbon placed eighty heads on stakes.

Atrocities were not restricted to what are sometimes considered religious wars. During the Hundred Years War between England and France, the English garrison besieged at Auberoche attempted to slip a messenger through French lines; he was caught and catapulted alive back into the town. At Brescia in 1238, Emperor Frederick II tied hostages to his siege machines in the hope of deterring enemy bombardments on them – a tactic that had failed before with murderous consequences; the Brescians in turn lowered live prisoners down their walls in front of Frederick's battering rams. An example from the siege of Crema in 1159 demonstrates the urge for reprisal seen so frequently in Languedoc:

> It was a pitiable sight when those outside cut off the heads of the slain and played ball with them, tossing them from the right hand into the left, and used them in mocking display. But those in the town, thinking it shameful to dare less, afforded a heart-rending spectacle by tearing limb from limb upon their walls prisoners from our army, without mercy.[201]

If anything, the accounts of atrocities at Toulouse are restrained; it is likely that far worse things happened and went unrecorded.

Too much had been invested in the war for it to stop now. Even more than that of King Peter II of Aragon, the death of Montfort changed the dynamics of the situation, causing a temporary hiatus, but plans were immediately made for the future. The southerners were quick to capitalise on the crusaders' disarray. 'Now is the time to attack', declares the Anonymous, 'and conquer and kill the French.'[202] Lombres and Pamiers defected from Count Amaury, and no doubt many others also rode the wave of the new momentum. Papal letters to Toulouse demanding that its citizens renounce Count Raymond fell on the deaf ears of a newly confident and re-emerging power.

Though Amaury was now the region's military commander, the northerners needed the help of the French crown to supply the influx of pilgrims required for campaigning, as demand exceeded supply with the Fifth Crusade now bogged down in the massive siege of Damietta on the Nile delta. Nevertheless, when Pope Honorius heard of Montfort's death over a month later, he generously issued another indulgence for those taking up the cross in Languedoc. He co-ordinated his response with the legate Bertrand to appeal to Philip II in mid-August to send his son Louis to lead an army south, while the legate sent Bishop Fulkes of Toulouse and Countess Alice de Montfort to the French court to make personal pleas for royal intervention.

Although Philip would in many ways prefer a northern Frenchman loyal to him to rule the south rather than the independently minded counts of Toulouse, who would continue their alliance with England, the ever-cautious Philip was reluctant to respond. However, Bertrand's offer (be it genuine or crafty) to the teenaged Count Theobald of Champagne to lead a new crusade decided the Capetian's mind. As Count of Champagne, Theobald was already one of the most powerful noblemen in France; his prospects as heir to the throne of Navarre and now potential great power across Languedoc, added to his vast lands and wealth in Champagne, raised the prospect of an overmighty noble that Philip chose not to ignore. The offer from the pope to grant Philip half of the Egyptian crusading tax he was collecting from the clergy in France also helped in the king's decision. The king instructed his son to lead a crusading expedition. There are some indications that Louis may have been reluctant to go, but the ambitious and chivalrous prince would have also seen the planned campaign as a chance to reassert his reputation after the defeat in England the previous year. On 20 November, Louis 'took the cross, for the glory of God and the suppression of heresy in Toulouse'.[203] The might of the French throne was about to be brought to bear on Languedoc.

But it would be another six months before Louis arrived, as he prepared the logistics and recruitment of his campaign and arranged his affairs in France. Meanwhile, the chronicles report sporadic military activity. As the crusade temporarily broke up for winter in the wake of their great loss, one of their allies called Joris, a southerner, made an incursion into the lands of Comminges. He and his men ravaged their way to Meilhan, where the castrum had risen against the northerners, and set to besieging the garrison in the tower. The Count of Comminges's son, also Bernard, made a forced march to launch a successful surprise attack on Joris and his troops at the town, killing many and taking their commanders prisoner.

Dates are unspecified and unclear during the winter of 1218–19, but the final recorded engagement of the fateful year in 1218 was probably at Cazères. Here the crusaders under Amaury had better luck as he laid waste the lands of the Count of Foix. He regained many castra that had seceded from him before he arrived there. And it is here that Peter of Vaux de Cernay writes the closing lines of his epic chronicle. A bigoted fanatic he might have been, but his colourful and detailed account of the Albigensian Crusade will be sorely missed hereafter. It is unknown why he stopped at this point: perhaps he died; perhaps he had lost interest now that his hero was no longer the focus of his story. Peter's very last words refer to the actions of Montfort's son and heir at Cazères; they reflect the unrelenting and unforgiving nature and content of the monk's great work: 'Within a few days he took it and burnt it, and killed the occupants. Proceeding further he severely harassed the enemy by destroying their castra and slaying unbelievers.'[204]

8

1219–29: 'THEY COMPLETED THE WORK OF DESTRUCTION'

The year 1219 ushered in a new era of the Albigensian Crusade: now the enterprise was to fall under the aegis of the dominant force in Europe. Philip Augustus's great victory over his English and imperial enemies at Bouvines in 1214 had left France the foremost power in Christendom. While the king had previously permitted his subjects to participate in the crusade in Languedoc, now he was about to throw the huge weight of the crown behind it. It was no longer just one noble's quest for dominance and the papacy's quest for spiritual orthodoxy; from this time onwards the subjugation of the south became the policy of Europe's mightiest throne.

Before Louis's arrival in Languedoc in May, a fresh round of fighting had broken out. All knew the French were about to descend on the south with massive forces. The south had to make the most of the lull before the new storm broke by winning back fortified places to deny them to the fresh wave of northern reinforcements. For the crusaders, the task was to contain and push back these advances so that Toulouse could be the main focus of their whole campaign. Nîmes and Castelnaudary were added to the growing list of their losses; Quercy and the Rouergue rallied to Raymond the Younger. There was to be no let-up in the cycle of atrocities: in Provence, one of the leading nobles, William des Baux, had been captured by southerners, burnt alive and his body cut into pieces. Even high-ranking elements within the Church in Languedoc were not just coming to terms with Count Raymond's new position, but actively helping the southerners against the crusaders: the Abbot of Lagrasse was accused of this while a Cistercian was found guilty of recruiting mercenaries for the Count of Toulouse. The French needed to prevent these serious reverses from gaining momentum in the wake of Montfort's death.

The Last Battle in the South: Baziège, Spring 1219

The first major clash of the new year occurred at Marmande, lying on the Garonne nearly halfway between Bordeaux and Agen and right on the north-western edge of the area of conflict, approaching the western seaboard. Alice de Montfort and Bouchard de Marly had returned from the north with enough men for Amaury to continue campaigning. Following up his successes in Comminges, he reached Marmande sometime at the end of December or the start of January. He had a substantial force, augmented by local levies, but not large enough to invest the place tightly. Raymond (as we shall call the son to distinguish him from his father Count Raymond) had organised the defence of the town well, garrisoning it with Brabançon and German mercenaries and archers with Turkish bows, under the command of Centule d'Astarac, son-in-law of Count Bernard of Comminges and a veteran of Muret and Las Navas de Tolosa. A storming attempt across the river and from land failed and so the besiegers dug in and waited for Louis to turn up and press 'this savage and deadly siege'. [205]

Meanwhile, some 100 miles to the south-east the Lauragais had been given over to near anarchy, so often the fate of contested areas in lengthy conflicts. Here the Count of Foix was raiding the land comprehensively, whether as a second front or as a diversionary manoeuvre to help Marmande, or both, is not clear. They 'seized cows and oxen, villeins and peasants'. [206] But French troops under the command of the Berzy brothers – 'men of vigorous and warlike disposition' – were also operating similarly here, adding to the widespread disorder. They may well have been taking some action under their own initiative, or combining crusading activity – stemming the ravaging of the Count of Foix and plundering supplies for their men – with their own private enterprise as 'they rode about the country round Toulouse in an audacious manner, and gathered together booty in the form of sheep'. [207] The Anonymous says that the hard, daring and tough Foucaud de Berzy was seeking out Count Raymond Roger to attack him; William of Puylaurens says it was the other way round.

Foucaud may have been unaware that the count had been joined by Raymond from his base in Toulouse with Hugh d'Alfaro, Hugh de la Mota and a large number of Spanish mercenaries; the southerners now had a major presence in the field. Some time in spring at Baziège, 14 miles south-east of Toulouse, the two sides met. The French had some powerful knights among them – Alan de Roucy, Hugh de Lacy, Sicard de Montaut – but they were heavily outnumbered. The Count of Foix gave his battle orders: his son, Roger Bernard, and Arnald de Villemur were to lead the charge with Hugh d'Alfaro and the best men and horses, while the count would follow up with Bertrand, an illegitimate son of Count Raymond. Any man who disobeyed orders would lose his land for his lifetime.

The Anonymous's account says first that Foucaud and his men stood fast in their ranks, indicating that they were ready to receive the enemy charge on foot; knights frequently dismounted to face cavalry charges. But later in his description he says that both sides rode across the open field to attack each other in a full mounted combat. A plausible interpretation would be that the bulk of the French fought as footsoldiers, with a smaller cavalry contingent performing their normal role. One of the tasks of the French cavalry was to make for Raymond and 'bring him down', thus hopefully putting the enemy to flight. The lines clashed and thus began the last major battle of the Albigensian Crusade.

The Anonymous claims that Raymond, a hero to him as Montfort was to Peter of Vaux de Cernay, rode at John de Berzy and unhorsed him with a skilful lance blow, piercing his armour into the padded gambeson worn underneath. John struggled to his feet and broke his sword defending himself. (Many writers often depicted combats in this way: the most chivalric leaders sparring with their opposite number in battle. This is often stylised reporting; it is more probable that it was one of Raymond's men who had knocked John from his mount.) Peter William of Séguret, an Occitanian knight who had gone over to the French, then attacked Raymond, his blow slashing the straps of his hauberk and cutting his belt. The outnumbered northerners were now hard pressed. Foucaud once again ordered his men to 'stand firm!' and they 'took their stand on the field'.

The southerners' light cavalry, comprising javelin throwers and crossbowmen, circled the French, their missiles inflicting heavy casualties and breaking up their ranks. As this was going on, the heavy cavalry regrouped and then unleashed a shock charge in serried ranks that penetrated the French line. They then 'rode around and outflanked them'. The southern infantry moved in to engage the enemy footsoldiers and 'to kill the fallen' as 'livers and guts were sliced up and tossed about'.[208] The crusaders were overwhelmed. Those who could fled on their horses. The southerners had won the last pitched battle of the Albigensian war.

The victory had cost them the life of only one squire, who had ridden too far ahead of his comrades. The Foucaud brothers and at least one other knight were taken prisoner; the rest were massacred. John was imprisoned at Niort and Foucaud in the Château Narbonnais, both to be held for a later prisoner exchange. Peter William, deemed a traitor, was hanged. The battlefield dead were stripped of weapons, armour and clothes. William of Puylaurens opines that the French might have escaped unharmed had they been willing to abandon the booty they had amassed. This, combined with the southerners' wish to fight on open ground, suggests that the Berzy brothers would have avoided the battle had they the choice. Thus the Occitanians had successfully employed a battle-seeking strategy. The French, lacking troop numbers until reinforcements arrived later, may have been better off consolidating their forces into one, rather than having them split up and exposed between Marmande and Baziège; as a general rule, Montfort had concentrated his forces in difficult times such as these, as at Toulouse and Beaucaire. The extent of the massive revolt against Amaury, growing all the time, and the pressure this put on securing provisions, may have persuaded the crusaders that the decision to split their forces, though risky, was necessary. Such a victory on the field of battle greatly boosted the morale of the resurgent resistance across Languedoc and added further significant weight to their growing momentum.

The Anonymous drily commented that Count Amaury did not feel like laughing when a messenger brought him news of the disaster at Marmande. The thoughts of the veterans with him would have turned back to the slaughter at Montgey in 1211. His response – partly in anger, but more to counter the negative impact of this latest blow – was to make another storming attempt on the town by land and river. It failed again. But help was on the way.

The Arrival of Prince Louis's Army and the Massacre at Marmande

It arrived in two waves. The first reinforcements came with Bishop Pons of Saintes and the leading knight William des Roches, Seneschal of Anjou.

With these Amaury was able to tighten the siege of Marmande, the crusader camp now expanded substantially and the river now filled with their boats. The main army under Louis turned up on 2 or 3 June. He had set out on 16 May with a huge force, possibly the largest seen on crusade since 1209. The Anonymous claims there were many thousands of knights with too many footsoldiers to count. The continuator of William the Breton offers a realistic figure of 200 knights, both he and William saying that the infantry numbered 10,000; William is keen to point out that these were sent at Philip's 'own expense'.[209] The lengthy preparations had ensured that the campaign was abundantly supplied with food, armour and weapons. The strength of this formidable force was reinforced by the calibre of its men: veterans of the wars with England and the Bouvines campaign: Bishop Guérin of Senlis, a former Knight Hospitaller and one of the chief architects of the victory at Bouvines; Count Peter de Dreux of Brittany; the counts of St Pol and Guînes; Arnold d'Oudernarde; and, of course, Louis himself. This constituted an impressive concentration of French chivalry all focused on defeating the southerners.

With the French sprawled out around the town, the southerners had never been in a siege situation against such overwhelming odds. They could not resist for long. An all-out assault made immediate gains, capturing the ditches and breaking down bridges and barricades. The imminent prospect of a successful storm, with all the horrors that could entail, persuaded the garrison commander Centule to seek terms and surrender. What the exact terms were is unknown, but they were certainly not adhered to by the crusaders.

The Bishop of Saintes argued strongly that the Count of Astarac should not be exchanged, but killed, along with the townspeople. Count Gaucher of St Pol and Count Peter de Dreux were seemingly horrified at this proposed transgression of chivalry; Gaucher had been at the siege of Acre on the Third Crusade, where over 2,500 Muslim prisoners had been decapitated, but he baulked at a slaughter here. The counts feared that such an action would 'disgrace France for ever', claims the Anonymous. The Bishop of Auch rightly pointed out that, should Centule and leading knights be killed, so would be the fate of the Berzy brothers and others in the hand of the southerners; he well understood the rules of reprisal. Thus Centule and four other nobles were spared execution and exchanged for the Berzys.

The rest of the garrison and the townspeople were not so lucky. Either as these discussions were taking place, or – more sinisterly and more likely

– after they were concluded, French soldiers started shouting and set upon the castrum. They slaughtered the inhabitants comprehensively and indiscriminately: 'Lords, ladies and their little children, women and men stripped naked, all these slashed and cut to pieces with keen-edged swords. Flesh, blood and brains, trunks, limbs and faces hacked in two, lungs, livers and guts torn out … Not a man or woman was left alive.'[210] Even William the Breton openly admits that the women and children were not spared. After the butchery, the town was razed to the ground. Louis may well have been shaken by the experience. He had been an active campaigner and seen death before, but this was his first taste of a massacre, and one of non-combatants, too. There were no reports of heresy in Marmande, so there was nothing to justify the slaughter except for the perceived necessities of the military imperative. Ten years after Béziers, the policy of terror still held good.

The destruction at Marmande may well have been an impulse move by soldiers eager for plunder before their forty days' service expired. The detail of men and women being stripped naked – in part, as the Nazis knew all too well, because naked victims were less likely to resist; but also because their clothes would not be ruined by cuts and gore and thus lose value – reveals this aspect. It is worth remembering the case of Fronsac in 1451 during the Hundred Years War. Here the English surrendered under terms that guaranteed the town's protection from being plundered; but some French soldiers contrived an incident to appear as if the English had gone back on their word. They used this as an excuse to sack the town and fill their pockets, something that should not have happened under the terms of the surrender. It is possible that while Louis was still pondering how to treat the town, certain elements among his captains gave the order to start the massacre. Amaury and his men no doubt wanted revenge for the humiliation and bloodletting at Baziège.

Shortly afterwards, Louis departed for Toulouse, arriving there with his huge army on 16 June. The hills and plains and roads and paths to the city were crammed with French, Flemish, English and German crusaders with their baggage trains. They made the journey in small stages so that the columns did not become too stretched out. William of Puylaurens captures the expanse of Louis's force before Toulouse: 'His army was truly immense. His camp extended around the whole of Toulouse, in a circuit formed by the suburb, part of the Cité, and the far side of the Garonne.'[211] This is the army that Montfort had dreamed of leading on his fateful siege.

The resolve of the Toulousains as they faced their third siege had been hardened by four factors. First, the victory at Baziège had shown them that the south could beat the northerners in a pitched battle. Secondly, the inept slaughter at Marmande taught them that even a negotiated surrender was not a guarantee of safety; thirdly, the crusading force, as huge as it was, was nearing the end of the forty-day service period and so might be waited out. Fourthly, though this was a much larger army than Montfort had threatened them with, they had had a year to rebuild their formidable defences and strengthen them further, as well as to reinforce the city with soldiers to defend it. Marmande had bought them time to bring in these extra troops.

In the last few pages of the *Song*, the anonymous author recounts these preparations. He tells of the citizens' fear and how the consuls sent out the call to arms to all feudal levies, mercenaries, sergeants and archers, and of how 1,000 cavalry and 500 javelin men poured into the city. Raymond, responsible for the defence of the city, was advised to recognise King Philip as his lord now that Montfort was dead; but he refused. Raymond's stature and confidence was growing all the time and he was more than ready for the new challenge faced by the south. The city was stocked with everything its inhabitants and garrison could want for another long siege: bread, meat, wine, oats, barley, dried fruit. Carpenters and engineers went to work under the expert supervision of Bernard Parayre and Master Garnier constructing catapults and mangonels. The town was organised into defensive units for separate quarters, each responsible for the gate and walls in their sector. Once again a huge communal effort went into the defences: barricades, ditches, walls, barbicans, fighting platforms, arrow loops, covered pathways to the battlements and outer fortifications. Such is the detail he even lists the names of the dozens of knights deployed to take command of some seventeen specified defensive points – gates, bridges, barbicans – around the city. He offers deep insights into the defence of a major city facing a siege. Toulouse was in a far stronger position than it had been for Montfort's investiture.

The Anonymous now leaves us with the city facing the fearful proclamation by Bertrand, the papal legate, that 'death and slaughter must lead the way, that in and around Toulouse there shall remain no living man, neither noble lady, girl nor pregnant woman, no created thing, no child at the breast, but all must die in the flames'. But, in his very final words, he adds: 'The young count and the saints will defend them.'[212] With that, the Anonymous departs the scene, leaving us with just William of Puylaurens of our original war reporters. William's chronology is confused and disjointed for this period, but as events progress towards his time of composition later in the century, so his account becomes richer in detail. Our sources now become more diffuse and episodes more obscure as the Albigensian Crusade entered a period dominated more by politics and diplomacy than by major campaigns.

This period is presaged by the third siege of Toulouse. William tells us that Louis led a determined bombardment of the city followed up by direct assaults. If he did, he had little to show for it. On 1 August, after six weeks, Louis and the French destroyed their siege engines and struck camp and headed home to France. William says that this was not only because they had fulfilled their period of service, but also because their adversaries 'had mounted a courageous and effective defence'.[213] Northern chroniclers such as the continuator of Robert of Auxerre, Alberic de Trois Fontaines and the Dunstable annalist offer another reason for Louis's failure at Toulouse, hinting at treachery among the French ranks, a reason given again in 1226 with more foundation. William the Breton says that Louis conducted the siege only half-heartedly. Roger of Wendover, whose chronology here is confused, conflating the second and third sieges of Toulouse, blames Louis's failure on an acute lack of supplies that caused famine among his troops. Papal letters point to other possible explanations, revealing concern that Louis might use his army to invade Poitou and Gascony. At Marmande he had drawn so close to English-held territory that the garrison and castrum of La Réole made ready to withstand a siege. England always remained the Capetians' military priority. Louis's intervention in the summer of 1219 had made only superficial gains; his departure opened the floodgates for an overwhelming southern resurgence.

The Southern Tide, 1219–24

The years that followed Louis's exit from the scene are, after an initial outburst of intense warfare, ones in which the scrappy, sporadic nature of military affairs is inextricably intertwined with complex political and diplomatic wrangling. Louis's great army was gone, inadequately replaced by occasional trickles of crusaders seeking their indulgences in Languedoc. The prince had left Amaury 200 knights for a year, but this was woefully insufficient to stem the southern tide surging in and washing across the region during that time. In December 1219, Pope Honorius replaced Bertrand with a new legate, the aggressive German Cistercian and Bishop of Porto, Cardinal Conrad von Urach, who attempted to revitalise the crusaders' cause with a new source of manpower by establishing the Order of the Faith of Jesus Christ in the south, based on the model of the Knights Templar; there were few takers. Meanwhile, the Fifth Crusade in Egypt was making no progress and needed its own reinforcements. Amaury and his men were pretty much left to their own devices.

The Berzy brothers' reign of terror indicates the increasing level of anarchy in various areas, as the northerners and their allies often became robber barons to sustain their positions in a war-weary and economically depleted south. Having been exchanged for the commanders of Marmande, Foucaud and John Berzy were once more free to ravage the land. Foucaud comes in for particular opprobrium from William of Puylaurens, who accuses this 'extremely cruel and arrogant man' of a number of crimes, the least of which was his and his men's licentious behaviour and seizure of married women. Any of his prisoners who could not come up with a 100 sous ransom was killed. Captives were tortured by flinging them into underground pits and starving them; those dead or dying were hauled out and flung onto dung heaps. During his last raiding party over the winter he had a father hang his son before he was himself hung next to him. (Such actions were repeated in the Jacquerie peasants' uprising in the fourteenth century and at the guillotine in revolutionary France.) Montfort had made Foucaud lord of Puylaurens, so William knew his man well. As the chronicler dismissively says of the Berzys and the other crusaders, 'They did not perform the tasks for which they had come originally; the end did not match the beginning.'[214] Few shed a tear for the Berzys when they were caught by Raymond on their last, brutal plundering mission and were dragged to Toulouse, where Raymond had them decapitated. Their heads were placed on stakes by one of the city's gates.

Place after place went over to Raymond the Younger or were taken by him and his allies. The sources give only glimpses of the warfare that took place; there is nothing of the abundance of detail provided in the *Song* of William of Tudela and the Anonymous or the *History* of Peter of Vaux de Cernay. The terse coverage we have tends to give a perhaps misleading picture of the great speed at which events occurred. Nonetheless, the southerners were indeed swift in their decisive advances; Amaury was permanently on the defensive and always losing ground.

The lords of Penne had already paid homage to the Count of Toulouse by the time Raymond, with Hugh d'Alfaro and often Roger Bernard of Foix, went on the campaign trail early in 1220. Over the next year and a half he met with little but success. Servian paid homage to Toulouse. At Lavaur, almost all of the crusader garrison was killed, a few escaping by swimming across the river. Puylaurens, held by Foucaud's widow Ermengarde, surrendered under the promise of safe passage out of the castrum following a short siege. Montauban, as ever, was all too ready to give its allegiance to Count Raymond. Castelnaudary hardly waited for Amaury to leave before it, too, went over to Raymond. Amaury attempted to break Raymond's momentum with a prolonged siege on Castelnaudary from about July 1220 until February 1221. Not only did the assault fail, but his younger brother Guy de Montfort was killed in an attack at the very start of the operation.

In February the veteran crusader Alan de Roucy was besieged in his castrum of Montréal; he carried on fighting from the tower after the town had been taken and its walls destroyed. He hoped to hold out until Amaury sent help from nearby Carcassonne. It never came. In the heat of the combat, Alan was mortally wounded in the same way as his former master – a siege machine hurled a stone that cracked open his head. Without their leader, the men of the garrison negotiated a surrender and safe conduct to Carcassonne. It was another high-ranking fatality and another serious strategic loss. Meanwhile, the Count of Foix continued to contribute to the military success of the south, with Fanjeaux, Limoux and Prioulle all going over to him. Some northern reinforcements sent in July into the Agenais failed to make any gains; this area and Quercy were now almost entirely in Raymond's hands. The French were being pushed ever further east, holding on only to Carcassonne, Narbonne and a few other places such as Penne in the west.

Militarily all but defeated, exhausted and financially broken by his efforts, Amaury had to hope for political and diplomatic support that might translate into significant numbers of soldiers on the ground. This avenue did not start well, when, in spring 1220, the legate Conrad was chased out of Béziers and forced to take refuge in Narbonne. What victories Amaury had in this field were hollow ones, as strong words from the pope were blithely ignored by the victors on the ground. When Honorius angrily removed Raymond's rights to his land in October 1221, no one paid much attention. More were agitated by the failure of the Fifth Crusade at this time; indeed, Honorius himself now turned his focus once more to the planning of another crusade in the Middle East and, like Innocent III before him, began vacillating on what to do with Languedoc. In the meantime, Moissac re-established its allegiance to the counts of Toulouse.

Hope was once again placed in the intervention of the French crown. Huge financial and massive territorial incentives were presented to King Philip by the papacy in May 1222: if only he would march south, all was his for the taking. Amaury did not take much persuasion by Honorius to offer his few remaining strongholds to the Capetian monarch in May and December, for without him he would be left with nothing. Philip still would not budge. He did not wish to antagonise his English allies in the south while there was work to be done against his Angevin enemy; the latter, under Henry III's minority government, still harboured designs to win back the lands taken by Philip in France. In fact, the Capetians' position was stronger than they realised; but caution was ever Philip's watchword.

The next twelve months saw the deaths of Count Raymond, Count Raymond Roger of Foix, Count Bernard of Comminges and King Philip Augustus. Count Raymond died suddenly in August 1222 in Toulouse at the age of 66, from a stroke. The Church was in no mood to treat this egregious thorn in their side with any clemency. Still an excommunicant since before the battle of Muret in 1213, and unable to confess his sins on his deathbed as the stroke had deprived him of speech, Count Raymond was refused a Christian burial. His body was left in a coffin outside the Hospitallers' priory in Toulouse. Sometime over the next few years his bones disappeared, whether taken by trophy hunters or removed to be buried by sympathisers is unknown. Raymond was followed by the Count of Foix early in 1223 and the Count of Comminges not long afterwards; the King of France died in July. Along with the deaths of Montfort, and veterans such as Alan de Roucy, this period confirmed the bitter inheritance of the conflict by the next generation.

Count Raymond had long since passed over the reins of active power to his more able son, who now began targeting isolated enemy towns and villages with his allies. Just before his death, the Count of Foix had retaken Pamiers and, in March 1223, was on the point of retaking Mirepoix. He died at the siege there, not in action, but due to an ulcer. Guy de Lévis, Simon de Montfort's venerable marshal, was taken prisoner here, in another sweeping aside of the old guard. The only setbacks were the results of Raymond's siege of Penne d'Agenais. Amaury returned from peace talks near Paris with a large force, a rare if fleeting luxury for him, to raise the siege. Marching through Albi, it enabled him to demolish the castrum of Lescure and to capture the garrison and *bastide* of Déodat Alaman. As they approached Penne, Raymond beat a tactical retreat.

It was while in this position that Amaury agreed to a truce with Raymond while talks were undertaken to bring the war to its conclusion. As the proposal was King Philip's, Raymond did not wish to antagonise him and bring him into the conflict when things had been going so well, so he acquiesced, but from a position of overwhelming strength. The truce that summer saw a more amiable connection made between Count Raymond VII of Toulouse and Viscount Amaury de Montfort, both 25 years of age. They met in Carcassonne, where Raymond, 'a man given to jesting', pretended to his comrades that he had been arrested; these, 'stupefied by terror ... sought refuge in flight until they realised that the report had been put about as a jest. The two counts enjoyed the joke together.'[215] It was a soldier's dark humour for dark times.

In Béziers, the legate Conrad wrote in desperation to King Philip for help: 'We expect death at any moment ... all around us the enemies of peace and the faith wave their swords about our heads.'[216] Here and throughout the region, Cathars felt safe enough to emerge back into the open, and perfects such as Guilhabert de Castres began administering once more to the heretical faithful. But the French king did not act. On 14 July King Philip Augustus died at the age of 58 after forty-three years on the throne of France, having led his country to become the foremost power in Europe. Thus the peace talks he had arranged at Sens between the two counts had to proceed without his imposing presence. There was no agreement here and both sides once more made ready for war after the expiry of the truce.

Amaury's preparations were optimistic and small scale. Prince Louis now became King Louis VIII of France and donated 10,000 marks to Amaury's cause, adding to money contributed by the crusade's first legate, Arnald Amalric; this proved sufficient to see off the siege of Carcassonne conducted by Count Raymond and Count Roger Bernard of Foix at the end of the year. Arnald's contribution seemed to be bringing the crusade around full circle, for Béziers, the town that had experienced the horror of the crusade's brutality on its very first day of operation, now had its ruling family restored: the teenaged Raymond Trencavel, only an infant when his father died in mysterious circumstances at the hand of the first crusaders some fourteen years earlier, had campaigned successfully to finally regain his father's inheritance.

By this stage the crusaders were reduced mainly to veterans of Simon de Montfort's time holding a handful of isolated places dispersed widely across Languedoc. Amaury had not been in Carcassonne at the time of the siege; he was probably trying to hold the final line elsewhere while simultaneously seeking a decisive battle such as Muret that might dramatically rescue him from his forlorn position. Everywhere he found all the towns and castles ranged against him; he attempted to besiege one unspecified place in the hope that it might surrender quickly, but it resisted and he simply had neither the time nor the resources to press it. As William of Puylaurens laconically notes of the territory: 'he was unable to defend it, nor were his funds sufficient to maintain knights.' Now Viscount Aimery of Narbonne, ever fickle and non-committal, paid homage to Raymond. Arnald Amalric wrote that 'total ruin menaced the few remaining with the Church' and that Amaury was hard pressed to withdraw his troops and their families to places of relative safety as the enemy was everywhere.[217]

All could sense total defeat in the air. Pope Honorius's fraught exhortations to rally the crusade were ignored. Nothing could persuade knights to stay with Amaury; the danger was simply too great. But, as Arnald had warned, even leaving was fraught with danger. Sixty knights who had served Amaury had to fight their way back to France. When they were confronted by Raymond, they offered him their warhorses and arms to allow them to pass in peace. Raymond rejected the offer as he wished not only to take their equipment but also to haul in the substantial ransom that could be collected on so many knights. They withstood a cavalry charge by the southerners and provided a rearguard for their servants and pack animals sent on ahead. They then launched a deadly counter-attack in which they killed many of their foes, some possibly after they had been taken prisoner. The French made their way to safety.

The complete hopelessness of Amaury's position was made clear by the count's few remaining supporters: he now had left with him only twenty-three knights. Among them were those old veterans who had fought their way to astonishing victories with his father: his uncle Guy, Lambert de Thury and Guy de Lévis. They had come through the conflict to witness total triumph and now total defeat. On 14 January 1224, Amaury sued for peace.

Facing Count Raymond and Count Roger Bernard, Amaury agreed to surrender Minerve, Penne d'Agenais and, crucially, Carcassonne, the crusaders' headquarters since 1209. The southerners agreed not to attack his castra and territory of Narbonne, Agde, Penne d'Albigeois, La Roque de Valsergue and Termes for the two months of the truce. They also promised 10,000 marks to him if a reconciliation was forged with the Church; this was a priority for Raymond as it would preclude the possibility of any further crusades. This permitted Amaury to receive generous terms for what was a comprehensive military defeat. The Montforts' crusading era was over. Languedoc was forever lost to them, as were the lives of their patriarch and one of his sons. The bodies of Amaury's two relatives were sealed in oxhides in readiness for their last journey back north. Their blood and that of thousands of others had been spilled in vain. The next day, 'the count, distressed and under duress, sad and doleful, abandoned the country with his people and returned to France'.[218]

The Diplomatic Scramble and Preparations for a New Crusade, 1224-26

As the south celebrated the handover of the last remnants of the Montfortian empire on 14 March, the episcopate of Languedoc bewailed the open return of heresy in the region. An active correspondence between the bishops, the pope and King Louis VIII was in full flow, the former two trying to draw the French crown back into the conflict. Louis was prepared to listen. In February Amaury had ceded his southern lands to the French crown on the condition that Louis should lead a crusade there; Louis eagerly sized up the prospect of incorporating the wealthy region and its lucrative trade routes into his kingdom. That same month, he wrote to the pope to set out his terms for undertaking a new crusade and geared his government towards the forthcoming enterprise.

But the pope was also writing to Raymond at the end of January, promising a friendly hearing for his delegation in Rome, and in April on the matter of reconciliation with the Church; Raymond was all too eager to promise the full suppression of heresy if it kept another invasion at bay. The vacillations of the pope, emulating his predecessor, were influenced by two main factors: his hopes for the next crusade in the Middle East under Emperor Frederick II, and the thought that King Louis would be less compliant with papal policy in Languedoc than Raymond would be with the carrot of a rapprochement with the Church being dangled before him. Honorius therefore put the proposed crusade on hold, much to Louis's complete exasperation. Writing to the legate Conrad on 5 May, the king rid himself of the whole damned project: 'From now on [you] should write nothing further to us about the Albigensian business, since we are now entirely disengaged from it.'[219]

The political and diplomatic games continued for over a year before a determined course of action was settled upon in the second half of 1225. Worried by the proximity of Louis's armies, which were conquering Poitou and much of Gascony from the English, Raymond moved closer to an accommodation with the Church in the summer of 1224, agreeing (along with Count Roger Bernard of Foix and Viscount Raymond Roger of Carcassonne and Béziers) at the council of Montpellier in August to extirpate heretics and mercenaries and recompense the local churches. But in October a Montfortian delegation of bishops to Rome warned the pope that all their gains and wealth were at risk. Honorius, suspicious of Raymond's good intent, dispatched a new legate to France in the new year, Cardinal Romanus of St Angelo, a severe and unbending prelate who instigated the major council of Bourges at the very end of November 1225. In September, Arnald Amalric, Abbot of Cîteaux, Archbishop and Duke of Narbonne, first papal legate of the Albigensian Crusade and the person to whom the chilling command of 'Kill them all!' is attributed, died.

Romanus was charged with bringing King Louis back on board for another crusade, now that Honorius had finally made up his mind. Raymond, under safe conduct, pleaded his case, proclaiming that 'he would do whatever he ought towards the French King and the Church to retain his inheritance'.[220] Count Amaury was also there, still holding out for a restoration of his title of Count of Toulouse and Viscount of Carcassonne and Béziers: this was less a fanciful dream than a ploy to assert Louis's claims as overlord to the region (Amaury was to be rewarded in 1230 with the post of Constable of France). The council's decision had been reached before it began: it was convened to give Louis legal grounds for taking Languedoc. The council withheld its verdict until 28 January 1226, after Raymond had left. His submission to the Church was deemed insincere and of no consequence unless he restored Amaury's lands – an intentionally excessive demand they knew full well would not be met. This was the *casus belli*. Immediately after Raymond's departure, they decreed that he was not absolved from excommunication – instead, it was loudly reaffirmed – and his allies the Count of Foix and Raymond Roger of Trencavel suffered the same indignity. Amaury sold all his interests and titles in the south to Louis, and the council, under the guidance of the legate Romanus, acknowledged

Louis as the one legitimate suzerain of Languedoc. A new crusade was proclaimed.

There were good reasons for Louis to become enmeshed with the 'Albigensian business' once more. In August 1224 he had achieved new successes in his war against the English, taking the vital Atlantic seaport of La Rochelle and large swathes of Poitou. This was the Angevins' entry point for placing its army in western France – King John had taken refuge there after his defeat by Louis at La Roche au Moine in 1214 – and so Louis had greater protection from any southern expeditions by the Angevins. Between Amaury and the council, Louis also now been granted both comital and monarchical rights in the south, an extremely powerful and almost unchallengeable combination.

On the day of the council of Bourges's verdict, Louis announced a baronial council to be held in Paris to prepare for a southern campaign. Two days later he officially took the cross. A truce with England was arranged so that the old conflict should not impede the new one. The crusade was preached throughout France and Europe. The Church granted Louis a tenth of ecclesiastical incomes in France for five years and all the usual accompanying crusading indulgences and privileges. But although the expedition was cloaked in the mantle of pilgrimage – the chronicler Philip Mousket exalted that now 'the Albigensians should be destroyed!' – it was in fact a matter of the French crown setting out to annex the south and bring it under monarchical rule. Many were unenthused or unconvinced by the veneer of this new crusade; most recognised that the French were now fully committed to conquest.

The Siege of Avignon, 1226

The army of King Louis VIII mustered at Bourges on 17 May. Louis, 38 years of age, small and wiry, was at the head of a huge army, one designed to intimidate and to conquer. The sources attest to the imposing size of the expedition, its magnitude increased by extensive financial backing from the papacy. Some historians estimate that it comprised 20,000 fighting men and believe that it may have been up to twice the size of the force that headed south in 1209. This is not unrealistic for now it was led by the King of Europe's leading power. Amaury de Montfort and his uncle Guy were present to offer invaluable intelligence and advice, learnt the hard way from their experiences in the south. The veteran crusader Bouchard de Marly was also among them, as was their erstwhile enemy, Savary de Mauléon. Powerful counts such as those of Brittany and Champagne put in a brief appearance (they were more concerned with affairs in their own lands) and the throng was made all the greater by the vast numbers of bishops accompanying the host (motivated by the incentive of a tax exemption).

The army achieved most of its objectives before even setting off. Its sheer scale cowed most of the south into submission. Lord after lord fell over each other as they sent word to Louis in Bourges that they recognised him as their overlord and wished to nestle under the protection of his wings, as Bernard Otto of Laurac, a well-known heretic, put it. Even Nunó Sanchez, Count of Rousillon, defected. Count Raymond was even abandoned by King James I of Aragon, who forbade his subjects to aid the enemies of the crusade. Catalan lords offered their support to Louis. As more lords rendered submission to Louis, the momentum grew: nobody wanted to be left alone and exposed on the shore after the tide had gone out. The towns followed. Stalwarts of southern resistance were among those who made almost unseemly haste in changing their allegiance: Béziers, Castres, Nîmes and Puylaurens before Louis had even arrived; these were followed by Carcassonne, Beaucaire, Tarascon, Narbonne, Orange, Marseille, Albi, Arles and Termes after he had.

Why the massive capitulation? It was a recognition that the politics of the situation had been transformed in a way that could not be realistically countered. As outlined above, Louis's position as both comital and royal sovereign was an overwhelming combination. The crusade was no longer a messy and disorganised collection of various lords and soldiers making their way south; now it had the full weight of the French crown behind a government-backed enterprise that had months of meticulous planning and co-ordination behind it. This power was made all the more dreadful because of the recent victories won by France over the previous twelve years: the hope of English intervention was seemingly insufficient to rally widespread southern resistance. Henry III of England, seeing an opportunity to thwart his Capetian foe, did wish to aid Raymond; but papal pressure, plus a suspiciously sanguine report from the king's brother in Languedoc, Richard of Cornwall, that Count Raymond would do just fine without English help, saw this plan come to nothing – for the moment at least. Louis did not have to worry about England in the same way his father had before 1214;

he could turn his attention to fresh conquests. For the south, submission to a dominant French king seemed a surer bet than submission to a vulnerable southern count.

There were other reasons, too. One was sheer war-weariness and exhaustion. Count Raymond's remarkable sweep back into power in Languedoc had been met with joy and optimism as the crusaders under Amaury de Montfort had been comprehensively defeated and driven out of the south. But, two years on, the crusade was coming back, and this time stronger than it had ever been before. If this was the northerners' response to complete defeat, then what hope could there ever possibly be to stop the relentless invasions of the south? Resistance had simply been ground down. And there was also fear. This was palpable. The horrific events at Marmande were fresh in the minds of the people of the south, who obviously associated Louis with the massacre there. The magnitude of the imminent expedition also seemed reminiscent of the first crusade with all the horrors that that had entailed. The expulsion of the crusaders from the south almost rendered the region one massive area for conquest and offered *carte blanche* for military operations with little adherence to chivalry and restraint deemed necessary. Most of the south had simply had enough.

All Count Raymond had with him was the counts of Foix and Carcassonne and a few other lesser lords, and the towns of Agen and Limoux, plus, of course, the considerable resources of Toulouse. His city, however, gearing itself to prepare for the prospect of its greatest challenge yet, had lost some of its unity: social divisions within the city and banditry outside it were causes of serious agitation and unquiet. This put Raymond in a difficult position, as he needed all elements of the Toulousain to be united behind him. Two years earlier he was regarded as the hero and the saviour of the south; now, in the face of French royal vengeance, he had been all but deserted.

But Raymond knew well enough by now how the fluctuations of war went. If he could resist for long enough, the crusading forces would be depleted; Louis might lose interest; a resurgent England trying to reclaim its lost French lands might drag the king back north at any time; and the innumerable uncertainties and exigencies of campaigning might lead anywhere. Or so he hoped. His own advances to Louis spurned, Raymond knew that if he did not fight, all his lands would be lost forever. To save them, he had to destroy some of them: he began a scorched earth policy so that the crusaders advanced into a wasteland.

Louis arrived at the traditional staging post of Lyons on 28 May. There was no resistance: 'the consuls of towns and fortified places belonging to the Count of Toulouse came to meet him, handed over their fortifications and gave hostages at his discretion.'[221] From here, the heavier equipment was loaded onto boats and barges to be taken down the Rhône to Avignon, where Louis arrived on 7 June. This city, such a prominent and active supporter of Raymond and an instigator of his counter-attack ten years earlier, had long since come to terms with Louis's army. Avignon was a powerful, almost independent city (despite being a holding of the empire) protected with high towers and a long double curtain wall and double moats, so Louis was relieved that this centre of resistance had agreed his passage across the Rhône. But the plan soon went awry.

The chronicles disagree slightly on what went wrong. What is clear is that the problem centred on the crossing of the Rhône over the stone St Bézénet Bridge, which could be reached only by moving through the city. The king and a small part of his entourage were granted this concession, but the rest of his army had to cross a pontoon bridge constructed for this purpose; Louis received this as an insult as it cast aspersions on his intentions. The chronicles report the anxiety and deep mistrust between the city and the crusaders, each side accusing the other of treachery: some think that Louis wished to take the town, others that the Avignonnais planned an ambush all along. Nicholas de Bray wrote:

> The people of the town, confident in the strength of their position, and their hearts infected with venom and treason, held counsel and decided that when the king had entered into the town with some of his troops, they would close the gates in secret, shackle his arms and hold him prisoner, and those remaining outside, finding themselves deprived of their leader and divided in two, would immediately be killed.[222]

But this is almost certainly Nicholas de Bray being painfully melodramatic and overblown, as usual. Some troubadour songs seem to suggest that Avignon planned resistance at the last moment: 'Although Frederick, the ruler of Germany, tolerates Louis unpicking his empire, the king from beyond Brittany [England] will be most upset by it. Let us be firm my lords, and let us count on powerful support.'[223] There may be some truth in such lyrics; as we shall see, they may help solve the mystery of why Avignon suddenly resisted. Roger of Wendover claims that it was the consuls' fear of

Louis's intentions that dominated their meeting. The crusaders complained that Avignon had not honoured its hostage criteria: too few of them were of sufficient social standing and there were just too few generally. For whatever reason, Louis, the legate Romanus and the royal contingent were denied entry into the city. The certainty is that the mutual suspicions led to a point of crisis triggered by a misunderstanding.

This trigger point seems to have come when a section of the French army under the command of Walter d'Avesnes, the Count of Blois, had crossed over the river and flew their banners before the city walls. The *Chronicle of Tours* suggests that Walter might have crossed not appreciating that the talks between the city and the king had not been settled, which might have prompted the inhabitants to see his move and display of banners as a pre-emptive move on them while their consuls were deliberately distracted by diversionary negotiations. The crossing was regarded by the citizens as either a provocation or, more ominously, a prelude to an attack on the city and its sack. Another Béziers was feared. The citizens struck first.

Already armed and ready in preparation for emergencies, some of the soldiers and citizens unleashed a hail of stones, spears and arrows at Walter's men, killing a number of them. Louis immediately sent the Count of St Pol to aid Walter, but the Avignonnais successfully broke the pontoon bridge, though not before the count had reached an island in the Rhône, which he then held. This left Walter's contingent seriously exposed. The outbreak of hostilities may have been the response of a panicked commander guarding that section of walls, or even the action of the anti-crusade faction within the city determined on a confrontation. Amidst the immediate recriminations, attempts were made to mend the ruptured truce. The legate demanded satisfaction, but none was forthcoming. Although the prisoners taken in the fighting were released, the provisions already gathered in the city in readiness for their arrival, together with the money to buy them, were withheld. Louis, furious at this completely unexpected reversal and obstruction at the very start of his expedition, began his siege on 10 June.

Besieging the city was difficult enough given its defences and the two rivers – the Rhône and the Durance – that made the approach very difficult. But there were diplomatic issues, too. Avignon's suzerain was Emperor Frederick II. Pope Honorius had warned the crusaders not to antagonise him, not least because the papacy depended on the emperor for the next crusade to the Middle East (Frederick was to win Jerusalem by negotiation by the end of the decade). So Louis was treading on delicate ground. He had letters sent to Frederick explaining his actions, blaming the perfidy of the Avignonnais for going back on their agreement. The *Chronicle of Tours* and other Latin sources are quick, of course, to raise the heretical tendencies of the city as further justification for the military action: they were accomplices of Raymond VII, and had 'for a very long time welcomed Waldensian heretics'.[224]

Louis had to make an example of Avignon: if it became a symbol of prolonged resistance it could easily become a rallying point for southerners and make the crusade yet another long, drawn-out slogging match. By besieging it, Louis was demonstrating his resolve to settle the matter in Languedoc once and for all. Southerners understood the message: when the siege began, so did a new wave of capitulations. During the three-month course of the encirclement, Count Bernard of Comminges, whose father had been an ardent anti-northerner, made his submission to Louis in August. Even Count Roger of Bernard of Foix, kicked out of Carcassonne by its citizens who wished to capitulate, attempted to do the same, but his approach was rejected; the few veteran crusaders remaining in the French army would not easily have stomached a reconciliation with this family.

There are a number of sources that cover the siege, but none with the immediacy and detail of either Peter of Vaux de Cernay or the two authors of the *Song*. Storming the formidable city was not a prospect in the early stages, so a massive engineering operation began: belfries, mangonels, trebuchets and moveable pontoon bridges were all drawn into position and miners deployed under the orders of Louis's chief engineer, Amaury Copeau. The bridges allowed the two halves of the army to be reunited. The entire region outside Avignon was stripped bare by the crusaders as they gathered in food, vines and timber. As the siege was pressed, so the defenders responded with equal aggression, their own machines, archers and slingshots 'unceasingly carrying wounds and cruel death from a distance'.[225] One of the victims was Amaury Copeau, hit by a stone as he conducted his engineering operations. The city's two great towers – Quiquenparle and Quiquenrogne, proudly displayed on the city's seal – were full of Brabançon and Flemish mercenaries, who also manned the ramparts beside the militia. There would be no quick solution.

As the attrition dragged on, the crusaders suffered heavy losses. Powerful elements of the French army were quick to head back north as soon as they had served their time: the Count of la Marche, the Duke of Burgundy and also Count Theobald of Champagne, despite the king forbidding his departure. Effective sorties caused many casualties and burned some of the siege machines. One particularly damaging sortie caught the French while eating, and many of them were slain. This forced the French to construct a deep defensive trench between them and the city, meaning that many operations were then carried out further from the outer defences of the city. A boatload of knights was ambushed by mercenaries and the occupants massacred, among them the famous knight Pierre de Tournelle. On 8 August an assault was launched under the command of the Count of St Pol, but as the French stormed across a bridge it broke – either from the weight of numbers or from enemy sabotage – and hundreds fell into the river, where many drowned. The assault continued with some success, Count Gaucher of St Pol leading the way through the storm of missiles. Nicholas de Bray almost fell victim: stuck in the crush of the troops surging forward, he saw an arrow flying directly at him; only by a quick shove of those in front could he move forward just enough to avoid it striking him. The defenders began to withdraw from the battlements. As the Count of St Pol climbed the siege ladder to the top of the ramparts, 'he fell, mortally struck by an enormous block of stone'.[226] Louis, a close friend of Gaucher, was deeply upset. He immediately called off the attack.

Unable to make much headway, the legate and whole assembly of prelates gathered, excommunicating their enemies, as they had 'no other means of punishment'.[227] The consuls of Avignon attempted to send out 'useless mouths' – the old, women and the young – as the first step towards a negotiated settlement, but Louis refused their egress. He and the legate argued over the prospective spoils of the city: the legate demanded half, much to Louis's disgust, the king reminding the legate that he did not need him to take the town.

Beyond Avignon, the military picture was not reassuring. The English had launched a raid on La Rochelle; despite the truce, Louis being bogged down in Avignon was too good a chance to miss. Some of the port's leading bourgeoisie attempted to hand over the city's keys to the English, but their efforts failed; some escaped, but four were hung. This may indicate that the troubadour's song above referring to help from King Henry III of England was accurate. I would suggest that the mystery of why Avignon suddenly defended itself may be solved in light of this: the Avignonnais may well have decided to resist once they knew that the English had planned this operation and thus co-ordinated their defence with the English attack.

Count Raymond was active closer by in the region around Avignon. Although not strong enough to raise the siege by direct force, he nevertheless caused great problems for the French, as one chronicler reports:

> The provisions of the [French] soldiers failed them and numbers of the troops died; for the Count of Toulouse, like a skilful soldier, had, before the arrival of the French, removed out of their way all kinds of provisions, together with the old men, women, children, and the horses and cattle, so that they were deprived of all kind of sustenance. And it was not only the men who suffered, but also the horses and cattle of the army perished from hunger; for the count had ordered all the fields throughout the district to be ploughed up, so that there was no supply of fodder for the cattle except what had been brought from the French provinces; therefore large bodies of troops were obliged to leave the camp to seek provisions for the men and food for the horses, and on these trips … they often suffered great losses from attacks by the Count of Toulouse who, with his troops, lay in ambush for them.[228]

Louis's men, horses and animals (both for transport and for eating) were thus deprived of food and were weakened accordingly. This required the French to forage in territory where Raymond's men operated, leading to French prisoners being killed or mutilated. Even the people had been removed, partly for their own safety and partly so they would not be held for ransom.

While famine hit the ordinary soldier hardest – food became simply too expensive – the whole army's woes were compounded by the spread of disease. Bodies polluted the river while the intense summer heat made conditions in the siege camp ripe for dysentery: mass open graves were overflowing with bodies before corpses were disposed of in the Rhône.

Roger of Wendover reports that the camp was plagued by a swarm of huge black flies working their way into tents, contaminating water and food. Bouchard de Marly, one of the few remaining original Montfortians, succumbed, as later did the Archbishop of Reims and the Count of Namur. Louis himself fell ill and was left permanently weakened. Philip Mousket confirms the fatalities caused by 'disease and famine and the filth of vermin' and reports that those in the city were also suffering from lack of food.[229] By the start of September both sides were worn down. The longer the siege went on, the greater the prospect of a brutal sack, as the frustrations and deprivations of the crusaders could only exacerbate the consequences of a storm. The Avignonnais sought terms.

Roger of Wendover believes that when the city opened its gates to allow in the legate and his delegation of churchmen for negotiations, the crusaders broke their word and poured into the city, taking it by force. But had this been the case we would no doubt hear of a merciless sack. The reality was that a negotiated settlement had been reached. Anywhere between 150 and 300 hostages were handed over to the crusaders; the city's proud defences were levelled; Louis was compensated with 6,000 silver marks and all the arms, armour and siege weaponry within the walls; and the citizens had to bear the cost of constructing a large royal castle nearby as sentinel over them. Practical penitence for their spiritual transgressions came in the form of 1,000 silver marks to be handed over to their new (irreproachably orthodox) bishop and the funding of thirty knights to spend three years on crusade in the Holy Land. The penalties were stiff, but Avignon had escaped a potentially far worse fate. By 9 September Louis occupied the city. It was the last major confrontation of the Albigensian Crusade.

Louis was finally free to proceed across the region. For all the hardships of the siege, the constant flood of capitulations throughout its duration ensured that his progress was triumphal as the few towns, strongholds and castles that had not already surrendered peacefully to him did so now. The roads were lined with nervously cheering southerners greeting their king. The southerners who continued to resist did so as a guerrilla force, harassing French movement and laying ambushes. Louis appointed seneschals and royal officials throughout the region. Guy de Montfort returned as Lord of Castres. Toulouse had fortified itself for a fresh onslaught – but it never came. That city was to be the objective of a new campaign after winter, which, this being October, was not far off. Louis began his journey back to France, leaving behind his 30-year-old cousin Humbert de Beaujeu in charge of military operations, supported by a large force of knights. Louis left Languedoc as conqueror, vowing to return in the spring to finish off Toulouse and the remnants of resistance.

But Louis did not return. On his return journey to France he fell increasingly ill. Rumours spread that he had been poisoned by the Count of Champagne, who was purportedly in love with the king's wife, Blanche, but the truth was far more prosaic than that. The dysentery that took hold of Louis at Avignon had not yet finished with him. Already so weak he could not stay on his horse, he died at Montpensier on 8 November. He left in his place his 12-year-old son Louis on the throne, a minority rule with his mother Queen Blanche guiding the kingdom through its factional machinations. For the south, this was an opportunity to make one last attempt at freedom.

The Conquest Completed, 1226–29

Fighting remained to be done. But it was relatively small scale, if no less savage. As usual when a crusading army departed, the south saw a fresh wave of uprisings. But they were fewer this time: now that the French crown had a direct interest and significant investment in the region, the *ad hoc* nature of crusades had been replaced by a permanent opposition force. Homages made to a king held more weight than those made to an upstart count like Simon de Montfort. Nonetheless, Raymond made one more attempt to finally turn the tide. He began at Auterive, 16 miles south of Toulouse, which he besieged during the winter following Louis's death. The French garrison was unable to wait for assistance from Humbert and surrendered so that their lives would be spared. One of the count's men, a noble by the name of Stephen Ferréol, was killed during the siege by a crossbow bolt.

The count then fortified Labécède, just north of Castelnaudary and thus an important satellite fort for the route between Carcassonne and Toulouse. Raymond had placed it under the command of Pons of Villeneuve and Oliver de Termes, both staunch opponents of the crusaders, the former with particularly close ties to the Cathars. Humbert be Beaujeu headed here in the summer of 1217 with the Archbishop of Narbonne and the Bishop of Toulouse to retake the place. Bishop Fulkes was taunted from the battlements with the cry that he was 'the bishop of devils'; Fulkes's riposte was that they were correct: 'Indeed they speak the truth; they are devils and I am their bishop.' The small castrum did not withhold against the crusaders' siege engines for long. When defeat looked imminent, the commanders and some of their knights fled under cover of darkness. Humbert's men entered the village and massacred all the men, 'some by the sword, some by being impaled on stakes'.[230] It was only the intervention of the bishop that prevented the women and children from suffering the same fate. The Cathar deacon Gerald de Lamothe was found in the village with some fellow heretics; they were all burnt at the stake.

Sporadic military operations occurred throughout 1227 and early 1228, of which we know little. Humbert was active with a large army in Cordes, Albi and Lagrave, attempting to stamp out fires of resistance wherever they flared up, as at St Paul Cap de Joux, where the castrum paid homage to

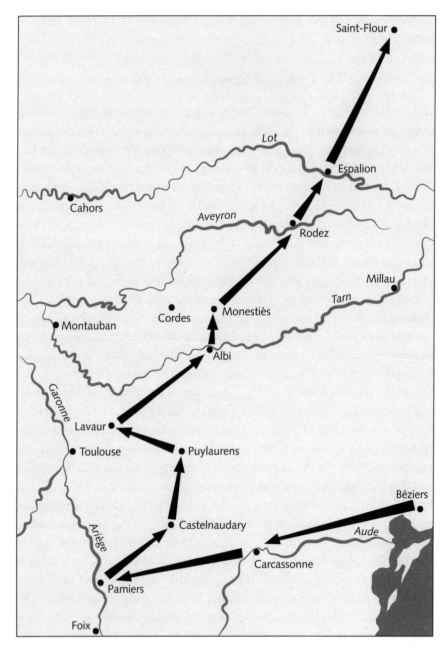

Louis's crusading movements after Avignon, 1226.

Count Raymond as, possibly, did Puylaurens once more. But Humbert jumped on most of these quickly (St Paul had to wait for the time being) and thus denied Raymond any possibility, slim as it already was, of building up a momentum of resistance in any meaningful way. The highest profile casualty of this period of warfare was none other than Guy de Montfort, killed near Pamiers on 31 January 1228. Once again, that deadliest of weapons, the bow, had claimed another victim. In Rome the previous March, Pope Honorius III had died, to be succeeded by Gregory IX. The new pope wanted the Albigensian business finished quickly. He did not have too long to wait.

Raymond's most notable victory from this period occurred in the spring at Castelsarrasin, just south of Moissac. He took the castrum while the garrison held out in the tower. Crusaders who held lands nearby were summoned to their aid, but these were kept at a distance by the palisade that blockaded the garrison in and kept the would-be rescuers out, a stratagem that had served Raymond well at Beaucaire. Humbert de Beaujeu arrived with the Archbishop of Narbonne and the bishops of Toulouse, Carcassonne and Bourges (the last bringing troops), indicating a large-scale operation. But they were still unable to lift the siege. As a diversionary tactic in the hope of drawing Raymond off, the crusaders turned their attention to Montech, which surrendered after a few days of siege. It did not help: the garrison at Castelsarrasin was starved into submission.

Roger of Wendover attributes a further intriguing victory to Raymond at the siege. In his account, Raymond learned of the approaching relief force from France and, on 18 May, laid a devastating ambush for it in a wood, killing or capturing scores, if not hundreds, of French troops. The knights taken were held for ransom while many of the surviving footsoldiers were mutilated:

> After they had all been stripped to their skin, the count ordered that the eyes of some be gouged out, the ears and noses of others to be slit, and the feet and hands of others to be cut off; after thus shamefully mutilating them, he sent them home, a deformed spectacle to their fellow Frenchmen.[231]

William of Puylaurens does not mention this episode, but we should not dismiss it; William was closer to events geographically, but Roger was much closer in time. Humbert actually made his way to the siege from France, where he had been at its start, compatible with Roger's report. A serious ambush with heavy losses may also have been the real reason why Humbert was unable to raise the siege, especially as he would otherwise have had a large force. That the mutilations bear a resemblance to those that Montfort inflicted at Bram is neither here nor there: such disfigurements were common throughout this and other wars. If it did occur, as I suspect it did, it was to be the last large-scale military atrocity of the Albigensian Crusade.

Raymond handed over Castelsarrasin to Bernard de Cazenac, a monster to Peter of Vaux de Cernay, a hero to the Anonymous. After Humbert's reversal at Castelsarrasin, he had headed to Lavaur with the intention of retaking St Paul Cap de Joux. However, here there was a major change of plan: all efforts would instead be put into laying waste the land around Toulouse. Some ravaging was already in progress – it was, after all, a mainstay of campaigning – but now it would become the overriding priority: economic warfare was the new strategy for the summer of 1228.

Humbert mustered his forces from all around for this undertaking. The archbishops of Auch and Bordeaux arrived, as did some barons and the last pilgrim crusaders to set out for Languedoc. Toulouse was not placed under formal siege, but it must have felt that way to its citizens, surrounded as they were by forces whose sole purpose was not to attack the city, but to destroy the livelihoods and the crops of its people. The crusaders set about their task like a workforce clearing land rather than an army. William of Puylaurens gives a detailed account of their 'threefold form of destruction': 'They set a large number of men to mow down the corn; others to pulling down the towers and walls of fortified places with pick-axes; many others were employed on destroying the vines.' Throughout the summer the destruction of immense economic wealth was carried out to the same format on a daily basis: after mass and breakfast, crossbowmen would go ahead in advance to check that the way was clear while knights escorted the work crews in case protection was needed; then, starting nearest the walls of Toulouse and working backwards towards their own camp, they would destroy all the vines they could find. This process went on for three months. This caused Bishop Fulkes of Toulouse to remark: 'How extraordinary it is that we are overcoming our adversaries by fleeing from them!'[232]

The idea of soldiers ravaging in the Middle Ages is still sometimes regarded by some as mindless destruction performed for want of any better ideas on how to wage war. But here we see the methodical approach taken to systematically destroy the enemy's economic base. If his land could not produce crops and vines, Count Raymond would not have the money to hire mercenaries, reward his followers or buy the costly materiel necessary for war. Just as serious as the depletion of resources were the political implications for Toulouse: day after day the citizens could see their food supplies being hacked down or going up in smoke; the prospect of starvation would create greater factional unrest and test their loyalty to the count. The French were also exposing the weakness of the count, demonstrating to the people that he was unable to protect their lands while simultaneously displaying the power of the French to destroy it. The count was therefore failing in his first duty as lord. As the thirteenth-century *Schwabenspiegel* states: 'We should serve our lords for they protect us; if they do not protect us, justice does not oblige us to serve them.' A key purpose of the crusaders was therefore to terrify the populace into changing their allegiance. Raymond was not in Toulouse at this time, or fighting the crusaders outside its walls; the damage done to his reputation was as catastrophic as that done to his fields.

This had always been the way of warfare: the famous *chevauchées* of Edward the Black Prince across France in the Hundred Years War were nothing new; in fact Anglo-French texts from the early thirteenth century use exactly this term to describe ravaging. One medieval Latin term for it was *depopulare*, ominously indicating vast tracts of smoking land emptied of people and with villages abandoned and fields uncultivated, growing only weeds. This was Count Raymond's own scorched earth policy in 1226 as he burnt the land the crusaders would march through. The late twelfth-century poet Jordan Fantosme offers this military advice to those about to go to war:

> Destroy your enemy and lay waste their land: let it all be consumed in fire and flames! Do not leave them, outside their castles, in wood or meadow, as much as will furnish a meal on the morrow … That is the way to fight them, to my way of thinking: first lay waste the land, then destroy one's enemies.[233]

The effects of such actions were often, quite literally, devastating. William the Conqueror's harrying of the north in England during the winter of 1069–70 left the Yorkshire economy crippled for years, local people moving south as refugees and some even resorting to cannibalism due to the consequent famine. Languedoc would again see massive destruction in the next century, when the Black Prince went on his infamous *chevauchée* across Languedoc in 1355 from sea to sea, from Bordeaux via Fanjeaux, and Limoux (which he burned), Carcassonne (where the suburbs were destroyed) to Narbonne, and back again. He deployed his men and incendiaries in three columns abreast to maximise the swathe of destruction.

The desolation being caused around Toulouse was happening elsewhere in France and England at around the same time. In Champagne, French troops 'were cutting down the vine and fruit trees, sparing nothing', while in England Henry III waged war against his enemies by 'cutting down their woods and fruit trees, and destroying their parks and lakes … and warrens'. The intent, as at Toulouse, was to undermine the enemy's economy. When Louis invaded England and both he and King John were ravaging the land, 'markets and trades ceased … agriculture was at a standstill'.[234] It could be a highly efficient method of warfare and proved to be so here.

The real damage was done, as indicated above, by Raymond's absence: he does not seem to have made even a show of protecting his people. Why was the energetic and tenacious Raymond of Auterive and Castelsarrasin just a few months earlier so conspicuous by his absence now? We know he was in Gaillac in June receiving the homage of thirty-three knights, but the crisis was in his home city of Toulouse. In all probability, he could see the writing on the wall. The successes in winter and spring were the last forlorn, desperate and wishful attempts of a defeated force. The momentum of defections to the French was just too great to turn around. He had failed to bring about a general uprising in a region weary of war; the consequence of further resistance was utter ruin, as the French were so emphatically demonstrating outside his city walls. Thirty-three knights were a drop in the ocean of French troops and desertions. This fatalistic awareness had seen even the Count of Comminges pay homage to Louis in 1226 and, more shockingly still, the Count of Foix's attempts to do so; in the autumn of 1228 even Oliver de Termes had changed sides, too. Raymond was simply too weak to do anything about the widespread French ravaging. He knew it; the French knew it; and the people of Languedoc knew it, too.

'After completing this work of destruction', the pilgrims in the army that surrounded Toulouse returned home.[235] There was nothing left worth destroying. Humbert de Beaujeu's troops then set about crushing the few remaining pockets of notable resistance. Cabaret, that perennial centre of southerner independence, fell about this time. Around October or November, in the very last military operation of the Albigensian Crusade, the French took Pamiers and moved southwards deep into the territory of the Count of Foix, garrisoning the whole region with their men. The Toulousains were left bereft of any significant allies. There was also the terrifying prospect of facing a fresh crusade and another royal expedition the following year. Alone and isolated, and 'much shaken by the many reverses they had suffered, a foretaste of what might be to come, they agreed to make peace'.[236]

When Elie Garin, the Cistercian Abbot of Grandselve, was sent to Languedoc to offer peace terms, Raymond rushed to meet him. A final truce was declared while negotiations took place. Preliminary terms were agreed at Meaux in January 1229 and, after some revisions that were not in Raymond's favour, finalised in the Treaty of Paris on 12 April. The terms were considered by many to be harsh, but they might have been a lot worse. Raymond was to remain count during his lifetime. After his death, his 9-year-old daughter Joan, his only child, was to inherit his lands. But Joan was to marry Alphonse de Poitiers, brother of King Louis IX, and if they were childless (as was to be the case) the lands would revert to the French crown. The dispossessed knights, the *faidits*, were to regain their lands as long as they were not tainted by heresy. Some thirty castra were to have their defences destroyed; among these Montauban, Fanjeaux, Castelsarrasin, Avignonet, Moissac, Castelnaudary, Labécède, Lavaur, Puylaurens, Agen and Auterive. The demilitarisation of suspect places was also carried out in Toulouse, which once more lost its walls; the Château Narbonnais was to be strengthened by Raymond at the cost of 6,000 marks and handed over to the crown for the next decade. Another 14,000 marks were to recompense the Church. The sums were steep, made all the more so by the requirement that they be paid within four years. Raymond and his officials were to be active in extirpating heresy and thus to aid the Inquisition, which was about to take root now that the peaceful conditions allowed it to do so. In another attempt to combat heresy, 4,000 marks were paid to establish a school of orthodox theology in the heretical heartlands. Raymond's personal penance was to be five years spent on crusade in the Holy Land, this time fighting a non-Christian enemy.

The Trencavels were the worst hit: they were disinherited and their lands went to France. Count Raymond was, for the time being, still left with the Toulousain and Lauragais and places in Agen and Cahors, plus some castles west of the River Tarn. In effect, he lost all his lands in the east of the region: west of the Rhône to the French crown, east of it to the Church. He now ruled over only half the area his father had. Worse, he was to be a caretaker count for the French. No one was in any doubt that the French crown was now the dominant power in the south of France.

On 12 April all that was left of the submission of Count Raymond was his public humiliation. This took place in Notre Dame Cathedral in Paris. He walked along the central aisle to the altar in front of the cardinal legates Romanus and Conrad and an array of high churchmen. This was the price of reconciliation with the Church and the implementation of the Treaty of Paris. William of Puylaurens wrote of the pathos of the occasion: 'It was pitiful to see such a great man, who for so long had been able to withstand so many powerful adversaries and nations, led to the altar barefooted and naked except for his shirt and breeches.'[237] With this mortifying ceremony, the Albigensian war ended.

EPILOGUE: 1230–40 – 'THE SYNAGOGUE OF SATAN'

L anguedoc was not going to be rendered instantly and comprehensively subservient by a peace treaty signed by the defeated Count Raymond in Paris. Many southerners continued to resent the French takeover, a resentment that was exacerbated by the imposition of the Inquisition to destroy heresy, which followed immediately in the wake of the 1229 settlement. Count Raymond was only entering his thirties when he made his submission to the French crown. He had agreed terms as a reflection of his hopeless position at that time, but that did not mean he no longer harboured thoughts of regaining what he had lost. Who knew where the political unrest and rebellion in northern France might lead, or if the French would be forced to divert all their energies and attention to a revanchist England fighting to win its lost lands in France? Count Raymond bided his time in the hope that the wheel of fortune would once more turn his way.

But there were to be no more periods of extended military activity in full-scale war. The bloody violence that erupted sporadically over the next fifteen years had more of the characteristics of baronial and municipal unrest than of a serious conflict between major powers. In the tense aftermath of the Treaty of Paris in 1229, the localised fighting that did occur represented a threat of another general uprising and widespread massacres of the French; any disturbances were therefore responded to with the utmost gravity and severity. Thus Humbert de Beaujeu, whom Louis VIII appointed as the French Captain-General of Languedoc, pursued the enemy to the very bitter end at Montségur in 1244.

This closing chapter looks at these outbreaks as an epilogue to twenty years of war in Languedoc. The Albigensian Crusade was over. But there was still bloodshed and atrocity to come.

Revolt and Rebellion: Toulouse and Carcassonne, 1235 and 1240

A major condition of the Treaty of Paris was the complete extirpation of heresy in Languedoc. In Toulouse, the new bishop, the Dominican Raymond du Fauga (Fulkes had died in 1231), started off with a vengeance, launching a night raid on a Cathar prayer gathering, capturing nineteen heretics and burning them all at the stake. Count Raymond VII had accompanied him; one of the victims was Pagan, the elderly lord of Labécède, who had defended the castle for Raymond against Humbert de Beaujeu in 1227. Thereafter, the bishop was less assiduous, becoming more comfortably accommodated within Raymond's circle and less prone to display militant orthodoxy.

By 1233 the pope had set up the Grand Inquisition to quash heresy. The Dominican order was responsible for running the Inquisition in Languedoc and set about their task with an unbecoming zeal. The friars earned their nickname 'the hounds of God' (derived from a pun on their Latin name rendering *Dominicani* as *Domini canes*) for their dogged pursuit of any scent of heresy and the hunting down of Cathars. They set up in Toulouse as many Cathars once more took to remote mountain and forest villages to escape persecution, torture and death; their stronghold became the mighty fortress of Montségur, to the east of Foix. Across the south, neighbour denounced neighbour and personal enemies were accused to do them down. Erstwhile friends and co-religionists could no longer be trusted. A man called Doumenge, accused of heresy, betrayed a group of ten perfects to save himself (three of these managed to escape; the rest were burnt). Robert le Petit, nicknamed 'the Bugger', was a former Cathar who now joined the Dominicans and persecuted the heretics; such insider knowledge was invaluable, as it was reported that Robert could recognise Cathars just by their gestures and speech and that 'within two or three months he had caused about fifty people to be burnt or buried alive'.[238]

This oppressive air of uncertainty and seemingly arbitrary wielding of power provoked deep resentment in an already resentful people. The inquisitors exacerbated this with some foolish acts of vindictive and crassly insensitive behaviour: an old Cathar lady on her deathbed was dragged out of the city to be burned alive at the stake; the bodies of buried heretics were frequently exhumed and, after 'their bones and stinking bodies were dragged through the town', they were ritually burned.[239] And there were still the burnings: a staggering 210 went to the stake at Moissac alone during the Inquisitors' first visit there. Count Raymond wrote to the pope warning that such excess would be counterproductive and was raising the hostility of the people. The warning signs were present: in 1233 at Cordes the townspeople threw a couple of Dominicans down a well; in Albi an inquisitorial exhumation party was attacked and was lucky to avoid decapitation and drowning. In 1235 the people of Toulouse rose up – not against their rulers but against the Inquisition. They first besieged the Dominican convent and then its forty friars were carried out of the city by their head and feet. The city was excommunicated once more for a year, until it conceded to the Inquisitors' return.

Count Raymond was meanwhile making the most of his position as a vassal of Emperor Frederick II for his lands in Provençal. The empire and the papacy were locked in a vicious power struggle, so Pope Gregory IX tended to be lenient towards Raymond in return for his support. Raymond was thus able to extend a three-month suspension of the Inquisition in his city to three years. His plan was that the declared deracination of unorthodoxy should be placed in the hands of more malleable bishops than the Dominicans. The great lords of the region, meanwhile, were ready to exploit the unrest.

In 1240 we see the last major attempt to rid the south of both the French and now the Inquisition too. Count Raymond, hopeful of winning back his lands in the east, allied with his suzerain the Emperor Frederick in the latter's struggle against the papacy and Marquis Raymond Berengar of Provence, who had close family ties to Louis IX of France. Raymond gathered a large army and headed east with the counts of Comminges and Rodez and Oliver de Termes. He had his eyes set on Arles, Narbonne and Marseille, the last of which offered itself to his lordship and provided him with help in his siege of Arles. The convoluted power games of France, the papacy and the empire provided gates of opportunity for the Occitanians. Raymond Trencavel, the disinherited Viscount of Carcassonne and Béziers, seized the moment to storm through one such gateway in 1240. In the alliance of the Count of Toulouse and the emperor, Trencavel saw a golden opening to be a useful pawn of powerful friends and thus perhaps regain his lands. In August he invaded.

Trencavel had been living in exile in the court of King James I of Aragon. Now he returned with a considerable army of *faidits* and Aragonese and Catalan soldiers. Roger of Wendover (whose dating is hopelessly confused here) says that this army entered southern France 'burning churches and slaying the Christians of both sexes and all ages without mercy'.[240] Joining him now was Oliver de Termes, son of the veteran southern warrior. Whether this was with the approval of the Count of Toulouse or not is open to conjecture; certainly the count was trying to hedge his bets. Languedoc welcomed Trencavel back with open arms as a liberator. Castrum after castrum went over to him; Montréal, Saissac, Limoux, Azille, Laure and 'such was the turmoil caused by his invasion, every place he wished he took under his control'.[241] Montoulieu put up a fight and for that its inhabitants were massacred as a warning to others.

It was a moment of great crisis for the French crown as Carcassonne once more became a place of refuge. Here the bishops encouraged the citadel and the suburbs to withstand any onslaughts and wait for the help of King Louis. The city prepared itself with 'all preparations made in anticipation of the forthcoming battle', stocking itself with the harvest and an early gathering of the vines (which would otherwise have been destroyed), building siege engines and constructing hoardings for the battlements.[242] There were rumours of betrayal as men from the *bourg* held secret talks with Trencavel to allow his men into the city. Count Raymond, who had been ravaging the countryside on his return from the Camargue, was approached near Carcassonne by the French seneschal William des Ormes. William demanded that Raymond, as a vassal of the King of France, drive out the invaders. Raymond was determined to sit on the fence and watch as events played out, so he promised that he would return to Toulouse and take counsel there on how to proceed. Once back home in the first week of September, he did nothing except wait.

The siege began around 7 September. The southerner forces must have been very large to take on the principal fortress of Languedoc. The rumours of the *bourg* residents' complicity with the enemy proved to be well founded, as the southerners entered and took control of the place. The clergy took refuge in the church, and emerged when they were given a promise of safe conduct to Narbonne. However, thirty-three of them were seized near the gate and slaughtered. Oliver de Termes and his men set up camp between the River Aude and the city walls and burned one of the city's mills, killing the young defenders inside. In a letter to the regent Blanche de Castile, which provides us with the most detailed account of the siege, William des Ormes says that he had already levelled the suburb of Granoillant and taken from there 'a great quantity of wood which was very useful' for defensive purposes in the city.[243] He said that it was hard to reach the enemy because they had destroyed the routes to the outer defences.

Another detachment positioned itself in front of the barbican before the Narbonne Gate with a large force of crossbowmen to prevent sorties being made from there. They drew up a mangonel facing the barbican and began pounding away; however, William set up his own stone thrower to counter it, so successfully that the besiegers were driven back and abandoned their machine. The southerners then concentrated their efforts on a mine against the barbican; William responded to this threat by ordering the excavation of a counter-mine and the construction of a dry stone wall. Despite his efforts, the wooden supports to one tunnel were fired, bringing down part of the barbican; William had already anticipated this with the new stone wall he had erected to protect the other half. Further along the wall, the besiegers had started another mine against a tower and the defenders responded with one of their own. The defenders entered theirs and engaged with the enemy in a subterranean combat, and drove them out. A third mine brought down a section of the wall but Oliver and his men were faced with a strong palisade they could not get past.

On the *bourg* side, a fourth mine was threatening the citadel. Trencavel had obviously come prepared with a large contingent of engineers needed to supervise these delicate operations. Both William's letter and the chronicle of William of Puylaurens give an account of events here. The attackers began mining from further away and using circuitous routes in the hope of avoiding detection; we hear of no fewer than seven such mines at the siege. Mining could still be detected by pails of water on the walls, ripples indicating activity underground. Noise could also give them away, as happened at Carcassonne. The besiegers' mines caused more damage, but once again rushed but strongly made improvised defensive palisades with arrow loops were erected and these kept the enemy at bay. Counter-attacks were also made in the tunnels: 'the enemy attempted to invade the Cité by burrowing like moles; however our men met them under the ground, using the same method, and drove them back either by wounding them or using smoke and lime, forcing them to abandon their attack.'[244]

The fighting remained fierce on all sides. Trencavel pressed the siege hard as he wanted to retake his city before French reinforcements arrived from the north. Close-quarters fighting was both frequent and intense. William of Puylaurens reminds us that 'the houses of the Bourg were virtually attached to the Cité and the enemy could use them as a platform from which to attack the Cité with crossbows and also a means of secretly opening up gaps without the knowledge of the defenders'.[245] But William des Ormes had prepared Carcassonne as best he could in the short time available to him when he learned of Trencavel's invasion. He informs Blanche that 'since the start of the siege they did not cease from launching assaults against us. But we had a large number of good crossbowmen as well as courageous people and decided to defend ourselves so, with each assault, the enemy lost many men.'[246] On the third Sunday of the siege, the southerners regrouped their forces for a major frontal assault on the barbican, but they were driven back by a barrage of stones and crossbow bolts. An even bigger storm attempt occurred the following Saturday but that too was repulsed, with heavy casualties among the besiegers and none among the defenders. Then, on the Thursday evening of the fourth and final week, a large force arrived from France. Learning of its approach, Trencavel lifted the siege.

As the southerners departed, they burned the *bourg* and, to further establish their hostility towards the Dominican friars, totally destroyed all their buildings (or what was left of them after they had stripped them of wood for their palisades). They also burned the castra and villages they came across in their retreat to Montréal. William was keen to inform the regent that he had prepared the city so well that 'even the poorest survived. Indeed, Madam, we had such great quantities of grain and meat that we could have waited for your help for a very long time, had that been necessary.'[247] The southerners knew that Carcassonne could not be starved out in the short time they had available to them, so they had made great efforts with their mining operations and costly frontal assaults to take the citadel quickly.

The southerners now found themselves pursued and besieged in Montréal. After a few days a negotiated settlement was brokered by the counts of Toulouse and Foix, and Oliver de Termes and the other lords and knights were permitted to go free with their horses and arms. Nonetheless, the French imposed harsh repercussions on the towns around Carcassonne and Béziers and many less powerful lords were permanently dispossessed.

The inhabitants at Montréal were driven out and their town destroyed. The French also began a mopping-up campaign across the south, implementing further repressive measures. Some pockets of resistance remained, such as the mighty castles of Peyrepertuse and Quéribus, but these were isolated. The loss of the minor lords was probably more serious for the Cathars, as it left them fewer and fewer places in which to find refuge. The French crown, meanwhile, continued to assert its authority in the region by building castles, such as Tour Régine at Lastours by the end of the next decade, and at Carcassonne, building an additional curtain wall and transferring the suburbs across the Aude to the *bastide*, where the new town lies today. Count Raymond and Trencavel knew time was against them as the French grew stronger and they grew weaker. They were to throw the dice one more time.

The Last Revolt: The Massacre at Avignonet and the Battles of Taillebourg and Saintes, 1242

The year 1242 was when the last nails were hammered into the coffin of southern independence. Count Raymond, now 42, realised if he were to have any hope at all he would need the aid of prominent figures on the national stage, and not just southern lords. To this end, with Roger Trencavel and the counts of Foix, Comminges and Provence, and other southern lords, he forged an alliance with King Henry III of England, who was still trying to win back lands in France, and with Hugh de Lusignan, the powerful Count of la Marche, who was trying to stem further French dominance of Poitou. The plan was for a multi-front attack on the King of France, 'relying on the belief that if he were assailed from many sides he would be less able to mount a defence'.[248] In May, Count Raymond declared war on France.

While preparations were in progress and an English force landed on the west coast, a brutal drama unfolded at Avignonet, deep in the heart of a heretical area 25 miles south-east of Toulouse. Here on the night of 28/29 May, a massacre of the Inquisitors took place, signalling the start of the last revolt. It is not known whether Count Raymond ordered the massacre – his tracks are once more concealed – but witnesses at the time implicate him as the man behind it. The act itself can be blamed squarely on two men: Raymond d'Alfaro, the count's nephew and bailiff, and Peter Roger of Mirepoix, the garrison commander of the Cathar stronghold of Montségur. Raymond sent word to Peter Roger of the opportunity to kill the Inquisitors; the latter responded willingly, being a Cathar himself and the military leader of the largest single group of remaining fundamentalists. With fifteen knights and just over forty mounted sergeants – half of his total garrison – Peter Roger rode the 60 miles to Avignonet.

In the town, the Inquisitors' party was residing in Count Raymond's hall. Foremost among the group of eleven were Brother William Arnold of the Dominicans, Brother Stephen de St Thibéry of the Franciscans, the Archdeacon of Lézat and the castrum's own prior. Just outside the town, in the abattoir, Peter Roger was joined by other knights and more soldiers. Twelve axes were handed out as Raymond led a dozen men plus fifteen townspeople armed with hatchets and clubs to the back door of the building where the Inquisitors were sleeping. The door was kicked down and the men rushed in. The Inquisitors went on their knees and prayed and screamed; there was no doubt as to their immediate fate when Raymond cried out, 'This is it!' A sergeant was later reported to have made the mocking comment about their cries of fear: 'Come and listen to the sermon of Brother William Arnold!'[249] The party was wiped out; the killers gleefully shared out the booty with their comrades. For many, the greatest success here was the destruction of the inquisitorial lists of Cathar suspects.

The official inquest into the massacre that followed soon after went into great detail, naming all the men involved and listing who got exactly what from the spoils of murder. The only disappointment was for Peter Roger, as no one brought him back the skull cap (or perhaps even the entire head) of William Arnold so that he could drink from it. Count Raymond soon found himself excommunicated yet again for a year, until he reconciled with the Church, not least by hanging some of those involved in the murder. In a region used to slaughter, this massacre of churchmen was still able to shock, and 'this atrocity caused some persons to draw back from the war against the king'; no doubt they were fearful of the reprisals to come.[250]

Nonetheless, Count Raymond's hopes were high that summer as, for the last time, he saw a sweep of gains across the region where he was once more accepted as lord: Termenès, Razès, the Minervois and, at Narbonne, Viscount Aimery paid him homage and Raymond reclaimed the title of Duke of Narbonne. It was not to last. His fate was to be decided by his allies in the Poitou–Charentes region outside the furthest boundaries of the Albigensian theatre of war. The battles of Taillebourg and Saintes are rarely associated with the struggle for independence in southern France, but their outcomes decided Raymond's final fate.

Henry III of England had arrived in France with an army of 200 knights. Raymond hoped that Henry's presence would keep the French king from intervening in the events of the south and so allow his offensive to continue unchecked. Henry was expecting to augment his force with recruits from Gascony and a large contingent of Hugh de Lusignan's men from his county of La Marche. However, this latter contingent was much smaller than Henry had been anticipating and a quarrel broke out reflecting English disappointment. As Henry delayed moving forward through waiting for extra troops and time-wasting diplomacy, he lost the initiative to Louis IX. The French king, now in his mid-twenties, was able to muster a large army and march south-west to meet Henry in Poitou–Charentes. The English went to block his progress over the River Charente at Taillebourg. The two sides confronted each other on 20 July. Thus 'there was a king on one side near the river, and on the other side, similarly close to the river, was the other king'.[251]

Matthew Paris puts the English numbers at this stage as being 1,600 knights, 700 crossbowmen and 20,000 infantry. The numbers of cavalry and infantry are probably exaggerated (especially the latter). The French chronicler Joinville implausibly claims that they outnumbered Louis's men by twenty-to-one. In fact, events at Taillebourg suggest that it was the English who had a disadvantage in numbers. But both sides fielded large royal armies as befitted a major campaign led by monarchs. The English protected the bridge and held the castle as the French approached. However, at the last moment, Geoffrey de Rançon, the Lord of Taillebourg, deserted the English and handed over his town and castle to Louis, leaving the English dangerously exposed to a flanking manoeuvre.

Joinville depicts the French heroically eager for the fray:

> Our men, who were on the other side of the river where the castle stood, spared no efforts to get across to the other side. With great risk to themselves they passed over the river in boats and on pontoon bridges, to fling themselves on the English. Then a fierce and furious fight began.[252]

The English were quickly hard pressed; some French sources say they had hoped to be able to defend the bridge but soon realised that they did not have sufficient troops for the task. Henry's brother, Richard of Cornwall, crossed the bridge alone to seek a truce. Reluctantly, the French agreed to one for twenty-four hours; they were showing Richard respect for his status as a crusader and because it was a Sunday, a matter of concern for the pious French king, later to become St Louis. The English seized the opportunity to beat a rapid retreat to Saintes.

The encounter here took place two days later, on 22 July. The French followed them, reinforced further in the meantime with more men and a baggage train comprising, it is claimed, 1,600 wagons which, says Matthew Paris, 'extended along the road for about three miles'. A French foraging party outside the town was ambushed by Hugh de Lusignan, 'who wished to either lose his life or redeem his fame'. As the cries of combat went up, so others rushed to the scene to engage in a vicious combat along the narrow roads between the vineyards. Paris points out that the English were still outnumbered here. One of the knights he picks out for mention on account of his heroic prowess is Simon de Montfort, named after his great crusading father. The English were defeated, despite Henry's dishonest attempt in a letter to persuade Emperor Frederick II that the French had retreated to their tents in confusion. Henry, one of England's most militarily inept kings, withdrew to Bordeaux. As William de Nangis said of these events: 'King Louis powerfully vanquished the English, putting them to flight, and took a great number of prisoners.'[253]

Count Raymond's hopes of wrestling back his ancestral lands from the ever-tightening clutches of the French monarchy disappeared from view along with Henry during the latter's precipitous retreat from Saintes. The coalition he had built up, so powerful on paper, rapidly dissolved. Henry's failure sent out waves of defeatism. With nothing to show for their ally's massive campaign, the King of Aragon and the Count of Provence distanced themselves from Raymond. His vassals tripped over themselves in their rush to come to terms with the French crown: if even the King of England could do nothing to so much as delay the advance of Louis, then what hope had they? Their best interests were now served by paying homage to Louis; not to do so was by now both counterproductive and potentially very dangerous. Hugh de Lusignan came to terms, as did even the Count of Foix. It was time for Count Raymond VII of Toulouse to do so as well, for the final time. And he did so. No more would he try to resist the might of the French crown. Raymond spent the last seven years of his life in local obscurity, giving support to the Inquisition, and unable to prevent the ultimate fate of his lands: their incorporation into the French kingdom. Occitanian independence was now just a memory.

Montségur: The Last Stand of the Cathars, 1244

Montségur itself is not one of the more impressive castles of Languedoc; little more than a stone fort, even after its later renovations, it lacks the brooding power and imperiousness of the mighty fortresses such as Peyrepertuse, Puilaurens and Quéribus. But its positioning just south of Lavalenet on the edge of the Pyrénées makes it one of the most striking and formidable. It sits atop a rocky crag some 3,500ft high. The only approach to it is from the west side, difficult enough even today; its other sides are prohibitively steep, especially the east, which is practically a vertical sheer. Inside the defences were two wells, so the Cathars could not be parched out as happened on the first surrender of Termes; skeletons, probably from the siege, were later found down one of the wells. Outside the castle and clinging to the rock on the northern and western faces, often extending over the sheer drop below, were the huts and buildings of a small village; here, and in the larger village lying at the base of the mountain, were the homes of some 400 Cathars. Outer defences included a barbican on the eastern side and a small tower, the aptly named Roc de Tour, to the east and slightly northward on the outer perimeter, the defences being connected by a series of wooden palisades. Montségur's position was deemed so impregnable neither the crusaders nor the French had deemed it worth taking: the task was simply too great an effort for a place of little strategic value, when other places needed conquering first.

It was designed as a Cathar sanctuary, hence its name, meaning 'safe mountain'. Guilhabert de Castres, the Cathar Bishop of Toulouse, had declared it the diocesan seat. Its lord, Raymond de Péreille, a defender of heresy in every sense and the son of a perfect, had overseen its reconstruction in 1204. In 1243 his son-in-law Peter Roger of Mirepoix, an instigator of the Avignonet massacre, shared lordship of the place. In some ways it was a Cathar equivalent of a Catholic place of pilgrimage, its holy reputation amongst heretics causing it to become a vibrant marketplace. For orthodox writers, it was 'the synagogue of Satan'.[254]

Now it stood as an affront not just to the Catholic faith, but to the French crown, especially after the rebellion of 1242 and the massacre of the inquisitors at Avignonet. Count Raymond had made a token gesture of besieging the place to pacify his new masters and the Church, and Humbert de Beaujeu had menaced the castle for a while, but now the authorities were determined to eradicate this stain against God once and for all. A meeting of prelates at Béziers in April 1243 demanded that action be taken against Montségur. Hugh des Arcis, the new French Seneschal of Carcassonne, gathered a large army, perhaps 5–6,000 strong at its peak, and set out to eliminate this last bastion of heretical defiance. With him were the archbishops of Narbonne and Albi. With this move, the Albigensian Crusade was in a way coming full circle back to its original intent, for this last major military action of the war was prompted as much by religious concerns as by strategic ones.

The siege began by the end of May. It was to last an astonishing ten months. Peter Roger had prepared well: he and his men had bought up vast supplies of grain, flour, beans and vegetables; he needed to feed the villagers and perfects he was protecting, plus his garrison of about ninety-seven soldiers, of whom at least twelve were knights. Weaponry was also hoarded. Despite the large numbers of the French army, they were not enough to completely blockade the castrum on the crag. There were many Cathar villages around Montségur prepared to smuggle through extra supplies to the defenders; small numbers of reinforcements could also get through; and there seemed to have been sympathisers within the besieging army among those recruited locally. The Cathars also had the advantage of an intimate knowledge of the difficult landscape. The permeability of the French lines allowed Cathars, perfects, soldiers and mercenaries to slip through. Although they were vastly outnumbered, the looseness of the siege, the inaccessible, natural strength of their position, and the hold of their spiritual beliefs, offered reassurance to the Cathars. That reassurance was bolstered by the presence among the defenders of two aged Cathar bishops, Bernard Marty and Raymond Aguilher, the latter a sparring partner of Dominic nearly four decades earlier.

The French army probed the outer defences throughout the summer and autumn to no avail. The defenders were well stocked with food, water and weapons. Of the 400 people immured there, the women did their part by tending to wounds and by manning the defenders' siege engines, under the guidance of the engineer Bertrande de Vacalerie after he was smuggled into the castle in January; the French, meanwhile, were having great difficulty bringing their own engines to bear and were severely feeling their want. By October we learn of only three fatalities among the defenders; all received the Cathars' last rite of *consolamentum*. The sheer vertical protection of the mountain, crested by strong palisades, continued to keep the attackers at bay. The French would get nowhere until they had surmounted the cliffs and placed siege engines on the slopes at the top of the ridge on which the castle stood.

In January 1244 they put in motion an operation to achieve this. Under cover of night, a group of lightly armed Gascons were led by others, who knew Montségur, up the eastern cliff, 'a terrifyingly precipitous slope'. They battled through the darkness, freezing cold and fear to reach the Roc de Tour on top undetected: 'they took the guards by surprise and were able to capture the tower; they put the occupants to the sword'. The next morning when they looked down on the climb they had made they could hardly believe what they had achieved. Others from the French army were quickly brought up so that they finally occupied the same ridge as the castle. This meant that siege engines could finally be erected within effective striking distance of the besieged. Bishop Durand of Albi, in the best tradition of Archdeacon William of Paris, oversaw the artillery operation. The eastern wall began to take a battering.

The barbican could now be assaulted. It was taken by mid-February by a bloody escalade. Around this time the southern knights Bertrand de Bardenac, Jordan de Mas and two others were killed, possibly while defending the barbican. With so few knights in the first place, such losses were heavy. By now there were at least thirteen fatalities amongst the garrison. There was still a deep crevasse protecting the approach to the castle but Peter Roger and Raymond's only viable hope was that someone – Count Raymond, Emperor Frederick, even – would come to their rescue. But all knew the situation was now one of imminent peril.

Morale dropped. Peter Roger had to command that any approaches by the northerners to open discussion should be met with a barrage of crossbow bolts. Imbert de Salles, one of the garrison sergeants later interrogated, claimed that before the siege tightened further, two perfects were sent out with the Cathars' treasure to slip through enemy lines and hide the hoard in the caves near Foix. The only reinforcements that now got through were two crossbowmen and a third man. A plan for an Aragonese mercenary captain to break through the French lines with twenty-five experienced soldiers and thus bolster the defenders came to nothing. Rationing was restricted further. A sortie on foot to retake the barbican and destroy the siege engine positioned there was a costly failure.

Within the castle, heated disagreements broke out about what to do; crammed within the tight confines of the castle and the few huts on the northern and western cliffs, many were asking to receive the *consolamentum* in case they were struck down in a storming. They were preparing for the worst. They were exhausted as they 'were given no respite from attack, by day or by night'. The northerners could rotate their men between combat and rest; the Cathars had no such option. On 1 March, Peter Roger's official Peter Ferrer was killed. He is the last person we know of who lost his life during the siege's final combat. The next day Peter Roger surrendered the Cathar fortress of Montségur.

The garrison had made the decision: they could lose their lives in a storm or save them through negotiation. They chose the latter, thereby guaranteeing their safety. Many had been involved in the Avignonet massacre, so to escape execution for this crime was no small thing. The soldiers could leave the castle with their arms and goods, only needing to undertake a light spiritual penance. The castle was to come under royal control. The Inquisition would impose only light penances on those who abjured Catharism; those who refused to recant would be burnt. These were remarkably lenient terms given the question of heresy, the rigours and length of the siege and the atrocity of the Avignonet massacre.

Before the terms were enacted, the Cathars and garrison were to remain fifteen days in the castle. The anguished turmoil among the faithful was considerable: to recant and live; or remain true to their faith and die. Most chose the latter. Remarkably, a dozen soldiers of the garrison, including two knights, chose the same fate; some wished to die with their wives. On 16 March, the garrison and Cathars left the castle. Over 200 heretics were asked one last time to reject their heretical beliefs and save their lives; they refused. Among these were the two Cathar bishops and many women. All were 'confined to an enclosure made of pales and stakes' which was then set on fire. 'They were burnt and passed on to the fires of Tartarus.'

Catharism as a cohesive religion was now broken and driven underground. The Inquisition picked up the pieces left behind in the wake of Montségur – the last time the heresy found armed protection. Some perfects found temporary refuge in the castles of Puilaurens and Quéribus, but by the middle of the next decade these too were in royal hands, surrendered to the French crown without a fight. And so it was that the military problem of the southern heretics had arrived at its final solution. It had started with a massacre at Béziers in 1209 and had ended with a massacre at Montségur in 1244. The years between had been filled with many others. Thirty-five years after the first crusading army had marched south, there was no one left to kill.

APPENDIX 1

THE CATHAR CONTROVERSY

One of the most heated and perhaps surprising recent debates in medieval heresy has centred on the Cathar heresy: was there such a thing at all? I touch on this debate in a paragraph early on in *Kill Them All*; it is worth expanding on a little here for the book's second edition as the controversy is an impassioned and fascinating one. As R.I. Moore, the figurehead of the revisionist school, has noted, disagreement on this subject has always been 'attended' by 'acrimony'. Indeed, a conference in 2003 led to revisionist methodology being likened by some to that of holocaust deniers!

The revisionist school, led by R.I. Moore and Mark Pegg, proffered the thesis that medieval heresy, especially as practised by the Cathars, did not really exist; instead it was a construct by a Church resistant to the notions of reform movements that it labelled, unoriginally, as heretical in the Manichean tradition. Pegg's books – *The Corruption of Angels: The Great Inquisition* (2001) and *A Most Holy War: The Albigensian Crusade and the Battle for Christendom* (2008) – and articles have been endorsed by Moore, a central figure and guiding light in pioneering heresy studies. In the second edition of his seminal *The Formation of a Persecuting Society: Power and Deviance in Western Europe, 950–1250* (2006), Moore writes of 'the bitterly resisted but ultimately irresistible critique, most powerfully marshalled by Mark Pegg (2001), of the idea that "Catharism" ever constituted a unified or coherent alternative to Catholicism, let alone an organised counter-Church'. (He adds that '"Waldensianism" was an equal and similarly artificial construct'.) 'Catharism', argues Pegg, was little more than a local Occitan expression of folk religion in the twelfth century. He and Moore believe that it was the crusade and subsequent persecution that promoted the actual manifestation of Catharism later in the thirteenth century.

The debate really took off when Moore expressed his controversial change of views on Catharism in *The War on Heresy: Faith and Power in Medieval Europe* (2012; 2014) in which, as he writes, he has 'denied, or set aside, in whole or in part, almost everything that most readers (including many academic readers) thought they knew about [the war on heresy]'. In claiming that Catharism was a construction, Moore believes that it was 'contrived from the resources of the well-stocked imaginations' of Church writers 'with occasional reinforcement from miscellaneous and independent manifestation of local anticlericalism or apostolic enthusiasm, and confirmed from the 1230s onwards by the ingenuity and assiduity of the Dominican inquisitors'. I have long held the conviction, expressed clearly in *Kill Them All*, that, as Moore states in the 2014 edition of his book, 'contrary to the common presumption this war was not mainly about the "Cathars"'; however, on the matter of heresy itself, I agree with Peter Biller, Bernard Hamilton and others that the dilution of the Cathars' spiritual challenge does go too far.

This is not to say that Moore, Pegg and others have not made a very valuable contribution and corrective to an *over-emphasis* on Cathar unification; and they are right to stress, as Moore does in his book, that early accounts of heresy were often 'drawn from the common stock of patristic theology and of rhetorical conventions and techniques'. Moore and Pegg have persuaded many scholars of their case. (See Moore's website for a full engagement between his views and those that contest it: www.rimoore.net.)

The nature of the debate is caught in two review articles of Moore's *The War on Heresy*. (The lengthy reviews afforded it marked the importance and impact of the work.) In *The Times Literary Supplement* (20 December 2012), Diarmaid MacCulloch responds positively to Moore's changed views. Moore, he says, 'argues with the zeal of a convert' that the Gregorian Reform movement of the late eleventh century unleashed radicals that took reform too far, as was the case with the Patarenes. Indeed, the name 'Patarene' became synonymous with 'Cathar' by the early thirteenth century. Similarly, MacCulloch sees as 'significant' Moore's focus on the reformist Premonstratensian Order of monks (also known as the Norbertines) and its communities that involved married preachers 'whose wives were inspired to embrace the ascetic lives of their husbands'. The Church's resistance to wandering preachers meant that 'many would-be friars' (like the Dominicans and Franciscans whose mission it was to extirpate heresy) 'ended up burned at the stake as heretics'. Moore believes that many twelfth-century heretics were 'disappointed Premonstratensians'.

MacCulloch concludes with a firm endorsement of Moore's thesis:

It is difficult to fault the logic of his observation that to ask how many heretics there were in the Midi before the Albigensian Crusade is like asking how many witches were in Europe on the eve of the early modern witch craze. The great virtue of this major recasting of Western history over three centuries is that it sounds right. It sums up more than a decade's worth of growing doubts among many medieval historians about the reality of Cathar dualism. It takes due note of the untidiness of historical developments, and the almost limitless capacity of human beings to believe and internalise the most risible nonsense if it suits them.

The last sentence is very strongly put, and there is much truth in it. However, it does not necessarily mean that it can be fully applied to the Cathar question.

In *Reviews in History* (www.history.ac.uk/reviews), leading medieval heresy scholar Peter Biller offers a more critical response to Moore – and the revisionist school in general (especially Pegg and Hilbert Chiu). He starts with the historiographical dispute and then moves onto the realities of Catharism as reported in and beyond the inquisitorial records: theological disputations between Cathars and churchmen; the detailed penances of individuals; the heretics' petitions of their lords to use Montségur as their headquarters; Cathar organisational evidence. Biller calls Moore's new views 'jaw-dropping', sensibly arguing against the notion 'that whenever an inquisitor ordered someone to be burnt to death his own imagination had conjured up what the person believed'. On a centrally important human note, he warns of the cost in 'denying to men and women in thirteenth-century Languedoc what they believed in when they chose an agonising death'. This injects some common sense into the debate amidst the complex scholarly positioning.

Readers should also consult Moore's spirited, urbane and detailed response to Biller's review (that follows on the website) which takes the intense scholarly argument further. Here, Moore reasserts that the term 'Cathar' is an 'outmoded and superfluous epithet' and gently reproaches Biller who, he believes, 'comes close to charging me not with intellectual error, but with rank incompetence and outright dishonesty'. (This is still a very low-key engagement by comparison with other academic historical debates!) To Biller's relevant point about belief and death above, Moore says he and fellow revisionists do not deny what they (the heretics) believed in; instead, 'we try to get what they believed in right'. Moore concludes his response with a reference to 'the abyss across which Biller and I find ourselves confronting one another', and reminds the reader that 'history is dangerous stuff'.

More recently, as is the way of academic debates, the counter-response has gathered pace to halt the momentum of more radical revisionist view. Chris Sparks, in *Heresy, Inquisition and Life Cycle in Medieval Languedoc* (2014) counters

Pegg's positing of a 'constructed' and 'fictional "Cathar church"' which did not exist in the minds of its supposed ministers', saying that Pegg's 'arguments are powerful, but not entirely convincing'. Sparks warns that 'the following points should be noted':

> first, that there is significant counter evidence to his claims; second, that much of the evidence can be found in the testimonies of ordinary men and women collected by the Languedocian inquisitors (some within the registers he used); and, finally, that Pegg does not seriously engage with the problems this material presents to demolish the idea of 'Catharism'.

Peter Biller has also raised the same points.

Claire Taylor, in 'Evidence for Dualism in Inquisitorial Registers of the 1240s: A Contribution to a Debate' (2013), uses the evidence to show convincingly that Catharism was a very real phenomenon, concluding: 'Far from being the creation of inquisitors, Catharism's core doctrines had flowered in the twelfth century but, although adherence to the heresy had remained strong, the structures of doctrinal leadership had been somewhat dislodged in the process of invasion by the crusaders.' This is exactly what we would expect from the major enterprise that was the Albigensian Crusade, which pushed Catharism underground. Taylor's research also convinces her that the traditional view of Catharism is the right one, the evidence showing 'that there was dualism in the Languedoc and that it did not originate there'.

This long, smouldering controversy is brought fully and comprehensively up to date in a volume of papers by leading scholars of heresy which directly addresses this lively debate: Antonio Sennis (ed.), *Cathars in Question* (2016) brings together opposing camps in the debate, brought face to face at a conference in London in 2013. The balance of the papers adheres to the traditionalist view, which I think is right.

The crusaders on the brutal Albigensian campaigns might not have had the destruction of heresy at the very top of their list of motivations, but they were correct in thinking that when they fought against the southerners of Occitania they were also combatting heretics in their enemy's midst.

APPENDIX 2

THE STATUTES OF PAMIERS (1 DECEMBER 1212)

A Translation[1] by G.E.M. Lippiatt

In the name of our Lord Jesus Christ do we always proceed to all our decisions and acts, for through the same we have been appointed to this, no petty seat of justice, that by our foresight and solicitude, we may restore to the path[2] of righteousness those things that have been undertaken against God, the

---

1   This translation has been taken from my own transcription of the original (under digital reproduction), catalogued as Archives nationales, AE ii, n° 207 (formerly J 890, n° 6). The printed version found in C. de Vic and J. Vaissète (eds), *Histoire Générale de Languedoc*, 2nd edn, viii (Toulouse, 1879), cc. 625–35, which serves as the basis for the only other English translation of the Statutes (Peter of Vaux-de-Cernay, *The History of Albigensian Crusade*, trans. W.A. Sibly and M.D. Sibly (Woodbridge, Suff., 1998), pp. 321–9) is defective in a number of places. I am currently preparing a critical edition of the Statutes intended for publication with a monograph study of the document and its context. The translation is quite literal, leading to obtuse language in places, but I have tried to preserve the legalese that characterises the original Latin. I am very grateful to Andres Reyes and Hugh Reid for their comments on the original draft of this translation.

2   I have preferred the reading *tramitem*, found in later royal copies, to *transmittere*, found in the original, in order to make sense of this sentence: de Vic and Vaissète, *Histoire générale*, viii c. 626.

Roman Church, and justice, and that we may hold them firmly so restored, especially the abolition of the depravity of the heretics and the extirpation of the wickedness of brigands and all evildoers. Therefore, we, Simon, earl of Leicester, lord of Montfort, and by the providence of God viscount of Béziers and Carcassonne and lord of Albi and the Razès, desiring to accomplish all the aforesaid, to hold the land in peace and quiet, and to preserve it for the honour of God, the Holy Roman Church, and the lord king of the French and the advantage of all our subjects, by the counsel of venerable lords – namely the archbishop of Bordeaux,[3] the bishops of Toulouse,[4] Carcassonne,[5] Agen,[6] Perigueux,[7] Couserans,[8] Comminges,[9] and Bigorre,[10] wise men, other barons, and our nobles – establish such general customs in all our land, and order that they be inviolably observed by all. The customs are these:

1.[11] Let all privileges of churches and religious houses, whether granted by canon or human law, and the liberties of the same be observed and guarded by everyone everywhere.

2. We forbid churches to be fortified and reduced to servitude by laymen; moreover, we order that those that have been fortified be pulled down or kept at the judgement of the bishops; but in the walled villages and towns of other lords, the bishops shall not be able to retain such fortifications.

3. Likewise, let all first-fruits be rendered without any difficulty to the churches as they have been customarily rendered in these parts, and all tithes be rendered as it has been written[12] and is ordered by the lord pope.

4. Likewise, no clerk shall be tallaged, even if he may have had an occasion to inherit, unless he is a merchant or married; and the same applies to a poor widow.

---

3   William II.
4   Fulk.
5   Guy.
6   Arnold IV.
7   Ralph I.
8   Navarre.
9   Garsia.
10 Arnold II.
11 The original document does not number the statutes nor separate them by paragraphs. This has been done for the convenience of the reader.
12 I.e. in the Bible and canon law.

5. Likewise, henceforth let no public market be held on Sundays, and if it is discovered that a market has been thus established, let it be moved to another day, at the judgement of the lord of the land and the count.

6. Likewise, let whoever shall have captured a clerk in any crime or other manner – even if he should have naught but a tonsure[13] – render him to the bishop, archdeacon, or their deputy without delay; for if he retain him, he shall be immediately excommunicated, and compelled to render the clerk by his superior lord.

7. Likewise, let any inhabited house in the land conquered in common[14] pay 3*d*. melgorian[15] annually to the lord pope and the Holy Roman Church, as a sign and perpetual memory that by her help the land was conquered from the heretics and granted in perpetuity and confirmed to the count and his successors. The term for this manner of collection of pennies will be from the beginning of Lent until Easter.

8. Likewise, let no barons or knight compel men of the churches or religious houses – that is to say, those men whom they possess by the donation or concession of kings, princes, and other territorial lords, or by other just means, who were free until that time from all exaction of the lords in whose lands or towns they live – to give tallage. If, however, the possession of these men has been interrupted in this region by the wickedness of the heretics and other evil princes, and for this reason doubt has arisen, let the truth be investigated without delay, or proof admitted without evasion, and if violence be truly found to have occurred, let the lords of the walled villages or towns in which they live thenceforth abstain from all exaction and tallage.

9. Likewise, parishioners are to be compelled to come to church on Sundays and feast days; on these days they will cease their work and instead hear the Mass and preaching in their entirety. Therefore, if on such feast days the lord and lady of any house should not come to church – and they had been present in the town and had not been hindered by illness or another reasonable cause –

---

13 I here follow the Siblys' interpretation of *etiam si non haberet nisi coronam*: Peter of Vaux-de-Cernay, *History of the Albigensian Crusade*, p. 322; *pace* M. Roquebert, *L'Épopée Cathare*, i (Toulouse, 1970), p. 500.
14 I.e. the viscounties granted to Simon in 1209, as opposed to his subsequent acquisitions further afield (of which Pamiers was one example).
15 The dominant currency of the Midi, minted in Melgeuil.

they shall pay 6*d*. tournois,[16] half of which will be for the lord of the town and the other half divided between the priest and the church.

10. Likewise, in all towns in which there are no churches and in which houses of the heretics exist, let one house which is most suitable be given to be made into a church, and another be given to the priest for a home. If, however, there has been a church there, and the priest has not had a house, let one house which is reasonably near to the church be given in perpetuity for a presbytery.

11. Likewise, whoever will henceforth knowingly allow a heretic to remain in his land, whether for money or for any other cause, and will then have confessed or been convicted, for this cause alone he will forfeit all his land in perpetuity, and his body will be in the possession of his lord for redemption according to his will.

12. Likewise, it will be allowed to whomever, whether knight or peasant, to bequeath alms from his own estate, up to the fifth part according to the custom and usage of France around Paris, saving in baronies and castles, and save foreign rights and the entire service of the superior lord, which the lord ought to have in the residual land which remains for the heirs as an inheritance.

13. Likewise, let there be no exaction from the parties in the provision of justice or the giving of judgement under the pretext of any custom or on the occasion of advocates or assessors, but let justice be provided free for all, and with regard to a poor man who has no advocate, let him be given one by the court.

14. Likewise, let no heretical believer, although he be reconciled, be made provost, bailiff, or judge, or assessor in a judgement or witness, or advocate, and let the same apply to Jews, except that a Jew will be able to bear witness against a Jew.

15. Likewise, let no robed[17] and reconciled[18] heretic have licence to remain in the town in which he dwelt in that perverse perfection, but he will be able to dwell outside that town where the count permits him.

---

16 A currency common throughout the kingdom of France, minted at Tours.
17 I.e. 'consoled' or 'perfected'.
18 This is a necessary condition in the Latin, rather than simply a possible one as in the Siblys' translation: Peter of Vaux-de-Cernay, *History of the Albigensian Crusade*, p. 323. The error has confused some scholars: e.g. D. Brown, *Hugh de Lacy, First Earl of Ulster: Rising and Falling in Angevin Ireland* (Woodbridge, Suff., 2016), p. 130.

16. Likewise, let clerks, any religious man,[19] pilgrims, and knights pass through all our land free and immune from the exaction of any toll, unless they be merchants.

17. Likewise, all barons and knights of France are held to serve the count in this land when and wherever he will have war against his person by reason of this land, conquered or yet to be conquered, and this with the number of knights according to the obligation on which the count gave to them their land and revenues. In this way, if the revenues have been adequately assigned according to the promise in its entirety, then the baron or knight will be held to serve with the promised number of knights as assigned for as long as the lord count will have war for this conquered land as has been said. However, that knight to whom the assignment has not been made in full according to the prior agreement shall not be held to serve with the entire number of knights, but the number of knights for service ought to be fixed according to the proportion and amount of the assignment made. However, if the count – not from his own necessity nor that of his land, but of his own will – should wish to aid another or others, whether nearby or distant, in war, his aforesaid knights are not held to follow him in this or to serve him themselves or through others, unless they should do so from their love and goodwill.

18. Likewise, French knights who owe service to the count are held to serve him with French knights. They are not able to provide knights of this land in place of French knights for his service for twenty years, but after this anyone will serve him with such suitable knights as he can find in the land.

19. Likewise, knights authorised by the count to be in France ought not to remain there longer than the term set for them beforehand by the count without reasonable cause, and yet the count is held to wait for them, saving his service, for four months after the expiry of this limit; but after this the count will be able to seize their land in his possession without any protest, and thence freely to do his will, unless they can show the count in full a sufficient or inevitable cause for why they were not able to come more quickly.

20. Likewise, all barons, knights and other lords in the land of the count are held to render walled villages and castles of the count without any delay or contradiction, in dispute or peace, to his will, that is, whenever he might want those walled villages and the castles which they hold from him, and the same count, as a good lord, is held to return these to them in the same state and

---

19 I.e., a monk or canon regular.

value in which he received them, without diminution or damage, his business being concluded.

21. Likewise, all barons, knights, and men of greater and lesser rank who may be summoned are held in common to go to open battle (whether in declared war or not), or to the aid of the count if he may be besieged, or to a general levy. And if a baron, knight, or other lord of the land should be proved not to have come to give aid to the count in this supreme necessity – unless he can be excused by sufficient cause[20] – one half of his moveable goods will be in the possession and will of the count and the lord under whom he lives.

22. Likewise, barons, knights, and other lords of the lands who owe service to the count, if, having been summoned to fifteen days' service, they should not come to the place set beforehand by the count for the army, provided that he[21]

---

20 In a seventeenth-century copy (taken from a different original or another thirteenth-century copy, now housed in the Bibliothèque municipale de Toulouse, ms. 639, pp. 68–75) in place of the final sentence this statute reads: 'And if a baron, knight, or other lord of the land should be proved not to have come to give aid to the count in this supreme necessity – unless he could be excused by sufficient cause – the land which he holds from the count will be in the possession and will of the count. However, other lesser men, namely, burghers and rural peasants, are held to go in the aforesaid articles if reasonably summoned: they should be the two best of any given household if they are there, if, however, there should not be but one in the household, he himself will be held to go. Whoever should not go – unless he will be able to be excused by sufficient cause – to the extent of one half of his moveable goods will be in the possession and will of the count and the lord under whom he lives, and to the extent of one half of his other goods will be in the possession of the count and the lord under whom he lives.' This is likely an interpolation, as the language differs from the formulations of the surviving original; it may have been inserted when the Statutes were inherited by the royal seneschalty of Carcassonne.

21 The count. If Simon or his successor has not actually begun his campaign within the fifteen days of the muster obligation, presumably the penalty is waived. The wording here is vague, and the subject might be thought here to be the offending lord who arrives to the muster late, but still within fifteen days. However, pace the Siblys in Peter of Vaux-de-Cernay, *History of the Albigensian Crusade*, p. 325n. 6, the consistent reference throughout this sentence (though not in the following one) to the potential offenders in the plural, alongside the lack of articulation of a penalty for those who do not set out within fifteen days, argues for the subject being the count.

has set out on the way within fifteen days, the fifth part of all their revenues for one year, that is, from their lands which they hold from the count, will be in the possession and will of the count as an indemnity, unless they can be excused by sufficient cause. If, however, he should come, but not with the number of knights owed, for every knight that is lacking he shall give double wages[22] on the spot for as long for as he shall be without the number of knights owed. The same penalty will apply to indigenous barons and knights, if they do not[23] render their service owed to the count.

23. Likewise, let no one in the land of the count who is subject to his dominion and power attempt to build a new castle or rebuild one which has been razed, without the assent of the count.

24. Likewise, indigenous knights who have been Catholics and have hitherto persevered in the Catholic Faith are held to fulfil service to their lords, to the count, or to others as they were obligated to fulfil it to their own indigenous lords before the crusaders came. However, those who were believers of the heretics are held to serve at the judgement of the count and his barons.

25. Likewise, let none be judged to have been believers of the heretics or to have been heretics[24] unless by the testimony of bishops or priests.

26. Likewise, no baron, knight or any other lord to whom the count has given land in these parts shall be able to demand beyond the measure of tallage established and confirmed by the letters of the same lords and the count, whether in the name of tallage or revenue, or in the name of bounty or of any other cause whatsoever, saving rents, other revenues from lands, vineyards, houses, and other property, and legal penalties. Indeed, this tallage was established and measured for all other tallage, whether revenue or redress; beyond this let it not be allowed for anything further to be demanded or extorted from anyone. And if anyone should be proved to have demanded beyond this, and there is a complaint as a result, the count will be held to send to the town and the lord of the town in which this was done, and the lord will be compelled by him to raise or release what he has demanded beyond his charter, and he will be compelled to observe his charter.

---

22 Presumably, to the count.
23 A double negative here that would otherwise reverse the meaning seems obviously in error and has been ignored.
24 I.e., those who are 'perfected' or 'consoled'.

27. Likewise, it will be allowed to all men who can be tallaged to cross from one lord to the lordship of another lord according to his will. Thus, those who are called free will be able to cross without any contradiction to another lord with their moveables, leaving behind their inheritance and dwelling to their previous lord, along with all that they hold from others. Others, however, who are called owned men or serfs will similarly be able to cross to another lord, leaving not only their inheritance and dwelling, but also their moveables, to their previous lord. As such the previous lord will not be able to demand anything further from him wherever he may be on occasion of the moveables or revenues or another thing afterwards; having left his lord he shall remain under the lordship of the other. However, they will not be able to cross into the lordship of clerks or churches, until they[25] consent to this, and have given their letters on the subject to the count and his barons.

28. Likewise, let no man be sent to prison or kept captive so long as he can give sufficient pledges that he will stand in court.

29. Likewise, let no lord receive from his men pledges or any security that they do not withdraw from his lordship – under the terms written above[26] – when they might wish.

30. Likewise, according to the ancient custom of the lands and towns, let lords receive the owed daily labour from their men and, according to custom, give them food.

31. Likewise, if the men of the indigenous princes and lords in this land should be heavily oppressed with tallages and exactions, and they complain to the count, the count ought to convene the lords and knights, that they might keep an appropriate and reasonable measure of tallages and exactions, and, if it should be necessary, he will be able to compel them to observe this, that their subjects may not be heavily oppressed on account of the excessive wickedness of their lords.

32. Likewise, in woods, waters, and pastures, let the men of the towns have their usage as they have had for the past thirty years. And if a dispute should arise over this between the people and the lord, let whoever is in possession remain so until the truth may be investigated through the sworn statements of the elders who are in the same land or by some other means.

---

25 Presumably, the clerks.
26 See statute 27.

33. Likewise, let no man be taken for the debt of his lord unless he be a pledge or debtor.

34. Likewise, let no baron, knight, burgher, or peasant dare to pillage or take the property of another by violence, nor let him to whom injury has been done dare to avenge himself without the licence of his superior, but let them bring their complaint to their superior. If, however, they may be convicted of or confess to having done contrary to this, he who first took the goods of the other will give as an indemnity to his superior lord: if a baron, it will be 20*l*.; if a knight, let it be 10*l*.; if a burgher, 100*s*.; if a peasant, 20*s*.; and furthermore at the order of the lord he will render all that he took to the one who suffered the injury, and as for him, let it fully satisfy him for any damage that he had. Whoever revenges himself in the same way will entirely redress it to his superior lord, and moreover let him pay an indemnity of 60*s*. to him on whom he avenged himself, making restitution of stolen goods and damage, with this exception: it is allowed for anyone to repel force with force without delay.

35. Likewise, let no barons, knights, burghers, or peasants dare in any way to assemble themselves by means of faith or oath, or to make any conspiracy even under the pretext of a confraternity or another good, except with the assent and will of the count. But if any should be proved to have so conspired against their lord both they and their property will be in the possession and will of the lord. If, however, they have conspired not against their lord but for the injury of others, if they should be convicted of or confess to this, each will give: 10*l*. if they are barons; 100*s*. if simple knights; 60*s*. if burghers; 20*s*. if peasants. Merchants or pilgrims who swear among themselves in order to preserve their fellowship have been exempted from this penalty.

36. Likewise, whoever shall henceforth, without the knowledge of the count, transport provisions, anything else whatsoever, or men, whomever they may be, to Toulouse or to any other enemies of Christ or the count and shall be convicted of or confess to this, they will for this reason alone lose their inheritance with all their goods in perpetuity. If, however, any sergeant or bailiff should do this without the knowledge of his lord, he will lose all his goods and his body will be in the possession and mercy of the count. However, all men and property taken in such transportation will belong, without subtraction or protest, to the one who may capture them.

37. Likewise, anyone in the land of the count who is able to capture enemies of the Faith and the count, and does not capture them, and can be proved or convicted of it, his land will be attacked and his body in the possession and mercy

of the count; the same will befall one who might see such men and not wish to publish and pursue them according to the custom of the land in good faith.

38. Likewise, let bakers make and sell bread according to the manner and measure or weight given to them by their lord, and if they should not observe this, as often as they may act contrary to this, they shall lose all their bread, and let the same apply to innkeepers.

39. Likewise, let public prostitutes be placed without the walls in all towns.

40. Let tolls which have been instituted by princes and other lords in the past thirty-four years be entirely abolished without any delay.

41. Likewise, let farmed possessions not be given nor sold to the diminution of the superior lord.

42. Likewise, let rents be rendered to lords in their courts in the established terms, and as often as they should surpass a term, for each term thus passed, let them pay the lords 5s. as an indemnity. And if he[27] should allow three years to pass without the payment of the rent, the lord will be able to give [the farm] to another or sell it without protest from him; but if he[28] should retain it in his possession, he will be held to return it if it is paid to him for every year or term that has passed, with the penalty of 5s., as has been said.

43. Likewise, let heirs, both among barons and knights and among burghers and peasants, succeed to their inheritances according to the custom and use of France around Paris.

44. Likewise, let the dowries of women revert to their heirs, and let them be able to make a will on this subject if they should wish.

45. Likewise, let all wives of those traitors and enemies of the count – even if they should be found to be Catholics – leave the the land of the count, so that suspicion may not fall on them, and they will have the lands and revenues of their dowry, but under oath that they will make over no part of it to their husbands so long as they should remain at war with Christianity and the count.

---

27 The tenant.
28 The lord.

46. Likewise, for ten years let no great widows or noble heiresses who have fortifications or walled villages dare to marry, without the licence of the count and of their own will, indigenous men of this land, on account of the danger to the land; but they will be able to marry Frenchmen as they wish, not requiring the licence of the count or another; but after the term elapses, they will be able to marry among themselves.

And therefore I, Simon, earl of Leicester, lord of Montfort, by the providence of God viscount of Béziers and Carcassonne and also lord of Albi and the Razès, have confirmed by means of an oath that I will observe the general customs written above in good faith, and all my barons have similarly confirmed under oath that they will observe them, obviously saving improvement or amendment by Holy Church or our barons, and also saving conventions and privileges conceded, oaths made in other places, and other established customs, should they not be contrary to these. Done at Pamiers in our palace, in the year of the Incarnation of the Lord 1212, on the first day of the month of December.

Appendix:[29]
These are the customs which the lord count ought to observe between himself, his barons of France, and others to whom he has given land in these parts.

a.[30] Let heirs, both among barons and knights and among burghers and peasants, succeed to their inheritances according to the custom and use of France around Paris.

b. Likewise, let no baron or knight or any other lord in our land accept a duel in his court for any cause, except for treason, theft, rape,[31] or murder.

c. Likewise, in pleas, judgements, dowers, fiefs, and distributions of lands, the count is held to observe for his barons of France and others to whom he has given land in these parts the same use and custom that are observed in France around Paris.

Done at Pamiers in my palace, in the year of the Incarnation of the Lord 1212, on the first day of the month of December.

---

29 Separate parchment attached to the queue of Simon's seal, written in a different hand.
30 Again, there are no markers separating clauses in the original.
31 I.e. in its traditional, more expansive sense, including sexual violation but also any violent abduction of persons or property.

[I am greatly indebted to Gregory Lippiatt for this fine translation and scholarly annotation of the Statutes of Pamiers which he kindly prepared exclusively for the second edition of *Kill Them All*. I draw readers' attention to his important and original monograph, published two years after the first edition of *Kill Them All* in 2015: *Simon V of Montfort and Baronial Government, 1195–1218* (Oxford, 2017). This detailed study offers invaluable insights into Montfort's career, shedding much-needed light on, among other things, the complex land issues (and associated financial aspects) that so often motivated and shaped his decision-making and actions. As such, it is a highly significant contribution to the literature not only on Montfort but also the Albigensian Crusade in general. Lippiatt offers an excellent analysis of the Statues of Pamiers on pp. 161–9.]

APPENDIX 3

THE TREATY OF PARIS 1229

A Translation by W.A. Sibly and M.D. Sibly

The text is that printed in HGL (*Historie Générale du Languedoc* – see Bibliography), vol. VIII, 883–93, and dated 12 April 1229.

The document occupies ten columns of HGL VIII, about 3,000 words. It is written in good Latin, and for the most part clearly expressed, and in translating we have attempted to follow the Latin closely. Each item is set out with careful precision and in very elaborate detail, presumable to ensure that Raymond VII would have little chance of disputing the terms at a later time. Roquebert's *L'Epopée Cathare*, vol. III: Le Lys et la Croix (see Bibliography) in chapter 29 first provides a full French translation both of the preliminary document agreed at Meaux (HGL VIII, 878–83) and the treaty itself, and then proceeds to give a detailed analysis, inter alia pointing out that the terms of the treaty are much more stringent than those agreed at Meaux. In his chapter 30 he discusses the implementation of the treaty. The paragraph numbering follows Roquebert's.

Summarised sections are in italics.

The treaty begins:

Raymond, by God's grace Count of Toulouse, gives greetings in the Lord's name to all those to whom the document may be presented.

Let all know that, whereas a state of war has for a long time existed between the Holy Roman Church and Louis, King of France, on the one part, and ourselves on the other, we now sincerely inspire to live in unity with the Holy Roman Church and remain loyally devoted to the service of our lord the King of France; and have made every effort, in person and through the agency of others, to ensure the maintenance of the peace which has been arranged between the Holy Roman Church and the King of France on the one part and ourselves on the other part.

[1 and 2] We therefore promise Romanus, Cardinal-deacon of St Angelo, legate of the Apostolic See, in the name of the Roman Church, that we will unto death remain faithful to and loyally support the Church and our lord Louis, King of France; and that we will always use every endeavour to expel from the territories which we or our people hold (or may hold in future) heretics and their believers, supporters and receivers; in this not sparing neighbours, vassals, kinsfolk or friends. We will also purge these territories which the King may hold.

[3] We promise moreover that we will immediately do due justice to manifest heretics, or see to it that our bailiffs ('ballivos nostros') will do justice to them, and vigorously arrange for enquiries to be made and ourselves diligently make such enquiries with a view to seeking out heretics, their believers, supporters and receivers, according to such arrangement as the legate may make in this matter. Also, to encourage and facilitate the search for heretics we promise to pay two silver marks for two years to anyone who brings about the arrest of a heretic, and thereafter to pay one mark in perpetuity if the heretic who has been arrested is condemned for heresy by the Bishop of the area or any other person with the necessary authority; if several heretics are arrested, we will give the same amount for each. In regard to heretics who are not manifest heretics, and the believers, receivers and supporters of heretics, we will carry out, and see to it that the others carry out, whatever instructions are laid down by the said legate or the Roman Church.

[4] Item, we will keep the peace in the territories which we and our people hold, and see to it that others do so, and will also help to keep the peace in territories which the King holds in his own hands. We will also expel mercenaries and mete out due punishment to them and their receivers.

[5] We will defend the Church and men of the Church and ensure that our people do so. We will protect and firmly ensure the protection of their rights, liberties and immunities. Also, to ensure that the keys of the Church's authority are not scorned in the future, we will observe sentences of excommunication and ensure they are observed by our people and through our people; we will shun excommunicates and ensure they are shunned by

others, as it is laid down in Holy ordinances, and if any persons obstinately remain in a state of excommunication for a year, then, following the Church's instructions, we will compel them to return to the bosom of the Mother Church, seizing their property both moveable and immoveable which we will hold until they give full satisfaction in the matter for which they were bound with the chain of excommunication and for any wrongs done in association with their excommunication.

[6] We will ensure that an oath is sworn by all our bailiffs, whether already appointed or to be appointed in future (in the latter case the oath to be taken at the time of appointment) to observe faithfully everything set out as above; if they are found to be neglectful in this respect we will punish them according to their error, and if they are found to be blameworthy we will punish them by depriving them of all of their goods. We will appoint as bailiffs no Jews, but only Catholics of local origin who are untainted by any suspicion of heresy. Jews or any suspected heretics will not be allowed to acquire the revenues of cities, towns or *castra* or road tolls. Should we unwittingly appoint any such person we will dismiss him and punish him when the facts are made known to us.

[7] Item, we promise that we will at once restore all immoveable properties and all rights belonging to churches or men of the Church, and we will also ensure their full restoration by our people and throughout the territories which we or our people shall hold; namely properties and rights which were held by churches or persons of the Church before the advent of the crusaders, or which it is agreed were seized for them. In regard to other properties we will stand in judgment before ordinaries or the legate or persons delegated to him or by the Apostolic See.

[8] We promise also that we will in future pay tithes in their entirety, and will ensure that our people also pay them in their entirety and in good faith, and that we will not allow knights and other lay persons to possess tithes in the territories which we and our people hold or may hold in future, and that the tithes will revert to the churches in their entirety as instructed by the legate or Roman Church.

[9] Turning now to losses caused by ourselves and our people to churches and men of the church, as regards moveable property and houses or vills or other properties which were destroyed (leaving aside immoveable properties, for which restitution is to be made as set out above) we will pay ten thousand silver marks, to be allocated to persons of standing, who are suitable and true

to the faith, as may be chosen by the legate himself or the Roman Church, whose task it will be to distribute the said sum, on the advice of men of good standing, in due proportion and with due care, in accordance with the amount of harm incurred. Neither we nor our people will be held liable to make reparations in excess of this sum, as is set out above, in regard to harm done to moveable property or the destruction of houses or vills or other properties.

[10] Item, we will pay:
– to the Abbot of Cîteaux two thousand silver marks to be used to acquire revenues to support the abbots and brothers when they gather for the Chapter General;
– to the Abbot of Clairvaux five hundred marks to support the abbots and brothers when they meet on the feast day of the Blessed Virgin Mary;
– to the Abbot of Grandselve one thousand marks, to the Abbot of Belleperche three hundred marks, and to the Abbot of Candeil two hundred marks; these amounts being intended for building works at the three monasteries.
We make these payments both for restitution for harm done to moveable properties, and for the salvation of our soul.

[11] Item, we will pay six thousand marks, to be used as may be seen to be appropriate to fortify, strengthen and garrison the Château Narbonnais and other castles which the King intends to hold for a ten-year period (as will be set out below) for the Church's security and his own.

[12] We will pay the above total sum of twenty thousand marks over a four-year period, i.e. at the rate of five thousand marks each year.

[13] Item, we will assign four thousand marks to four masters in theology, two decretalists, six masters in the liberal arts and two masters in grammar teaching at Toulouse.

The detailed allocation of this amount follows; in each case payments are for ten years: fifty marks to the masters in theology; thirty to each decretalist; twenty to each master in arts; ten to each master in grammar.

[14] The Count then gives an undertaking (which in event was not carried out) to go on Crusade in Outremer for five years, by way of penance. The Treaty continues:

[15] We shall not harass those who sided with the Church, the King, his father, the Counts of Montfort and their supporters, on the grounds of their

having sided with the Church, the King, his father, but will treat them kindly as friends as if they had not been opponents, always excepting heretics and heretical believers. Also the Church will deal similarly with those who sided with us against the King and the Church always excepting those who are unwilling to join us in making peace with the Church and the King.

[16] The King, having regard to the humility we have displayed and hoping that we will faithfully maintain our devotion to the Church and our loyalty to him, and wishing also to show favour to us, will arrange for the marriage of our daughter (whom we will hand over to him) to one of his brothers, after obtaining a dispensation from the Church. He will then hand over to us the whole bishopric of Toulouse ('episcopatum Tholosanum'), excepting territories of the Marshal which the Marshal holds from the King. However, after our death the bishopric of Toulouse and Toulouse itself will come into the possession of the King's brother who is married to our daughter or any sons of the two. If, however, the King's brother should die without issue (may this not be) Toulouse and the bishopric of Toulouse will revert to the King and his heirs, and our daughter and any other sons or daughters of ours or our heirs will have no right to reclaim these possessions. And if our daughter herself dies without issue fathered by the King's brother, similarly Toulouse and the bishopric of Toulouse will revert to the King and his heirs after our death and no one will be able to claim any right there save sons or daughters descended from the King's brother and our daughter, as set out above.

[17] Item, the King leaves ('dimittit') to us the bishoprics of Agen and Cahors. Of the bishopric of Albi he leaves to us that part which lies beyond the Tarn viz. from the area of Gaillac; and the city of Albi will remained with the King, with whatever of the Bishopric which lies beyond that river towards Carcassonne. The King will hold the river bank and the water up to the middle of the river, and similarly we will hold the river bank on our side up to the middle of the river; always subject to the rights and possessions of others, and provided those in the King's area perform their duty to him and those on our side similarly perform their duty to us.

[18] The King leaves us the bishopric of Cahors, excepting the city of Cahors and any fiefs which King Philip, the King's grandfather, had in the bishopric at the time of his death.

[19] If we die without issue from a legal marriage the whole of the said territory will remain with our daughter, who is to be married to the King's brother, and their heirs.

[20] This all to be on the basis that we, as the true lord, will have full legal powers and free rights of lordship in the territories left to us, on the conditions stated above, in regard to the city and bishopric of Toulouse and the other territory named above, and at our death will be able to make charitable bequests according to the uses and customs of the other barons of the French kingdoms. The King leaves all of the above to us without prejudice to the rights of the churches and men of the Church, as laid down above.

[21–2] *The position of Verfeil as a possession of the Bishop of Toulouse and his son ('episcopo Tholosano & filio O.de Lyliers') (subject to homage to Raymond) is confirmed. Other gifts made by the King or his father or the Counts of Montfort in the territories left to Raymond or his people are revoked. Raymond is to do homage to the King for all these territories according to the practice of the barons of the kingdom of France.*
The Treaty continues:

[23] All other territories on the nearer side of the Rhône within the French kingdom and all rights therein appertaining to us, or which might appertain to us, we now yield absolutely to the King and his heirs in perpetuity.

[24] Imperial territories beyond the Rhône and all rights therein appertaining to us, or which might appertain to us, we now yield absolutely to the legate to hold us in perpetuity in the name of the Church.

[25] Item, local lords who were driven from the territory as *faidits* in the interests of the Church, the King or his father, or the Counts of Montfort and their adherents, or who left voluntarily, are to have their rights and possessions restored to them, unless they are condemned as heretics by the Church; this to exclude possessions gifted by the King, his father or the Counts of Montfort.

[26] If any men remaining in the territories which are handed to us refuse to revert to obedience ['redire ad mandatum'] to the Church and the King, more especially the Count of Foix and others, we will engage them in open warfare ['faciemus eis vivam guerram'] and not make peace or a truce with them without the assent of the Church and the King.
If their territories are occupied, they will remain in our control, but before that all castles and forts ['munitionibus & fortericiis'], walls and ditches will be destroyed, unless the King wishes to retain them for a period of up to ten years during which he will retain the revenues and profits from these places.

[27] Item, we will arrange for the walls of Toulouse to be completely pulled down and the diches to be filled up, as instructed by the legate.

Item, we will have the walls pulled down and the ditches filled up of the following thirty towns and *castra,* namely:

Fanjeaux, Castelnaudary, Labécède, Avignonet, Puylaurens, Saint-Paul-Cap-de-Joux, Lauvar, Rabastens, Gaillac, Montégut, Puycelsi, Verdun, Castelsarrasin, Moissac, Montauban, Montcuq, Agen, Condom, Saverdun, Auterive, Casseneuil, Pujols, Auvillar, Peyrisse, Laurac and five others as determined by the legate.

These places will not be refortified without the consent of the Church and the King, nor will new fortifications be erected elsewhere.

However, we will be allowed to build unfortified towns in the territories left to us. If any of the towns or *castra* which were due to have their fortifications destroyed (as set out above) belonged to our people and they refuse to allow this to be done, we will engage them in open warfare and will not make peace or agree a truce with any of them without the approval of the Church and the King, until their walls have been pulled down and their ditches filled in.

[28–29] The Count then undertakes to abide by all the above and ensure that his vassals will do the same. He will ensure that the citizens of Toulouse and the inhabitants of his other remaining territories will swear to abide by what has been agreed. The consequences he will face should he fail to keep to his promises then follow:

It will be set out in their oath that they will themselves take effective measures to ensure that we ourselves keep to our undertakings; and that if we go against the above provisions or any part of them they will ipso facto be released from any obligation to us and henceforward ['exnunc'] we will release them from the loyalty and homage due to us and all other ties, and they will join the Church and the King in opposing us, unless within forty days of receiving warning we make due amends or stand under the law before the Church on matters concerning the Church, or before the King in matters concerning him; and the whole territory left to us will pass in trust ['in commissum'] to the King and we shall revert to out present condition in regard to the King and our excommunication and in regard to all other decisions made concerning us and our father at the General (sc. Fourth Lateran) Council and subsequently.

The oaths to be sworn will include an undertaking to help the Church and the King against heretics and their supporters, to the extent of taking up arms. The oaths are to be renewed every five years as the King might require. The Treaty continues:

[30] To ensure that all the above requirements will be implemented and fully adhered to for the benefit of the Church and the King, and to ensure the security of the Church and the King, we will hand over to the King the Château Narbonnais, which he will hold for ten years and garrison and fortify if he considers this to be desirable.

Item, to ensure the security of the Church and the King we will hand to him the keeps of Lavaur and Castelnaudary, the *castrum* of Montégut, Penne d'Agenais, the *castrum* of Cordes, Peyrusse-le-Roc, and the *castra* of Verdun and Villemur. He is to hold these places for up to ten years, and in the first five years to cover the expenses of maintaining garrisons these places we will pay him fifteen hundred livres tournois, this not to be included in the six thousand marks previously referred to; for the following five years the King will himself cover these costs. However, the King will (should this be the wish of the Church and himself) be allowed to demolish four of the *castra* referred to above, viz. the keep of Castelnaudary, the keep of Lavaur, Villemur and Verdun, and this will not result in a reduction in the sum of fifteen hundred livres tournois. The revenues and returns from the places and all else relating to the rights of seigneury will be ours, and the King will hold the keeps of these *castra*, and also Cordes. We will install bailiffs (to be men not suspect in the eyes of the Church and the King), who will administer justice and collect the said revenues. After ten years the King will return to us the said keep, and Cordes, on the conditions set out above and provided all undertakings given to the Church and King have been observed.

[31] There is then a full column of text dealing with Penne d'Albigeois, which at the time had not yet submitted to the King. The Treaty continues:

[32] The King releases the citizens of Toulouse and other men of the territory which is being given to us from all obligations made to himself and his father and the Counts of Montfort or to others on their behalf, also from the penalties and forfeitures they agreed they would pay to the King or his father or the Bishop of Toulouse or other prelates in the event of their ever reverting to our rule or our father's, and any oath applying to the King, always subject in every respect of the above conditions.

The Treaty concludes with formalities. There is then a further section of text, not part of the Treaty proper, dealing with arrangement for twenty citizens of Toulouse to be held in French custody until the city walls have been pulled down.

HGL VIII, 893–4, also dated 12 April, deals with Raymond's absolution by Cardinal Romanus.

Translated (and abridged in italics) by W.A. Sibly and M.D. Sibly (eds and trans.), *The Chronicle of William of Puylaurens* (Woodbridge, 2003).

[My profound gratitude to Michael Sibly for his kindness in permitting this extremely useful translation to be reprinted here. As I point out in the main text, scholars of the Albigensian Crusade are indebted to the translations, editing and annotations undertaken by Michael and his father of the two key Latin chronicles of the crusade. I would also like to take this opportunity to thank Michael for coming to Strode College to give our undergraduate students on the History, Heritage and Archaeology degree course an inspirational talk on Catharism and the crusade.]

APPENDIX 4

LIKE FATHER, LIKE SON: THE OTHER SIMON DE MONTFORT

In France, the name Simon de Montfort is synonymous with the general who led the crusade against the Cathars and their supporters in Languedoc; in Britain, the name instantly recalls one of Simon's younger sons who loomed every bit as large in that country's history, and arguably even more so. Father and son shared not just their names but many dominating character traits: a deep, even fervid faith; undoubted bravery and dedication to the hardships of military campaigning; ruthlessness and single-mindedness; and an all-consuming, unlimited ambition. The younger Simon was to be loved and loathed in equal measure as either a hero or selfish rebel.

Simon the Younger's parents had a strong relationship; indeed, the uxorious Simon the Elder was noted for his closeness to his wife Alice. Together, like any dutiful and successful noble dynasty, they hatched a large nest of offspring. There were two daughters: Amicie, born around 1200, who married Gaucher de Joigny, Lord of Château-Renard (he had participated in the Albigensian Crusade in 1209), and died in 1253; and Petronilla, born in 1211 and who became Abbess of the Cistercian convent of St Antoine. Of their four sons, little is known of the youngest, Robert, who died sometime after 1226. As we have seen, the second son, Guy (named for his uncle and Simon the Elder's indispensable brother and captain), died in 1220 in the early stages of military action at Castelnaudary.

Amaury, born in 1195, was the eldest of the four. He inherited his father's roles as Count of Toulouse and leader of the Albigensian Crusade following

314

Simon's death at Toulouse in 1218. In some ways he was poorly suited to leadership; but, as shown in the book, he was ineluctably bypassed by the growing involvement and gravitational pull of the French crown in the suppression of Languedocian resistance. Amaury was rewarded for stepping to one side – not least in relinquishing the county of Toulouse to King Louis VIII – by going on to become Constable of France in 1230. He experienced severe financial difficulties and in 1239 the Church stepped in to settle his debts; it was no coincidence that Amaury embarked on the Barons' Crusade that year. Joining the powerful contingent of Theobald, Count of Champagne, he fought with notable bravery, his eagerness to engage in combat leading to his capture at Gaza in November. (At least one contemporary noticed in Amaury's behaviour the pride and arrogance associated with his father.) Amaury languished in captivity in Cairo for nearly eighteen months before the release of crusader prisoners in Spring 1241 negotiated by Richard, Duke of Cornwall, during his contribution to the campaign. (Richard was the younger brother of King Henry III of England, the monarch who was to be all but usurped by Amaury's own younger brother, Simon.) It was thus left to the third son, Simon the Younger, to carry the de Montfort banner to new heights with the succeeding generation.

Simon's early life is shrouded in ignorance. He was born around 1208 and seems to have been raised in southern France, accompanying his parents during Simon the Elder's campaigning there. Peter of Vaux de Cernay informs us that he was present with them at the siege of Toulouse in 1218 when his father was killed there. His name first appears in a charter of his mother that year. With his older brother Guy dying in 1220 followed by his mother in 1221, it is probable that thereafter Simon was raised in the household of his surviving older brother, Amaury. He pops up only twice in the sources during the 1220s, attesting to two of Amaury's charters in 1222 and 1226. It is thought, with reasonable assumption, that Simon gained military experience during the 1226–29 phase of the Albigensian Crusade.

He came to England in 1230 as a 'tall, handsome and energetic' young man, says a contemporary, to lay claim to and gain (though his maternal side, and also through the payment and transferring of rights) the honour of Leicester, buttering up Henry III as a means to this end. (His first act was to expel the Jews from the town.) Henceforth, Montfort's ambitions became increasingly focused on England, incrementally advancing his position at Henry's court, especially in the aftermath of the struggle between Hubert de Burgh and Peter des Roches that brought down these two great ministers of state by 1234. By the second half of the decade he was close to the king, with Henry dangling the prospect of the earldom of Leicester enticingly before him. Personable, articulate and with close ties to intellectual and cultural circles, Montfort also had the practical advantages that came with having family lands situated strategically between Paris and the borders of Normandy, something of keen interest to the English king trying to regain lands lost there by his father, the inept King John; Montfort was therefore a valuable ally. In 1238 Montfort's ambitions appeared, at that time, to have summited: he married Henry's sister, Eleanor, whom Montfort had pursued to the point of possible seduction (despite her earlier vow of chastity). Eleanor held many obvious attractions for Montfort: she was fair, a young widow (twenty-three, having lost her husband, the powerful William Marshal, Earl of Pembroke – son of the regent of the same name who was renowned for his chivalric accomplishments – in 1231) and doubled, perhaps even trebled, Montfort's landed income. And it made him brother-in-law to the king.

Montfort's march to the top meant stepping on many toes along the way. There were numerous magnates who resented the rise of yet another foreigner over the heads of home-grown talent who felt that they were more deserving and, more to the point, more entitled to these favours of royal patronage. Montfort's marriage was so secret that even Henry's brother, Richard, Duke of Cornwall, did not know of it until after the event. A short revolt ensued, led by Richard and the Earl of Pembroke. But Montfort stayed close to the king, naming his son after him and officially gaining the title of the Earl of Leicester in 1239. Nonetheless, Montfort was proving himself to be a divisive figure. Despite his favoured position, he was to remain anxious over his finances, as Eleanor's lands were not transferrable to Montfort's family after her death, whether she predeceased him or not.

It was money, almost inevitably, that led to Montfort falling out with the king only the next year. In a serious misjudgement – not his last – he named, without permission, the king as a guarantor for a loan. This blunder of presumption was met with a furious response by Henry, who accused Montfort of having made Eleanor pregnant before the marriage (the timing between their marriage in January and their first-born in November would indicate that any pre-marital foreknowledge of pregnancy was unlikely). As a precautionary consequence, Montfort and his bride sensibly departed for the continent.

Now was a good time for Montfort to honour his crusading vow, following his brother on the Barons' Crusade. This enhanced both his political and military reputation enormously, and perhaps also his ego. Henry, in need of Montfort's French connections, summoned him to his disastrous Poitevin campaign in 1242 which ended in the battle of Saintes (discussed in the book's final chapter). Back in England, Montfort was restored to favour, if not to the king's complete confidence. In what was to prove an expensive move, Henry granted the powerful castle of Kenilworth in Warwickshire to Montfort. (It was to undergo a six-month royalist siege in 1266 – the longest siege in English history.) There was still little real reason either for Montfort to be other than grateful to the king for his largesse or to side with those grumbling at Henry's rule. That was about to change.

In 1248, Henry sent Montfort to take charge of Gascony, the English duchy in south-west France under internal and external threat. His rule there was effective overall, but high-handed and draconian ('brutal', says the historian Stephen Church), his successes coming at a high cost both financially and politically. This resulted in Montfort having to answer the charges raised against him in London in 1252; he smarted at the dishonourable mortification of this and the king's shameful undermining of his position. Although the result of the trial was to distance crown and magnate even further and with a new heightened degree of enmity, Henry and Montfort continued to co-operate for a time thereafter to mutual advantage, but not with mutual respect. The financial difficulties of both caused further antagonistic crossings of paths. Thus Montfort eventually began to align himself with the baronial discontents in England. At first his motivations were more financial and personal, but later he embodied what for many was a moral programme against Henry's policies.

As was so often the case in such matters, the problem of patronage was very much to the fore (among other issues such as financial incompetence, the Sicilian Business and Henry's overly ambitious foreign policy objectives). Henry favoured familial connections with the Lusignans and promoted these foreigners over English lords. In April 1258 a baronial party called for reform and a change in direction of Henry's government. These barons entered Westminster Hall in their armour. The response of the startled king was to ask: 'Am I your prisoner?' Montfort reassured him, somewhat unconvincingly, that this was not the case. In effect, the baronial coalition had seized the reins of power. The legal manifestation of this came in the radical Provisions of Oxford from June 1258 under which Henry had to concede a number of startling restrictions on his power through submission to the baronial council. For J.R. Maddicott, the foremost authority on Montfort, these 'constituted something like a revolution [...] a quasi-republican constitution, even going beyond what had been attempted by King John's opponents in 1215'.

The reform movement met with widespread support across the social orders. But individual interests, infighting, international affairs and an inherent sense of loyalty to the monarchy led to splits within the coalition, and from 1261, when the king exploited these differences to regain some measure of control, Montfort assumed leadership of its more hard-line (or pure, depending on one's point of view) elements, even proposing that parliament could meet without the presence of the monarch. Matters came to a head in 1263 when Henry refused to bow to pressure over the Provisions; military activity broke out. All-out civil war was about to begin.

It is a testament to Montfort's skills as a general and to his unrelenting drive that he was able to take on the King of England and all his resources. Deprived of the erstwhile support of King Louis IX, the most powerful monarch in western Christendom, Montfort nevertheless rallied sufficient popular support from beyond the ranks of the aristocratic elites and inspired many with his ideals of reforms (and followers did believe that these were indeed ideals). An anti-foreign, pro-nationalist stance reinforced this support. As the contemporary, pro-Montfortian *Song of Lewes* opines, Henry and his foreign-dominated court wished to 'blot out the name of the English'. There was therefore no little irony in the fact that Montfort, a Frenchman who was not fluent in English, used as an exhortation the rallying cry, 'Down with the foreigners!'

When open hostilities broke out early in 1264, Montfort demonstrated resilience at initial setbacks and went on to gain a huge victory at the battle of Lewes in May 1264. Here not only Henry but his heir Edward and brother Richard of Cornwall were all taken prisoner. Montfort was supreme, if not entirely secure. As David Carpenter observes: 'he was the first noble in English history to seize power and rule the country in the name of the king.' Montfort consolidated his position among the populace by the calling of two parliaments in June 1264 and January 1265, which decentralised some powers to the shires and commons, represented by knights and burgesses. These measures earned him a reputation from some for creating the House of Commons (a reputation that is, needless to say, a matter of debate among some historians). He achieved this against the background of a potential invasion from France, another factor which helped to rally support around him and his reform programme. Montfort's boldness, defiance and pursuance of the rights expressed in the Provisions sustained his leadership at this crucial juncture, elevating his positive status across broad swathes of popular opinion, while repulsing others; Montfort was nothing if not a truly divisive figure. That the royal family were also in his grasp afforded further political advantage. Montfort was now king in all but name.

But it was not to last. A damaging feature of Montfortian rule was its avaricious procurement of wealth and lands for family members before all others. This may have been an over-compensating action for years of financial insecurity. An obvious consequence of this was to alienate supporters such as the young but powerful Gilbert de Clare, Earl of Gloucester, and to open Montfort up to charges of self-interest over national interest. Clare deserted to the royalist side, a serious blow for Montfort and a marker for the way things were going. As Stephen Church wrote in 2017, 'hubris [...] brought about Simon's downfall'. In May 1265, worse was to come: the Lord Edward made a dramatic escape – a high-speed getaway on horseback that outpaced his pursuers – having linked up with the Clares. Edward presented a potent figurehead for royalists and anti-Montfortians, being both a competent heir to the throne who inspired confidence as well as offering a reassuring reputation for military ability. Everything now unravelled for Montfort.

On 4 August 1265, Montfort's small army was trapped and annihilated at the battle of Evesham. According to some reports, Montfort either saw his son Henry killed or heard of his death. His response was: 'Then it is time for us to die.' Montfort, unhorsed and fighting on foot, was struck down in the thick of the action. With him fell at least thirty other knights – an unparalleled number for a battle between Englishmen in this age of 'chivalry'. The Montfortian infantry fared even worse and was massacred in droves. Those who desperately sought sanctuary in Evesham Abbey did so in vain; here the slaughter continued. The contemporary chronicler Robert of Gloucester writes: 'Such was the murder of Evesham, for battle it was none.'

Like his father, then, Montfort died as a knight fighting in battle. Unlike his father, his body was not treated with respect. The Osney chronicler writes:

> After the battle, certain friends of the earl, weeping and lamenting [...] came into the field and collected, on an old and shaky ladder, the remains of his body which lay abandoned under the sky. They covered it with an old cheap cloak, and brought it back to the conventual church of Evesham where, wrapping it in a pure, clean cloth, they placed it in a new grave.

The reality was more horrific: Montfort's corpse was desecrated. He was comprehensively dismembered; his son, Simon, witnessed his father's head being paraded on a spear. Montfort's testicles were cut off, strung across his nose and then stuffed into his mouth. Revenge and anger did nothing to stay the victors' swords. Such vindictive violence was matched by the spiritual devotion of Montfort's followers. They saw him as a martyr, the scene of his death becoming a place of pilgrimage and miracles.

As Church has recently written, 'Simon de Montfort was a controversial figure in his own time and has continued to be so ever since'. This might be an understatement for a man remembered as both 'The First Dictator of England' and 'The Father of Parliament'. Montfort does indeed remain a fascinating character for historians, not least for the paradoxes he presents. An extremely devout, hairshirt-wearing individual, he was lacking in Christian charity. While pursuing relentlessly his own financial ends, he often ignored the needs of others, being hard and miserly and rarely generous. His stubbornness and single-mindedness proved both a handicap and a virtue. Maddicott observes that Montfort's pursuit of self-interest also constituted 'the interests of reform [...] and he really persuaded himself that reform was best served by his own promotion'. There is much truth in this; indeed, the reforms of Montfort and his council were later legally enshrined in the Statute of Marlborough in 1267. As Maddicott notes, 'the posthumous Montfort was thus more successfully than his bloody end at Evesham might have led any of his friends or enemies to expect'.

Maddicott judged that 'in the end, we should perhaps see Montfort as a classical tragic hero, a man of high abilities, a master of men and figure of weight and moral worth, who in the end overreached himself and was brought down by his ambitions and personal failings'. This is a judicious assessment of the man. In his aspirations, energy, tenacity, ruthlessness and generalship, Simon de Montfort was indeed his father's son. The fruit had not fallen far from the tree.

Further reading on Simon de Montfort, Earl of Leicester (*c.* 1208–65) can be found in the comprehensive bibliography in J.R. Maddicott's *Simon de Montfort* (Cambridge, 1994), which deservedly remains the standard biography. Maddicott's 'Who Was Simon de Montfort, Earl of Leicester?', in *Transactions of the Royal Historical Society*, sixth series, vol. 26 (Cambridge, 2016) offers an updated summary with more recent publications cited. Since then there have been further publications of note. On Montfort there is Lucy Hennings's 'Simon de Montfort and the Ambiguity of Ethnicity in Thirteenth-Century Politics', in Andrew Spencer and Carl Watkins (eds), *Thirteenth Century England XVI* (Woodbridge, 2017). On the great crisis of mid-thirteenth century England there is the important collection of papers: Adrian Jobson (ed.), *Baronial Reform and Revolution in England, 1258–1267* (Woodbridge, 2016). The most up-to-date studies of Henry III's reign are David Crook and Louise J. Wilkinson (eds), *The Growth of Royal Government Under Henry III* (Woodbridge, 2015) and Stephen Church, *Henry III: A Simple and God-Fearing King* (London, 2017).

NOTES

Abbreviations

Chronicle   William of Puylaurens, *The Chronicle of William Puylaurens*, ed. and trans. W. and M. Sibly, Woodbridge, 2003

History   Peter of Vaux de Cernay, *The History of the Albigensian Crusade*, ed. and trans. W. and M. Sibly, Woodbridge, 1998

RW   Roger of Wendover, *Rogeri de Wendover Liber Qui Dicitur Flores Historiarum*, ed. H. Hewlett, Rolls Series, ii and iii, London, 1886–87

Song   William of Tudela and Anonymous, *The Song of the Cathar Wars*, ed. and trans. J. Shirley, Aldershot, 1996

WB   William the Breton, *Oeuvres de Rigord et de Guillaume le Breton*, 2 vols, ed. H. Delaborde, Paris, 1882

1. Cathars, Catholics and Crusaders: 'The Generation of Vipers'

1   *Song*, 13.
2   W. Wakefield and A. Evans, *Heresies of the High Middle Ages*, New York, 1969, 72–73.
3   Gervase of Canterbury, *The Historical Works of Gervase of Canterbury*, ed. W. Stubbs, Rolls Series, London 1880, i, 270.
4   E. Le Roy Ladurie, *Montaillou*, London, 1978, 212.
5   Le Roy Ladurie, *Montaillou*, 157.
6   *Chronicle*, 25.
7   Roger of Howden, *Chronica*, ed. W. Stubbs, Rolls Series, London, 1868–71, ii, 160–61.

8   M. Barber, *The Cathars: Dualist Heretics in Languedoc in the High Middle Ages*, Harlow, 2000, 112–13.
9   *History*, 24–25.
10 Barber, *The Cathars*, 117.
11 *Chronicle*, 26.
12 *Chronicle*, 23.
13 *History*, 32.
14 *History*, 32.
15 *Song*, 14.
16 *History*, 37–38.
17 *Song*, 15.
18 *History*, 45.
19 WB, i, 229.
20 *Song*, 17.
21 *Song*, 13.

2.   1209: 'Kill Them All! God Will Know His Own!'

22 *Song*, 18.
23 *History*, 48–49.
24 T. Reuter, '*Episcopi cum sua militia*: The Prelate as Warrior in the Early Staufer Era', in T. Reuter (ed.), *Warriors and Churchmen in the Middle Ages*, London, 1992, 93.
25 *Song*, 18.
26 *Song*, 18.
27 *Song*, 19–22 for this and William's following quotes on Béziers.
28 *History*, 50.
29 *History*, 50, 289.
30 *Chronicle*, 33.
31 Barber, *The Cathars*, 211 n. 20.
32 *History*, 50–51.
33 RW, ii, 89.
34 WB, i, 230.
35 R. Hill (ed. and trans.), *Gesta Francorum*, 1962, 91–92; E. Peters (ed. and trans.), *The First Crusade: The Chronicle of Fulcher of Chartres and Other Source Materials*, Philadelphia, Pennsylvania, 1998, 92, 260–61.
36 Barber, *The Cathars*, 211 n. 20.
37 *Song*, 13.
38 *Song*, 21.
39 WB, i, 230.
40 *Chronicle*, 33.

41   *History*, 51.

42   *History of William Marshal*, ed. A. Holden, D. Crouch and S. Gregory, Anglo-Norman Text Society, London, 2002–06, ii, 301.

43   Hill, *Gesta Francorum*, 19–30; W. Zajac, 'Captured Property on the First Crusade', in J. Phillips (ed.), *The First Crusade: Origins and Impact*, Manchester, 1997, 155.

44   Froissart, *Chronicles*, trans. G. Brereton, Harmondsworth, 1978, 151.

45   RW, ii, 218.

46   *Song*, 22.

47   RW, ii, 89.

48   *Song*, 22–26 (for this and William's following quotes on Carcassonne).

49   *History*, 52–53 (for this and Peter's following quotes on Carcassonne).

50   WB, i, 231.

51   RW, ii, 90.

52   WB, i, 231.

53   *Chronicle*, 34.

54   *Song*, 29.

55   *Song*, 28, 29; *Chronicle*, 34.

3.   1209–10: 'Frantic Men of an Evil Kind and Crazy Women Who Shrieked Among the Flames'

56   *History*, 56.

57   *Song*, 27.

58   WB, 231; Guillaume de Nangis, *Chroniques Capétiennes*, Clermont, 2002, 124.

59   *Song*, 27.

60   *History*, 63.

61   Gilbert of Mons, *Chronicle of Hainaut*, ed. and trans. L. Napran, Woodbridge, 2005, 101.

62   *Song*, 30.

63   *History*, 70.

64   WB, 136–37.

65   Suger, *Vita Ludovici Grossi Regis*, ed. H. Waquet, Paris, 1964 edn, 8–9.

66   RW, 217.

67   *Song*, 30.

68   *Song*, 32.

69   *History*, 79.

70   Froissart, *Chronicles*, 106.

71   RW, 339.

72   *History*, 83; *Song*, 33.

73   *Song*, 33.

74   *Song*, 33.

75   *History*, 91; *Song*, 36.

76   *History*, 94–95.

77   Joinville and Villehardouin, *Chronicles of the Crusades*, ed. and trans. M. Shaw, Harmondsworth, 1963, 215.

78   RW, 201.

79   *History*, 100.

80   *History*, 96.

81   *Song*, 36.

82   *Song*, 37.

83   *Song*, 37.

4.   1211: 'There Was So Great a Slaughter it Will Be Talked of Until the End of the World'

84   *Song*, 38.

85   *Song*, 39.

86   *Chronicle*, 39.

87   *History*, 114.

88   For this and Peter's following quotes from Lavaur, see *History*, 115–17.

89   *Chronicle*, 39.

90   *Song*, 42; *History*, 113.

91   Robert of Auxerre, *Roberti Canonici Sancti Mariani Autissiodorensis Chronicon*, ed. O. Holder-Egger, Monumenta Germaniae Historica Scriptores, Paris, xvi, 1882, 276.

92   *Song*, 42.

93   RW, ii, 219.

94   *Song*, 42.

95   *Song*, 41.

96   *Song*, 41; Suger, 141.

97   Robert of Auxerre, 276.

98   Robert of Auxerre, 276.

99   *Song*, 42.

100   *Chronicle*, 40.

101   *Chronicle*, 41.

102   *Chronicle*, 41.

103   *Song*, 46.

104   *History*, 126.

105   *History*, 127.

106   *Song*, 49.

107   *History*, 131–39 for this and Peter's following quotes on Castelnaudary.

108   *Song*, 51–55 for this and William's following quotes on the battle.

109   *Chronicle*, 42.

110   *History*, 142.

5.   1212–13: 'All Were Seized Without Mercy and Put to the Sword'

111   *Song*, 56.

112   *Song*, 57.

113   *History*, 152.

114   *History*, 152.

115   *History*, 157.

116   WB, ii, 200.

117   *Song*, 60.

118   *History*, 163.

119   *Song*, 64.

120   *History*, 169.

121   *History*, 309, 310.

122   *Song*, 64.

123   *History*, 195.

124   *Chronicle*, 43.

125   *Song*, 67.

126   *Chronicle*, 64; *History*, 198.

127   *History*, 201.

128   *Song*, 69–71 for this and following quotes from the Anonymous on Muret.

129   *Chronicle*, 46–47. For further quotes from William on Muret, see his account of the battle, *Chronicle*, 46–49.

130   *The Deeds of James I of Aragon*, ed. and trans. D. Smith and H. Buffery, Farnham, 2010, 24.

131   *History*, 208. For Peter's account of Muret and other quotes cited here, see *History*, 208–17.

132   WB, ii, 235. For the longer of William's two accounts of Muret, and for other quotes cited here, see WB, ii, 233–45.

133   RW, ii, 93. See also *History*, 217.

134   *The Deeds of James I of Aragon*, 24.

135   *History of William Marshal*, i, 395.

6.   1214–17: 'We Shall Carry Death Across Your Land'

136   *History*, 222.
137   *The Deeds of James I of Aragon*, 25.
138   *History*, 224–45 for this and the following quotes from Peter on the Baldwin affair.
139   *Chronicle*, 50.
140   *Chronicle*, 50.
141   *History*, 103, 106.
142   *The Deeds of James I of Aragon*, 25.
143   *History*, 231.
144   *History*, 235.
145   *History*, 236.
146   *History*, 238.
147   *Song*, 158.
148   *History*, 239.
149   *History*, 247.
150   *Song*, 72; *Chronicle*, 54.
151   *History*, 252.
152   *Song*, 73.
153   *History*, 311.
154   *Chronicle*, 54.
155   *History*, 255.
156   *Song*, 82.
157   *Song*, 84.
158   *Song*, 85.
159   *Song*, 87–88. For other quotes from the *Song* relating to events at Beaucaire, see 87–105.
160   *History*, 259.
161   RW, ii, 149.
162   *History*, 262.
163   *Chronicle*, 57.
164   *Chronicle*, 57.
165   *Song*, 116.
166   *History*, 265.
167   *History*, 268.

7.   1217–18: 'Who Could Fail to Dissolve in Tears?'

168   For this and other quotes from the Anonymous at Toulouse, see *Song*, 122–30.

169   *Chronicle*, 59.

170   *Chronicle*, 60.

171   *History*, 270.

172   *Song*, 132.

173   *History*, 271.

174   *Song*, 135.

175   *Song*, 137.

176   RW, ii, 191–92.

177   *History*, 271.

178   *History*, 273.

179   *Song*, 142.

180   *Song*, 149–50 for this and the following quotes from the Anonymous on this combat.

181   *History*, 273.

182   *Chronicle*, 61.

183   *Song*, 151–52 for this and the following quote from the Anonymous.

184   *History*, 273.

185   *Song*, 157.

186   *Song*, 163.

187   *Song*, 164.

188   *Song*, 166.

189   Raymond Escrivain, 'Senhors, l'autrier vi ses falhida', in C. Léglu, R. Rist and C. Taylor, *The Cathars and the Albigensian Crusade: A Sourcebook*, Abingdon, 2013, 99.

190   *History*, 275.

191   *Song*, 170.

192   *History*, 276.

193   *Song*, 172.

194   *Song*, 172.

195   *History*, 277.

196   *Chronicle*, 61.

197   *Song*, 175.

198   *Song*, 176.

199   *Song*, 176.

200   William de Nangis, 145; WB, i, 316; Matthew Paris, *Chronica Majora*, ed. H. R. Luard, London, 1876, iii, 57.

201   Otto of Freising, *The Deeds of Frederick Barbarossa*, trans. C. Mierow, Toronto, 1994, 284.

202   *Song*, 178.

203   *History*, 279.

204   *History*, 279.

8. 1219-29: 'They Completed the Work of Destruction'

205   Song, 181.

206   Song, 182.

207   Chronicle, 63.

208   Song, 186.

209   WB, i, 331; WB, ii, 361.

210   Song, 188–89.

211   Chronicle, 65.

212   Song, 194.

213   Chronicle, 65.

214   Chronicle, 66.

215   Chronicle, 69.

216   Histoire Générale du Languedoc, ed. C. de Vic and J. Vaissète, revised A. Molinier, Toulouse, 1879, vi, 553.

217   Chronicle, 69; Histoire Générale du Languedoc, viii, 785.

218   Histoire Générale du Languedoc, viii, 796.

219   Chronicle, 136.

220   RW, ii, 300.

221   Chronicle, 71.

222   Nicholas de Bray, La Geste de Louis VIII, Clermont, 2004, 67.

223   Tomier and Palaizi, 'De chanter farai una esdemess', in Léglu et al., The Cathars and the Albigensian Crusade: A Sourcebook, 101.

224   Chronicon Turonensis, in Recueil des Historiens des Gaules et de la France, ed. M. Bouquet and L. Delisle, xviii, Paris, 1869–1904, 315.

225   Nicholas de Bray, 75.

226   Nicholas de Bray, 86.

227   RW, ii, 312.

228   RW, ii, 311.

229   Philip Mousket, Chronique Rimée, ed. Reiffenberg, Brussels 1836–38, v. 26783–4.

230   Chronicle, 76.

231   RW, ii, 347.

232   Chronicle, 78.

233   Jordan Fantosme's Chronicle, ed. R. Johnston, Oxford, 1981, 33–35.

234   RW, iii, 3–4, 53, 58; ii, 166–7.

235   Chronicle, 79.

236   Chronicle, 79.

237   Chronicle, 80.

Epilogue: 1230–40 – 'The Synagogue of Satan'

238 Matthew Paris, *Chronica Majora*, iii, 361.

239 *Chronicle of William Pelhisson*, in W. Wakefield, *Heresy, Crusade and Inquisition in Southern France, 1110–1250*, Berkeley, 1974, 224.

240 Matthew Paris, *Chronica Majora*, iii, 267.

241 *Chronicle*, 96.

242 *Chronicle*, 97.

243 William des Ormes's letter to Blanche de Castile is reproduced in full in G. Langlis, 'La Rébellion Contre le Roi: Le Siége de la Cité de Carcassonne (9 Septembre–11 Octobre)', in L. Albaret and N. Gouzy (eds), *La Grandes Batailles Méridionales (1209–1271)*, Toulouse, 2005, 174–76; the quotation here is from 174.

244 *Chronicle*, 97.

245 *Chronicle*, 98.

246 William des Ormes, 175.

247 William des Ormes, 176.

248 *Chronicle*, 102.

249 Manuscrits du Fonds Doat, Paris, Bibliothèque Nationale, xx, 258a.

250 *Chronicle*, 104.

251 Matthew Paris, *Chronica Majora*, iv, 209–14 for this and following quotes from Matthew Paris on Taillebourg and Saintes.

252 Jean de Joinville in Joinville and Villehardouin, *Chronicles of the Crusade*, 189.

253 William de Nangis, 180.

254 *Chronicle*, 108 for this and the following quotes.

BIBLIOGRAPHY

Place of publication London unless otherwise stated.

1. The Albigensian Crusade and Heresy

Albaret, L., and Gouzy, N. (eds), *Les Grandes Batailles Méridionales, 1209–1271*, Toulouse, 2005

Arnold, J., *Belief and Unbelief in Medieval Europe*, 2005

Barber, M., 'The Albigensian Crusades: Wars Like Any Other?', in M. Balard et al. (eds), *Dei Gesta per Francos: Crusade Studies in Honour of Jean Richard*, Aldershot, 2001

—, 'Catharism and the Occitan Nobility: The Lordships of Cabaret, Minerve and Termes', in C. Harper-Bill and R. Harvey (eds), *The Ideals and Practice of Medieval Knighthood, 3: Papers from the Fourth Strawberry Hill Conference, 1988*, Woodbridge, 1990

—, *Crusaders and Heretics: Twelfth to Fourteenth Centuries*, Aldershot, 1995

—, *The Cathars: Dualist Heretics in Languedoc in the High Middle Ages*, Harlow, 2000

Belperron, P., *La Croisade Contre les Albigeois 1209–1249*, Paris, 1942

Biller, P., and Hudson, A., *Heresy and Literacy, 1000–1530*, Cambridge, 1994

Bonde, S., *Fortress-Churches of Languedoc: Architecture, Religion and Conflict in the High Middle Ages*, Cambridge, 1994

Burl, A., *God's Heretics: The Albigensian Crusade*, Stroud, 2002

Costen, M., *The Cathars and the Albigensian Crusade*, Manchester, 1997

Cowper, M., *Cathar Castles: Fortresses of the Albigensian Crusade, 1209–1300*, Oxford, 2006

Dean, J., *A History of Medieval Heresy and the Inquisition*, Lanham, 2011

Fichtenau, H., *Heretics and Scholars in the High Middle Ages, 1000–1200*, University Park, Pennslyvania, 1998

Girou, J., *Simon de Montfort du Catharisme à la Conquête*, Paris, 1953

Given, J., *Inquisition and Medieval Society: Power, Discipline and Resistance in Languedoc*, Ithaca, New York, 1997

Gougad, H., and Zink, M. (trans. and ed.), *Chanson de la Croisade Albigeoise*, Paris, 1989

Graham-Leigh, E., *The Southern French Nobility and the Albigensian Crusade*, Woodbridge, 2005

Hamilton, B., *The Albigensian Crusade*, 1974

—, 'The Albigensian Crusade', in his *Monastic Reform, Catharism and the Crusades, 900–1300*, Aldershot, 1999

—, 'The Albigensian Crusade and Heresy', in D. Abulafia (ed.), *The New Cambridge Medieval History, V, c. 1198–c. 1300*, Cambridge, 2009

—, *The Medieval Inquisition*, 1981

Harper-Bill, C., and R. Harvey (eds), *The Ideals and Practices of Medieval Knighthood, 3: Papers from the Fourth Strawberry Hill Conference, 1988*, Woodbridge, 1990

Jenkins, E., *The Mediterranean World of Alfonso II and Peter II of Aragon, 1162–1213*, New York, 2012

Lambert, M., *The Cathars*, Oxford, 1998

Langlois, G., 'Le Siège du Château de Termes par Simon de Montfort en 1210: Problèmes Topographiques et Historiques', in *Heresis*, 22, 1994

Le Roy Laderie, E., *Montaillou*, 1978

Léglu, C., Rist, R., and Taylor, C., *The Cathars and the Albigensian Crusade: A Sourcebook*, Abingdon, 2014

Madaule, J., *The Albigensian Crusade*, trans. B. Wall, New York, 1961

Marvin, L., 'Siege of Carcassonne', 'Siege and Battle of Castelnaudary', 'Simon de Montfort IV', 'Siege of Montségur', 'Battle of Muret', 'Siege of Termes', in C. Rogers (ed.), *The Oxford Encyclopedia of Medieval Warfare and Medieval Technology*, 3 vols, Oxford, 2010

Marvin, L., *The Occitan War: A Military and Political History of the Albigensian Crusade, 1209–1218*, Cambridge, 2009

—, 'Thirty-Nine Days and a Wake-Up: The Impact of the Indulgence and Forty Days Service on the Albigensian Crusade, 1209–1218', *The Historian*, 65 (1), 2002

McGlynn, S., 'Battle of Taillebourg', 'Battle of Saintes', in C. Rogers (ed.), *The Oxford Encyclopedia of Medieval Warfare and Medieval Technology*, 3 vols, Oxford, 2010

—, 'Kill Them All! Cruelty and Atrocity in Medieval Warfare', *BBC History*, 10 (8), 2009

Medieval Warfare, 3 (4), 2013 [Albigensian Crusade special issue]

Moore, R., *The Formation of a Persecuting Society: Power and Deviance in Western Europe, 950–1250*, Oxford, 1987, 2006

—, *The Origins of European Dissent*, 1977

—, *The War on Heresy: Faith and Power in Medieval Europe*, 2012, 2014

Mundy, J., *Liberty and Political Power in Toulouse, 1050–1230*, New York, 1954

O'Shea, S., *The Friar of Carcassonne: The Last Days of the Cathars*, 2011

—, *The Perfect Heresy: The Life and Death of the Cathars*, 2000

Oldenbourg, Z., *Massacre at Montségur: A History of the Albigensian Crusade*, 1961

Paterson, L., *The World of the Troubadours: Medieval Occitan Society,*
c. 1100–c. 1300, Cambridge, 1993

Pegg, M., *The Corruption of Angels: The Great Inquisition of 1245–6*, Princeton,
2001

Pegg, M., *A Most Holy War: The Albigensian Crusade and the Battle for*
Christendom, Oxford, 2008

Peter of Vaux de Cernay, *The History of the Albigensian Crusade*, ed. and trans.
W. and M. Sibley, Woodbridge, 1998

Pladihle, D., *Simon de Montfort et le Drame Cathare*, Paris, 1988

Rist, R., 'Papal Policy and the Albigensian Crusades: Continuity or Change?',
Crusades, 2, 2003

Roach, A., *The Devil's World: Heresy and Society, 1100–1320*, Harlow, 2005

Roca, J., *Xacbert de Barbera: Lion de Combat, 1185–1275*, Barcelona, 1989

Roquebert, M. (ed.), *La Croisade Albigeoise*, Carcassonne, 2004

—, *L'Epopée Cathare*, 5 vols, Toulouse, 1970–98

—, *Simon de Montfort*, Toulouse, 2005

Sackville, L., *Heresy and Heretics in the Thirteenth Century: The Textual*
Representations, Woodbridge, 2011

Sennis, Antonio (ed.), *Cathars in Question*, Woodbridge, 2016

Sparks, Chris, *Heresy, Inquisition and Life Cycle in Medieval Languedoc*, Suffolk,
2014

Strayer, J., *The Albigensian Crusades*, New York, 1971

Sumption, J., *The Albigensian Crusade*, 1978

Taylor, C., 'Evidence for Dualism in Inquisitorial Registers of the 1240s: A
Contribution to a Debate', in *History*, 98 (3), 2013

—, *Heresy, Crusade and Inquisition in Medieval Quercy*, Woodbridge, 2011

—, *Heresy in Medieval France: Dualism in Aquitaine and the Agenais,*
c. 1000–c. 1250, Woodbridge, 2005

—, 'Pope Innocent III, John of England and the Albigensian Crusade, 1209–
1216', in J. Moore (ed.), *Pope Innocent III and His World*, Aldershot, 1999

Vincent, N., 'England and the Albigensian Crusade', in B. Weiler and
I. Rowlands (eds), *England and Europe in the Reign of Henry III*, Aldershot,
2002

Wakefield, W., *Heresy, Crusade and Inquisition in Southern France, 1100–1250*,
Berkeley, 1974

Wakefield, W., and Evans, A., *Heresies of the High Middle Ages*, New York, 1969

Waugh, S., and Diehl, P. (eds), *Christendom and Its Discontents: Exclusion, Persecution and Rebellion, 1000–1500*, Cambridge, 1996

William of Pelhisson, *Chronique 1229–1244*, ed. and trans. J. Duvernoy, Paris, 1994

William of Puylaurens, *The Chronicle of William Puylaurens*, ed. and trans. W. and M. Sibly, Woodbridge, 2003

William of Tudela and Anonymous, *The Song of the Cathar Wars*, ed. and trans. J. Shirley, Aldershot, 1996

Wolfe, P., 'Une Discussion de Témoignes: Le Massacre de Béziers en 1209', in P. Wolfe (ed.), *Documents de l'Histoire du Languedoc*, Toulouse, 1969

Zerner-Cahrdavoine, M., *La Croisade Albigeoise*, Paris, 1979

2. Medieval Warfare

Allmand, C. (ed.), *Henry V*, 1992

—, *Society at War: The Experience of England and France during the Hundred Years War*, Woodbridge, 1998

—, *The Hundred Years War: England and France at War, c.1300–c.1450*, Cambridge, 1988

—, 'The Reporting of War in the Middle Ages', in D. Dunn (ed.), *War and Society in Medieval and Early Modern Britain*, Liverpool, 2000

Audouin, E., *Essai sur l'Armée Royale au Temps de Philippe Auguste*, Paris, 1913

Ayton, A., *Knights and Warhorses: Military Service and the English Aristocracy under Edward III*, Woodbridge, 1994

Baraz, D., *Medieval Cruelty*, Ithaca, New York, 2003

Barber, M., *The New Knighthood: A History of the Order of the Temple*, Cambridge, 1994

Barber, R. (ed.), *Edward III and the Triumph of England*, 2013

—, *Life and Campaigns of the Black Prince*, 1979

—, *The Knight and Chivalry*, Woodbridge, 1995

Barnie, J., *War in Medieval English Society: Social Values in the Hundred Years War, 1377–99*, New York, 1974

Bautier, R.-H. (ed.), *La France de Philippe Auguste: Le Temps des Mutations*, Paris, 1982

Bennett, M., *Agincourt 1415: Triumph against the Odds*, 1991

—, 'Military Masculinity in England and Northern France, c.1050–c.1215', in D. Hadley (ed.), *Masculinity in Medieval Europe*, 1999

Bradbury, J., *Stephen and Matilda: The Civil War of 1139–53*, Gloucester, 1996

—, *The Battle of Hastings*, Gloucester, 1999

—, *The Medieval Archer*, Woodbridge, 1985

—, *The Medieval Siege*, Woodbridge, 1992

Brooks, F., *The English Naval Forces, 1199–1272*, 1933

Contamine, P., and Guyotjeannin, D. (eds), *La Guerre et la Paix: Frontières et Violences au Moyen Age*, Paris, 1978

—, *La Guerre, la Violence, et Les Gens au Moyen Âge* (2 vols), Paris, 1996

—, 'L'Armée de Philippe Auguste', in R.-H. Bautier (ed.), *La France de Philippe Auguste*, Paris, 1982

—, 'Rançons et Butins dans la Normandie Anglaise, 1424–1444', in *Actes du 101e Congrès National des Sociétés Savantes*, Lille, 1976

—, *War in the Middle Ages*, Oxford, 1984

Contamine, P., Giry-Deloison, C., and Keen, M. (eds), *Guerre et Société en France, en Angleterre et en Bourgogne, XIVe–XVe Siècle*, Lille, 1991

Coss, P., *The Knight in Medieval England, 1000–1400*, Stroud, 1993

Coulson, C., *Castles in Medieval Society: Fortresses in England, France, and Ireland in the Central Middle Ages*, Oxford, 2003

—, '"National" Requisitioning for "Public" Use of "Private" Castles in Pre-Nation State France', in Alfred Smyth (ed.), *Medieval Europeans: Studies in Ethnic Identity and National Perspectives in Medieval Europe*, 1998

Curnow, P., 'Some Developments in Military Architecture c. 1200: Le Courdray-Salbart', *Anglo-Norman Studies*, 2, 1979

Curry, A., *Agincourt: A New History*, Stroud, 2005

—, 'Medieval Warfare: England and Her Continental Neighbours, Eleventh to the Fourteenth Centuries', *Journal of Medieval History*, 21 (3), 1997

Duby, G., *The Legend of Bouvines*, Cambridge, 1990

Dunbabin, J., *Captivity and Imprisonment in Medieval Europe, 1000–1300*, Basingstoke, 2002

Erlande-Brandenburg, A., 'L'Architecture Militaire au Temps de Philippe Auguste: une Nouvelle Conception de la Défense', in R.-H. Bautier (ed.), *La France de Philippe Auguste*, Paris, 1982

—, 'Organisation du Conseil d'Architecture et des Corps des Spécialistes sous Philippe Auguste', in X. Altet (ed.), *Artistes, Artisans et Productions Artistique au Moyen Age*, Paris, 1987

Fino, J., *Forteresses de la France Médiévale*, Paris, 1967

Foley, V., Palmer, G., and Soedel, W., 'The Crossbow', *Scientific American*, 1985

Forey, A., *The Military Orders: From the Twelfth to the Early Fourteenth Centuries*, 1992

France, J. (ed.), *Medieval Warfare 1000–1300*, Farnham, 2006

—, 'Recent Writing on Medieval Warfare: From the Fall of Rome to c. 1300', *Journal of Military History*, 65 (2), 2001

—, *Western Warfare in the Age of the Crusades, 1000–1300*, 1999

Gillingham, J., 'Richard I, Galley Warfare and Portsmouth: The Beginnings of a Royal Navy', *Thirteenth Century England*, 6, 1997.

—, *The Wars of the Roses: Peace and Conflict in Fifteenth-Century England*, 1981

Gillingham, J., and Holt, J. (eds), *War and Government in the Middle Ages*, Woodbridge, 1984

Green, D., *Edward the Black Prince*, Harlow, 2007

—, *The Battle of Poitiers, 1356*, 2002

Hajdu, R., 'Castles, Castellans and the Structure of Politics in Poitou, 1152–1271', *Journal of Medieval Military History*, 4, 1978

Hanley, C., *War and Combat, 1150–1270: The Evidence of Old French Literature*, Woodbridge, 2003

Hattendorf, J., and Unger, R. (eds), *War at Sea in the Middle Ages and Renaissance*, Woodbridge, 2003

Hollister, C.W., *The Military Organization of Norman England*, Oxford, 1965

Hosler, J., *Henry II: A Medieval Soldier at War, 1147–1189*, Woodbridge, 2007

Kaeuper, R., *Chivalry and Violence in Medieval Europe*, Oxford, 1999

—, *War, Justice and Public Order: England and France in the Later Middle Ages*, Oxford, 1988

Kagay, D., and Villalon, L., *The Circle of War in the Middle Ages*, Woodbridge, 1999

—, (eds), *The Final Argument: The Imprint of Violence on Society in Medieval and Early Modern Europe*, Woodbridge, 1998

Kapelle, W.E., *The Norman Conquest of the North, 1000–1135*, 1979

Keen, M., *Chivalry*, 1984

—, 'Chivalry, Nobility and the Man-at-Arms', in C. Allmand (ed.), *War, Literature and Politics in the Late Middle Ages*, Liverpool, 1976

— (ed.), *Medieval Warfare: A History*, Oxford, 1999

—, *Nobles, Knights and Men-at-Arms*, 1996

—, *The Laws of War in the Later Middle Ages*, 1965

Lawson, M., *The Battle of Hastings 1066*, Gloucester, 2002

Marvin, L., 'Warfare and the Composition of Armies in France, 1100–1218: An Emphasis on the Common Soldier', unpublished PhD thesis, University of Illinois, 1996

McGlynn, S., 'A War without Quarter: The Scottish Invasion of England in 1138', *Medieval Warfare*, 3 (3), 2013

—, *Blood Cries Afar: The Forgotten French Invasion of England, 1216*, Stroud, 2011

—, *By Sword and Fire: Cruelty and Atrocity in Medieval Warfare*, 2008

—, *Henry V and the Agincourt Massacre*, 2015

—, 'King John and the French Invasion of England', *BBC History*, 11 (6), 2010

—, 'Land Warfare, 1000–1500', 'Siege Warfare', 'Richard I (The Lionheart)', in C. Messenger (ed.), *Reader's Guide to Military History*, 2001

—, *Medieval Generals*, 2015

—, 'Medieval Warfare', *European Review of History–Revue Européenne d'Histoire*, 4 (2), 1997

—, 'Philip Augustus: Too Soft a King?', *Medieval Life*, 7, 1997

—, 'Politics and Violence in the Late Middle Ages', *Canadian Journal of History*, 26 (3), 2001

—, 'Research on Medieval Warfare, Past and Present', *European Review of History–Revue Européenne d'Histoire*, 20 (1), 2013

—, 'Roger of Wendover and the Wars of Henry III, 1216–1234', in B. Weiler and I. W. Rowlands (eds), *England and Europe in the Reign of Henry III, 1216–1272*, Aldershot, 2002

—, '*Servicium Debitum*', 'Otto IV', 'William Marshal', 'Philip II of France', 'John, King of England', 'Louis VII of France', 'Louis VIII of France', 'Marshal, William', 'Richard I of England and Anjou', 'Sandwich, Battle of', 'Siege Warfare: Tactics and Technology', in C. Rogers (ed.), *Oxford Encyclopedia of Medieval Warfare*

—, '"Sheer Terror" and the Black Prince's *Grand Chevauchée* of 1355', in D. Kagay and A. Villalon (eds), *The Hundred Years War: Volume 3*, Leiden, 2011

—, 'The Myths of Medieval Warfare', *History Today*, 44 (1), 1994

—, 'Violence and the Law: Popular Attitudes to Judicial Violence in Medieval England', *History Today*, 57 (4), 2008

—, 'War Crimes', in G. Martel (ed.), *Blackwell Encyclopedia of War*, Oxford, 2011

Messenger, C. (ed.), *Reader's Guide to Military History*, London, 2001

Meron, T., *Henry's Wars and Shakespeare's Laws: Perspectives on the Law of War in the Middle Ages*, Oxford, 1993

Milner, N. (ed. and trans.), *Vegetius: Epitome of Military Science*, Liverpool, 1993

Moore, J., 'Anglo-Norman Garrisons', *Anglo-Norman Studies*, 22, 2000

Morillo, S. (ed.), *The Battle of Hastings*, Woodbridge, 1996

—, *Warfare Under the Anglo-Norman Kings*, Woodbridge, 1994

Nicholson, H., *Medieval Warfare*, Basingstoke, 2004

—, *Templars, Hospitallers and Teutonic Knights: Images of the Military Orders, 1128–1291*, Leicester, 1995

Nicolle, D., *Arms and Armour of the Crusading Era, 1050–1350: Western Europe and the Crusader States*, 1999

Palmer, J., 'War and Domesday Waste', in M. Strickland (ed.), *Armies, Chivalry and Warfare in Medieval Britain and France*, Stamford, 1998

Peters, E. (ed. and trans.), *The First Crusade: The Chronicle of Fulcher of Chartres and Other Source Materials*, Philadelphia, Pennsylvania, 1998

Pitte, D., 'Château-Gaillard dans la Défense de la Normandie orientale (1196–1204)', *Anglo-Norman Studies*, 24, 2002

Powicke, M., *Military Obligation in Medieval England*, Oxford, 1962

Prestwich, J. O., 'Military Intelligence under the Norman and Angevin Kings', in G. Garnett and J. Hudson (eds), *Law and Government in Medieval England and Normandy*, Cambridge, 1994

Prestwich, M., *Armies and Warfare in the Middle Ages: The English Experience*, 1996

—, 'The Garrisoning of English Medieval Castles', in R. Abels and B. Bachrach (eds), *The Normans and Their Adversaries at War*, Woodbridge, 2001

—, 'The Victualling of Castles', in P. Coss and C. Tyerman (eds), *Soldiers, Nobles and Gentlemen: Essays in Honour of Maurice Keen*, Woodbridge, 2009

Purton, P., *A History of the Early Medieval Siege, Volume I: c. 450–1200*, Woodbridge, 2010

—, *A History of the Late Medieval Siege, Volume II: 1200–1500*, Woodbridge, 2010

Reuter, T., '*Episcopi cum sua militia*: The Prelate as Warrior in the Early Staufer Era', in T. Reuter (ed.), *Warriors and Churchmen in the Middle Ages*, 1992

Rogers, C., 'By Fire and Sword: *Bellum Hostile* and "Civilians" in the Hundred Years War', in M. Grimsley and C. Rogers (eds), *Civilians in the Path of War*, Lincoln, 2002

— (ed.), *Oxford Encylcopedia of Medieval Warfare and Military Technology*, Oxford, 2010

— (ed.), *The Wars of Edward III: Sources and Interpretations*, Woodbridge, 1999

—, *War Cruel and Sharp: English Strategy under Edward III, 1327–1360*, Woodbridge, 2000

Russell, F., *The Just War in the Middle Ages*, Cambridge, 1976

Saunders, C., Le Saux, F., and Thomas, N., *Writing War: Medieval Literary Responses to War*, Woodbridge, 2004

Smail, R. C., *Crusading Warfare, 1097–1193*, Cambridge, 1956

Speed, P. (ed.), *Those Who Fought: An Anthology of Medieval Sources*, New York, 1996

Stacey, R., 'The Age of Chivalry', in M. Howard, G. Andreopoulis and M. Shulman (eds), *The Laws of War: Constraints on Warfare in the Western World*, New Haven, Connecticut, 1994

Strickland, M., 'A Law of Arms or a Law of Treason? Conduct in War in Edward I's Campaigns in Scotland, 1296–1307', in R. Kaeuper (ed.), *Violence in Medieval Society*, Woodbridge, 2000

—, 'Against the Lord's Anointed: Aspects of Warfare and Baronial Rebellion in England and Normandy, 1075–1265', in G. Garnett and J. Hudson (eds), *Law and Government in Medieval England and Normandy*, Cambridge, 1994

— (ed.), *Anglo-Norman Warfare: Studies in Late Anglo-Saxon and Anglo-Norman Military Organization and Warfare*, Woodbridge, 1992

—, 'Arms and the Men: Loyalty and Lordship in Jordan Fantasome's Chronicle', in C. Harper-Bill and R. Harvey (eds), *Medieval Knighthood, 4*, Woodbridge, 1992

—, 'Killing or Clemency? Ransom, Chivalry and Changing Attitudes to Defeated Opponents in Britain and Northern France, 7–12th Centuries', in H. Kortum (ed.), *Krieg im Mittelalter*, 2001 (from www.deremilitari.org/strickland)

—, *War and Chivalry: The Conduct and Perception of War in England and Normandy, 1066–1217*, Cambridge, 1996

Strickland, M., and Hardy, R., *The Great Warbow*, Stroud, 2005

Stringer, K.J., 'The War of 1215–17 in its Context', in R. Oram (ed.), *The Reign of Alexander II, 1214–49*, Leiden, 2005

Suppe, F., *Military Institutions on the Welsh Marches: Shropshire, 1066–1300*, Woodbridge, 1994

—, 'The Cultural Significance of Decapitation in High Medieval Wales and the Marches', *Bulletin of the Board of Celtic Studies*, 36, 1989

Thomas, H., 'Violent Disorder in King Stephen's England: A Maximum Argument', in P. Dalton and G. White (eds), *King Stephen's Reign, 1135–1154*, Woodbridge, 2008

Upton-Ward, J. (ed.), *The Military Orders: Volume IV*, Ashgate, 2008

Vale, M., *War and Chivalry: Warfare and Aristocratic Culture in England, France and Burgundy at the End of the Middle Ages*, Athens, Georgia, 1981

Verbruggen, J., *The Art of Warfare in Western Europe during the Middle Ages from the Eighth Century to 1340*, trans. S. Willard and R. Southern, 2nd edn, Woodbridge, 1997

Viollet le Duc, E., *Military Architecture*, London, 1990, 80–94 [1860]

Vries, K. de, *Medieval Military Technology*, Peterborough, 1992

— (ed.), *Medieval Warfare, 1300–1450*, Farnham, 2010

—, 'The Use of Chronicles in Recreating Medieval Military History', *JMMH*, 2, 2004

Wright, N., *Knights and Peasants: The Hundred Years War in the French Countryside*, Woodbridge, 1998

Zajac, W., 'Captured Property on the First Crusade', in J. Phillips (ed.), *The First Crusade: Origins and Impact*, Manchester, 1997

3.   General

Abulafia, D., *Frederick II: A Medieval Emperor*, Harmondsworth, 1988

Alberic de Trois Fontaines, *Chronica*, ed. P. Scheffer-Boichorst, Monumenta Germaniae Historica Scriptores, xxiii, 1863

Annales Monastici, ed. H.R. Luard, Rolls Series, 1864–69

Anonymous of Béthune, *Chroniques des Rois de France*, in *Recueil des Historiens de Gaules et de la France*, xxiv, ed. L. Delisle, Paris, 1904

—, *Histoire des Ducs de Normandie et des Rois d'Angleterre*, ed. F. Michelet, Paris, 1840

Aurell, M., *Des Chrétiens Contre les Croisades, XII–XIII Siècle*, Paris, 2013

Baldwin, J., 'Le Sens du Bouvines', *Cahiers de Civilisation Médiévale*, 30, 1987

—, *The Government of Philip Augustus*, Berkeley, 1986

Bartlett, R., *England Under the Norman and Angevin Kings, 1075–1225*, Oxford, 2000

—, *The Making of Europe: Conquest, Colonization and Cultural Challenge, 950–1350*, Harmondsworth, 1993

Bautier, R.-H. (ed.), *La France de Philippe Auguste: Le Temps des Mutations*, Paris, 1982

Benjamin, R., 'The Angevin Empire', in N. Saul (ed.), *England in Europe, 1066–1453*, 1994

Bolton, B., 'Philip Augustus and John: Two Sons in Innocent III's Vineyard?', *Innocent III: Studies on Papal Authority and Pastoral Care*, Aldershot, 1995

Bordonove, G., *Philippe Auguste*, Paris, 1986

Caesarius of Heisterbach, *Dialogus Miraculorum*, ed. J. Strange, 2 vols, Cologne, 1851

Carpenter, D., *The Minority of Henry III*, 1990

Chalk, F., and Jonahsson, K., *The History and Sociology of Genocide: Analyses and Case Studies*, New Haven, Connecticut, 1990

Chaytor, H., *Savaric de Mauléon*, Cambridge, 1939

Choffel, J., *Louis le Lion: Roi de France Méconnu, Roi d'Angleterre Ignoré*, Paris, 1983

Chronicon Turonense Magnum, ed. A. Salmon, Tours, 1854

Chroniques des Comtes d'Anjou et des Seigneurs d'Amboise, ed. L. Halphen and R. Poupardin, Paris, 1913

Cowdrey, H., *Popes, Monks and Crusaders*, 1984

Duby, G., *France in the Middle Ages, 987–1460*, Oxford, 1991

—, *The Early Growth of the European Economy: Warriors and Peasants from the Seventh to the Twelfth Centuries*, Ithaca, New York, 1974

Duggan, A. (ed.), *Kings and Kingship in Medieval Europe*, 1993

Dunabin, J. *France in the Making, 843–1180*, Oxford, 1985

Fawtier, R., *The Capetian Kings of France: Monarchy and Nation, 987–1328*, Basingstoke, 1960

Forde, S., Johnson, L., and Murray, A., *Concepts of National Identity in the Middle Ages*, Leeds, 1995

Foreville, R., *Le Pape Innocent III et la France*, Stuttgart, 1992

Fuhrman, H., *Germany in the High Middle Ages*, trans. T. Reuter, Cambridge, 1986

Gauthier, G., *Philippe Auguste*, Paris, 2002

Gauvard, C., 'Justification and Theory of the Death Penalty at the *Parlement* of Paris in the Late Middle Ages', in C. Allmand (ed.), *War, Government and Power in Late Medieval France*, Liverpool, 2000

Gervase of Canterbury, *The Historical Works of Gervase of Canterbury*, ed. W. Stubbs, Rolls Series, 1880

Gesta Stephani, eds. K. Potter and R. Davis, Oxford, 1976

Gilbert of Mons, *Chronicle of Hainaut*, ed. and trans. L. Napran, Woodbridge, 2005

Gillingham, J., *Richard Cœur de Lion*, 1994

—, *The Angevin Empire*, 2nd edn, 2001

—, *The English in the Twelfth Century: Imperialism, National Identity and Politics*, Woodbridge, 2000

Gobry, I., *Les Capétiens*, Paris, 2001

Goff, J. Le, *Saint Louis*, Paris, 1996

Gonthier, N., *Le Châtiment du Crime au Moyen Âge*, Rennes, 1998

Goodall, J., 'Dover Castle and the Great Siege of 1216', *Château Gaillard XIX: Études de Castellologie Médiévale. Actes de Colloque International de Graz (Autriche), 22–29 Août 1998*, Caen, 2000

Gorby, I., *Louis VIII, 1223–1226: Fils de Philippe II*, Paris, 2009

Guillaume de Nangis, *Chroniques Capétiennes*, Clermont, 2002

Hadenague, A., *Philippe Auguste et Bouvines*, Paris, 1978 [1935]

Haverkampf, A., *Medieval Germany, 1056–1273*, trans. H. Braun and R. Mortimer, Oxford, 1988

Histoire Générale du Languedoc, 6 vols, eds C. de Vic and J. Vaissète, revised A. Molinier, Toulouse, 1879

History of William Marshal, ed. A. Holden, D. Crouch and S. Gregory, Anglo-Norman Text Society, 2002–06

Howlett, R. (ed.), *Chronicles of the Reigns of Stephen, Henry II and Richard I*, 4 vols, Rolls Series, 1884

Hutton, W., *Philip Augustus*, 1896

Johnston, R. (ed. and trans.), *Jordan Fantosme's Chronicle*, Oxford, 1981

Joinville and Villehardouin, *Chronicles of the Crusades*, ed. and trans. M. Shaw, Harmondsworth, 1963

Jordan, W., *Europe in the High Middle Ages*, 2001

Llobera, J., 'State and Nation in Medieval France', *Journal of Historical Sociology*, 7 (3), 1994

Loengard, J. (ed.) *Magna Carta and the England of King John*, Woodbridge, 2010

Luchaire, A., *Philippe Auguste et son Temps*, Paris, 1980 [1902]

—, *Social France at the Time of Philip Augustus*, 1912

Lyons, M., 'The Capetian Conquest of Anjou', unpublished PhD thesis, Johns Hopkins University, 1976

McGlynn, S., 'Britain and Europe: A Medieval Comparison', *Politics*, 16 (3), 1996

—, *The Life and Reign of King John: Tyrant of Magna Carta*, forthcoming, 2015

Meyerson, D., Thiery, D., and Falk, O., *'A Great Effusion of Blood?': Interpreting Medieval Violence*, Toronto, 2004

Michel, F. (ed.), *Histoire des Ducs de Normandie et des Rois d'Angleterre*, Paris, 1840

Mousket, P., *Chronique Rimée*, ed. de Reifenberg, 2 vols, Brussels, 1836–38

Nicholas de Bray, *La Geste de Louis VIII*, Clermont, 2004

Norgate, K., *England under the Angevin Kings*, 2 vols, 1887

—, *John Lackland*, 1902

Otto of Freising, *The Deeds of Frederick Barbarossa*, trans. C. Mierow, Toronto, 1994

Paden, W., Sankovitch, T., and Stalein, P. (eds.), *The Poems of Bertran de Born*, Los Angeles, 1986

Painter, S., *The Reign of King John*, Baltimore, 1949

Paris, Matthew, *Chronica Majora*, ed. H. Luard, Rolls Series, 1884–89

—, *Matthei Parisiensis Historia Anglorum*, ed. F. Maddern, Rolls Series, 1866–69

Pernoud, R., *Blanche of Castile*, Paris, 1975

Petit-Dutaillis, C., *Étude sur la Vie et le Règne de Louis VIII 1187–1226*, Paris, 1894

Pinker, S., *The Better Angels of Our Nature: A History of Violence*, 2011

Potter, D., *France in the Later Middle Ages*, Oxford, 2002

Powell, J. (ed.), *Innocent III: Vicar of Christ or Lord of the World?*, Boston, 1963

Power, D., *The Central Middle Ages*, Oxford, 2006

Powicke, F.M., *King Henry III and the Lord Edward*, 2 vols, Oxford, 1947

—, *The Loss of Normandy*, 2nd edn, Manchester, 1961

Ralph of Coggeshall, *Radulphi de Coggeshall Chronicon Anglicanum*, ed. J. Stevenson, Rolls Series, 1875

Robert of Auxerre, *Roberti Canonici Sancti Mariani Autissiodorensis Chronicon*, ed. O. Holder-Egger, Monumenta Germaniae Historica Scriptores, xvi, 1882

Roger of Howden, *Chronica*, ed. W. Stubbs, 4 vols, Rolls Series, 1868–71

Roger of Wendover, *Rogeri de Wendover Liber Qui Dicitur Flores Historiarum*, ed. H. Hewlett, Rolls Series, 1886–87

Rosenwein, B. (ed.), *Anger's Past: The Social Uses of an Emotion in the Middle Ages*, Ithaca, New York, 1998

Rummel, R., *Statistics of Democide*, Piscataway, New Jersey, 1997

Sassier, Y., *Louis VII*, Paris, 1991

Sayers, J., *Innocent III: Leader of Europe, 1198–1216*, 1994

Scales, L., 'Bread, Cheese and Genocide: Imagining the Destruction of Peoples in Medieval Western Europe', *History*, 92 (3), 2007

—, 'Identifying "France" and "Germany": Medieval Nation-Making in Some Recent Publications', *Bulletin of International Medieval Research*, 6, 2000

Scales, L., and Zimmer, O. (eds), *Power and Nation in European History*,
    Cambridge, 2005

Sivéry, G., *Blanche de Castille*, Paris, 1990

—, *Philippe Auguste*, Paris, 1993

Smith, A., *National Identity*, 1991

— (ed.), *Medieval Europeans: Studies in Ethnic Identity and National Perspectives in
    Medieval Europe*, Basingstoke, 1998

Spiegel, G., *Romancing the Past: The Rise of Vernacular Prose Historiography in
    Thirteenth-Century France*, Berkeley, 1993

Stacey, R., *Politics, Policy and Finance under Henry III, 1216–45*, Oxford, 1987

Stephenson, J. (ed.), *Radulphi de Coggeshall Chronicon Anglicanum*, Rolls Series,
    1875

Suger, *Vita Ludovici Grossi Regis*, ed. H. Waquet, Paris, 1964 edn

The Book of Deeds of James I of Aragon, ed. and trans. D. Smith and H. Buffery,
    Aldershot, 2003

Turner, R., *King John*, Harlow, 1994

Tyerman, C., *England and the Crusades, 1095–1588*, Chicago, 1988

Weiler, B., *Henry III of England and the Staufen Empire, 1216–1272*,
    Woodbridge, 2006

William the Breton, *Oeuvres de Rigord et de Guillaume le Breton*, 2 vols,
    ed. H. Delaborde, Paris, 1882

INDEX

You may also enjoy …

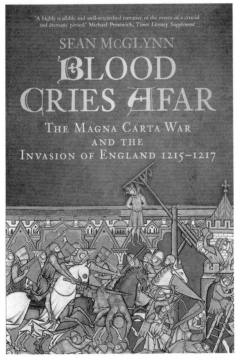

978 0 7509 6391 6

'McGlynn tells a dashing story with gusto … an entertaining military history of a very exciting reign.'– *The Spectator*

'A spirited narrative … A highly readable and well-researched narrative of the events of a crucial and dramatic period.' – *Times Literary Supplement*

'A powerful and gripping read showing a mastery of the sources … A lively and wide-ranging study.' – *History Today*